DEATH
INVESTIGATIONS

James M. Adcock, PhD
The Center for the Resolution of Unresolved Crimes

Arthur S. Chancellor, MCJA
Special Agent
US Army Criminal Investigation Command (CID)

JONES & BARTLETT
LEARNING

World Headquarters
Jones & Bartlett Learning
5 Wall Street
Burlington, MA 01803
978-443-5000
info@jblearning.com
www.jblearning.com

Jones & Bartlett Learning books and products are available through most bookstores and online booksellers. To contact Jones & Bartlett Learning directly, call 800-832-0034, fax 978-443-8000, or visit our website, www.jblearning.com.

This publication is designed to provide accurate and authoritative information in regard to the Subject Matter covered. It is sold with the understanding that the publisher is not engaged in rendering legal, accounting, or other professional service. If legal advice or other expert assistance is required, the service of a competent professional person should be sought.

Unless otherwise indicated, all photographs and illustrations are under copyright of Jones & Bartlett Learning, or have been provided by the authors.

Production Credits
Publisher: Cathleen Sether
Acquisitions Editor: Sean Connelly
Editorial Assistant: Caitlin Murphy
Production Manager: Tracey McCrea
Marketing Manager: Lindsay White
Manufacturing and Inventory Control Supervisor: Amy Bacus
Composition: DSCS Composition and Publishing Services
Cover Design: Kristin E. Parker
Rights and Photo Research Supervisor: Anna Genoese
Cover Image: © Warren Goldswain/ShutterStock, Inc.
Printing and Binding: Malloy, Inc.
Cover Printing: Malloy, Inc.

Some images in this book feature models. These models do not necessarily endorse, represent, or participate in the activities represented in the images.

Library of Congress Cataloging-in-Publication Data
Adcock, James M.
  Death investigations / James M. Adcock, Arthur S. Chancellor.
    p. cm.—(Jones & Bartlett Learning guides to law enforcement investigation) (The law enforcement guide to investigations)
  Includes bibliographical references and index.
    ISBN 978-1-4496-2674-7 (pbk.)
1. Homicide investigation. 2. Death—Causes. 3. Criminal investigation. 4. Medical examiners (Law) I. Chancellor, Arthur S. II. Title.
  HV8079.H6A36 2013
  363.25′952—dc23
                                        2011037933

6048
Printed in the United States of America
16 15 14 13 12   10 9 8 7 6 5 4 3 2 1

BRIEF TABLE OF CONTENTS

TABLE OF CONTENTS

FOREWORD

Death Investigation
by James M. Adcock & Arthur S. Chancellor

The first of a series of books from Jones & Bartlett Learning entitled "Jones & Bartlett Learning Guides to Law Enforcement Investigation".

This book on death investigation is the first of a series of books that will serve as a guide for criminal investigations. The series editor, James M. Adcock, designed this concept believing that a return to basics as they relate to individual crimes will increase awareness and solvability or clearances of these types of cases.

Both Dr. Adcock and Mr. Chancellor are retired U.S. Army CID agents who collectively have over 60 years of experience in conducting investigations and teaching students as well as the nuances of conducting criminal investigations. Adcock went from retirement to being a Chief Deputy Coroner and moved on into academia where he has touched the lives of many forensic scientists, criminal justice students, and detectives around the country. This all coincided with his position as a professor at the University of New Haven and his Fellow status and teachings with the Henry C. Lee Institute of Forensic Science. He recently published a book, *Cold Cases: An Evaluation Model with Follow-up Strategies for Investigators* and has now embarked upon making the investigative process better through this series of books.

After his retirement from the U.S. Army, Mr. Chancellor went to work for the Mississippi State Crime Lab as a Senior Crime Scene Analyst and later transferred to the Mississippi Bureau of Investigation where he created and managed the MBI's cold case unit. Mr. Chancellor has also served as an adjunct instructor for the University of Mississippi, at Clayton State University, Marrow, GA, and as a certified instructor at the Mississippi State Police Academy. He is also a graduate of the FBI National Academy. From Mississippi Mr. Chancellor went back to the U.S. Army CID as a civilian investigator where he is operationally responsible for the review of death investigations for completeness and accuracy as well as supervising CID agents in their day-to-day investigative activities. While he is the coauthor with Adcock on this book, he has also taken on the task of writing another book on the investigation of sexual assaults. Both he and Dr. Adcock are members of the American Academy of Forensic Sciences.

The authors have done a superb job in this book to bring theory, science, and practical experience to the forefront while promoting the "basics" of conducting a criminal investigation with an emphasis on death investigation. It is a refreshing approach to the subject using experience and basic logic to demonstrate how one should go about working a death investigation. The authors make their points without getting hung up on the many technical issues better covered in separate texts and case examples.

The authors have run the gamut from understanding death, to conceptualizing the investigative process from utilization of the scientific method, to first responder duties, from the crime scene to the investigation. They then cover the importance of developing a good victimology report, and provide information regarding autopsy and interpreting injuries, interviewing witnesses and suspects, reconstructing the information where theories of the crime can be validated, and investigating the most difficult cases—those deaths that are equivocal in nature. They thoroughly address investigative and supervisory mistakes found in death investigations and discuss legal responsibilities surrounding these types of cases. The authors have provided a sample of the Behavioral Analysis Interview as it relates to a homicide; a suspect identification model utilizing pre-crime behavior, peri-crime behavior, and post-crime behavior; and lastly, a sample of an equivocal death analysis.

Readers of this book will be well informed about the basics of conducting death investigations, not just homicides, but suicides and accidental deaths as well. It will become a worthwhile reference for all practitioners.

Dr. Henry C. Lee, Distinguished Chair Professor
University of New Haven
Founder, Henry C. Lee Institute of Forensic Science

PREFACE

James M. Adcock, PhD
Series Editor

For many years as both an investigator and an academician, I have seen the need for a series of books that would specifically address the investigative process in more detail than what had been previously provided. Most texts on criminal investigation discuss the process and all crimes in one book as if all types of investigations are conducted in the same exact manner. In my view this is far from the case and while some steps are the same, each crime type brings a different perspective to the forefront. Furthermore, over some thirty plus years of experience as an investigator I have also come to realize "we" as investigators and supervisors of investigators have to be held accountable for some if not many of the unsolved cases that exist today, especially with homicides. Hence, the creation of this book series entitled *Jones & Bartlett Learning Guides to Law Enforcement Investigation* in which there will be several books addressing specific types of crimes and the investigative processes that should be applied.

The first of these is this book on death investigation that I have coauthored with Arthur S. Chancellor, another thirty-year-plus veteran of conducting criminal investigations. I use the title *Death Investigation* because it is more encompassing of what a death detective actually does. While most books on homicide investigation are valuable resources they tend to be too technical and do not focus on the basics. Therefore, this book outlines the process of conducting a death investigation in a simple and easy to follow manner.

Following this collaboration, Mr. Chancellor is taking on the task of writing a book on sexual assault investigations. Other topics in the series will eventually include interviewing children in criminal cases; investigating missing persons and children; and hopefully other topics such as computer crime investigations, and managing the investigative process, all with the goal of providing specific information that is directly related to the investigation of the type of crime at hand.

ACKNOWLEDGMENTS

We would like to thank the following reviewer for his feedback:

James Smith, Troy University

   No venture of this nature can be successful without the assistance of many individuals. First and foremost I want to thank my former step-son George David Johnson whose artful talents were put to use many years ago to draw the numerous illustrations found in Chapter Seven. Initially these were created to make my death investigation presentations easier to understand, especially when it came to interpreting various types of injuries. At that time I had no idea that I would be writing this book and would need these again.

   I need to also acknowledge Sean Connelly and the editorial staff at Jones & Bartlett Learning for their hard work helping me to get this book off the ground and published on schedule.

James M. Adcock, PhD

   I would like to thank CW5 Ricky L. Sanders (ret) and CW4 David C. Allen (ret), two of the best CID agents I have had the pleasure to work for during my 20 years with Army CID. Their time and effort to teach, train, and mentor me meant all the difference in the world in my career. Thanks Chiefs. I would also like to thank my family and wife, Tracy, for all their support and putting up with the whole process. I especially want to thank my dad, James Shanda, for pushing, prodding, and nudging me to always do my best throughout my life and career.

   "Here you go Pop—I finally did it!"
Arthur S. Chancellor

INTRODUCTION

According to Scripps News Service,[1] 185,000 murders since 1980 remain unsolved. This staggering figure should cause anyone to take note and ask why we are in such a state of affairs as it relates to the death investigation process in the United States. The factors contributing to this dilemma are many and they range from societal changes, to economics, to drugs, gangs, etc. However, as the authors of this book we also strongly believe some of the responsibility for the lack of solving these cases belongs on the shoulders of the supervisors and the detectives charged to investigate these cases. Frequently the investigative agencies do not have the resources nor adequate training and the supervisory oversight required to become more successful at accurately resolving death cases.

Many books on the market delve into the investigative and forensic aspects of homicides but singularly, do not adequately address death investigation as a whole. For many years the authors have been teaching the investigative aspects associated with all death cases, not just homicides. Understanding the entire process and event (whether it be homicide, suicide, accident, or natural) with all of its nuances makes the detectives better death investigators. It is true however, that any death case should be approached from the standpoint that it is a homicide until the facts and circumstances prove otherwise. The forming of "tunnel vision" may cause the demise of the investigation and result in the waste of time and resources not to mention the fact that the case may remain unresolved.

Statistically, natural deaths represent approximately 90% of all deaths that occur, and as long as there is a medical doctor willing to certify that the death is from natural causes, then all is well and good. The problems that arise do not normally involve natural deaths but rather become complicated when the death hovers between suicide and accident or homicide and suicide or even homicide and accident. These are equivocal cases because it is not readily apparent what happened, how, and why. Therefore, the goal of the death investigator is to first determine "what" happened.

In this book, the authors provide the readers information about the death process and concepts known to be productive for those charged with investigating such cases. In Chapter 1 we have started with "Understanding Death" as a lead-in as to how this part of our system functions. It will include cause and manner of death determinations, physiological changes that occur to the body once death has occurred, and will end with a discussion about the medico-legal death investigation system.

Chapter 2 enlightens the reader to the three investigative components—physical, informational, and behavioral. Then we provide a description of the four phases of homicide and lastly, the scientific method for investigators. The next chapter discusses the responsibilities of first responders at death cases, outlining such things as dying declarations, scene security, interviews of witnesses, proper note taking, and the establishment of a security or contamination log.

In Chapter 4, the intricacies of investigating a death crime scene are detailed. This is followed by a discussion of how to conduct the preliminary investigation and develop investigative leads for the follow-up investigation. In Chapter 6 we have detailed the process for developing a victimology report, the importance of which cannot be over stated for s/he who knows the victim also knows the perpetrator.

As we progress into Chapter 7, the autopsy along with the interpretation of various injuries are all discussed. The correct interpretation of these injuries is critical if one is to attain an accurate manner of death determination. From types of injuries and their interpretation, the book goes to the interview process and the gathering of information from witnesses and suspects. This is followed by the reconstruction phase of any death investigation where timelines are created and hypotheses of what happened are either verified or invalidated.

Since suicides are far more common than homicides and because many such cases become very equivocal, we have dedicated a chapter to the investigation of equivocal deaths with an emphasis on investigating these potentially problematic cases. From there we have gone into describing some of the common mistakes made during death investigation in hopes that you do not fall victim to these. The final chapter brings to light the very important report writing aspect of any investigation, but particularly a death case and the critical phase of coordinating the investigation with the prosecution.

In the three appendices, we have included one that uses a homicide to illustrate how the Behavioral Analysis Interview should be used; another one on suspect identification through pre-, peri-, and post-offense behaviors; and, the equivocal death analysis of a case where the manner of death (homicide versus suicide) was at question.

All twelve chapters were jointly written by the authors while the appendices were provided separately. Appendix A came from the Inbau, Reid, Buckley, and Jayne book, *Criminal Interrogations and Confessions*; Appendix B was put together by Richard D. Walter and Sarah L. Stein; and Appendix C was my equivocal death analysis of the Hess case which was initially published by the *Investigative Sciences Journal* in March 2011.

Ultimately, we are hopeful that this book will fill a void in the topic of death or homicide investigation by providing a fresh approach. Many previous writings, while informative, do not address all of the investigative processes necessary for an investigation to be thorough and complete. In fact, this book will go a long way to augmenting those writings and will make the reader a better death detective.

James M. Adcock
Arthur S. Chancellor

Notes

1. Hargrove, T., *Nearly 185,000 homicides since 1980 remain unsolved.* Retrieved from http://www.scrippsnews.com/projects/murder-mysteries/nearly-185000-homicides-1980-remain-unsolved.

CHAPTER ONE

Understanding Death and the Death Investigation System

Death is referred to as "the permanent cessation of all vital functions; the end of life"[1] and while most of us probably know that we felt it necessary to start off with a simple definition. Most of the time the end of life comes after many years of living when someone dies of natural causes. Well over 90% of all deaths are what we call a "natural" death. Sometimes it is just old age but many others succumb to things like cancer, brain hemorrhages, or some other physiological or disease process. It is interesting to note that only about 1% of all deaths are homicides, 2–3% are suicides, and the rest are either accidental or equivocal where we do not know what happened. Therefore, the object of this chapter will be to build the foundation or knowledge base which the death investigator will utilize in analyzing and interpreting facts and circumstances to determine what we call the manner of death (homicide, suicide, accident, natural or undetermined), who did it, when, how, and why.

▶ Cause and Manner of Death

It is important to understand the difference between cause of death and manner of death. Cause of death is the medical reason for the death; e.g. gunshot wound to the chest, stab wound to the abdomen, blunt force trauma to the head, etc. This is determined by the coroner and/or medical examiner (ME) serving in specific jurisdictions. This person is also legally responsible for making the final manner of death determination of either homicide, suicide, accident, natural or undetermined. It was mentioned previously that the death investigator is charged with "analyzing and interpreting facts and circumstances to determine what we call the manner of death." However, the actual label placed on the death certificate is the responsibility of the coroner or medical examiner. The death investigator provides the critical information necessary for an accurate determination in conjunction with either a medical evaluation and/or autopsy of the

1

deceased. It is extremely important that the police and the coroner/ME work together as a team.

While the cause of death can be almost anything, the manner of death focuses on the five possibilities mentioned previously. The manner of death determination should be based on the totality of the circumstances and not a guess based on limited information. Homicide is basically defined as one taking the life of another without any consideration for which statute may have been violated (i.e. first degree murder versus manslaughter or negligent homicide). Suicide is one taking the life of oneself or as Freud would call it, "selbstmord" or self-murder. Accidental deaths are exactly that—an accident in which a set of circumstances occurred that lead to a death. In some jurisdictions charges may still be filed as in motor vehicle accidents (MVA) but the death certificate will still read accident MVA. The degree of fault or negligence is not something the coroner/ME are concerned with. Natural deaths have already been explained and absent any evidence to the contrary these types of deaths will be labeled natural. The last category is "undetermined" and these can be undetermined cause and/or undetermined manner of death. In these cases, the coroner/ME does not have sufficient information to accurately label the death.

Legal Definitions

As previously stated, if the manner of death is determined to be homicide, then that is the label placed on the death certificate and basically means one taking the life of another. But when one is arrested by law enforcement and subsequently charged for a statute violation the label is different and more comprehensive in considering the circumstances involved. These labels can vary from jurisdiction to jurisdiction but the elements of proof are all very similar. They may include labels such as, homicide, criminal homicide, negligent homicide, reckless homicide, vehicular homicide, felony DUI, murder, felony murder, first degree murder, second degree murder, voluntary or involuntary manslaughter, and justifiable homicide.

For the purposes of this text we will describe the most common according to Black's Law Dictionary[2]. Murder is defined as "the killing of a human being with malice aforethought." A person is guilty of murder if he or she: (1) caused the victim's death or serious bodily injury that then resulted in the victim's death, and (2) did so purposely or knowingly. In order for a defendant to be found guilty of murder, the State is required to prove these elements beyond a reasonable doubt: (1) that the defendant caused the victims death or serious bodily injury that then resulted in the death, and (2) that the defendant did so purposely or knowingly. A person acts purposely when it is that person's conscious objective to cause death or the serious bodily injury that results in death. A person acts knowingly when that person is aware of the likelihood that his conduct will cause death or serious bodily injury resulting in death.[3]

- First-degree murder—murder that is willful, deliberate, or premeditated; or that is committed during the course of another dangerous felony.
- Second-degree murder—murder that is not aggravated by any of the circumstances of first-degree murder.
- Felony murder—murder that occurs during the commission of a dangerous felony (often limited to rape, kidnapping, robbery, burglary and arson).
- Voluntary manslaughter—an act of murder may be reduced to manslaughter because of extenuating circumstances such as adequate provocation (arousing the heat of passion) or diminished capacity.
- Involuntary manslaughter—homicide in which there is no intention to kill or do grievous bodily harm, but that is committed with criminal negligence or during the commission of as crime not included within the felony murder rule.
- Negligent homicide—homicide resulting from the careless performance of a legal or illegal act in which the danger of death is apparent.
- Justifiable homicide—the killing of another in self-defense when faced with the danger of death or serious bodily injury.

▶ Coroner and Medical Examiner

While these terms may be familiar to some, there are those who may not fully comprehend the differences. The medico-legal death investigation system in the United States legally defines death investigation and death certification responsibility as being within the jurisdiction of a coroner, medical examiner or combination of the two. The statutes usually state that the coroner or medical examiner has investigative responsibility over all violent, unattended, unexpected or questionable deaths that occur within their jurisdiction.

The coroner is usually elected, is a political entity and may or may not be a medical doctor. The medical examiner, or ME, on the other hand, is normally appointed and is a medical doctor. The ME is usually a pathologist, specially trained and board certified in forensic pathology. In many jurisdictions the coroner utilizes the expertise of a pathologist or forensic pathologist to medically evaluate the body of the deceased and for the purpose of conducting an autopsy. In some jurisdictions these pathologists are not board certified in forensic pathology but may have some forensic experience. Both systems have their own unique problems, and issues may arise in either one that could adversely affect the outcome of a death investigation. Remember, the coroner and medical examiner have complete authority and jurisdiction over the body—it is *their* crime scene. Therefore, complete cooperation and collaboration between them and the law enforcement death investigator is paramount for a successful investigation.

▶ Forensic Autopsy

An autopsy is defined as "an examination of a body after death to determine the cause of death or the character and extent of changes produced by disease".[4] The practice of forensic pathology as applied in the forensic autopsy is defined as "a branch of medicine that applies the principles and knowledge of the medical sciences to problems in the field of law".[5] It is a sub-specialty of pathology that goes beyond the basic education and training of the average pathologist, who is primarily clinical. To be more specific, the forensic autopsy usually includes the following determinations[6]:

1. Identity of the deceased
2. Time of injury or time of onset of illness
3. The causative agent or object
4. The dynamics of the injury-direction, position, magnitude
5. Other contributing causes
6. Duration and quality of survival after injury or illness
7. Time of death
8. Cause of death
9. Manner of death

In order to accomplish this task, the forensic pathologist needs to be able to evaluate the entire situation including observations at the scene, statements from witnesses, historical information about all participants, and the evidence collected. In order to ensure a successful outcome, all agencies involved must work together cooperatively.

▶ Identification of the Deceased

Accurate identification of the deceased is imperative. Knowing the identity of the victim is critical in determining what happened to him, why, and who did it. There are five basic ways to identify the victim at autopsy. These are: (1) latent fingerprints, (2) dental records, (3) DNA, (4) surgical procedures, such as implants, scars, marks, tattoos, and (5) personal documents or personal recognition.

Fingerprints are the best method we have to identify a person, because there are no two fingerprints alike in the world. However, in order to make identification through latent prints, the victim's prints must have been obtained while the victim was still alive and a record of them must exist. Then post mortem prints (those taken during autopsy) may be compared to those earlier prints. Automated systems like AFIS are extremely helpful but the person must already be in the system while living for this to be effective. Another method utilizing prints can be found in **Case Study 1-1**.

Dental records are the second best method. Although humans tend to have the same number and type of teeth, through use they tend to become very individualized. Such individual markers may include overbite, crooked or chipped teeth, periodontal disease, cavities and fillings, other specialized reconstructive work such as bridges, or even false teeth. However, the difficulty remains that we must have previous records to use in comparison to the victim at autopsy.

Although DNA is one of the newest forensic developments especially in identifying suspects from crime scenes, it can be problematic because one cannot be identified to the exclusion of all others, but can be very significant statistically. This is particularly true with identical twins. They both have the same exact DNA because they were formed initially by the same egg and sperm cell and therefore have the same genetic markers. However, in the absence of fingerprints and dental identification, DNA is still a good choice.

Scars, particularly surgical scars, may also be used but it is the unusual scars or a series of surgical scars that should be used to identify a victim. The same can be said with dentures, false limbs, and pacemakers. Previously healed broken bones, or other medical procedures should be used in conjunction with medical records as a further means to identify the victim. Radiographic films taken during life may also be helpful when compared to those taken after death. An example of the utilization of x-rays coupled with a previously healed broken bone, is described and illustrated in **Case Study 1-2**.

Case Study 1-1

During the Oklahoma City bombing investigation, it was very difficult to accurately identify some of the deceased children because there were no recorded prints available for comparison. Therefore, several different methods were used. Some were able to be identified through their birth certificates that had an imprint of their foot. For some of the others, police actually obtained latent prints on personal possessions obtained from their homes. In one case, toys inside a damaged vehicle across the street from the destroyed building were obtained and latent prints recovered from them were used to identify one victim from post mortem prints.

Case Study 1-2

A farmer notified the coroner's office that along the side of a creek on his property he found what he believed to be a human leg bone. A forensic anthropologist confirmed that the initial bone was in fact human and as a result, a systematic search of the area was conducted over the next three days. Participants in the search were members of the sheriff's office crime scene unit, the coroner's office and two graduate students studying forensic anthropology under the supervision of the anthropologist. The initial observations by the anthropologist of the skeletal material indicated to him that the deceased person was most likely 40–50 years old and male. Armed with this information, as the search continued and more material was collected (see **Figure 1-1**). Detectives from the sheriff's office began canvassing the area and gathered reports of missing persons that coincided with the description.

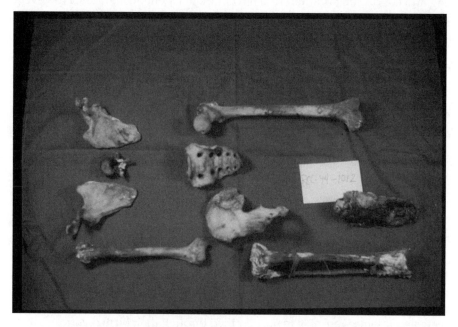

FIGURE 1-1. Case Study 1-2, identification made from limited skeletal material. See Color Plate 1.

The search ended with only those bones reflected in Figure 1-1. During a subsequent examination of these it was determined that the decedent had a plate surgically placed on his leg to possibly repair a broken ankle (see **Figure 1-2**). In the meantime the detectives located a missing persons report

FIGURE 1-2. Case Study 1-2, metal brace surgically placed on victim's broken ankle. See Color Plate 2.

from 3 months prior of a black male, 40–50 years old, last seen alive walking away from the home he was living in not far from the location of the skeletal material. Interviews of the occupants of the home confirmed this and that the deceased had in fact had an operation for a broken ankle sometime in the past.

The medical records of the deceased were located at a local hospital and a review of those records reflected he had in fact undergone surgery for a broken ankle and a plate had been placed on his leg to stabilize the leg and ankle. Radiographs taken at the time of the surgery were obtained and compared to those taken after death. There was no question that the two were identical and that the recovered remains were this person (see **Figure 1-3**). No other skeletal material was found and it could only be assumed that animals took them. Based on what was collected the person was positively identified; the cause and manner of death were undetermined, and the belief that it was most likely a natural death. That was all based on information gathered by the sheriff's department and the coroner in which there were no indications of foul play. The deceased was known to have heart problems; was known to take long walks in the rural area where he lived, and there were no indications that he had any enemies.

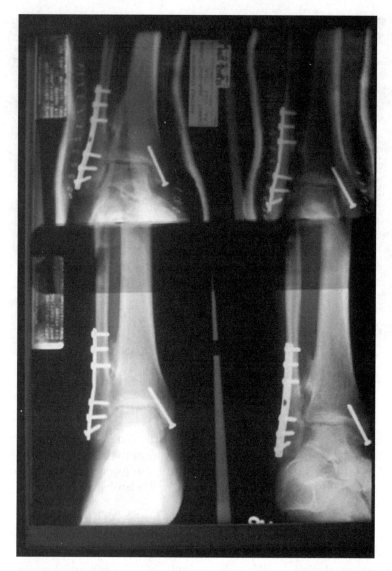

FIGURE 1-3. Case Study 1-2, ante mortem and post morten x-rays compared. See Color Plate 3.

At one time tattoos were a good source for identification but in recent years with the number of persons engaging in tattooing they're becoming more and more common. The more unusual or unique the tattoo, the more likely it can be used to identify the victim, particularly if the tattoo contained specific information such as children's names, or specific dates that can be compared with other information as a means to identify the owner. Certain birth marks may also be used.

Body piercings are another means of identification. These include those clearly visible such as tongue, ears, navel, nose, eyebrows, but might also include the penis or the nipples. One problem with the piercings of private areas is that the family may not be aware of them and therefore might not be able to confirm their location.

The least reliable of all methods of identification is the utilization of personal effects or documents found on or near the deceased. Clothing can be changed, wallets or personal effects can be stolen or planted on the body. If a tentative identification is made based on scars, marks, tattoos or personal identification/documents, be sure to confirm it through latent prints, dental, or DNA. This might avoid problems such as those described in **Case Study 1-3**.

Regardless of the method utilized, the investigator, in conjunction with the pathologist, should always seek to identify the decedent through one of the more reliable methods. Failing that, as many of the other methods as possible should be used to have a collective confirmation of identity.

If the identity cannot be established at the autopsy through one of the previously mentioned methods, steps may need to be taken to preserve the body for an extended period of time until it has been positively identified. This could range from a refrigerated morgue to a freezer specifically designed to maintain unidentified bodies and/or body parts. Once the body has been buried or the decaying process has begun, the identification becomes more difficult. The old adage "do it right the first time" is paramount because you may not ever get a second chance. With unidentified remains, an investigator will have to expand the search to other areas that might include records and information contained in the NCIC, VICAP, and missing person's reports; or use the media to broadcast a photograph or sketch of the unidentified person. It is important to remember that in over half of all murders committed the victim knew the assailant. Identification is critical in order for the investigation to proceed in the right direction. It is from this point that the operational plan is designed.

Case Study 1-3

Two teenage females were involved in a motor vehicle accident where one was seriously injured and the other was pronounced dead. Both were disfigured to the extent that identification was based on general appearance and clothing they were wearing at the time of the accident. Sadly, the deceased's parents took the girl identified as their daughter and buried her. Once the girl in the hospital woke up it was discovered that they had buried the wrong girl, and that their daughter was the one who had survived. As tragic as this scenario is, imagine the difficulties that may take place when the victim of a homicide cannot be properly identified or is incorrectly identified.

▶ Time of Death

The next major area of concern for the investigator and the forensic patholo-gist is the time of death. This is absolutely critical to the investigation espe-cially when attempting to evaluate alibis of persons of interest. Having not only the means and the motive to kill someone but also the opportunity are all a part of what the investigation needs to determine. However, time of death determination, without an eyewitness to the incident, is fraught with complications and is an educated guess based on the physiological changes the body goes through at the onset of death. Furthermore, information gath-ered from witnesses as to the last time the victim was seen alive must also be considered. Collectively, this information and the physiological changes in the body can provide a reasonably accurate time of death. The remaining investigative process will focus on and revolve around this determination.

These physiological changes incorporate a series of actions that take place at the onset of death. The primary three are algor mortis, livor mortis, and rigor mortis. An overall view of these can be found in **Figure 1-4**.

Keep in mind that none of these changes, in and of themselves, is that ac-curate but collectively they can be of great help. Algor mortis is the cooling of the body after death (Figure 1-4, Body Temp.). The body will cool, but no cooler than the ambient temperature and is affected in numerous ways by activity of the person just prior to the death, illness, infection, changes in the temperature surrounding the body, clothing, etc. A classic example of this can be found in **Figure 1-5**.[7] Therefore, careful consideration of these factors and

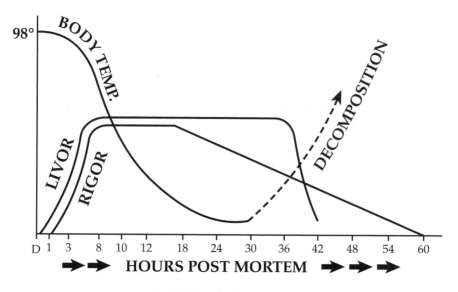

FIGURE 1-4. Physiological changes.

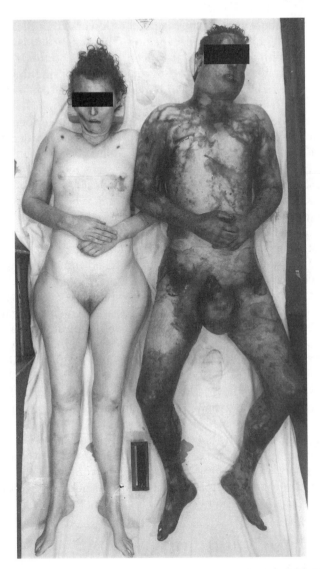

FIGURE 1-5. This couple was killed at the same time by a mentally deranged son. The body of the mother was found in the cool basement, while the body of the father was discovered in a warm upstairs room. Outside temperature was 90°, post mortem interval was forty-eight hours. (Reprinted with permission from Dr. Werner U. Spitz and Charles C. Thomas, Publisher.)

of the scene is important in determining the post mortem interval or time since death. The rule of thumb, under normal conditions, is that the body should be about 98.6°F and that once death occurs the temperature drops about 1.5°F each hour up to four hours; then drops about 1°F per hour. Body temperature however will never drop below the ambient temperature of the environment.

Livor mortis is the settling of the blood to the lower extremities of the body in accordance with gravity. The onset begins immediately and is advanced in 2–4 hours to a point of "fixation" between 8 and 12 hours. If the body is moved prior to fixation an incomplete development or positioning of the livor pattern may be seen. If this does occur it may also be helpful in narrowing the time of death; therefore full and complete documentation, including colored photographs of the body at the scene prior to removal are imperative.

Rigor mortis is the gradual onset of rigidity of the muscles after death. Also referred to as the stiffening of the body and while it begins in all muscles simultaneously, it is quickly evident and sometimes more prominent in the smaller muscles earlier than in the larger muscles.[8] Although this process starts almost immediately it may take up to 6 hours to become readily identifiable and up to 24 hours to complete rigor, or the entire body rigidity. It then will begin to dissipate after an additional 12–36 hours, dependent on the environment, temperature, etc., as stated earlier. Again, neither rigor mortis, nor livor mortis, nor algor mortis should be relied upon separately as sole determinant but collectively can be a strong indicator of the time of death.

Other determinants that the forensic pathologist may choose to evaluate in conjunction with the physiological changes are scene investigation information, ocular changes, vitreous potassium levels, the autopsy findings, and food in the stomach. However, when the discovery of the body is days to weeks after death the determination becomes more difficult. Rigor mortis may have come and gone, body temperature will have lost its value and decomposition may become evident internally as well as externally. The first stage of decomposition is usually the blue to green discoloration of the skin and abdomen and can be seen 24–36 hours after death. Other characteristics are marbling, bloating of the body, and skin slippage. Also noted may be insect activity on or in any injured areas of the body first where entrance to the body is facilitated. Any manifestation of maggots would be a clue to possible injury especially if not at a location of a normal body orifice or opening (mouth, eyes, etc.). At this point consultation with a forensic entomologist is highly suggested.

▶Skeletal Remains

Bodies that are extremely decayed or reduced to skeletal material present a challenge to the investigator. Care must be taken with the scene of the remains and the manner in which the material is collected. It is suggested that the investigator solicit assistance from either a forensic anthropologist or a forensic archeologist to ensure all human specimens are collected and that nothing with evidentiary value is left behind. Once collection is completed, the forensic anthropologist is asked to examine and evaluate the skeletal material looking for means of identification, signs of injury, or other information that may lead to the identity of the deceased.

In situations where skeletal material is found expect to spend hours to days processing the scene correctly. As stated above experts, are very helpful in these cases as the scene needs to be methodically processed to ensure the collection of all available pieces of bone, clothing, jewelry, projectiles, etc. It is suggested that the investigators secure and margin off the area into three separate levels of security (scene, search area, and control area). This will be discussed in later sections of this text that pertain to crime scenes and physical evidence.

References

1. Merriam-Webster (2010). Retrieved from http://www.merriam-webster.com.
2. Garner, B. A. (Ed.). (2004). *Black's law dictionary.* (8th ed.). St. Paul, MN: West Publishing.
3. New Jersey Statutes Annotated (2004). Retrieved from http://www.judiciary.state.nj.us/criminal/charges/homicide2.doc.
4. Merriam Webster (2010). Retrieved from http://www.merriam-webster.com.
5. Di Maio, D. J., & Di Maio, V. J. M. (1989). *Forensic pathology.* New York, NY: Elsevier Publishing. p. 1.
6. Froede, R. C., (Ed.). (2003). (2nd ed.). *Handbook of forensic pathology.* Northfield, IL: College of American Pathologists. p. 140.
7. Spitz, W. U., & Fisher, R. S. (2006). (4th ed.). *Medicolegal Investigation of Death.* Springfield, IL: Charles C. Thomas Pub. Ltd. p. 108. Reprinted with permission.
8. Spitz, W. U., & Fisher, R. S. p. 72.

Conceptualizing and Applying the Investigative Process in Death Cases

Prior to entering the investigative phase of any case, particularly death scenarios, it is critical that detectives fully comprehend the conceptual framework of the investigative process and of the crime itself. In this chapter, the investigative process will be disaggregated into four sections. The first section will describe the three components of information pertinent to an investigation—physical, behavioral, and informational evidence, as well as each component's relevance to answering the questions that comprise the second section of the process—what happened, to whom, when, where, how and why—that are critical to the resolution of a case. Thirdly, to assist investigators in their efforts to comprehend the conceptual framework of homicide, we will discuss the four behavioral phases typically observed within the context of murder. Finally, the scientific method for investigators will be examined. It is an invaluable tool in accurately determining what happened and who did it.

▶ The Three Components—Physical, Informational, and Behavioral

Keep in mind that the purpose of this chapter is to put in place the conceptual framework of the investigative process as it relates specifically to death investigation. Subsequent chapters will be more specific and thoroughly address the physical evidence and crime scene concerns as well the interview and interrogation processes.

As we look over the many available textbooks and classes offering information on the investigative process we find that they all emphasize the physical and informational aspects of the investigation as they relate to individual types of crime—homicide, rape, etc. However, in this book, we are suggesting that all investigations are comprised of three major components, not just two (see **Figure 2-1**). These would include the physical aspects and all the items of physical evidence that have evidentiary value, and the informational pieces as they relate to not only interviews and interrogations, but also retrieved documents and records that contain information about the actors involved. The component that is frequently overlooked is the behavioral element—those behaviors exhibited by the victim and especially by persons of interest.

The structure of most criminal investigation courses, whether taught at a university or in a police academy, still place emphasis on the crime scene with its physical evidence possibilities and the information gleaned from the interviews and interrogation processes. This makes sense because physical evidence can tie a suspect to a particular person or a crime scene, while the interview process can identify other potential witnesses. Additionally the interrogation has the potential to produce an admission or confession. When these elements (physical and informational) are linked together they carry a lot of weight in a court proceeding.

So why worry about the behavioral elements? Because physical evidence is not always properly collected and secured from the crime scene, and may only circumstantially link the suspect to the scene. DNA testing only

The Three Components of an Investigation

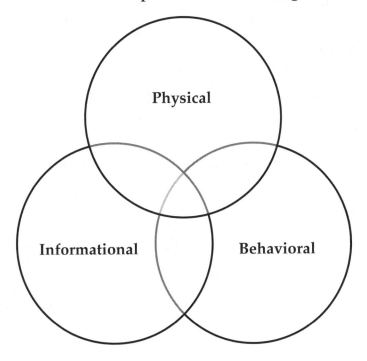

FIGURE 2-1. The three components of an investigation.

resolves about 27% of all cases but does eliminate far more than it identifies. Eyewitnesses and regular witnesses have been known to be wrong and false confessions do occur. As evidence of this, consider that since 1980 we have accumulated nearly 185,000 unresolved murders and throughout those decades to the present day, we traditionally only clear about two thirds of all homicides. This is an alarming figure that should cause us to question how and why we got into this predicament and is there anything we can do about it?

Our suggestion, while not a panacea, is to include in the investigative process the behavioral aspects as portrayed by the victim and persons of interest. Including this element in the three components results in a better and more thorough investigative end product. From the standpoint of the victim we are referring to the victimology (as will be discussed in subsequent material). We need to ask and answer the question—why this victim? As you will learn in that discussion, knowing your victim helps you to know and understand your perpetrator.

While keeping within the structure of the victimology report the investigator needs to closely evaluate the behavioral characteristics of all persons of interest, searching for key element(s) that may connect the victim and the crime typology to a particular person. What this entails is the gathering of information that will delineate the actions and behavior of your persons of interest into three types of behavior: (1) *pre-offense behavior*, (2) *peri or crime behavior*, and (3) *post-offense behavior*. This goes back to the old adage that with every crime the investigator needs to develop knowledge regarding what happened before, what happened during and what happened after the crime was committed. One way to accomplish this task is to categorize the crime/death into a particular typology. This will be the beginning of developing your hypothesis of how and why the crime was committed; in other words the start of a behavioral view of the crime that may assist in the identification of a specific perpetrator or the motive behind the death. If the physical evidence and informational pieces acquired through interviews are sound, then the behavioral analysis will significantly add to the case. But if the physical and informational are equivocal, the behavioral analysis may be the only link to a proper identification of the offender and successful case resolution.

To illustrate this concept we look to Groth's[1] research on rapes and rapists published in the late 1970s. Groth developed rape typologies and coined the terms that described a rapist as being a Power Rapist, an Anger Rapist or a Sadistic Rapist. In the years that followed, the FBI (specifically, what used to be called the FBI Behavioral Science Unit) realigned these into four categories known as Power Assertive (PA), Power Reassurance (PR), Anger Retaliatory (AR) or Anger Excitation (AE). Then in the late 1990s Keppel and Walter[2] illustrated how these same four typologies can be applied to murder investigations as well.

A good reference for these is the Crime Classification Manual.[3] These typologies will be further described and detailed in later material on conducting the suspect interview. The key is, at the onset, investigators need to be aware of behavioral traits, understand the typologies and know what to look for during the initial stages of the investigation that includes crime scene specifics.

▶Who, What, When, Where, How, and Why?

In any reported crime the investigator attempts to answer these questions; who did what to whom, when, where, how and why? The first question that should come to your mind is "What happened?" Do not let the scene overwhelm you to the point of thinking something like, "who could do such a thing to a child?" Determining what happened first is critical and foremost as this sets the foundation for you to work towards answering the other questions. Eventually, if not readily identified, the perpetrator should surface through the investigative process if it is followed correctly.

As you interview witnesses you will constantly ask them questions like, "What did you see?", "Where were you when the shots were fired?", "How do you know that person?", or "Do you know why?" These go on and on and relate in one form or another to answering the questions needed to accurately determine what happened, who did it, when, where, how and hopefully determine why they committed the crime. Other examples of the questions that need to be answered can be found in **Figure 2-2**.

Keep in mind that the three components—physical, informational and behavioral—are determined through these questions and the answers you ascertain during the investigative process. Whether it is the physical evidence that tells you how the victim died or a confession from the shooter that states why he shot the person, they all accumulate, if done correctly, into an accurate determination of the facts associated with case.

▶The Four Phases of Homicide

In a lecture by Keppel on serial killers,[4] he began by describing how, in sexual serial killings; there are four phases of homicide: (1) the antecedent phase, (2) the homicide, (3) the body disposal and (4) the post-offense behavior. While his lecture focused on sexual serial killers, it became apparent that the same four phases could also apply to other homicides, especially if they contained a sexual element (but do not necessarily have to be serial killings). The following is a thumbnail sketch of the general type of questions that need answering to establish the four phases.

Who?
Who was the victim?
Who made the report?
Who discovered the offense?
Who saw or heard something of
   importance?
Who had a motive for committing the
   offense?
Who committed the offense?
Who helped the offender?
Who was interviewed?
Who worked on the case?
Who marked the evidence?
Who received the evidence?

What?
What happened?
What type of offense was committed?
What actions were taken by the
   suspect and using what methods?
What do the witnesses know about it?
What evidence was obtained?
What was done with the evidence?
What tools or weapons were used?
What actions did you take?
What further action is needed?
What knowledge, skill, or strength
   was needed to commit the crime?
What other agencies were notified?
What witnesses were not contacted?
What time was the offense committed?
What time was the offense reported?
What was the time of your arrival?
What time did you contact witnesses?

Where?
Where was the offense discovered?
Where was the offense committed?
Where were the tools or weapons
   found?
Where was the victim?
Where was the suspect seen?
Where were the witnesses?
Where does the perpetrator live or
   frequently go?
Where is the perpetrator?
Where would the perpetrator be most
   likely to go?

Where was the perpetrator
   apprehended?
Where was the evidence marked?
Where was the evidence stored?

When?
When did the crime occur?
When was the victim last seen?
When was the perpetrator arrested?
When did help arrive?

How?
How was the offense committed?
How did the perpetrator get to and
   from the scene?
How did the perpetrator obtain
   information needed to commit the
   offense?
How were the tools or weapons
   obtained?
How did you get your information
   regarding the offense?
How did you affect the arrest?
With what trade or profession are the
   tools associated?
With what other offense is this one
   associated?

Why?
Why was the offense committed?
Why were particular tools or weapons
   used?
Why was the offense reported?
Why were the witnesses reluctant to
   talk?
Why was the witness eager to point
   out the perpetrator?
Why was there a delay in reporting
   this offense?

WITH WHOM
With whom does the perpetrator
   associate?
With whom was the victim last seen?
With whom are the witnesses
   connected?
With whom do you expect to locate
   the suspect?

FIGURE 2-2. Who, What, Where, When, How, Why?

Phase one (the antecedent phase)—the perpetrators behavior prior to the crime is what is important. As we look at the investigation, crime scene, evidence, the body site, etc., are there any indications of prior planning? What types of pre-crime stressors occurred in this person's life that were the catalyst for him moving into phase two and the murder? For example: a change in his mental or emotional state; a conflict with a significant other; loss of job; an argument with family or parents; or financial problems.

Phase two (the homicide)—the actual murder takes place. Questions that need answering are: How was the victim selected? Why this victim over any other? What was the method of abduction and why that over any other method? What did he do to the victim and how did he do it? Where did he go to commit the murder? Did he leave his "signature" or calling card at the scene?[5] Were there any post mortem injuries?

Phase three (the body disposal)—related to the body disposal and disposal site. This stage is especially important because up to the actual murder, the offender was engaged in planning or constructing a fantasy about committing a murder. However, now the offender must deal with the result of these actions, resulting in more displayed behavior. Here the investigators need to determine how the body was transported to this location? Why this site over any other site? Were there any attempts to conceal the body or was it open to public view? Was the victim posed in a certain manner (sexually suggestive or not, state of dress or undress, etc.)? Many of these could be important issues to the killer. He may want the victim discovered and/or he may want to shock the conscience of society with his acts.

Phase four (the post offense behavior)—What did s/he do after disposing of the body—flee, get sick, over indulge in alcohol or drugs, not show up for work or school, or return to the disposal site? Typically there are also personality changes that those close to the offender may recognize.

If while conducting the investigation we can attune ourselves to these phases it will go a long way to determining the facts of the incident and help us to develop a behavioral profile of the perpetrator. Looking for the post-offense behaviors as described in phase four, while not absolute, can provide an excellent indicator for possible inclusion of a certain person as a potential suspect.

▶ The Scientific Method for Investigators

The scientific method is valorized in both academia and the hard sciences. If followed properly, it is the only methodology that is nearly impervious to scrutiny from fellow experts. As such, it is important for investigators to consider the utilization of this method to deter criticism from colleagues, attorneys, the court system, and juries. In the arena of forensic science for example, a landmark ruling by the Supreme Court that elevated the standards for expert testimony was the *Daubert* decision. In *Daubert*, seven members of the court agreed on the following guidelines for admitting scientific expert testimony:

Judge is gatekeeper—Under Rule 702*, the task of "gatekeeping," or assuring that scientific expert testimony truly proceeds from "scientific knowledge", rests on the trial judge.

Relevance and reliability—This requires the trial judge to ensure that the expert's testimony is "relevant to the task at hand" and that it rests "on a reliable foundation."[6] Concerns about expert testimony cannot be simply referred to the jury as a question of weight.

Scientific knowledge = scientific method/methodology—A conclusion will qualify as *scientific knowledge* if the proponent can demonstrate that it is the product of sound "scientific methodology," derived from the scientific method.

Factors relevant—The Court has defined "scientific methodology" as the process of formulating hypotheses and then conducting experiments to prove or falsify the hypothesis, and provided a nondispositive, nonexclusive, "flexible" test for establishing its "validity" consisting of:

1. Empirical testing: the theory or technique must be falsifiable, refutable, and testable
2. Subjected to peer review and publication
3. Known or potential error rate
4. The existence and maintenance of standards and controls concerning its operation
5. Degree to which the theory and technique is generally accepted by a relevant scientific community

The argument could be made that the *Daubert* standards are only applicable to crime scene technicians and or crime laboratory personnel; in other words, those individuals associated with hard sciences. However, it is imperative that investigators are held to the same level of accountability regarding *Daubert*. This point is made given the fact that historically, there have been several cases where convictions have been overturned because law enforcement officials gave testimony based solely upon their preceding experience and without further validation of their opinions. By validation, we mean that the hypotheses of the crime have been empirically scrutinized, and all other

---

*In 2000, Rule 702 was amended in an attempt to codify and structure the "*Daubert* trilogy." Rule 702 now includes the additional provisions which state that a witness may testify only if
  1) the testimony is based upon sufficient facts or data
  2) the testimony is the product of reliable principles and methods, and
  3) the witness has applied the principles and methods reliably to the facts of the case

Case Study 2-1

A classic example of the type of testimony mentioned above, where an investigator relies exclusively upon previous experience as a law enforcement official, occurred in a murder trial in which a detective testified regarding a bloody knife that had been recovered from the carpeted floor outside the bedroom of the suspect. The detective stated that in his opinion, based on his experience, the knife had been placed as an attempt at crime scene staging, rather than having been dropped by the perpetrator as the defendant had alleged. Prior to trial, no empirical reconstruction of the crime scene had been attempted, for example, by using a similar weapon, dipped in blood, and dropped onto a similar carpet to try and replicate the defendant's account of events. The defendant in this case was convicted initially, but later received another trial and was acquitted for various reasons. The point implicit to this case study is that any testimonial blunders made by law enforcement could have been easily avoided via the use of the scientific method in recreating the crime scene.

possibilities, within reason, have been eliminated. Keeping this in mind, the utilization of the scientific method during the course of an investigation is paramount.

While the scientific method generally applies to those engaged in hard sciences, it is strongly recommended that investigators use the technique as well, whenever possible, to validate hypotheses of the crime. With the recent attacks of "hired guns" within the criminal justice system, why provide defense attorneys the ammunition to strike down your case? It is better instead, to eliminate opposing theories while simultaneously affirming the ones you, as an investigator proffer, in pre-adjudication phases of the investigation.

The scientific method adheres strictly to the laws of logic when discovering and testing scientific truth. However, in its most raw and basic form, it can be somewhat muddled when investigators confront the scene of a death. Forensic pathologist Dr. Thomas Young[7] argues that "past events cannot be observed, cannot be predicted or deduced from physical evidence, and cannot be tested experimentally." We respectfully disagree with Dr. Young in the context of the assertion that while facts cannot be deduced from physical evidence; in many scenarios, it is possible via crime scene reconstruction to affirm the occurrence of past events with a reasonable amount of certainty. However, Dr. Young is correct to the point that even given the best reconstruction efforts, investigators can never be absolutely certain of a sequence and or occurrence of events in the context of empirical standards. As such, it is prudent for investigators to be conscious of utilizing terms of uncertainty such as, "probably", "might have", "could have", "consistent with," etc. when recording events and providing subsequent testimony.

Young further enumerates his recommended practice, which involves comparing "anamnestic evidence obtained by investigators with observable physical findings discovered at the crime scene, in the crime laboratory, or in the autopsy suite."[8] It is often proffered that forensic science (we can also add criminal investigation) studies the past and not the present; we cannot see the past nor can we predict it. We typically, as investigators, find ourselves using "scenario building" where we deduce the occurrence of certain events from the findings at the scene of a crime. Keep in mind however that the initial conclusions reached by investigators are not infallible; as time passes, other relevant evidence may avail itself, at which point investigators must be willing to re-evaluate certain hypotheses of the crime. If periodic reviews and reevaluations of a case are not undertaken, the end result that unfortunately may occur is "tunnel vision."

The method described by Young above helps investigators avoid the simple "scenario building" problem and the concept in and of itself does a better job of satisfying the legal precedent of "innocent until proven guilty." At the same time, Young's advice also recognizes the ability of the investigator to "reason from events to findings on the basis of his or her experience and expertise."[9] While experience can be an invaluable asset during the course of a death investigation; coupling expertise and experience with the core values of the scientific method provides a much more solid conceptual framework in conducting such an investigation. As we see it being applied to investigations, **Table 2-1** provides an outline of the suggested method for investigators; it will assist in ensuring that the correct perpetrator is identified while ameliorating the possibility of other scenarios having occurred.

If the investigative process depicted in the scientifically based model is followed correctly, it is believed that a larger percentage of cases will be successfully resolved. The investigator interviews people for information trying

TABLE 2-1. The Scientific Method for Investigators

1. Obtain from witnesses the accounts of what happened.

2. Based on these accounts anticipate the questions you will be asked by others so you can properly collect and record the physical evidence.

3. Collect and record the physical evidence.

4. Formulate hypotheses about the events that occurred and anticipate the questions you will be asked.

5. Determine whether or not the witness statements are consistent with the physical evidence; gather more information or evidence as needed.

6. Through the process of verifying witness statements, admissions/confessions, consider the evidence at hand and disprove as many hypotheses as you can.

7. Formulate an assessment (final hypothesis) to a reasonable degree of certainty, recognizing the existing limitations.

to answer the questions of what happened, when, where, how, by whom, and sometimes determines the why, and also collects the physical evidence that traditionally assist in making these determinations. In an effort to deconstruct and understand the process of events, a hypothesis is formulated. Anticipating future questions (No. 4 in the model), however, appears to be lacking in contemporary investigative practices. Investigators frequently tend to focus on a single-minded course of action without regard or consideration for other possible avenues of explanation. If an investigator makes a concerted effort to debunk (within reason) all other possibilities in an investigation, the hypothesis previously formulated will carry increased weight and satisfies the *Daubert* standard of being based on sufficient facts and data.

One of the more critical aspects inherent to basing a hypothesis upon sufficient facts and data, as well as the elimination of other explanations for the crime (via interviews and historical information), is the pairing of physical evidence with investigative beliefs to provide an empirical framework for your hypothesis. We turn to an old adage used to frame a case: "Can you believe what you see if you see what you believe?" That is, it is imperative for investigators to allow the evidence to guide the formulation of hypotheses, and not the opposite. Never try to make the evidence fit a theory; this is one of the quickest ways to invalidate the investigative process. In addition, keep in mind that despite the strength of the evidence, investigators must remain aware that very little in the world of investigations is absolute; we can never be certain, to an empirical standard, how past events occurred—we only endeavor to make sound, educated estimates after the elimination of other reasonable possibilities.

The solidification of the investigative process requires two additional tasks. The first is to verify witness statements and historical data with the comprehensive known facts and circumstances to validate or disprove previously discovered information. The second task is to falsify circumstantial evidence. This requires clarification: in this context, the word "falsify" means that if we are going to adhere to sound scientific principles, the investigative process must be able to withstand the rigors of scientific scrutiny and be grounded in empirical fact. Therefore, all investigative efforts, beyond the normal and advanced collection and evaluation phases, should be used to disprove (falsify) your hypothesis of how the crime occurred. If done correctly, this process will either affirm or cause you to reject the original hypothesis. If, when anticipating future questions, you are able to disprove all hypotheses external to yours, this will leave defense counsel at trial without ammunition for a mistrial, a theme to challenge the investigative theory, or worse, a "guilty" verdict.

In an effort to clarify this and provide a visual example of what this process might look like it is suggested that you carefully review the death investigation protocol in **Figure 2-3**. This protocol illustrates how behavioral actions by two people come together where an intervening event occurs that results in a death. From there the investigation has two prongs, one is giving attention to the scene and the physical evidence while the other is collecting the

Death Investigation Protocol

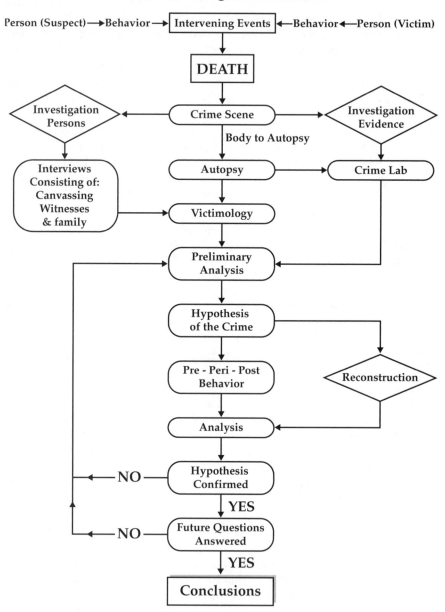

FIGURE 2-3. Death investigation protocol.

informational pieces of the puzzle, e.g. canvass, interviews of witness, etc. While the informational aspects continue, the body goes for an autopsy where more evidence is collected. Evidence from the scene and autopsy are sent to the crime lab for examination and analysis.

Many of the informational pieces will contribute to the victimology and eventually the known aspects of the evidence and information will come to a point where a preliminary analysis is conducted and a hypothesis or hypotheses are stated regarding what happened. While these hypotheses are tested through reconstruction of both the physical and informational pieces of the puzzle, the information regarding pre-offense behavior, crime behavior and post-offense behavior are evaluated. These behaviors are then reevaluated along with the reconstruction results to look for consistency and/or invalid pieces.

If a hypothesis is confirmed the investigation moves on to anticipating and answering future questions. If not confirmed then the process reverts back to the preliminary analysis where the process begins over again developing more ideas and testing them through reconstruction. This reverting back to the preliminary analysis may also occur if one is not able to anticipate and adequately answer future questions. The process is not finished until hypotheses are confirmed, within a reasonable amount of certainty, and all anticipated questions can be answered, also to a reasonable degree of certainty.

References

1. Groth, A. N. with Bernbaum, H. J. (1979). *Men who rape: The psychology of the offender.* New York, NY: Plenum Press.
2. Keppel, R. D., & Walter, R. D. (1999). Profiling Killers: A revised classification model for understanding sexual murder. *International Journal of Offender Therapy and Comparative Criminology, 43*(4), 317–337.
3. Douglas, J. E., Burgess, A. W., Burgess, A. G., & Ressler, R. K. (2006). *Crime classification manual.* (2nd ed.). San Francisco, CA: Jossey-Bass.
4. Keppel, R. D. 2005, Lecture on serial killers at the West Haven Police Department, West Haven, CT.
5. Keppel, R. D., & Birnes, W. J. (2009). *Serial violence, analysis of modus operandi and signature characteristics of killers.* Boca Raton, FL: CRC Press.
6. *Daubert v. Merrell Dow Pharms, Inc.,* 509 U.S. 579, 584-587.
7. Young, T. The Forensic Inference Series. *Forensic Science and the Scientific Method.* Retrieved from http://www.heartlandforensic.com/writing/forensic-inference/forensic-science-and-the-scientific-method.
8. Young, T. The Forensic Inference Series. *Forensic Science and the Scientific Method.*
9. Young, T. (2010). Email communication with Young in concert with information gleaned from the aforementioned website.

CHAPTER THREE

The First Responders

▶ Duties of the First Responders

The typical first responder to a reported death is the uniformed patrol officer who has some very important responsibilities and duties following highly emotional, often violent, and certainly tragic personal events. On his/her shoulders may rest the outcome of the investigation or the possibility of determining what happened.

There is no exact formula, protocol, or step-by-step instruction for responding to a reported death because the events and circumstances surrounding each event are different. Instead of detailed step-by-step instructions, the first responder has a wide range of both specific and general duties that are expected to be carried out as the situation dictates to the best of their ability. The most crucial of these duties are discussed in the following material.

Quickly But Safely Respond to the Scene and Take Charge

Upon dispatch the officer is expected to respond to the scene safely, evaluate the situation, and most importantly, to firmly take control. The obvious purpose of the quick response and taking control of the situation is to try to limit any type of damage or contamination of the scene. This is not always an easy task because death investigations are highly charged emotional events, especially when the body is found in a public place such as a residential neighborhood, involves multiple victims, the victim was killed in a particularly brutal manner, or the death involves the elderly or children. These are just a few of the many possible circumstances which can spark emotional responses.

Determine Status of Victim

Status refers to the basic medical condition of the victim and determining if the victim is actually dead or is still alive. If the victim is alive, then first aid and rapid evacuation of the victim to a medical facility is the absolute priority. In these circumstances, scene contamination by medical personnel is unavoidable and expected; but saving the victim's life is paramount. Any contamination by medical personnel such as opened or used medical equipment debris should be left in place and briefed to the responding detectives or crime scene technicians upon their arrival.

If the victim is still alive and able to talk, s/he may be able to provide very important information as to what happened and who was involved. This can be very crucial evidence and if the victim later dies, may be admissible in court under the hearsay exception as a *dying declaration*. The historical thought process for this exception is that no victim wants to go to their God with a "lie in their mouth." Therefore, the victim's last statement relating to what happened or who was involved is generally accepted as valid evidence in a subsequent trial.

In order for the dying declaration to be admissible, there are several factors that the court will consider.

1. Was the victim competent, rational, and in control of their mental faculties?
2. Did the victim believe there was no hope of recovery and that death was imminent?
3. Did the statement refer directly to what happened or who was involved?
4. The declaration is contingent upon victim's actual death.

If the victim expresses any hope of survival, does not acknowledge that death is imminent, or the victim does not actually die, the statements are likely inadmissible, especially in case of victim survival, because his testimony would render such declarations moot.

It is often advisable for a law enforcement official to accompany the victim in the ambulance or meet the victim at the hospital on the chance s/he may be able to talk and make a statement before death. Careful notes, or whenever possible a recording of the statement would be invaluable evidence in court. Although it is important to talk to the victim we must also balance our need and desire for information with the need to treat the victim for any injuries. We certainly do not want to be placed into a position where we have in any way interfered with the medical treatment of the victim just because we wanted to gain information.

In cases where it might not be clear if the victim is alive, it is expected of the first responder to check for any signs of life. Checking for life could include a check for pulse on the wrists, neck, or even placing a hand over the chest to feel for a heartbeat, listening or observing any breathing, pupils that are fixed and dilated and do not react to light. In cases where the victim is still alive the first responder would be responsible for initiating whatever first aid or life-saving measures are possible as well as ordering an ambulance to the scene.

In some circumstances the victim is clearly dead, either from extensive injuries such as decapitation or the presence of the early changes after death such as livor and rigor mortis, or even more obvious signs of death such as decomposition. In these cases, we want to try to limit the amount of additional contamination to the scene as much as possible and therefore, limit the number of persons allowed into the scene to attend and view the body.

Because of the medical protocols of many jurisdictions, a responding ambulance crew may still respond regardless of the condition of the body and want to check the victim for signs of life. In these obvious cases a compromise might be reached with the medical personnel to limit the number of persons entering the scene. Instead of two or three persons entering with all of their equipment, the initial responding officer may be able to escort just one of the ambulance crew with limited equipment inside to view the body, confirm the death of the victim, and thus limit the contamination of the scene.

Police humorously refer to actions of some medical personnel as the *Lazarus syndrome*, which is an apparent belief of some ambulance crews that they somehow have the ability to raise the victim back to life. We see evidence of this in many crime scene photos that depict the standard four adhesive pads placed on the victim to electronically record their vital signs. These actions seem incredulous to the police based on the extent of injuries to the victim. In one case a man placed a shotgun into his mouth and pulled the trigger and because of the extensive injury, literally had no head—but the pads were still placed on the body. In another case the pads were found by responding crime scene technicians on a body that was already in an advanced stage of decomposition. Pads were found on a body of a deceased female although a review of the ambulance call-out sheet reflects the attendants' own initial observations that the victim was "already cold and stiff to the touch." Yet, they still cut the victim's shirt open and placed the four pads on her chest and abdomen to tell them the obvious.

Arrest or Take Control of Suspect

Many times a suspect may still be at the scene upon the police officers' arrival and should be taken into custody as soon as practical. This is to prevent escape as well as prevent any other harm to other persons including the responding police officers. It is important to note that once the suspect has been taken into custody, searched, and handcuffed he should be removed from the scene as soon as possible. Obviously we do not want to stir up any additional emotions in witnesses or bystanders by his continued presence at the scene.

There are other important considerations as well, including important physical or forensic evidence which may be on the suspect's person that needs to be collected and protected for later examination. It is also desirable to interview the suspect as soon as possible after the event when s/he may be psychologically vulnerable and more likely to reveal important information.

In cases in which a suspect has already fled the scene but can be identified by a surviving victim or other witnesses, first responders need to ensure the information is properly relayed to the responding detectives and to the radio dispatch as soon as possible so an alert can be issued to look for the suspect. Again, the best chance of obtaining information and key evidence from the suspect is as soon after the offense as possible. So every effort should be expended to take him/her into custody as quickly as possible.

Regardless of the situation, whenever we are dealing with homicide suspects great care should be taken. Although they may appear to be in shock and quite docile, it is not uncommon for them to realize what has happened and suddenly decide to resist or attack further. This is an absolute officer safety issue that should not be ignored or discounted.

Additionally it is important to pay attention to anything the suspect might say or do and particularly any display of unusual behaviors or emotions such as crying, anger, excessive talking, or laughing. Although the initial responding officers are not going to interview, interrogate, or really interact with the suspect, it does not mean the suspect might not say or do something relevant to the event. It is quite common for suspects to make spontaneous statements as to what happened. These statements may range from providing explanations, "She reached for the gun and it went off," or "I didn't know it was loaded," to apologies, "I'm sorry, I'm so sorry it was an accident, I didn't mean to do it," to an outright admission, "I told her if she went out on me again I'd kill her." It is also not unusual for a suspect to provide unsolicited facts even providing an unsolicited alibi for his whereabouts "I just went to the store and came back and found her."

The value in these statements is that they are typically made spontaneously at the scene and not based on direct questioning. Because these statements are typically made on the spur of the moment before the suspect has a chance to sit down and think, they are generally considered reliable. These statements are referred to as *res gestae* or involuntary exclamations or excited utterances and are another exception to the hearsay rule. It is not unusual for suspects to change that initial statement or story completely during a more formal interview and thus create an inconsistency that can prove to be invaluable evidence. An example is an offender who at the scene may initially claim to have gone to the grocery store and in his absence his wife was murdered; but later under more formal questioning, says he went to the hardware store.

Secure the Scene

Securing the scene consists of the first steps taken to render the scene safe by determining if there are any other victims or witnesses located at the scene, and to make certain there is no one else in the area who could pose a threat to the first responder or other officers as they arrive at the scene. This would include a general walk through the area for that purpose. Care should always be exercised whenever walking through any crime scene to ensure the officers are not walking over or through possible evidence.

During these initial investigative steps there is no way to determine the actual extent of the scene or what may have happened prior to the reported death, so extreme caution must be taken by the initial responding officers to ensure that efforts to secure the scene do not actually contribute to damage of evidence or alteration of the scene. Therefore, use of a flashlight or available lighting is always advisable, rather than stumbling around and possibly destroying unseen evidence. There are many examples of officers walking around a crime scene in the dark only to later discover they have unknowingly stepped on or kicked pieces of evidence lying on the floor or walked through pools of blood tracking it throughout the entire scene.

This initial walkthrough is designed to be more of a safety issue rather than any search for potential evidence and therefore should be strictly limited in scope and duration—looking for other victims, suspects, and witnesses who may be present inside the scene or to identify any potential hazards inside the scene such as natural gas leaks, potential for fire, or presence of clandestine labs or other hazardous materials. Although we want to retain scene integrity as much as possible, the saving of human life and officer safety considerations takes precedence over any potential scene contamination.

Identify and Separate Any Witnesses

This is a critical step, because witnesses often disappear or suddenly decide against getting involved. If witnesses are identified early in the process and then disappear or leave the area before the detectives arrive, they can almost always be located and interviewed.

Although we do not expect or want the responding officers to conduct a detailed interview of any potential witnesses, it is certainly expected they will conduct at least a canvass type interview to identify those witnesses who can relate what happened or who was possibly involved. Those witnesses able to provide either first hand information, personal observations, or important information relative to the incident are known as *significant witnesses*. A brief interview is necessary especially if they are aware of what happened or they can identify a potential suspect. Any information obtained from these significant witnesses should be provided to the detectives upon their arrival at the scene and not just placed into a routine police report filed at a later time.

All witnesses, but especially significant witnesses, need to be separated from each other to keep them from comparing notes or discussing their observations with others. It is important to the investigation that each witness provide only what s/he saw, heard, felt, or did, and not fill in with information learned from other witnesses, or change his/her story because it does not seem to match what others are reporting. It is also very important to consider that an eye witness during the initial stages of the investigation may later turn out to be the prime suspect. Obviously we would not want the prime suspect to be talking to other witnesses to possibly influence what they might report to the police or to learn what other witnesses are going to report.

Protect and Define the Scene

There are actually several important steps in protecting and defining the crime scene—much more than simply rolling out the crime scene barrier tape. There are no hard and fast rules for defining the scene because each scene is different, and defining the scene, like many other responses in criminal investigations, depends upon the facts and circumstances of each incident. There are certain basics that we can use regardless of the specifics of any situation.

These same basic steps are used even with the most horrific of crimes such as the World Trade Center attack, the Lockerbie bombing, and the Oklahoma City bombing. These scenes literally expanded for multiple city blocks or as in the case of the Lockerbie bombing, may stretch over hundreds of square miles. Although they were enormous in magnitude, the same basic steps to define and secure the scene were used, even though at a much greater scale than the average or typical crime scene. In larger scenes however, it may take considerably more time and effort to determine the extent of the scene. This was the case in the Oklahoma City bombing, where the scene was expanded further out from the federal building as additional evidence was uncovered and continued increasing outward until such time as no more evidence was located, eventually taking in some sixteen square city blocks of Oklahoma City. That entire area was considered a crime scene and no access was granted until it was completely examined for any additional evidence.

As first responders our intent is to define the scene in a way that takes in what we believe encompasses the entire crime scene, or where any potential evidence may be found. Defining the scene is the first effort in protecting the scene. The general rule in defining a scene is, *it is always easier to collapse a scene or make it smaller than it is to expand it and make it larger*; particularly when onlookers or the media begin to show up.

The overall intent of scene definition and protection is to quickly establish a *double perimeter* around the scene consisting of an inter zone, or what we often refer to as an exclusion zone, with access limited only to detectives and crime scene personnel; and an outer perimeter established as an additional "standoff" barrier to prevent the public, media, or other officers from interfering with the scene examination or crime scene personnel. This double perimeter is the first step in defining the crime scene and essentially keeping anyone other than detectives and crime scene personnel from entering and further contaminating the scene.

The double perimeter concept is also important because eventually there is a need to conduct a search *beyond the scene*, which will include the area between the inner exclusion zone and the outer perimeter. With crimes scenes occurring inside a building it is fairly easy to establish the inner or exclusion zone, because as much as is practical, it is the building itself. The interior of the building becomes the exclusion zone and the outside perimeter is then enlarged around it. What this entails of course is entirely dependent upon the location and type of building.

In a single-family type residential neighborhood (see **Figure 3-1**), the house itself could be the exclusion zone and the front and backyards and driveway would be the outer perimeter. Adjustments will obviously have to be made in the case of multifamily and multistory residences. For multifamily structures such as apartments or row houses the interior of a particular house were the crime took place would be the exclusion zone and the exterior would have to be determined based on the individual circumstances. In the case of multistory apartments, hotels or motels, the inner zone would be the apartment or motel room itself and the outer perimeter may have to include the area from crime scene front door, to the elevator or entire stairway to the ground floor, and then into the parking lot—all should be considered part of the scene because this would be the pathway of the suspect arriving at and leaving the crime scene and therefore may contain important evidence.

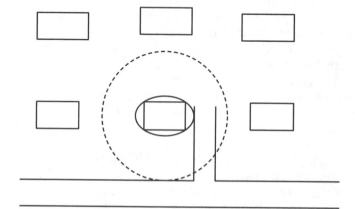

FIGURE 3-1. This sketch outlines a typical single family type residential neighborhood. The house itself has been established as the inner perimeter, the front and back yards and the driveway have all been included in the outer perimeter. If the scene already has fencing surrounding the property, it is even easier because the outer perimeter is already defined. It is then only a matter of keeping people out of it.

FIGURE 3-2. This image shows a crime scene outside a business establishment. Note the evidence tents that are placed on different items of evidence in the scene. It is spread out because of the actions of the suspect and the victims involved in a shootout. Evidence tents represent expended shell casings found at the scene. See Color Plate 4.

Figures **3-2** and **3-3** are examples of how a scene can expand based on the actions of the victim or offender or circumstances of the crime. In this example the victim was shot at as he ran across the front of the business; he was struck once and then ran around to the other side of the building where he finally collapsed and died of his wounds. This required an expansion of the crime scene as indicated by the barrier tape.

FIGURE 3-3. This photo shows the other side of the building with the double perimeter established. The inner perimeter was the location of the victim (already removed) and the outer perimeter can be seen in the background. These perimeters are not 'text book perfect' but based on the scene dynamics they were sufficient to keep the bystanders and others away from the body and the scene. Many times we are forced to do the best we can based on what is available at the scene. See Color Plate 5.

For outdoor scenes, we use concept of the "stone's throw rule," establishing the outer perimeter of the scene as far as you can throw a rock or stone, 360 degrees surrounding the crime scene or body location. The reasoning is, if one can throw a rock or stone that far then one can also throw evidence that far. The areas between the body and outer perimeter will have to be searched as well for any possible evidence that may have been thrown away.

Figures 3-4 and **3-5** demonstrate the stones throw rule in an open area. The victim was found in a stream bed (lower right) but was brought to the edge in a vehicle and dumped over the side. The scene was expanded (Figure 3-5) all the way out to the roadway to take in the stones throw concept.

Figure 3-6 shows what happens when a double perimeter is not properly established by the initial responding officers. In this case, the scene included both the interior of the house and extended outside to the driveway. Although a barrier was put into place, bystanders were still allowed to be within a few feet of the scene.

In those instances where a scene is established in a more public area such as a roadway, parking lot, or parking garage, defining the scene includes examining the area to insure the entire scene is included, not just the area around the body. Any vehicles or common areas such as elevators or stairwells, found within the exclusion zone should be protected. This includes movement of people or vehicles through or from that area until the arrival of crime scene personnel or detectives. Although this may interfere with someone's ability to gain control over his own property, such as a vehicle, or to enter his own residence, the delay is usually for a short time only. The decision

FIGURE 3-4. A well established outdoor scene, the victim is in the stream of water in the lower right corner. The inner perimeter, however, is actually established well above the ridge because items of evidence (see evidence flags in center of photo) were also discovered where the victim was unloaded from a vehicle and then rolled down the ravine into the water. See Color Plate 6.

FIGURE 3-5. This image depicts the outer perimeter of the same scene above the stream bed extending all the way to the roadway, a good example of an outdoor scene "stone's throw" perimeter. See Color Plate 7.

to release or not to release, or to grant access should remain with the detectives, not the first responder.

It is always best to defer these types of decisions to responding detectives. If the detectives determine a vehicle is not necessary to the investigation or there is no reason to keep other residents from their own homes, they can

FIGURE 3-6. This is an example of what can happen when an effective double perimeter is not quickly established by first responders. The crime scene actually includes the interior of the residence and extends outside to include the white truck and concrete parking pad in front of the house. This means the truck and parking area are also part of the exclusion zone. The people standing around outside the crime scene tape are the friends and neighbors of the victims, who arrived out of concern and interest but were never moved back by responding officers. There were so many persons and vehicles present at the scene that when the crime scene unit arrived they had to park almost 50 yards away and carry their equipment to the scene. See Color Plate 8.

permit access as they deem appropriate. In cases where the scene is in a public place, it is always a good idea to record the license plates of every vehicle within the area upon the first responder's arrival and to identify any residents that enter or leave a multifamily building.

Protecting the scene also includes recognizing and protecting any fragile evidence that may be at the scene. Fragile evidence includes anything that might be lost, damaged or destroyed if not immediately protected. Examples could include a tire or footwear impression or a murder weapon found outside during rainy weather. The initial responding officer may have to add additional crime scene tape surrounding the evidence to keep it from being walked on, or even place a box or other item over the evidence to keep it from being further damaged. We do not like to add anything to the scene, but sometimes we have no choice based on the circumstances. Always report anything that is added or altered at the scene to the responding detectives or crime scene technicians.

Contact Detectives and Crime Scene Personnel to Respond

One of the other key responsibilities of the first responders is to notify or request detectives and crime scene personnel to respond to the scene as rapidly as possible. Once the scene is secured and an initial evaluation of the facts and circumstances has been made, contact appropriate personnel to ensure detectives arrive at the scene as quickly as possible. The first responder is then charged to secure the scene as efficiently as possible and wait for the arrival of the responding detectives.

Note Taking

Among the most important tools available to the first responder are pen and paper. Note taking and recording of observations and activities is crucial. Particularly important is a record of any events that may have occurred at the scene after the responder's arrival, and before being relieved by responding detectives. Vital information would include a complete listing of those persons who were present at the scene, the various witnesses that have been identified, and any actions by the first responder in securing the scene or checking for other victims or suspects. Any statement made by the victim, the arrest of a suspect, or the identification of a fleeing suspect would also be of great interest to the responding detectives.

Note any changes to the scene made since the arrival of the responding officer, including during the initial walkthrough, any first aid or medical treatment, or when fragile evidence was found and protected. Note also other factors which might not be in evidence when the responding detectives arrive—such as lighting conditions, any unusual odors, and weather conditions. Depending on the type of scene itself, notes should include such things as if the doors were locked or unlocked, and who granted access to the scene.

A good chronology of events including the times they were noted is also critical, since a homicide investigation is focused a great deal on aspects of time, e.g., time of death, time of notification, time of arrival of first responders, and time of arrival of medical personnel. It is also important to collect information on anyone else that may have come to the scene such as ambulance or fire department personnel, or coroner, but have departed prior to the arrival of the detectives.

Establish a Scene Security Log

A security log is designed to document personnel who have entered or departed from the scene. It should be initiated as soon as practical and continued until the scene examination is completed. If the officer is relieved by another officer, the log is passed over and continued.

An entry log can be a formalized, agency preprinted document or can be created on a piece of scratch paper. It only requires the name of the persons entering the scene, their agency, the time they entered, the reason they entered, time they departed the scene, an agency contact number, and the purpose for entering the scene.

The security log is also very helpful in reducing the number of police "tourists," including other patrol officers and often high ranking officers who show up for no other reason but wanting to take a look at the scene. Bringing out the scene security log tends to limit the number of officers wanting to "check out the dead body." It becomes even more difficult to keep out police tourists when the scene is particularly odd, gruesome, or involves nudity of the victim.

Some agencies have gone even further by instituting a policy requiring a written report to be filed by every officer that appears on the crime scene log to validate the purpose for being at the scene. Other more experienced officers have started to call the crime scene log "the subpoena log," implying that anyone who signs in to the crime scene can expect to receive a subpoena to testify at a grand jury or trial proceeding about why they entered the scene. This is actually very effective in eliminating senior officers from entering into the scene.

The main purpose for keeping others out of the scene is to avoid as much crime scene contamination as possible based on the crime scene principal of *Locard's Law* or the *theory of transference*. This concept states a simple premise that whenever you enter a scene you bring something with you from the outside environment, such as any hairs or fibers and other items of trace evidence you may have on your clothing. A good example would be pet hair, lint, or dust from your residence or work place that is routinely and unknowingly deposited on your outer clothing as you go through your normal routine. As one enters another location or the crime scene those same hairs, fibers, lint, and dust will naturally fall off onto that other room or crime scene. Whenever you leave that other room or crime scene, you will also take something with you in the form of other hairs, fibers, or other items of trace evidence already inside the scene and now unknowingly attached to your clothing.

Theoretically, every time someone comes in and out of the scene he is bringing additional foreign objects into the scene and when leaving, taking some trace away from the scene.

Locard's Law is the basis of modern crime scene examination and is covered in much greater detail in subsequent discussions in this text.

▶ DO NOTs for First Responders to Remember

In addition to the many DOs or what should be accomplished by the first responder, there are several very important DO NOTs as well. DO NOTs are those things that should not be done except in extremely rare circumstances. The first responder DO NOTs include but are not necessarily limited to, the items discussed in the next section of this text.

DO NOT Talk to the Media, Witnesses, or Others About the Scene or Case

It is not the responsibility of the first responders to address the media about any aspect of the crime scene or evidence. It is not uncommon for the media to seek out lower ranking officers, especially first responders, and ask technical questions about the event hoping to get more information for their report. Unfortunately, because of their limited information first responders are not the best or most accurate source, but this is not always an important distinction for many media outlets which are only looking to get a quote for a story or a few seconds on tape for the nightly news. It is the job of the detectives or the agency public affairs officer to handle any media requests or to answer any questions relating to the investigation, and any questions or requests should be directed to them. Members of the media understand this policy and when the officers state unequivocally that all questions must be answered by the public affairs officer or responding detectives, they will usually desist.

All officers, first responders, and detectives should assume that the media are taking pictures or videotaping their every action. Therefore it is imperative to remain professional at all times. There have been many occasions when officers were caught in an unguarded moment, talking and laughing among themselves, and when displayed on television came across as very unprofessional. This is one of the more infamous media tactics used to critique the police or portray them in a bad light. Officers need to be aware and pay attention.

Other questions and comments by bystanders and witnesses are expected in these type of incidents, but the first responder needs to bear in mind at this stage of the investigation that it might not be clear exactly what happened or who may be involved. Needlessly offering comments or talking "out of school" about the scene could lead to problems later on, particularly if the questioner is actually a member of the media, or someone who later contacts the media. This is particularly important in this modern age when everyone has a camera phone with video recording capability. An extemporaneous or inappropriate comment about the victim, suspect, or scene; or offering of personal opinion as to what happened could easily find its way to the nightly news or even worse, to the internet.

DO NOT Use the Phone or Toilets at the Scene

Do not use the telephone, the toilet, get a drink of water, or eat inside the scene or use sheets or blankets from the scene to cover a body. Each example of using something from the scene, as mentioned previously, is likely to alter the scene and may create problems. A call using a telephone to the station may override the last outgoing and/or incoming. Using a toilet could cause a stoppage, could send something thrown into the toilet by the suspect into the sewer system. Eating or drinking something could change the appearance of the scene and mistakenly indicate another person might be involved or at least present prior to or during the crime.

The officer's actions in the following case study were wrong on so many levels it is really difficult to comprehend or further explain. But it is a good example of what not to do at a scene. As a side note, this same officer mentioned below was later fired from his agency after other instances of inappropriate conduct.

In addition to avoiding using the physical facilities, we do not want to use a blanket or sheet from a residence or scene to cover a body. Of course using something from inside the house could negate any potential hairs and fibers or other trace evidence that may be found on the body later on. If hairs or fibers were later recovered, the suspect need only claim they were possibly

---

Case Study 3-1

It took detectives a few hours to respond to a death scene late at night, but upon arrival there was no officer on duty outside to secure the scene. The detectives entered the scene and found the responding officer, who was supposed to be securing the scene, was actually sitting in a recliner in the living room, watching TV, drinking a soft drink, and eating a slice of pizza that he found in the refrigerator. The officer explained he was cold, tired, and hungry and "didn't think the victim would mind." Not only was this a somewhat callous thought and statement, it was also unprofessional, and by his actions he had essentially altered the scene. In this case it did not affect the outcome of the investigation, but there is no way to know at the initial stages what is important and what is not.

deposited onto the victim when the blanket was placed over the body. It is just as likely that any trace evidence on the body before the blanket was placed over the body could be transferred from the body to the blanket when it is removed, and thus lost as evidence. This is another example of *Locard's Law* or *the theory of transference* discussed earlier.

At this stage of the investigation there is no way to know what inside the scene is important or unimportant; but it is clear any change or alteration of any aspect of the scene could impact the later stages of the investigation. Therefore, regardless of the situation or circumstances, first responders should not use anything from within the scene until approved to do so by responding detectives. With rare exceptions, detectives or other patrol officers will be at the scene in a relatively short period of time and there is no need to use anything within the scene.

DO NOT Add Anything to the Crime Scene

Always use caution in determining the need to add things, change things, or otherwise alter the scene. Such changes should only be made when there is a specific need to do so and when failing to do so could result in loss of evidence. For example, there is seldom any reason for a first responder to add chalk lines around a body or in the case of outdoor scenes, spray paint to to identify the location of small items of physical evidence. Geberth refers to these actions as being accomplished by the "chalk fairy" because although chalk outlines are apparent around a body, no one at the scene admits to having placed them.[1] Thus they must have been drawn by the "chalk fairy," an entity who appears at many crime scenes.

Instead of protecting those items or aiding the examination by documenting the item's location at the scene, many times this marking may actually limit results from forensic examinations of the evidence. For instance, spray paint is often mistakenly used to mark the location of items of physical evidence, particularly in outdoor crime scenes but could possibly end up covering unseen latent prints on an item, making their development and identification more difficult. Red spray paint has been confused and misinterpreted as blood spatter at several scenes resulting in items being picked up that normally would not have been and creating confusion in interpreting the scene.

If deemed necessary or appropriate the detectives or crime scene personnel will outline the body upon their arrival, this is not the responsibility of the first responders.

Figure 3-7 demonstrates the mistaken belief that spray paint is helpful in identifying evidence at the crime scene, instead it is just as likely to add paint and damage the very item being marked.

On those rare occasions when it becomes necessary to mark evidence at the scene then a method should be used that causes the least damage and alters the scene as minimally as possible. In one example the first responders found

FIGURE 3-7. This is an example of spray paint used to mark the location of evidence at the scene. The problem is that the specks of paint may end up on the items of evidence and cover or damage other forensic evidence on the exterior of the items or be confused with blood spatter and cause misinterpretation of evidence. See Color Plate 9.

blood and brain tissue on a concrete pad outside a residence. They did not have any evidence tents or markers in their vehicles, so they improvised and placed sticky notes adjacent to the brain tissue to mark the location on the concrete pad so others arriving at the scene and beginning to place crime scene boundary tape out would be alerted to its presence and thus avoid stepping on or damaging it. The sticky notes were easily photographed by the arriving crime scene technicians and then easily replaced by evidence tents without causing any damage or alterations to the scene. Basic common sense must be used in all situations when dealing with adding to or altering the scene. Anything added to or altered in the scene should be reported to the responding detectives or crime scene technicians.

Adding to the crime scene also includes smoking; throwing down chewing gum wrappers, cigarette butts, other trash; or even spitting on the ground. There have been occasions when crime scene techs find spittle or a fresh cigarette butt within the scene and have collected them as evidence only to find out they were put there by responding police officers.

DO NOT Touch or Otherwise Move Weapons at the Scene

There also seems to be an almost universal belief and uncontrollable urge for the initial responding police officers to unload weapons found at a death scene, or take immediate custody of the weapons, or otherwise move them within the scene to somehow render them "safe." This is especially problematic when a weapon is removed from a deceased's hand. Many times this leads to a very confused interpretation of the scene and events. Therefore, a

FIGURE 3-8. This photo depicts a scene in which the first responding officer removed and unloaded the gun from a suicide victim's hand and placed it on the sofa, not only possibly destroying any fingerprints but also altering the scene. The gun was unloaded and moved because of "officer safety," but could have led to a completely different interpretation to the scene. The location of the gun so far away from the victim may have led detectives to look at the event as being more consistent with a homicide instead of a possible suicide. See Color Plate 10.

weapon found at the scene should be left untouched. There has never been a case when a dead person has fired off another round after they were dead; therefore if the scene has been cleared of other persons, there is no safety risk in leaving a weapon in a dead person's hand or at the scene. If safety is an issue with the weapon, then simply clear the area of anyone who does not belong.

Figure 3-8 is an example of the problem associated with removing a weapon from the victim's hand. In this case the responding officers removed the weapon, unloaded it and then placed it on the sofa in the background, thus altering the scene and its interpretation.

DO NOT Cover the Body

In general terms a body should never be covered and should be maintained in the same condition as it was initially found until detectives and crime scene personnel arrive and can take charge of the scene. Covering the body certainly alters the scene and may introduce scene contamination, in the form of trace evidence such as foreign hairs and fibers, through whatever medium is used to cover the body. If a body is out of the public eye and in a secured location, such as inside a building or residence, then there is no reason to ever cover the body. Although strongly discouraged as a matter of protocol there are a few limited legitimate reasons to cover a body. This should be the exception and not the rule.

There are times when covering the body that is in the public eye would be acceptable. **Figure 3-9** depicts a homicide victim that was killed in a residen-

FIGURE 3-9. The body was covered to calm down the other neighbors and family members in the area using a clean white sheet maintained in the crime scene equipment for this purpose. See Color Plate 11.

tial area, literally across the street from his own residence and in full view of his neighbors. In this case the body was covered because of the neighborhood's emotional reaction to their friend and neighbor's body just lying in the street. Rather than provoke further emotions within the neighborhood the first responders correctly covered the body with a clean sheet obtained from the responding ambulance crew. The on lookers calmed down almost immediately and a potential problem was avoided.

Other examples where it may be appropriate to cover a body in the public eye would include when the victim is a child, has been sexually displayed, or there are extensive injuries to the victim such as decapitation or evisceration. In the case of bodies located adjacent to a roadway, there is also a safety consideration because we also want to avoid rubber necking by other drivers as they slow down to drive past the scene.

Whenever a body is covered, it should only be covered with a clean white sheet obtained from an ambulance, medical examiner or coroner, or one already prepared in the first responder's vehicle. When the body is removed from the scene by the coroner, the sheet should accompany the body to be collected at autopsy or if removed at the scene should be collected and sent to the laboratory for possible trace evidence examination.

Figure 3-10 depicts another exception to the general rule of not covering the body. In this particular case the victim was found outside his home at the beginning of a torrential rain storm. First responders correctly contacted the responding crime scene technicians who based on the initial briefing of the scene, instructed them to place a plastic covering over the body. Normally we would not want to do this because the possibility that trace evidence could

FIGURE 3-10. Because of weather conditions, the first responders coordinated with the oncoming crime scene technicians who instructed them to cover the body with a plastic tarp to protect it from the heavy rain. See Color Plate 12.

be attracted to the plastic by static electricity and then lost when the plastic is removed. But, because of the extreme weather conditions, the exposed location of the scene, and the fact there was going to be a significant time lapse before the arrival of the crime scene team, covering the body was determined to be in the best interest of protecting the evidence. First responders were instructed to cover the body to protect it from the elements until the crime scene team arrived. It is important to note that the first responders correctly contacted the responding crime scene team to get their advice and instructions on how to properly protect the scene rather than make that decision on their own.

▶ Be Suspicious and Curious

Being curious and suspicious is an important aspect of general police investigation but especially for first responders at a death scene. There are many examples of suspects intentionally altering or staging a homicide crime scene to resemble a suicide or an accidental death. These types of offenders are hoping the first responding police officers believe their explanation of events and too quickly glance over and accept the scene as it has been staged. Offenders correctly recognize, in most cases, that in order to get away with a murder; they only have to get through the initial police response. Many times, based on agency policy and protocol, detectives may not even be called out for accidental deaths or even "obvious" suicides.

In an ideal world, every unattended death should be approached as a homicide until you can prove otherwise. However, in many large cities this is not always the case. Sadly, there are many instances in which the first responder was lured into believing the death was a suicide or a natural death only for detectives to discover years later that it was actually a homicide, and if the agency had responded with a minimum amount of investigative effort those facts would have been readily apparent. This is the reason why a correctly performed preliminary investigation is so vital in every reported death investigation.

References

1. Geberth, V. J. (2006). *Practical homicide investigation*. (4th ed.). Boca Raton, FL: CRC Press.

CHAPTER FOUR

The Crime Scene

Only a small proportion of deaths that occur in the United States every year actually require any additional investigation because most deaths can be attributed to disease, old age, some other natural occurrence such as weather (tornados, floods, lightening, or exposure), are self inflicted, or obvious accidents. There are actually relatively few homicides in comparison with the other manners of death.

Many times the only thing separating a criminal from being held responsible for his/her actions is a good scene examination and subsequent follow-up investigation. This is why we approach all deaths, regardless of how they are reported to the police, as if they were a homicide, until the true facts can be pieced together. This is an important concept because those offenders who try to stage a crime scene or otherwise misdirect a police investigation understand that to be successful in the crime, the offender only needs to get through the initial police response. If police suspicions are not aroused during the initial viewing of the scene, then it is likely the crime will never be investigated. The perpetrator is counting on his/her ability to alter the scene, police complacency, or a general lack of police training to get away with murder.

Most departments rely on uniformed personnel to respond to a scene and make an initial assessment of the basic facts of the death and the need for additional investigation. If the responding patrol officer is satisfied by the initial report to the police and the initial scene examination, it is likely no further police response will be forthcoming.

Unfortunately not all uniformed police officers have the experience and training necessary to make such on the spot determinations resulting in homicides or questionable deaths never being fully investigated. They may only come to light months or years later when the offender attempts a second or even a third homicide in the same manner. Suddenly background scrutiny of the suspect reveals association with two or three previous deaths which must now be reopened and worked as cold cases. The tragedy is the offender was able to murder one or more victims because of poor police procedure.

Case Study 4-1

A 30-year-old female divorced mother of one was found dead on the floor of the bedroom of her house by her 12-year-old son when he came home from school. She was suffering from Multiple Sclerosis (MS) but was fully capable and able to function normally. A uniformed police officer arrived at the scene, and after talking to her boyfriend, without any crime scene examination at all, determined the victim died of natural causes as a result of a seizure. The county coroner arrived to take control over the body and after speaking to the boyfriend, he also determined the death was natural and further determined no autopsy was necessary. The woman's family expressed concern and requested an autopsy so one was ordered. The state ME later conducted an autopsy and also concluded she had died of a seizure. Three years later, the boyfriend married, and several months after their marriage the woman simply disappeared. Weeks later, partial skeletal remains were recovered and identification was made based on dental records confirming the death of the missing woman. A subsequent homicide investigation centered almost immediately on the husband, especially after police learned he stood to gain a substantial amount of life insurance from the death of his wife. Further investigation turned up the name of the 30-year-old female who reportedly died from natural causes three years before. At the time, the suspect was this woman's boyfriend and had received a large insurance settlement following her death. A review of the autopsy file maintained at the ME's office noted the boyfriend had also called the ME's office prior to the autopsy and reported a history of seizures by the deceased woman. As part of the homicide investigation, the woman's family noted she had no such history of seizures. An exhumation of the body and re-autopsy noted distinct evidence, missed during the first autopsy, that the victim was manually strangled. The police report consisted of a two page brief report of the officer's arrival at the scene and conclusion it was a natural death based on a report by the boyfriend and that nothing unusual was noted at the scene.

In **Case Study 4-1**, had the police ever questioned the victim's family they would have learned the victim had no history of seizures, that her MS condition was not life threatening, and the boyfriend stood to gain a substantial life insurance settlement upon the victim's death. This basic information may have resulted in more focused attention placed on the death and potential motive of the boyfriend, and perhaps even prevented the murder of the second victim some years later.

In the vast majority of death investigations, the basic facts and persons involved in the criminal offense are identified to the police at the time the death is actually reported. This is because so many of these deaths are the end result of some type of interpersonal conflict between people who know each other. Examples of these relationships may include husbands and wives, boyfriends and girlfriends or lovers, family members, neighbors, or business associates. The general theme is a personal conflict, sometimes long standing, which escalates to physical conflict, and eventually ends with one person killing another.

Many times these deaths are actually reported by the person responsible or some other person familiar with the circumstances so when the police arrive at the scene they already know who is involved. In these situations the scene examination is essentially confined to proving or disproving whatever the surviving member of the conflict is reporting.

The scene examination is considered the bedrock or foundation for all criminal investigations and Gardner states its importance very clearly, "Crime scene processing is an inherent task and duty associated with most criminal investigations, for rarely does one encounter a crime without some kind of crime scene."[1]

For all crimes, the crime scene is perhaps the only observable instance in which both the victim and the offender, for whatever period of time, were together at one location. Therefore, it is the most logical place to find evidence linking all three—victim, offender, and location.

Obviously, the homicide detective is interested in proper crime scene examination including collection and documentation of as much physical and forensic evidence as possible. In contemporary practice this task is likely to be performed by specially trained and equipped crime scene personnel, rather than regular detectives. Depending upon the size of the department, these specially trained personnel may be other detectives specifically detailed to perform that function among their other investigative duties. In other departments, it might be uniformed officers who are specially trained to work scenes as an additional duty or responsibility. More and more departments however, are forming a specialized unit or are able to call on their servicing crime lab for trained personnel whose sole function is to process the scene and collect evidence.

There are inherent advantages and disadvantages to each of these scenarios, but often the size of the department and the size of the budget will determine the type and level of response.

In a major finding from Wellford and Cronin in their homicide clearance survey, those departments with specialized crime scene personnel or those who could call on a state or county crime scene unit to process their scenes, had much higher homicide clearance rates than those departments that used their own investigative personnel. The placement of specially trained personnel to document and process the scene freed up investigative personnel to concentrate on other aspects of the investigation.[2]

Theoretically, there should not be a great deal of confusion regarding who is in charge of the actual scene examination, but in reality, because of personality types involved and the lack of a clear established agency protocol, conflicts between the crime scene technicians and the case detectives are inevitable. Many times the most serious conflicts arise over something as simple as the detectives wanting the technicians to do or not to do something in particular at the scene, but the technicians insist on doing something else or doing it a different way. Imagine heated arguments between crime scene technicians and detectives at a death scene, over who is going to do what and how—a disturbing situation at such an important event. This of course does not happen at every scene or with every agency but it does happen often enough to merit addressing the problem. Most of these personality conflicts can be avoided by clearly written agency protocols or SOPs establishing individual responsibilities and supervisory authority at the scene.

Regardless of who is actually conducting the crime scene examination, traditionally the lead detective is ultimately responsible for the scene and the proper collection of evidence. The crime scene technicians work for the lead or case detective and should be responsive to his or her needs and any special requests. At the same time, detectives should listen to the crime scene technicians because they are the experts at their job. This should be a team effort and collaboration, not a contest over authority.

▶ Legal Considerations

There are some very important legal considerations to be addressed before any scene examination takes place. Of particular importance is the requirement to obtain a search warrant for the scene before any investigative action takes place. This requirement is based on three Supreme Court decisions decided during the last twenty years clearly establishing no crime scene or murder scene exception to the constitutional requirement for a search warrant. This was initially decided in *Mincey v. Arizona*[3], and has been reiterated and refined in *Thompson v. Louisiana*[4] and *Flippo v. West Virginia.*[5]

In *Mincey*, police officers were in the process of making a drug arrest inside the defendant's house, when an undercover officer was shot and killed by the defendant. Other police officers outside the house then forced entry and secured the scene. They immediately removed all occupants of the house including the defendant who was wounded. They then secured the house and processed it as a homicide scene for a period of four days. The Supreme Court held that the forced entry by police to rescue their colleague and arrest the suspects was permissible. Further, the arrest and/or removal of everyone else inside the house, a general exploratory search for other victims, witnesses, or offenders within the house, and securing the house for later examination were all permissible under one of the clearly defined exigent exceptions to the search warrant requirement. However, once the exigency was over and the scene secured, and there was no further chance of loss or destruction of evidence; the police were required to stop and obtain a search warrant to further process the house. The court unanimously refused to create an additional "murder scene exception" to the Fourth Amendment search warrant requirement.

This decision was reasserted again in *Thompson* under a slightly different context. In *Thompson*, the defendant shot and killed her husband in their house and then intended to take her own life by taking an overdose of pills. However, sometime after taking the pills she changed her mind and called her daughter for assistance. Her daughter arrived and called the police and an ambulance to take her mother to the hospital for treatment and report the death of her father. The police arrived and observed the deceased husband in another room and then conducted what they described as an "exploratory search" which lasted approximately two hours. The Supreme Court rejected the concept of a two-hour police "exploratory search" following their arrival at the scene, again ruling that having determined the scene was secure and no other emergency existed, police should have obtained a search warrant to proceed further with the scene examination.

Lastly, in *Flippo*, police were summoned to a cabin in a state park where a man claimed his wife had been attacked and murdered. The police found the woman inside with fatal head wounds and initiated a homicide scene examination. A briefcase was found on a table and upon opening it police found pictures indicating a possible homosexual relationship between the husband and another man. Police theorized this relationship may have provided a motive for murder of the wife. The state maintained that their examination of the briefcase was a standard police procedure at a homicide crime scene. Again, the Supreme Court ruled against any homicide crime scene exemption to the search warrant requirement.

In both *Thompson* and *Flippo*, there was an element of "consent" implied in the police actions because they were summoned to the scene by someone else and were actually invited into the scene. In *Thompson*, they were invited into the residence by a third person (daughter) to render assistance to the mother and to report the death of the father. In *Flippo*, the husband had invited the police into the cabin by reporting the murder of his wife. The court did not spend a great deal of time on the issue of consent because in each instance the state, in their appeal, relied on aspects of a homicide crime scene as their basis for an unwarranted search.

Any "consent" must be given by someone with standing to give consent. In the Thompson case it is clear the police were invited in by the daughter, but the question becomes: Did the daughter have any legal authority or standing in giving that consent to search her mother's house?" The answer is probably not. This issue can arise in other cases of domestic homicides or assaults, or in other crime locations where a suspect has Fourth Amendment protection equal to that of the victim. An illustration of the "consent" dilemma would be an instance in which the victim grants access to a house for a police search, but a suspect or other occupant with an equal right to privacy does not consent.

In *Flippo,* issues of consent were not as well defined because the husband did call the police and basically invited them into the scene by his report of the crime. But, did he consent to the actual crime scene search? The issue over consent could have been eliminated by obtaining a formal written consent from the husband outlining the police intent to search for evidence of the crime, and what that search would entail. However, based on the Supreme Court's steadfast opinion on the subject, it is better and easier in the long run to simply get a search warrant and avoid any such issues being raised at a later time.

Obtaining a crime scene search warrant is the responsibility of the police, not the crime scene technicians and not difficult to obtain. Many departments have a preprinted form requiring only the address and other specific data for that particular scene which is then presented to a magistrate or judge. In other jurisdictions a crime scene search warrant can actually be obtained by telephone from a magistrate and followed up by written memorandum.

Regardless of how the warrant is obtained, there is actually a very low threshold for probable cause in these cases. Establishing probable cause for a crime scene examination for most death investigations is essentially the report of an unexplained death or violent crime, at a particular place. That particular place needs to be examined, documented, and searched for evidence to determine if there is any criminality associated with the death.

If the scene is located in a place where the Supreme Court has previously determined there is no reasonable expectation of privacy, such as those areas accessible by the general public or in an area such as an open field, the Fourth Amendment does not apply; therefore, investigators need not be concerned with the warrant requirement.

When in doubt, the detective should always take the time to coordinate with the local district attorney's office to make certain they are proceeding legally. It is always better to delay the examination for a short period of time, than to have critical evidence suppressed during the trial or appeal because we have overstepped our legal bounds.

▶ Crime Scene Examination

The intent of this text is a general introduction to homicide and death investigation. The detailed step-by-step technical aspects of crime scene examination, documentation, and proper evidence collection cannot be fully covered here. This particular subject has become so technical that there are literally dozens of text books devoted to nothing but scene examinations and various aspects of forensic science. This chapter provides an overview of proper scene examination techniques and important general concepts.

An Opera, Not a Slam Dance

A crime scene is not just about taking pictures and throwing fingerprint powder around. Like an opera, the crime scene examination should be processed step-by-step based on an established and organized plan. Consider the opera—it is performed within a set program of music, singing, and stage movements. It is well organized and scripted and if the same opera were to be performed the following evening it would have the same music, singing, stage movements, and timing.

The crime scene examination generally takes place along a similar basic order of events with minor exceptions because of the particular individual dynamics of the scene. For example, before any examination of the scene takes place, it should be videotaped, photographed, and sketched before anything is touched or moved. Only after the scene is documented, does the actual search for evidence really begin.

The practice of following a set program and order of events is seen in our search for forensic or latent evidence. There is generally a particular order in which we search for and collect forensic and latent* type evidence. Typically we search for trace and biological evidence before we begin to search for latent prints and before introducing any chemicals or other potentially damaging examinations to the scene. The idea is to collect all those possible items of evidence that are readily observable and collectable before introducing any foreign substances to the scene.

A Marathon, Not a Sprint

There is, within reason, no real time limit to processing a scene. Therefore, there is no need to pressure or hurry the crime scene techs to complete their task and no reason to neglect specialized examinations or analysis if warranted. Sometimes this is a particularly difficult concept to teach and enforce because we, as Americans, tend to be rather impatient and therefore seek instantaneous answers and results. Even worse, many of us believe crime scene examination is like what we see on television—important evidence should be readily observable and found immediately.

The reality is that crime scene examination may take several days to several weeks, and in some cases much longer. It depends on the scene and the amount of evidence that is contained in the scene. The marathon vs sprint concept essentially reminds us we are under no time constraints and should never hurry through the processing of a scene.

---

*Latent evidence refers to something "hidden" or not visible to the naked eye; a good example is fingerprints which may not be visible until fingerprint powder is applied to develop them on an object.

▶ Locard's Law or the *Theory of Transference*

This general concept was initially discussed earlier in the text as an explanation for limiting the number of persons entering and exiting the scene, protecting the crime scene from contamination. Locard's Law or the *theory of transference* is the basis for modern crime scene examination and helps us understand the value of trace evidence as it is passed from one person to another, or to and from the scene by a person.

From a crime scene perspective we are interested in any potential transfer of evidence brought from the offender into the scene or taken from the offender away from the scene, as well as any potential biological evidence found at the scene or originating from the victim or the offender and transferred one to the other.

Some elements of Locard's Law are easily observable as seen in **Case Study 4-2**.

Case Study 4-2

An elderly man was found brutally stabbed and murdered at his residence in a rural area. From the initial observation of the scene it could be easily discerned that the victim was attacked while in his carport, stabbed multiple times, and then collapsed to the concrete floor where he remained for a period of time. He was then dragged partially into his house through the closest doorway and deposited on the floor of the laundry room. At this point he was apparently assaulted again and his throat was cut. He was on his stomach for some period of time while bleeding and at some time was turned over on his back by the offender and was found in this position. Based on the transference of evidence the offender's movements through the scene could be fairly easily determined. **Figure 4-1** depicts the crime scene in the car port showing bloody drag marks to the left and the offender's bloody footwear impressions in the right center of the photograph. These footwear impressions were obviously left by the offender as the victim's shoes did not match the impressions and he was clearly unable to walk after sustaining any of these injuries. The bloody footwear impressions were observed throughout the house as the offender walked through the various rooms and then again s/he must have stepped into the pool of blood as s/he exited the scene making additional impressions as s/he departed. During the examination of the interior of the house however, several drops of blood were discovered on the dining room floor located some distance away from the victim as depicted by the evidence tents in **Figure 4-2**. The drops of blood were too far away from the victim to have dripped from any weapon and were almost immediately thought to be from the offender. If this is blood from the offender, then the implication is the offender was likely injured during the assault. This is not uncommon

FIGURE 4-1. Large blood stain created as the victim was dragged across the concrete and footwear impressions in blood throughout the scene help identify movement and actions of the offender during the crime. See Color Plate 13.

when sharp force instruments are used in an attack. There were also several drops of blood found on the gravel driveway which again was consistent with the likelihood that the offender was injured during the assault. Based on these initial findings the victim was carefully examined and two drops of blood were found on the lower abdomen as shown in **Figure 4-3**. It was clear the

FIGURE 4-2. Drops of blood found a significant distance from the victim and assault location are consistent with possible injury to the suspect; especially when sharp force instruments are used. See Color Plate 14.

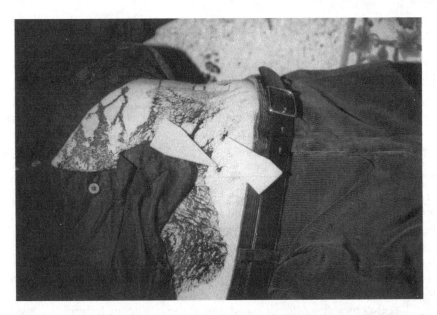

FIGURE 4-3. Example of Locard's Law or exchange principal of trace or other evidence between victim and suspect during a violent assault. The two drops of blood indicated by the markers, belonged to the suspect who was also injured during the assault. See Color Plate 15.

victim was at one time on his stomach in a pool of blood, as is evident from the smeared blood above the drops. These drops were photographed and collected as evidence. Later DNA analysis identified the drops of blood in the dining room and on the victim's lower abdomen as belonging to the offender. The offender was later convicted of the murder.

The preceding case study is a good demonstration of the theory of transference, in this case the transfer of blood or biological fluids from the victim onto the offender and from the offender onto the victim as well as throughout the scene. Based on the amount of blood found at the scene it can be reasonably assumed the offender also had blood on his/her clothing and certainly on the soles and perhaps on the tops of his/her shoes. It is also likely for both the offender and the victim to have exchanged hairs and fibers from their clothing between them because they were in such close personal contact during the attack.

This potential transference of evidence is the rationale behind our attempts to limit possible scene contamination by authorized persons. It also demonstrates the importance of collecting a suspect's clothing and possibly conducting a search of his/her residence and vehicle for possible evidence.

▶ Burned Bridges

This general concept deals with movement of things inside a crime scene and it essentially expresses an understanding that once an object is picked up or moved it can never be placed back exactly where it was when it was first found. Thus by picking up an item of evidence or moving the body, we have "burned the bridge," so to speak, of scene integrity. The item in question can be placed close to where it was; but never exactly where it was. No object or item of evidence should ever be touched or picked up until it has been thoroughly documented through photography and measurements for the crime scene sketch, and only picked up when you are ready to actually collect it as evidence. In other words, the one and only time an item of evidence should be picked up or moved, is when we are collecting it as evidence. Once we pick it up, it is then properly packaged and removed from the scene and any further contamination. If we need to photograph it, or collect something from it such as biological evidence or latent prints, it is done so as it is normally collected and then packaged and safeguarded.

Like other aspects of death investigation there is no such thing as a "typical" or "routine" scene. Although there are some standard procedures and protocols for scene examination, each reported death should be treated as an individual event with its own set of circumstances and dynamics for which the protocol must be adjusted. Detectives typically view the death scene from a different perspective than crime scene technicians. Crime scene technicians are concerned with physical and forensic evidence such as fingerprints, blood spatters, DNA, and properly documenting the scene. The detective is concerned with identifying the victim, the cause of death, and criminality of the act.

If the cause of death is determined to be from natural causes very little investigative effort is going to be necessary. In accidental death any subsequent investigation will likely be focused on criminal negligence determination. If no negligence is found, then there will be very limited investigation.

In cases involving domestic interpersonal conflicts which take place within the residence of the suspect and victim, there is a frequent professional disagreement between crime scene technicians and detectives relating to the actual value of the forensic evidence. Because both the victim and the offender have access to the same area, finding fingerprints, DNA, hairs and fibers, and other such trace evidence from both offender and victim would be expected, and thus may not have that much evidentiary value. Regardless of the possible limited value, the scene should be processed in the same general manner as if it were an unknown offender. The importance of this is demonstrated by several concepts.

Unless and until the scene is processed normally we really have no idea what type of forensic evidence is actually present at the scene Because the incident took place inside the home we may presume to know what evidence is there or what evidence may be found, but without processing the scene we truly do not know. We have no idea of the actual value of the evidence to the case. Unknown factors in the early stages of the investigation may later impact interpretation of the evidence. For example, at the time of the scene examination we might not know the couple was actually estranged, or that one of them had moved and had not lived at the residence for a period of time. The trace, biological, or other evidence may then become more valuable.

Processing might eliminate the possibility of successful defense or the CSI effect   In the initial stages of the investigation we have only a minimum amount of information regarding the facts and circumstances of the crime. If we do not process the scene as we normally would, we may unintentionally provide a foundation for a successful defense. A modern jury is likely familiar with various television programs involving forensic science and crime scenes, thus having a basic knowledge of crime scene investigation. They could very well be persuaded into believing the investigators did not do a thorough job. This is known as the *CSI effect* and it is a very real problem. This issue is covered in greater detail in subsequent material.

Every scene should be processed in the same manner because facts may change as new information or evidence is obtained   What is true and known on the first day is not necessarily what we know to be true several weeks later. By then it may be too late to go back and try to redo the scene. *It is always better to have evidence and not need it, than need it and not have it.*

Although every scene is different based on the individual circumstances of the scene and the crime itself, there are basic activities that must be accomplished regardless of the circumstances.

▶ Initial Walkthrough

Specially trained crime scene personnel should conduct the actual scene examination, but it is also important for the detective to observe the scene as well. This is accomplished in what is known as the initial walkthrough, the first chance for the detective to actually enter the scene.

Although not required, it is advisable that this walkthrough be conducted jointly with the detective and the senior crime scene technician. This is the best opportunity for the detective and the crime scene technician to discuss any particular examinations or to coordinate any special requests that may be recommended based on the scene dynamics or evidence. This initial walkthrough should be a very limited, hands-in-the-pocket tour by one or two senior persons. It is used to evaluate the scene and plan the formalized processing. This is a visual exercise, and not a time for anyone to pick up evidence, move items, or otherwise disturb the scene.

The detective and crime scene technicians each have different reasons for viewing the scene. The crime scene technician is primarily looking at the extent of the scene, determining the order in which the scene should be processed, if there is a need for specialized equipment, or if there are any other technical aspects related to documenting and examining the crime scene. This walkthrough is the opportunity for them to formulate their plan for the crime scene examination. The detectives should not only be observant of the physical and forensic evidence found throughout the scene but should also be focused on the wide range of possible offender behaviors which are also likely indicated by the evidence.

Method of Entry

Was the method of entry professional and experienced or clumsy and amateurish? This is often an indication of the experience level or criminal sophistication of the offender. If there were no signs of forced entry, entrance could have been granted because the victim knew the offender, or because the offender was able to "con" or convince the victim to allow entry into the house. The ability to con the victim or use a ruse to get access to the scene is very important behavior to note and understand and again speaks to the possible intelligence and confidence level of the offender.

Interaction With Victim

Interaction refers to anything said or done with or to the victim prior to death. This could include a wide range of possibilities such as ante mortem physical assault, efforts to control the victim by physical restraint or other immobilization, forcing the victim to open a safe or provide valuables; or other more serious behaviors such as torture, sexual assault, moving or posing of the body at the scene, or even post mortem mutilation of the victim. One of the keys to look for and understand is which offender interactions with the victim were ante mortem and which interactions were post mortem.

How Prepared Was the Offender?

This is perhaps one of the more important offender behaviors we can observe, it is an indication of the amount of thought and preparation by the offender before the crime was committed. An offender that is more prepared is one who brings the equipment and tools necessary to the scene, prepares an escape route out of the scene, tries to avoid leaving forensic evidence behind, or only strikes when ready or has some advantage over the victim.

This is in direct contrast to other offenders who seem to act impulsively, with little preparation or plan; using objects or tools found at the scene, and appear to be influenced by events and the victim's response rather than shape events to their advantage. There is often a great deal of forensic evidence left behind in these cases because they were not prepared to prevent it or did not think about it.

The two offenders described above represent the generic characteristics of the "organized" and "disorganized" type offenders. Through basic observation of the scene and the offender behavior you will identify these characteristics and thus form an impression about the offender. These impressions or observations of the scene are based on a combination of the detective's investigative experience and training, his own life experience, basic common sense, the testimonial evidence available, and physical and forensic evidence at the scene.

These impressions are formed by the detective looking through the scene for what is known as "Things that make you go hmmmmmm," meaning those things that make us pause and ask: What's that? Why did this happen? How does that fit in? Where did that come from? How prepared was the offender to commit the crime? Was the death a planned or spur of the moment event? What did the offender bring to the scene or take away with him? How was entry and escape made? What injuries were inflicted? Any signs of self defense injuries or signs of struggle? Were injuries inflicted ante mortem or post mortem? Were injuries inflicted more than what was needed to kill the victim? Did the offender maintain control over the victim? Is there any evidence of other crimes being committed such as theft, robbery, or sexual? What's present at the scene and what's missing?; along with a multitude other who, what, when, where, how, and why questions that are asked and answered during the course of every scene examination. These types of questions are routinely asked as the detective walks through the scene and observes the evidence that was left behind. Many times it is not possible to get complete answers for each of the questions arising from the initial walk through, so they are noted in the review or log of the scene and may become investigative leads in the subsequent investigation.

Following the initial walk through of the scene the detective by protocol should exit the scene and allow the crime scene technicians to document and collect whatever evidence is present. It is advisable for the detective and lead technician to discuss the scene examination to ensure there is a thorough understanding of any special requests by the detective or any special techniques required or suggested by the technicians.

Responsibility for the scene examination now shifts over to the crime scene technicians and the detective should actually exit the scene to get out of the way. Whenever possible it is always a good idea for at least one detective to remain at the scene, available to receive any information or critical evidence developed by the crime scene technicians. Many times this is dependent on the size of the agency and the number of detectives involved in the preliminary investigation. Regardless of whether the detective remains at the scene or not, there should always be at least one uniformed officer present to secure the scene from outsiders as the scene is examined.

▶ Crime Scene Documentation

One of the important tasks related to crime scene examination is the documentation of the scene as it is found prior to being disturbed. There are four main ways to document the crime scene (1) video tape, (2) photography, (3) sketching, and (4) written notes.

Video Tape

Video tape is actually a very good method for recording the scene as it is initially found. The greatest advantage of using video tape is that it takes in everything. Everything that is in the scene at the time the tape is made is going to be recorded on the video tape. It is not unusual for detectives to actually note things in the video tape when it is later played back or reviewed that they had not actually noticed when they were at the scene.

It is also beneficial to use the video tape as a means to identify important pieces of evidence, slowly zooming in towards the item and then back out again. It is especially valuable when filming a body to depict the injuries and location of any items of evidence on their clothing. Often when crime scene photographs are not available to show the medical examiner at autopsy the video tape can be used to familiarize the ME with the scene and the position of the body which may help in the interpretation of injuries.

The crime scene video tape, when done correctly, often plays very well with a jury during court presentation because we are living in a high tech era. The crime scene video will have a similar effect on the jurors as if they were watching one of the many television programs that concentrate on criminal investigations, crime scene examination, and forensic analysis. The jury members identify with and become part of the crime scene as they have seen on TV. It is a very good way to capture their attention and can be very valuable evidence when it is done correctly. When done incorrectly and unprofessionally then it will have the opposite effect and may prove to be detrimental to the prosecution's case.

The greatest advantage to videotaping is also its greatest disadvantage— the video tape takes in everything. It will faithfully capture any mistakes, movements, background noises or voices, comments or conversations by the participants. Most often an inappropriate comment is not an expression of disrespect or callousness, but more of a way to deal with stress and the horrific events that must be confronted on a daily basis. Obviously, to others unfamiliar with the need to relieve the stress, these comments could create problems when viewing the tape in court. Therefore, always turn down or disconnect the audio capabilities of the recorder.

It does take practice to learn how to properly video tape a scene but it is not difficult. The main issues are maintaining the camera in a stable position, avoiding jerky movements—very difficult when trying to walk and film at the same time. The effect is similar to trying to film while driving in a car on a bumpy road, the camera bouncing up and down or from side to side renders the video tape unusable as evidence. It is better to stand in one place, turn the camera on and slowly pan across the target space. It is recommended to pan at eye level, then pan around the same area towards the floor or ground, and if appropriate pan the ceiling in the same area.

Video photography is best when done as a singular activity; that is the videotaping is not done while the scene is actually being processed or evidence collected. It is best done first, before any other type of documentation is accomplished and before anything else is added or changed at the scene. Once the scene has been documented by the video tape, the next step is to begin the crime scene photography.

Photography

Crime scene photography is generally what comes to mind for most people when thinking about scene documentation. All four methods of crime scene documentation are important, but photography is probably the most vital aspect. Whenever we teach crime scene examination, we have always stated unequivocally if our agency had the money for one and only one piece of crime scene equipment; we would insist on a good camera.

What is a sufficient number of photos—50, 100, or even 200? There is of course no set number of photographs that you need for a particular scene. All aspects of the scene and all items of evidence must be properly documented, regardless of how many photos are exposed. Modern digital cameras permit shooting of hundreds of photographs before the images must be downloaded so there is no reason not to take a sufficient number of photographs of the scene. This is a huge advancement from the earlier 35 mm wet film cameras which allowed for 20–36 photos to be taken before the roll of film had to be changed. Additionally, there was no way to tell at the time if the photo was in correct focus, or the lighting conditions were adequate.

There are four general types of crime scene photographs: (1) overall, (2) establishment, (3) close up, and (4) close up with measuring device.

The *overall* type photographs are those generally taken from a distance and used to capture the overall nature of the scene. These are frequently discounted with very little attention given to their importance. As an example, **Figure 4-4** is a photograph of a deceased victim at a crime scene. Although we can tell from the photograph the victim was found in tall grass, we have no idea of what the surrounding area is like. Is this photo taken in a backyard or in an open field? We have no idea because there is no perspective or context to the photograph. If this is the only photograph of the area we are going to be extremely limited in learning anything else from the scene.

Figure 4-5 is the overall photo of the same victim taken from just a short distance away, but we can immediately tell the body is actually resting on the edge of an agricultural field. Other photos taken further back would clearly

FIGURE 4-4. Photos of the body are important, but without perspective of the entire area their value is diminished. See Color Plate 16.

establish the body was actually just a short distance from a dirt road. Taking a series of photographs from all cardinal directions would give a good perspective of where the body was located.

Figures 4-6 through **4-8** are a series of photographs taken using the *walk up* approach, which is a series of photographs taken starting from a distance

FIGURE 4-5. Through establishment photos the scene perspective is understood. It is clear the victim is at the edge of a agricultural field. See Color Plate 17.

FIGURE 4-6. Walk up technique, overall establishment photo of the entire area and then move up taking additional photos of the important areas or evidence. See Color Plate 18.

while approaching the main item of interest in the scene. Figure 4-8 is a close up of a spray-painted swastica on the siding of the house, which was the main item of interest at the scene.

Overall photographs taken inside a room or structure consist of a series of photographs to form a panorama 360 degrees around the entire room. The technique calls for the photographer to start at one point and then move horizontally in a circular clockwise or counter clockwise manner taking photographs of the room without changing the vertical orientation of the camera. Each new photograph should include approximately 10% of the preceding photograph, overlapping to create that panoramic effect. When the photographer has taken all of the photos needed from one position, he should then move to the opposite side of the room and continue in the same manner until the entire interior has been photographed. It is often necessary to repeat the

FIGURE 4-7. Walk up technique, after overall establishment photos, a series of photos are taken at decreasing ranges. See Color Plate 19.

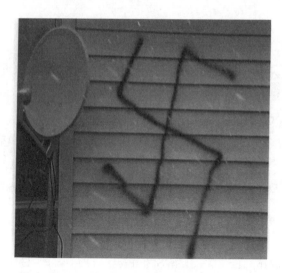

FIGURE 4-8. This is actually the main item of interest in the series of photographs, but if this were the only picture taken it may not have the same value when presented to a jury. See Color Plate 20.

process of the overall scene documentation by aiming the camera downward to photograph the floor and lower walls again using the panoramic technique. This process is continued until the scene has been properly documented. In enclosed areas, upper walls and ceiling would likely be documented in the same manner. Depending on the size of the room and the amount of evidence contained therein, the number of photos needed to document the room or interior scene will vary.

Only after the overall photography has been completed should photographers move on to the other types of scene photography.

The next type of photographs are known as *establishment* and are basically those photographs taken with attention to place a particular item of evidence into perspective with other items in the scene and the scene iteself. **Figure 4-9** shows a photograph of a cast off bloodstain on a wall. While this is an important photo and potentially valuable evidence, by itself the blood stains are diffiult to put into perspective or understand how they may actually fit into the scene because there is little context for the picture. In **Figure 4-10,** the establishment photo, we can now see where the stain is located within the scene and understand how it fits into the crime itself. This is one of the the purposes of taking establishment type photographs.

It is important to note that the overall and establishment photos should be taken before any evidence tents are placed down (**Figure 4-11**) to show the scene before anything was added to it even if it is marking important evidence. We first want to photograph the original scene as we found it. Then the evidence tents are placed down to mark whatever visible items of evi-

FIGURE 4-9. A bloodstain pattern is potentially important but with only this photo we cannot even tell exactly where the scene stain is located within the scene or why it is important. See Color Plate 21.

dence that we have seen and additional photos taken to show those various items of evidence and their location in the scene, as noted in **Figure 4-12**.

A *close up* photo is exactly that; photo of an individual item of evidence taken at a short distance. Because we have already established the overall scene in other photographs we can now concentrate on taking these close ups

FIGURE 4-10. With an establishment photo, the stains depicted in Figure 4-9 are now put into perspective within the total scene. See Color Plate 22.

FIGURE 4-11. Initial photographs are taken of the scene as it is found, before the scene is altered or anything is added to the scene. See Color Plate 23.

FIGURE 4-12. Evidence tents are used to accent or identify potential items of evidence noted within the scene. See Color Plate 24.

FIGURE 4-13. Potential evidence is first photographed as it is initially found. See Color Plate 25.

to identify and characterize items of evidence. **Figures 4-13, 4-14,** and **4-15** are examples of close up and close up with measuring device. Note that they were both taken directly over the item. Close up photos with a measuring device should always be taken at a 90 degree angle to the object. When taken at any other angle the object becomes distorted and accurate measurement is not

FIGURE 4-14. Evidence close up with measuring device. See Color Plate 26.

FIGURE 4-15. Close up with measuring device. See Color Plate 27.

possible. This is especially vital when taking photographs of bloodstains or latent prints for later analysis or comparison purposes.

In addition to the various establishment and close up photos there are also other "special" photographs which should be considered as part of the general crime scene documentation. These are photos which center on the victim and properly documenting the final position of the body. This includes photos of the full body from all possible angles, then separate photos of the body taken in thirds consisting of the lower portions of the legs, the abdomen and upper legs, and the chest and head. Identification photos should then be taken of the victim's head and face.

These photos of the victim's body are important because they capture not just the body's position, but also the clothing and any stains that may be present on the clothing before the body is moved or removed from the scene. It is not unusual once the body is picked up, placed into a body bag, and transported to the ME's office for autopsy that the clothing become saturated with blood or receive transfer bloodstains resulting in a very different interpretation of the stains.

Additional establishment and close up photographs of all visible injuries and photos of the hands including the backs, the palms, and fingers. Photos of the hands are especially important because defensive movements by the victim would most likely involve the hands in some manner, therefore these photos will help to validate the presence or absence of any injuries or identify other possible trace evidence.

When the body is eventually moved by the coroner or medical examiner we also want to photograph the unexposed side of the body, by turning it over or leaning it over and once the body is removed, to photograph the area underneath the body that was previously hidden from sight.

Depending on the scene and the types of forensic techniques used or evidence collected, it is often a good idea to take a few photographs of the condition of the scene as it was left, to prevent possible complaints by an offender or others of damage or destruction of personal property by the police during their examination.

Sketching

Sketching is the third method used in documenting a crime scene. This is a drawing of the scene typically from a bird's eye view as if looking straight down from on top of the scene. The sketch is used to show the spatial relationships between the various items of evidence and is an invaluable tool if the scene needs to be reconstructed at a later time.

Notes

Written notes are the last method of scene documentation and refer to the various observations made at the scene and recorded in the crime scene notes. The written descriptions and observations represent information that cannot be recorded or photographed. Examples would include the ambient temperature, humidity, and other weather considerations around the scene. Additionally the other documentation mediums cannot provide are specific information about any unusual noises or odors, or lighting conditions at the scene. These facts must be documented in written form based on the direct observations by the crime scene technician or detective at the scene.

The documentation of the scene is not a single phase of the initial examination that is performed and completed, but continues throughout the examination process. As additional evidence is located, it must be documented through the establishment, close up and close up with measuring device photos before it is collected, perhaps added to the sketch, and of course adequately described in the crime scene notes.

▶ Crime Scene from the Detective's Perspective

While the crime scene technician is ensuring the scene is properly documented and examined, the detective is also looking for other important factors that will add to the investigative effort. These special concerns include establishing the time of death, obtaining additional background information on the victim to assist in victimology assessment, the general assessment of the crime concerning a possible motive, as well as looking for other offender behavioral clues left behind.

When viewed from an investigative perspective, *the crime scene is the one time the offenders actually tell us all about themselves.* Unfortunately many detectives do not take the time to listen to what offenders are saying through their actions and behavior as evidenced in the scene.

Offenders do not always leave behind physical or forensic evidence, but almost always leave some clues about themselves at the crime scene. Sometimes this evidence is left behind quite unintentionally and the significance must be deduced from the totality of facts and circumstances found at the scene. Other times evidence is left behind quite purposely, as if to make a statement regarding the victim or the reason behind the crime. Other evidence left behind may be intended to cause a misinterpretation by police of the true evidence and events. What is left behind of course is always dependant upon the individual offender and the specific motive for the crime, the particular victim, and the location of the scene.

In addition to the behavioral evidence we are also concerned with some more basic facts and circumstances which are covered below.

Time of Death

Determining the time of death is a critical finding in any death investigation and should always be one of the main focuses of the detective during the crime scene examination and/or preliminary investigation. The time of death is going to be used to compare to any other event or information such as statements and alibis that are developed throughout the case. All other facts, circumstances, or evidence developed through the course of the investigation are going to be looked at as either *ante mortem*, before death or *post mortem*, after death.

Generally, the longer the time period between death and discovery of the body, the more difficult it is to determine the time of death. If the event is not observed by another person or somehow recorded by other means, any time of death determination is likely to be an educated guess covering a span of time. This educated guess can be determined from observation of the various physiological changes after death, such as algor, livor, and rigor mortis. These physiological changes are relevant and can be useful in determining the approximate time of death if the body is discovered within a few hours to 24 hours after death. But, generally if more than a day has passed then the time of death determination becomes somewhat more problematic and other available facts may have to be used.

Fortunately, in this modern age we have many different ways to track a person's whereabouts or activity. Even in a residence we have potential dated material. We may be able to determine if the mail was delivered or picked up, if there are telephone messages, cell phone text messages, or emails sent or received and opened. With a little extra effort we can also determine the last time a phone call was made to the victim and received, the last time the internet was accessed, and the last time the victim's ATM or credit cards were used.

Case Study 4-3

A mother and father were found murdered in their house on a Sunday afternoon by their two sons. The last contact with the parents was on Friday around 6:15 p.m. when the oldest son called to talk with them. During the call the father mentioned that the mother was in the kitchen cooking steak and potatoes, their typical Friday evening meal. During the crime scene examination of the kitchen area the police noted a steak was still in the skillet, nearly cooked, (see **Figure 4-16**) and there were potatoes still in the microwave. Based on the phone call and the steak still on the stove the police were able to circumstantially back up the time of the incident to sometime around 6:15 p.m. to 6:30 p.m. Although the time of death could not be limited to this time frame, it was a logical assumption that the victims were confronted by the offender and their death likely occurred sometime after the phone call. Although not perfect, it provided a fairly good estimated time frame the police could use.

FIGURE 4-16. Scene photograph in this case was used to circumstantially narrow the time of death of the victims. The victim told the last person he talked to that his wife was cooking steak and potatoes. Since the meal was cooked but not eaten the initial time of death was estimated to be approximately at the same time as the phone call. See Color Plate 28.

Many times an approximate time of death must be estimated through use of a combination of facts and events as noted in **Case Study 4-3**.

Victimology

A victimology assessment is a vital part of understanding the crime and is covered in greater detail in subsequent material. Sometimes a much more detailed victimology assessment is possible when the scene is at the victim's own residence, because it allows the detective to take a close look at how the victim lived and what was important to them. Take a look at your own residence and ask yourself: What does my house or apartment tell about me? Is it neat and orderly or is it messy? What books do I have, what other interests do I have? Who or what is important to me? What do I think is important in my life? These are all important factors to consider as we begin to look at the victim and understand particular offender behaviors.

▶ Evaluation of the Crime Location

Where the scene is located, meaning indoors or outdoors, and what other factors are present at the scene such as another crime, also impacts the initial evaluation. For indoor scenes one of the first investigative steps is to try to determine how entrance by the offender was gained and the motive for the homicide. The offender's entrance to the scene can be very important behavior as contrasted in the following scenarios.

Indoor Scene—Businesses

For public establishments such as restaurants, stores, or other businesses there are generally two main themes to homicides, interpersonal conflict within the business, and secondary to another crime. Interpersonal conflict may involve coworkers or past employees and usually some type of workplace violence. Many times these incidents are not very well planned out and consist of the offender simply returning to the work place and initiating some type of violent assault against co-workers. Many times the offender has not even planned or considered an escape and often the end result is suicide. In these cases offender behavior is going to be centered on ante mortem behaviors and what lead up to the incident or what steps they took to prepare for the event.

The second general theme in a business type homicide is the result of some other crime such as robbery. Entrance is generally made through the normal public entrance to the facility. This of course requires no special knowledge or equipment by the offender(s). It also allows them to rapidly take control of the situation and personnel, obtain the money and quickly depart from the scene.

During these types of robberies, actual harm to employees or customers is infrequent and generally not planned or intended, because the general goal is to steal money and leave. However, there are some exceptions to this general statement, such as if the offender is confronted or is somehow physically resisted by a customer or employee, an inexperienced offender panics, or if the offender is under the influence of alcohol or drugs. In these type of incidents the offenders may lash out at one particular person that attempted to physically confront them or one person they perceive as a threat to their escape. After eliminating the threat they may leave with or without even taking the money.

This is somewhat different from other robbery incidents in which the offender gains entrance from other than a public entrance, such as a rear door. Once inside s/he may gather everyone within the business and bring them to another location within the facility and tie them up or otherwise incapacitate them, thereby keeping them from interfering with the robbery. In some cases once all of the employees have been rounded up, they are then summarily murdered. This situation is not just a robbery with a motive to steal, this is also a premeditated murder committed in order to commit the robbery.

It is important to recognize we are dealing with two different types of offenders and their motivation and behaviors are quite different. In the first scenario the aspect of planning appears to be rather basic. They enter, show their weapon, and make their demands for money. If everything goes as planned, they flee the scene. There does not appear to be any real intent to cause harm and would likely not have committed any other crime if they were not resisted. In other cases the influence of drugs or some other factor may complicate the situation resulting in a homicide.

The second scenario describes a far different type of offender and one can assume much more planning and preparation was involved. There is a big difference between offenders who kill or injure a victim because of some immediate perceived threat to their safety or escape; and offenders who intentionally murder someone who actually cooperated or someone the offenders had already rendered incapable of posing a threat. An execution type murder of employees in a facility generally points to one of two possibilities. First, the perpetrator may be "a more experienced offender," someone who may have a lot of experience in these types of offenses and perhaps has been caught and punished in the past. This type of offender may believe there is really nothing to lose by committing a murder and does not want to chance leaving any witnesses around to testify against them. The second possibility is that it was an "inside job" meaning the robbery was perpetrated by someone who currently works at the facility, or may have worked there at sometime in the past, or knows someone currently or previously employed there. Therefore, the murder of the employees was necessary to prevent the identification of the offenders by eliminating any witnesses that could testify against them. Such inside knowledge may be demonstrated by offender behaviors such as knowledge of the surveillance system; knowledge of a back or side door entrance used by the employees; familiarity of the interior layout; or familiarity with employee habits, routines, or schedules.

Indoor Scene—Home or Residence

For homicides that take place inside a home or residence the method of entrance is also important. In these circumstances, we are looking for any signs or evidence of forced entry typically seen as a broken door, broken door jamb, pry marks, broken window, or other similar damage.

If there are no signs or indication that the offender gained forced entrance to the building and therefore access to the victim then it is traditionally assumed the victim and offender knew each other. This of course is not an absolute because an especially manipulative offender confronting a younger, more trusting, or naïve victim may be able to gain entry to the house and thus access to the victim without having to resort to force.

Forced entry therefore is something to look for and note one way or the other and then determine its significance as the investigation unfolds.

In all cases the detectives should be looking for any evidence that gives an indication that the offender may have previous knowledge of the scene or the victim. Such knowledge might be the location of a safe or other valuables, the presence and location of surveillance equipment or home alarm, or other particular information not known by the general public.

Additionally, the detective is concerned with the overall scene. Did it appear as if the offender was prepared to commit the crime? Does it appear the crime was thought out or planned? Did the offender bring whatever weapons or other equipment necessary to commit the crime with him? Did the offender have plans for an escape? Did the offender take measures to eliminate being identified or leaving evidence behind? This would include wearing a mask, wearing gloves, wearing a condom, or perhaps wiping the scene to eliminate the chance of leaving fingerprints.

Looking at the scene, did it appear the offender was able to maintain control over the situation and the victim? Control over the victim can be demonstrated by a lack of any efforts to escape, a lack of or limited defense wounds on the victim, lack of real resistance by the victim, or by using intermediate means of victim control such as tying the victim up. These are examples of what is referred to as an *organized scene.*

Conversely, a scene that appears messy and unplanned, where the offender uses material found at the scene as a weapon or perhaps to constrain the victim, or it appears the offender was unable to maintain control over the victim is referred to as a *disorganized scene*. With these disorganized type of scenes there is generally little concern shown by the offender for leaving any physical or forensic evidence behind.

Outdoor Scenes

For those crime scenes that are found outdoors, there are also some important considerations. First of course is to determine the departmental jurisdiction of the location where the body was found; or which department is responsible for the actual investigation into the death. There is an old adage used to describe investigative jurisdiction, "Like golf, you play bodies where they lay." In other words jurisdiction is traditionally established by the location where the body is found. If the location is within your jurisdiction the investigation is your responsibility unless some other department is able to assume responsibility.

This of course can present problems when the body is in one location and jurisdiction while the actual crime scene is in another jurisdiction. Some offenders, particularly serial offenders, are well aware of this and take great pains to transport their victims some distance away to cross these jurisdictional boundaries and thus create confusion for law enforcement.

There are some occasions in which an agency may already be investigating the suspected death, injury, or disappearance of a victim and instead of opening up a second investigation when the body is discovered, jurisdiction may be released to the agency covering that location.

Thus it is important to establish whether the location where the body is found was the actual murder scene or if the body was dumped—the victim was killed elsewhere and simply taken to another location and "dumped" as a means of disposal.

As previously mentioned, the location where the body is found, whether inside or outside, is referred to as the *primary scene*. If it appears the primary scene is actually just a body disposal site, then at a minimum there are probably at least two other likely crime scenes, known as *secondary scenes*. The first possibility is whatever vehicle was used to bring the body to the dump site. Even if it was only used to transport the body physical and forensic evidence may be recovered from the vehicle. Another secondary scene could be the murder scene or where the death took place. Depending on the actual events of the crime, there may even be more than two other scenes to consider, such as a victim that is kidnapped from their work or their vehicle, taken to another location and murdered. The place of work would then be a scene as well. The number of potential crime scenes can quickly expand based on the individual dynamics of the crime. **Case Study 4-4** illustrates how the number of scenes can quickly expand.

Case Study 4-4

A family of three was reported missing from their rural residence. Police responded to family friends who reported seeing the front door to the house standing open and the pickup truck parked in the front, opened for several hours on a Saturday morning. This was unusual for that family. They stopped by to check and although no one was present at the home, noted a small amount of blood in the kitchen and a large blood stain on the cement pad in front of the house. The initial crime scene investigation of the residence noted several bullet defects in the walls, expended shell casings, and blood in the hallway and kitchen. Examination of the vehicle pad in front of the house noted bloodstains, and what appeared to be brain tissue. Several bullet defects were found in the pickup truck and blood spatter on the undercarriage of the truck. The evidence was consistent with the possibility that the husband was shot outside, followed by the kidnapping, and based on the bloodstains, the possible shooting or injury of the wife and child inside. However, no bodies were present at the scene. Several days later, the main suspect, a relative, finally confessed to the murder of all three. He admitted he had shot the husband outside and then loaded his body in to his own vehicle. He had then entered the house to kidnap the wife and child. During the struggle he shot the wife in the arm and hit her several times in the head to gain control of them. He then forced the wife and child to literally sit on top of her husband in the car as he drove some 100 miles to his own house. He then took them to another building he owned, where he forced them inside and then killed them both. He then left all three bodies and went home, returned with another truck and loaded them into the truck bed. He then drove another 20 miles to an outside location in another county, where he buried all three bodies and covered them up.

The primary scene was the interior and exterior of the victims' house with numerous secondary scenes that required additional scene examination including:

- The husband's pickup truck parked outside the house
- The suspect's vehicle initially used to transport the victims away from their house
- The suspect's own residence (for his clothing and weapon)
- The second site where the wife and child were taken and actually murdered
- The second vehicle used to transport the bodies to the outdoor scene
- The outdoor area surrounding the clandestine grave
- The actual clandestine grave site
- The victims' bodies and clothing
- Outdoor scene where suspect was known to have fired the suspected murder weapon, looking for expended shell casings and projectiles to use as a match to those recovered during the primary scene examination.

At each scene, additional evidence was successfully gathered. This case study is an example of how the individual dynamics of the event may result in many additional scenes being uncovered requiring additional examination.

For outdoor scenes we also have to consider many other questions including: Why did the offender pick this particular location? What was it about this particular area? Did it have any particular advantages or disadvantages for the offender? As the case develops this might prove to be an important aspect of the investigation if it can be shown that the offender was somehow familiar with the area, or can be placed in the area at the time of the crime. This of course was a very important aspect in the well publicized Lacy Peterson homicide investigation, when the victim's body was later discovered in the water where the husband claims he was fishing the day of her disappearance.

What is the distance from last known location of victim and body discovery site? A distance of several blocks or even several miles may not be unusual, but any significant distances between the victim's last known location and body discovery site raises many other questions about the victim's and offender's last activity that need to be addressed. We also try to determine how much physical effort the offender had to exert in order to dispose of the body at a particular location. For example, consider the difference in effort between a body simply pushed out of a car at the side of the road as opposed to a body the offender must pick up and carry a considerable distance away and the terrain traversed. One method certainly takes more effort than the other.

The next series of questions are a sample of some of the important questions that should be part of a careful outdoor investigation that can help us understand the event dynamics and assist in developing the long term investigative plan.

Was the Body Hidden or Buried and Only Accidentally Found?

A body that is hidden or buried generally indicates an attempt at delaying discovery or an attempt to destroy evidence. Was the body carried into the woods and left on the surface? Was the body covered up by some other object to hide it? Deposited in an abandoned building? All of these are important offender behavior because it deals with the offender's post mortem activity.

It sometimes takes a lot of energy and planning to transport a body to another location and then dig a grave or otherwise hide it. This is again important offender behavior and also shows whether or not the offender is disciplined enough and strong enough to spend the time to dig an effective grave. Many times the body is discovered because the offender was impatient or too lazy to dig a proper grave and the body is exposed as the ground settles down around it.

Were Steps Taken by Offender to Delay Identification of the Victim?

There are many ways to delay the identification of the deceased, ranging from removing the various identification documents and or clothing from the victim, to more aggressive means such as removal of the hands or fingers to eliminate identification through fingerprints; decapitation to limit the ability of personal identification or use of possible dental records; or placing the victim in a fire to try to destroy the complete body.

Any effort to delay identification is important to note, but when the effort includes removal of body parts or burning, this could reflect on the offender's criminal experience level. Another indicator of experience might be the offender's willingness to touch, move, or otherwise interact with the body post mortem.

Was the Body Intentionally Placed in a Location Where Easily Found?

This includes placement in a public or high traffic area, with obvious intent that the body would be found easily and quickly. We see this many times in serial killers, one of the better examples is the Hillside Stranglers. The two subjects kidnapped, raped, sadistically tortured their victims, and intentionally placed the bodies along public streets or on an open hillside where they were observed and reported by neighbors. This of course is very important behavior, first for the ability to interact with a dead body and as a way to demonstrate power by their ability to murder at will and deposit the bodies in the open without being caught. This effort was also a way to taunt the police through media stories and public critique over their inability to protect the public.

Was the Body Posed in a Sexually Stylized or Provocative Position?

This activity would include not only outdoor but also indoor scenes, where the victim is often undressed and then posed in sexually stylized position, such as spread eagled, with foreign object insertion, or some other pose that is designed to humiliate and degrade the victim, and shock and offend society and the first responders who are called to the scene. It is also not uncommon for the body to have suffered post mortem mutilation in the form of sharp force injuries to the breasts or sexual organs.

This type of behavior is especially important to note because it is generally based on offender fantasies and therefore likely to be observed again in other cases occurring before or after the current case. This behavior is an example of what is known as the offender's "signature" and is one of the best methods we can use to link what may seem to be dissimilar cases together. An offender's signature is considered to be unique to a particular offender and it is essentially defined as "offender behavior that is above and beyond what is necessary to complete the crime."

For example, after the victim is murdered, what would be the purpose of posing the victim in a degrading position? It is not associated with effort to complete the crime, to escape detection, or aid in the offender's escape from the scene, therefore it is above and beyond what is necessary to complete the crime. It is important to note that the offender's action at the scene and his/her interactions with the victim may not be exactly the same in each case, but the general theme will remain the same. Changes are liable to be noted as the offender gains more experience with each subsequent victim or develops the fantasy further as s/he continues to offend.

Was Any Consideration Given to the Likelihood of Discovery of the Body?

For some bodies found in public but not necessarily intentionally placed there with the intent that it be found, perhaps there was no concern one way or another. We see this many times when a victim is murdered, driven a short distance away, and thrown from a vehicle. Other times the victim was just shot and left where they fell. There is a great difference between the offender who murders, undresses the victim, and leaves the body next to the road with the intention that it be found, creating fear within the community and an offender who simply leaves the victim without concern about discovery.

Does the Victim's Clothing Match the Area and Weather Conditions?

A victim found outdoors in cold weather without appropriate clothing could indicate removal from another environment to the outdoor scene. At the same time, a victim dressed as if for sleeping, such as in pajamas, robe, or nightgown, might also provide a clue to the time the victim was taken or murdered.

▶ Release of the Body

At sometime the scene examination will reach a point where it is safe to remove the body without the possibility of further contamination. Removal of the body is the responsibility of the county coroner or the ME and their assistants, but any time the body is moved or examined, it is a good idea for the detective to be present to observe. Our main interest of course is to document any additional injuries or determine if the body has any identification documents in their clothing, and observe the area underneath the body which was unobservable until the body was moved.

▶ Search Beyond the Scene

After the crime scene technicians have documented the scene, completed their forensic examination, have collected all of the visible physical and forensic evidence, and the body has been removed, it is recommended an additional more conventional search of the scene be conducted. This search is focused more on documenting and collecting the non forensic evidence at the scene and would include a general search through the scene such as desk drawers, closets, dressers, under mattresses or sofa cushions. Basically we want to look through the scene for any hidden evidence. It is not uncommon while conducting the search beyond the scene to find very important physical or forensic evidence in the most unusual places. There are many instances where looking in the refrigerator, police have found the suspect's bloody fingerprints on an item in the refrigerator; or the murder weapon is found in between the sofa cushions, or love letters between the mattress and box springs in the bedroom.

Characterization of non forensic evidence varies from scene to scene and is based on the individual facts of the crime. Several examples might include: personal day planners, day calendars, address books, notebooks, diaries, letters, phone records, checkbooks or registers, business records, tax records, medical records, personal photographs and papers, or other personal records. In the modern high tech era many documents will also be found in electronic media such as cellular telephones, blackberries, pagers, computers, portable hard drives and back up devices, recordable CDs, thumb drives, and other personal electronic devices. The seizure and later examination of these high tech items is very desirable and often very rewarding in the type and amount of evidence retrieved.

Although we might recover them during the scene examination under the authority of a crime scene search warrant, a second separate warrant authorizing the examination of the contents of this electronic media will be required. This is the responsibility of the police detective and must be completed before the media is examined.

▶ Completion of Crime Scene Examination

At the completion of the crime scene examination and after the scene is released, it is necessary for the detective to file a search warrant return in the same manner as other search warrants; advising the court of the items seized during the execution of the warrant.

It is also important to coordinate with the crime scene technicians to have a clear understanding of all of the items of evidence that have been collected for the search warrant return, as well as a clear understanding of the potential forensic examination at the crime lab. Evidence collected during the examination should be submitted expeditiously to the lab for examination. Typically there is a long waiting list of cases pending examination so it is beneficial to get the evidence into the queue as quickly as possible.

▶ Conclusions

One of our main concerns as detectives is to determine criminality associated with any reported death. It is very difficult to return or try to re-do a crime scene examination if it is not done correctly or if one is not conducted at all. We generally have one chance to process the scene with as little contamination as possible. We need to do it correctly. We need to work as a team. The key is always the basics—the scene documentation, avoiding scene contamination, and following a simple protocol.

Remember the mantra: *It is always better to have evidence and not need it, than to need it and not have it.*

References

1. Gardner, R. M. (2005). *Practical crime scene processing and investigation*. Boca Raton, FL: CRC Press.
2. Wellford, C., & Cronin, J. (1999). *Analysis of variables affecting the clearance of homicides*. Justice Research and Statistics Association, Washington DC. (NCJRS# 181356).
3. *Mincey v. Arizona*, 437 U.S. 385 (1978).
4. *Thompson v. Louisiana*, 469 U.S. 17 (1984).
5. *Flippo v. West Virginia*, 528 U.S 11 (1999).

Additional References

Fisher, Barry A. J., & Fisher, David. (2003). *Techniques of crime scene investigation*. (7th ed.). Boca Raton, FL: CRC Press.

CHAPTER FIVE

The Preliminary Investigation

The preliminary investigation is a distinct stage of every death investigation. It consists of those initial steps and activities taken to answer the six basic questions of who, what, when, where, how, and why of any event. There is no hard and fast rule signaling the end of the preliminary investigation and the beginning of the latent or follow up investigation, but generally speaking the first 48–72 hours is accepted as a normal uncomplicated preliminary investigation. Based on the circumstances it can be shorter or longer depending on what happened at the actual event and what evidence or information is available for the initial responding detectives.

The preliminary investigation consists of a wide variety of simultaneous activities including crime scene examination, collection of physical and forensic evidence, canvass interviews, interviews of significant witnesses, arrests and interviews of suspects, forensic autopsy, background investigation on the suspect, and initiation of a victimology assessment of the victim. This is only a short list of things requiring attention in a normal event without any of the various nuances that may confront the detectives within a particular scene or a particular event.

The list of possibilities confronting the detectives in any case is almost endless, which makes hard and fast rules for conducting a preliminary investigation very difficult to define. Possible difficulties in a preliminary investigation would include the addition of drugs or alcohol to the scene or event, the presence of other surviving victims, the discovery of additional missing persons or other potential victims, whether the scene is indoors or outdoors, if the identity of the victim cannot be quickly established, or if the crime scene also included arson, explosives, or some type of chemical contamination such as a clandestine laboratory. In cases of arson and explosives there is liable to be great damage to the crime scene and to physical and forensic evidence, which may have added even more evidence to the original scene. The presence of dangerous chemicals at a clandestine lab scene will also directly influence the ability to conduct a thorough scene examination.

The preliminary investigation also tends to set the tone of the entire investigation. Meaning, if the preliminary investigation is not taken seriously, not vigorously pursued, or is haphazard and incomplete; it is likely the investigation will be unsuccessful regardless of witnesses and evidence. If mistakes are made during the initial steps of the investigation, recovery may be very difficult.

▶ Notification of Death

The preliminary investigation actually begins with the initial notification to the police of a death or discovery of a body. This notification has great investigative value that is frequently not recognized by detectives.

There are a few automatic steps in the preliminary investigation, meaning those steps that are taken in every preliminary investigation. The first step includes obtaining a copy of the notification telephone call if it was recorded by the department or 911 call center. With the actual recording available, there is no doubt as to what exactly was reported to the police and it is also possible to actually hear such things as the tone of voice and excitability of the caller, other background noise, or other background voices that may prove to be important in later stages of the investigation.

When such a notification of a death takes place there are some very important questions that should be asked and answered; these initial questions should include but are not necessarily limited to:

- Who made the call?
- When was call made?
- What is the relationship to the deceased?
- What exactly was reported?
- How did the caller know or find out about the death?
- How was the report made, in person or by phone?
- Is there a copy of the 911 tape?

Eliminate the First Witness

This is a simple but important concept that is often ignored or underrated. The person who actually makes the report to the police or has found the body, may also be involved in the actual crime. This is not an absolute, but happens with enough frequency that it should be a solid first investigative step to take in all reported death investigations.

Although a criminal actually reporting the crime to the police may seem counterintuitive, consider why this may be important to the offender. This report to the police may serve as an attempt to explain the offender's presence at the scene in the first place. Other examples may include efforts to explain being observed at the scene by someone else, or the chance that the offender's DNA or fingerprints would be found at the scene. Additionally, the offender may attempt to explain the presence of blood or other evidence on his/her own clothing caused during the actual physical confrontation with the victim, through innocently touching of the injured victim, through embracing a dying victim, or even from attempts to render first aid.

In cases where the person reporting the crime or finding a body is not involved, they can be eliminated quite easily through a quick check of his/her alibi or through other factors. An example of of being able to quickly eliminate some persons is found in **Case Study 5-1**.

In the initial stages of the investigation we might not be aware of any potential motive the person who found the body (or reported the incident) might have to cause or be involved in the death of the victim. Immediately establishing and locking in the alibi, statement, potential physical evidence (such as clothing) from that person is critical. Failing to do so may impact the case at a later time when such motives or unusual behavior are uncovered, but the evidence is no longer available because it wasn't collected at the scene. If details surrounding the activities and whereabouts of the person reporting the death are not well documented it may be impossible to reconstruct the information at a later time.

Lastly, a red flag should be raised whenever it appears that efforts were made to have someone else find the body or to report the crime. This should be viewed with suspicion unless otherwise explained. **Case Study 5-2** provides a good example of this concept.

As the limited case study indicates, the first man manipulated the other man into actually finding the body as if somehow this was going to establish his own nonparticipation in the crime. The effort to engage someone else to

Case Study 5-1

A driver reportedly was traveling along a busy interstate highway when he had to urinate. He parked his vehicle, and stepping just into the nearby trees he observed a body in the woods. The driver notified the highway patrol through his cell phone and the authorities responded to the scene. The driver was looked at briefly but was eliminated very quickly. He was from out of state, he claimed to be en route to a business meeting some miles away which was quickly verified, his alibi for the previous several days was checked and verified through out of state motel receipts, his vehicle was checked and no sign of evidence was discovered, and he had no criminal background. He was rather quickly eliminated from any involvement and was allowed to proceed. The man had literally stumbled upon the dead body.

> ## Case Study 5-2

One morning a man called another man he had known for a long time and asked the acquaintance to accompany him to a car repair shop in the next small town. The second man agreed and several minutes later was picked up at his house by the first man. On the way, the first man said he first also wanted to go by his elderly mother-in-law's house to check on her, stating they had been calling her that morning but she hadn't answered the phone and wanted to make sure she was OK. The second man knew the mother-in-law as well and agreed to go with the first man and check on her. They drove over to her residence and upon arrival, the first man asked the second man to go to the front door and ring the doorbell while he waited in the car. The second man did so, but returned minutes later claiming there was no answer. The first man, still in the car, asked the second man to walk around to the back of the house and see if she was in a small shed located in the back yard. The second man walked to the shed door and looked inside and found the woman hanging by the neck from a rope affixed to the rafters, in what initially looked like a suicidal hanging. He hurried back to the first man still in his car and reported his finding. The first man refused to get out of the car to look for himself and instead called 911 on his cell phone to report the incident to the police. The first man never got out of his vehicle even when the police arrived and began to look at the scene. Shortly after the coroner arrived to remove the body, the first man left the scene, having never once gotten out of the vehicle. It was later determined that the woman was first strangled with a ligature and then positioned in the shed as if she hung herself. Suspicion fell on the first man and his wife.

find the body, and then never even getting out of the vehicle to see his mother-in-law who was reportedly hanging in the shed, is very important behavior that must be explained. Phone records were checked and confirmed no such efforts were made to contact the victim that particular morning.

▶ Agency Response

Other key factors influencing the outcome of cases may be based on agency protocol or how an agency actually responds to reported deaths. These basic responses were documented in the late 1990s in a fairly comprehensive study conducted by Wellford and Cronin[1] looking to identify specific agency responses that lead to a case being successfully resolved. The study went through the entire investigative process comparing agencies with a high solve rate with those with a lower solve rate, and found many variables that directly impacted the successful resolution of the case.

Their study determined the chances of resolving a homicide may actually rest with the actions of the department and the initial response to the scene, rather than any specific actions by any individual. Traditionally, the preliminary investigation starts with the quick arrival of the uniformed patrol officer who is able to take charge of the scene including apprehending suspects if possible, separating and identifying witnesses, protecting the scene, and then contacting detectives to respond to the scene.

Wellford and Cronin identified other very important departmental responses that led to successful outcomes.

- Detectives were immediately contacted by the uniformed patrol and arrived within the first 30 minutes and then took charge of the scene
- Trained crime scene technicians were called and responded to process the scene
- Medical examiners or coroners were contacted and responded to the scene promptly
- Significant witnesses were identified and interviewed and written statements taken
- Canvass interviews were conducted in a timely manner
- Background and criminal history checks were conducted of the suspect and victim

Perhaps one of the more important findings in the survey was the impact of the number of detectives who were assigned to work in the preliminary investigation. In their survey, Wellford and Cronin found the greatest successes involved three or four detectives participating in the preliminary investigation. Considering the number of things that must be accomplished in a short period of time it makes sense to provide sufficient personnel to accomplish these tasks.

There were no significant changes in the outcomes with the addition of more detectives unless more than eleven were assigned. Therefore, responding to a normal or uncomplicated homicide with at least 3 or 4 detectives to conduct the preliminary investigation gives an agency the best chance to resolve any death case successfully. Obviously a more complicated case with multiple victims, scenes, or offenders, may require more personnel to assist.

There are other standard basic investigative steps that are taken in every death investigation regardless of the circumstances. These steps include coordinating with the first responders and obtaining a briefing as to what happened upon their initial arrival, and what actions the first responders took to define and secure the scene. If not yet established, then a scene security log should be initiated.

A briefing should be conducted with any responding ambulance crew regarding any treatment and overall condition of the victim upon their arrival;

and if available, coordination with the responding member of the ME or coroner's office to obtain any history, injuries, or if possible a tentative cause of death.

In every case we are concerned with two very important facts—the time of death and the cause of death. Basically this is determining *when* the victim died and *what* mechanism was used to kill the victim or what caused their death. Establishing the time of death and cause of death is always critical regardless of the circumstances of the event.

It is important to coordinate with the crime scene technicians and conduct an initial walkthrough of the crime scene.

▶ Situational Dynamics

Other steps taken or emphasized during a preliminary investigation are based on the dynamics of the event and the conditions at the scene. The following examples describe situations routinely confronting detectives. Note the different initial approaches and priorities based on the different circumstances.

Fresh Scene with Identified Victim, Unknown Offender

When the body is discovered (or the crime is reported) relatively soon after the death and the victim is easily identified, the preliminary investigation tends to focus on the crime scene examination, canvass, and witness interviews to determine what happened and who may be involved.

Although the crime scene is always important, for a fresh scene it becomes even more important because there is a better chance to locate, identify, and collect physical and forensic evidence before it has a chance to become contaminated or otherwise damaged. Additionally, if the victim has not yet begun the late changes after death, such as decomposition, there is a greater chance of obtaining additional forensic evidence during autopsy.

The canvass interviews become more critical because we are also trying to locate potential eye witnesses and determine who may have been involved. A secondary goal is to attempt to narrow the time frame of the event as much as possible. There is a better chance of locating a potential witness or to obtain information about the victim and the scene in the immediate hours after the event rather than weeks or months later.

The other main focus in a fresh scene is the victim. The victimology assessment will be explained in greater detail in subsequent material.

Suspect Arrested at Scene

For those incidents in which a suspect or offender is actually found or taken into custody at the scene, or easily identified through eye witnesses or other evidence shortly thereafter, the actual thrust of the preliminary investigation will be somewhat different. Although activities would certainly include the crime scene itself, any physical and forensic evidence, and canvass interviews, our main focus will be on the suspect.

The focus of the preliminary investigation would shift to the expected interrogation of the suspect and other efforts concentrating on the individual suspect's background, criminal history, and the validity of any statements and alibis.

Outdoor Scene with Identified Victim

The preliminary investigation for outdoor scenes must quickly determine if the homicide or death actually occurred where the victim was found or if the victim was killed elsewhere and the body transported to this location and dumped. If the body was dumped, then there are likely other perhaps more significant crimes scenes to locate and process. The location of the body is referred to as the *primary scene*; other potential scenes are known as *secondary scenes*. These secondary scenes could include a wide range of locations including the vehicle used to transport the body to where it was dumped; the location where the murder actually took place; the last known location of the victim. (See **Case Study 5-3**.)

Elapsed time between time of death and time of discovery is also an important factor, including length of time the body has been at that particular location. Being exposed to the weather, insects, and possibly animals may make

Case Study 5-3

A teen age female called her mother to let her know that she was released from her job at a fast food restaurant early, was going to a small store to get a greeting card, and then would come home. Within an hour a neighbor stopped by the family home and inquired as to the safety of the teenager since her vehicle was parked a short distance away on the side of the road. The teenager never arrived home and a report was made to the sheriff's department. For three weeks the country sheriff and state police worked feverishly to find the teenager without success. Three weeks later her nude body was found in a shallow stream approximately 60 miles away. The body was in the early stages of decomposition, but the time of death was determined to be within a week of her discovery. This meant the victim was alive for at least two weeks after her disappearance and prior to her death. Based on the teenager's background and victimology, along with other evidence found in her vehicle, it was considered highly unlikely the victim had stayed away from her family intentionally. Therefore, there must be a secondary scene where the victim had been taken or held until her death. This of course added an entirely new dynamic to the investigation.

time of death determination much more problematic. Therefore one of the focuses on the crime scene is the overall condition of the body when it was found.

Decomposed Body of Identified Victim

If the body is already in an advanced decomposed state when discovered, this is an indication of elapsed time between the death and body discovery. If the victim can be identified, the initial focus tends to revolve around time. Specifically the time of death and the time and date the victim was last seen. Based on autopsy results we are likely to only get a range of time in days or weeks, even months in some cases, rather than anything more specific. Therefore, the preliminary investigation will need to focus on canvass interviews of the family, friends, and acquaintances to locate potential suspects, and to narrow down the time frame as much as possible.

If the victim can be positively identified there will likely be a missing person report filed by the next of kin or friends. This would be a key starting point for developing the time line and chronology of events leading back to the last time the victim was seen alive.

Skeletal Remains of Unknown Victim

If the body is found as skeletal remains, this presents another difficulty because of the added problems of collecting the remains and determining the time frame between death and discovery. Without any other information or evidence, the time of death will be an educated guess with a wide range of months or even years, depending on where and under what conditions the body was found and the weather and temperature conditions of that location. Additionally, it can be very difficult to make an accurate determination of the actual cause of death. There is often no soft tissue present for examination, usually extensive insect involvement, and possibly animal activity which could have spread the remains over a wide area.

If the victim died as a result of some type of trauma such as blunt or sharp force, or if firearms were used, evidence of that trauma may be found on the bones in the form of defects or fractures. But, if the cause of death was a result of injuries limited to the soft tissue, or nontraumatic death such as asphyxia it may be problematic to determine the cause of death and may lead to a listing of "undetermined."

Additionally, the length of time the body and scene are exposed to weather, insects, or animals may impact on the ability to collect forensic evidence from the surrounding area. It is not unusual for animals to have spread the remains over a great distance, which adds to the difficulties.

In the case of skeletal remains of an unknown person, the preliminary investigation will likely be centered on efforts to identify the deceased. Without victim identification we are likely to have no other starting point from which to conduct the investigation. Generally, attempts to identify the unknown victim revolve around missing person reports from the local area, then state, then surrounding states. It is good practice to place any available information about the victim into as many law enforcement databases as possible.

▶ Development of Theory

As demonstrated in the previous examples, how a preliminary investigation is conducted and prioritization of focus is directly related to the circumstances of the event and what evidence is presented. This is why hard and fast rules or procedures for conducting the preliminary investigation are difficult to apply. Detectives must be very flexible and adaptable and also must apply the very basic steps which are applicable to every scene.

One important goal during the preliminary investigation regardless of the circumstances is to begin to develop a theory of the crime: What was the motive? Why was the homicide committed? Who could be involved? Many homicides are related to some type of interpersonal conflict or are a part of some other criminal act, and in these cases the motives and identities of the players may be relatively clear.

There are others where we will need to take a step back and examine the totality of circumstances of the event including but not limited to the physical evidence, the offender's behavior, witness interviews, victimology, and our own investigative experience in order to fully understand what happened. In developing a theory of the crime we look at the totality of circumstances and then consider how the various facts are related and how best the events might be explained.

If during the course of our theory development we discover evidence conflicting with our theory of the crime, we cannot simply ignore or discount the evidence because it does not agree with our theory. Instead we must either prove or disprove the other facts. If the facts and circumstances are found to be invalid then we can proceed with our original theory of the crime. If we can prove the new facts are valid and conflict with our theory, then we must adjust the theory to take in that new evidence. There are investigators who decide upon a theory and accept as valid only evidence that fits into that particular theory, discounting any evidence or facts that do not agree. We refer to this effort as "practicing cafeteria investigations," that is, being able to pick and choose what to accept and what to discount. This is very much like the saying "don't confuse me with the facts," referring to someone who has a set belief and will not budge. This approach will likely lead to an unresolved investigation or to possibly identifying the wrong suspect.

There are also many instances where the events are not clear and multiple motives or suspects must be considered. During the preliminary investigation we are not limited to any particular theory; rather we consider each one and attempt to develop each one; adding and comparing new information and evidence as it is obtained. Generally speaking, as more and more information and evidence is collected the various theories and motives will start to either gain strength or start to weaken.

Regardless of the number of theories developed during the preliminary stage they are all subject to change and adjustment as new evidence is obtained or the initial facts and circumstances are validated or invalidated. We say that the initial theory is not "written in stone," rather it is "written in sand." We have to be flexible rather than rigid in our thought process. It is very common to go into an investigation thinking you understand what happened or being told one set of facts, and then quickly discovering your suspicions or information is not accurate or was purposely falsified. So, regardless of the circumstances you have to be prepared for the very real possibility your theory is no longer valid and you have to be able and willing to change course.

The development of a theory of the crime is important because it helps not just identify potential suspects who may be involved in the death, but also gives the investigation a pathway or direction. Developing a theory of the crime begins to shape the investigative plan of what needs to be done in order to prove or disprove the theory. There is a method of theory and in particular suspect development which is very effective not just in the preliminary stages, but throughout the investigation. We refer to this by the acronym *MOM* which stands for *motive, opportunity,* and *means.* In simplistic terms, we are looking for who has a reason or motive to murder, who has the chance to commit the crime, and who has the ability or tools necessary to commit the crime.

Motive

The motive is basically the actual underlying cause or reasons behind the death of the victim. While not a legal necessity to prove murder, motive is extremely important when it comes to identifying a potential suspect, and in the end it is vital for court. Although there is no legal requirement to show a motive, juries want to hear and understand what the motive was. They want to know and understand "why was this person killed?"

From an investigative perspective it is understanding or recognizing the general motive behind the homicide that will give us the first hints as to who may be involved or what type of person may be involved and start on our theory of the crime.

Therefore, motive development is going to be a very important part of the preliminary investigation and an extensive part of any follow up latent investigation. There are probably as many motives for homicide as there are homicides, but there are a few that are fairly well known and accepted because we see them so often.

Motives can include these possibilities and many others

Money/property	Revenge	Infidelity
Love/romance	Rivalry	Dishonor
Jealously	Power/domination	Business
Sexual motives	Interpersonal conflicts	Euthanasia
Political	Criminal acts	Punishment
Insurance	Inheritance	Work-related

Any of these motives can play out on friends, business partners, casual acquaintances, coworkers, total strangers, or family members. Because we see so many interfamilial homicides based on money, wealth, and revenge, there are a couple of popular sayings handed down from cop to cop and used frequently to explain these situations, "where there's a will, there's a relative" and "blood is thicker than water, unless money is involved." This explains why we always want to look at family members and those with a close personal or intimate relationship with the victim at the same time we look at strangers.

There are several important concepts to consider when trying to determine the motive for the crime, some of which are overlooked or misunderstood by some detectives.

It is not enough to simply allege or suspect a motive; it must be clearly established through investigation   The previous concept is really based on common sense and mirrors closely the earlier comments on theory development in that we must look at all aspects of the crime and base our decision or conclusions on all of the facts and evidence we have available. This includes the motive espoused by the suspect during his interview or interrogation. Although the suspect may admit to or claim a particular motive or offer an explanation, reason, or excuse for the murder, it must be carefully examined to determine if their claim is validated through other evidence.

A husband, after being identified as the actual offender, admits during his interrogation that he killed his wife in a jealous rage when he found out about her infidelity and confronted her. The investigation, however, noted no evidence of such activity by the wife, but did reveal evidence that the husband significantly increased the amount of a life insurance policy on the wife in the months or days leading up to her death. These facts may be used to invalidate his stated motive and establish another motive for the death.

Failing to establish a clear understandable motive will hamper your ability to convict in court   As stated previously, juries want to understand why the particular crime was committed and it is incumbent upon the prosecutor to be able to outline or explain the *why* of the murder. Strictly speaking there is no such thing as a motiveless crime. There is always a reason (motive) behind the perpetrator's actions, although it might not be readily apparent or understood by law enforcement at the scene. There are some crimes in which the actual or underlying motive is only understood by the perpetrator and may never be clarified until s/he is captured. Well known examples would include the well-publicized serial killer investigations of Son of Sam, the Tate-LaBianca murders committed by the so called Manson family, and the Zodiac murders. Each offender had a particular reason or motivation, but it wasn't understood until much later. The Zodiac serial murderer was never captured or brought to justice, so his specific motives for murdering his victims can only really be postulated.

Once the motive is identified or theorized we need to start looking at potential suspects who would match the motive and determine if those suspects also had the opportunity and means to commit the crime.

Opportunity

Opportunity is basically the chance to commit the crime and basically refers to whether or not the suspect had the time or was otherwise available to commit the crime. Generally speaking, a person cannot be in two places at the same time. This is why quick determination of time of death is so vital because all alibis of all witnesses and suspects will be compared against the time of death to see if it is possible for them to have had the opportunity to commit the crime.

Opportunity is generally not an issue when dealing with most interpersonal conflict type crimes, or murders committed during the commission of another crime. The opportunity in those situations is quite clear. The concept of opportunity becomes more important when dealing with premeditated type crimes. In those circumstances, the suspect may have gone through extraordinary efforts to establish an alibi to reflect s/he had no opportunity to commit the crime because s/he was somewhere else.

Establishing opportunity is one of the reasons to interview your suspects and witnesses as quickly as possible to get statements regarding their whereabouts or actions during the time the crime was committed or the time of death. It is important to lock in these times on tape or in writing as soon as possible

There is another aspect to opportunity that we must consider whenever we are dealing with a premeditated crime. With a premeditated crime the offender will likely understand s/he is probably going to be considered at least a logical suspect or even the most logical suspect. Therefore, the offender may go to extraordinary lengths to establish an alibi for his/her whereabouts at the time the actual crime was committed. Suspects who appear to be too ready with an alibi and names of verifying witnesses, voluntarily provide documentation or evidence as to their whereabouts without being first asked,

Case Study 5-4

An adult male and his female girlfriend were both murdered in the early morning hours as they were preparing to go to work. The female had driven to an isolated agricultural area where the male had parked his truck for the night. The female was shot while still in her car, through the driver side window. The male was shot as he tried to drive away. Suspicion almost immediately fell on the girlfriend's estranged husband. He claimed to be driving along an interstate some 40 miles away at the time of the murder and therefore could not have been involved. He said by way of verification he was talking on the cell phone to someone else around that time. His cell phone records were examined and there were several phone calls made to that person. However, one of the phone calls hit a cell phone tower located a mile from the crime scene at about the same time as the murders. The police were able to prove if he were traveling on the highway as he claimed, his cell phone signal would have hit a different cell phone tower and not the one near the crime scene. The husband was later convicted of the double murder.

---

or who are able to state with certainty and precise times their whereabouts during the crime should be looked at very carefully as seen in **Case Study 5-4**.

Means

Establishing the means for committing a murder is essentially being able to show the suspect had the ability to commit the murder. Depending on the method used to kill the victim, there is a wide range of possibilities for the definition of having the means to commit the crime. In certain circumstances it could merely reflect the physical size of the suspect in relation to the victim; in others it could reflect the suspect's possession of the murder weapon. It could also reflect specialized training, knowledge, or experience with the particular method of murder that was used. For example, if the victim was murdered through poisoning, and during a search of the suspect's residence, we found an online recipe, along with several chemicals needed to make the poison; we could conclude the suspect had the means with which to commit the crime.

At a more abstract level, means could also reflect the ability to pay someone else to commit the crime or the connections through personal relationships to locate someone else willing to commit the crime.

Case Study 5-5 demonstrates how using all aspects of MOM as a basis for theory development can help in identifying what happened and who may be involved.

Case Study 5-5

Friends found a victim lying on the kitchen floor inside his mobile home, dead. A review of the crime scene revealed he had been sitting at the table, dressed only in his underwear and t-shirt, eating a meal when he was shot in the back of the head then fell onto the floor where he was later found. The doors to the mobile home were all locked from the inside, and his friends had to force their way inside. Background information quickly established the victim was single and lived alone, normally worked a midnight shift and therefore did not normally get up until mid afternoon, and would then fix something to eat. The victim was also engaged in illegal small time gambling operations and sold beer in a dry county from inside his garage next to the mobile home. According to friends, the victim never allowed any of his gambling acquaintances or anyone he did not know very well into his home, because he was afraid of being robbed. Missing from the scene was the victim's .357 revolver, (the empty holster was found on the nightstand in his bedroom) and the small bank bag in which the victim normally kept his illegal profits. Using the concept of motive, opportunity, and means, it was clear that whoever murdered the victim was known and trusted enough by the victim to be allowed inside the residence in the first place. The suspect must also have been trusted to the point the victim allowed them to wander around the residence as he was sitting down eating and eventually get into a position behind him. In this case, the motive was clearly monetary, as the bank bag with his illegal profits was also missing. The means was also fairly clear as the victim's own .357 pistol was missing and was likely the weapon used to kill him. It was the opportunity to commit the crime however, that was so important in establishing the suspect. Based on the circumstances, the suspect would have to be someone that also knew about the existence of and whereabouts of the pistol. They would have to know about the existence of the bank bag and where it was kept and would have to be trusted enough to be allowed to walk through the house, get the weapon, and then be able to get behind the still eating victim without causing any concern. The suspect was rapidly identified as a close personal friend and was later convicted of the murder. The motive was stealing the money.

Regardless of the type of murder we are investigating, understanding and establishing the motive, opportunity, and means are critical steps in identifying the suspect. Whenever a potential suspect is identified, we must be able to clearly show and explain all three. If we cannot clearly demonstrate all three, then we need to continue the investigation to develop the evidence that is lacking or recognize we may have the wrong suspect and widen the search.

▶ Next of Kin Notification

The actual notification of the next of kin is not always carried out by detectives. In some jurisdictions, by legal requirements, local protocol, or agency agreement, notification of the next of kin is carried out by the medical examiner or county coroner. Families will want to know what happened to their family member, and detectives should be ready to provide them as much information about the incident as practical without divulging the key elements of the crime. This is also a good opportunity to provide the family with contact numbers to the detectives or to the agency's victim witness coordinator.

The notification of the family or next of kin is actually a very important aspect of the death investigation for a number of reasons. First, it is good to establish contact with the family as a way to help them through the traumatic situation. Establishing that personal contact will go a long way toward securing the continued assistance of the family during the subsequent investigation and also help greatly in gathering the necessary background information needed for the victimology study.

This contact also gives us an opportunity to observe the reactions of family members as they hear of the death or as the circumstances surrounding the death are first revealed. Spontaneous statements by family members can be very revealing. Many times we hear expressions of admonitions towards the victim because of past fears for their safety or because of their precrime activity. These are often expressed in statements such as: "I knew he was going to get into trouble", "I told him to stay away from those guys", or "I told her he was going to kill her one day." It's also not unusual to hear direct accusations towards a particular suspect such as: "It was John Smith", or "It was those boys from the corner", or other such positive accusatory statements.

This is important information because these statements are typically unplanned and unscripted and are revealed during a highly emotional time. Unfortunately, after a period of time when the emotions have died down it is not uncommon to approach the family and be met with more stoic responses or denial of knowledge of what might have happened. This is particularly noted in inner city residents who may retreat behind a general suspicion of the police or begin to fear for their own safety if they cooperate with the investigation.

It is important to realize how extremely stressful these notifications and subsequent interviews are for both the family, who are going to be shocked by the event and likely still in denial as well as for the detectives who must conduct the interviews. There is of course a wide range of possible reactions but we look for a reaction that does not seem to fit the circumstances. Examples would be a group of five or six family members who are all crying and genuinely upset, but one family member who is standoffish or seemingly unaffected by the news; reactions that are more a result of nervousness and anxiety rather than shock and grief; or reactions of sobbing and crying but without actual tears. None of these reactions are necessarily indicative of any guilty knowledge or evidence of any criminal act; but they are important enough to make a note of and possibly investigate as the case develops.

It would be inappropriate to question any unusual emotional reaction of any family members at the time of notification. If questions are raised by the responses it is best to note them down and then along with other investigative leads uncovered during the preliminary investigation enter it into the investigative plan.

▶ Investigative Plan

An investigative plan can be simply defined as a "to do list." It consists of any questions raised but not answered during the preliminary investigation and the many investigative leads or tasks that need to be completed to answer those questions. An investigative plan is an investigative tool which acts as a basic road map or reminder of things that need to be accomplished. An investigative plan is not an investigative report; rather it is a type of investigative note. It can be formalized by an agency on a preprinted form or can be completed on a piece of scratch paper. It should be a "living document" designed to be added to, updated, or edited as the case progresses.

Since it is an informal document it can be adjusted to the individual detective's own preference, and be either hand written or typed. We can use a simple bullet, phrase, or comment format or provide a detailed description of what needs to be accomplished. The real value of the investigative plan is to act as a reminder of the things that need to be accomplished in the case. Theoretically, the detective should be able to go to the investigative plan to quickly determine the tasks that need to be accomplished, rather than go back through the entire file or to try and recall through memory what is still remaining to be done. The investigative plan is especially helpful when dealing with multiple cases at the same time. The following example of a basic investigative plan uses short bullet statements to list the leads that need to be accomplished to keep the investigation on track.

Sample Investigative Plan

1. Interview John Smith—former employee
2. Obtain autopsy report—interview ME investigator
3. Obtain copy of 911 tape
4. Criminal background check of
   a. ~~Bob Jones~~ (done 9/2/09)
   b. Phil Johnson
5. Obtain victim's cell phone records # (000-000-0000)
6. Obtain ambulance run reports/interview attendants
7. ~~Interview Sally Smith~~ (done 9/1/09)
8. Check insurance policies of victim

As the leads are accomplished they are checked off or lined through. As new leads are developed they are simply added. With the computer age it is easy to go through once a week and edit the plan to take out those leads that have been completed or remove those leads that are determined as unnecessary, and to add those leads which were identified to be accomplished.

One of the last stages of the preliminary investigation is to sit down with all of the detectives involved and prepare the investigative plan. This allows all of the detectives to impute their questions or concerns that need to be clarified during the later stages of the investigation. It is also possible to prioritize the investigative leads to make certain the more important things are accomplished early in the investigation. Theoretically, at the end of the day or end of a stage of the investigation, the investigative plan should be reviewed and updated to reflect any new developments or information.

The investigative plan has two other important functions. It allows supervisors to review the file and determine if the detectives are on the right track or to insert their own requirements/leads that need to be accomplished and perhaps prioritize them. Just as important, if the case is ever reassigned to another detective for completion, the new detective will be able to very easily see the direction the case was going or how the theory of the crime was being developed.

References

1. Wellford, C., & Cronin, J. (1999). *Analysis of variables affecting the clearance of homicides: A multi site survey.* Washington, DC: U.S. Dept of Justice.

Additional References

Geberth, V. J. (2006). *Practical homicide investigation, tactics, procedures, and forensic techniques.* (4th ed.). Boca Raton, FL: CRC Press.

CHAPTER SIX

Victimology

Until very recently, assessing the victim in a death investigation was largely considered by detectives to be an unimportant but necessary part of the overall effort. The victim's background was deemed somewhat more important when dealing with the "who done its" or when confronted with unknown suspects. Generally, efforts to obtain background information were handled as a matter of routine and often resulted in only a cursory amount of information being developed or used. Obviously victims are the actual center of any death investigation, but delving into the victim's character, activities, behavior, and background traditionally played only a very minor role. This has begun to change with the increasing development and use of *victimology assessment*, or the study of the victim, their background, and personality characteristics, in order to understand how the victim came to be a victim of crime in the first place.

A victimology assessment has become a critical stage in every homicide or death investigation (especially in the vast majority of sex crime offenses) and is very beneficial when confronted with equivocal deaths, where the manner of death cannot be readily determined. This assessment is designed to give us a good insight into the victim and identify any risk factors that may have contributed to the victim's death or victimization.

▶ Risk Factors

Risk factors are intentional or unintentional circumstances of our lives that may be influenced by how we live or why we do certain things. For example, if our work is a great distance away and we travel on a highly congested interstate for an extended period of time in the mornings and in the evenings, we would likely be at greater risk of getting involved in an accident than someone who lived a short distance away and only had to deal with a small amount of traffic. As another example, if a person lived in a high crime area where many residential burglaries occur, they might expect to one day become a victim of such a crime. In both examples there is no implication based on the persons driving ability or the person's involvement with criminal activity; rather the normal and routine circumstances in their life have elevated those circumstances into what are known as *risk factors*.

Based on the evaluation of various risk factors, we can use this assessment not only to tell us about the victim; but it might also be able to help us determine why they were chosen as victims by an offender in the first place.

This information about the victim is gathered throughout the course of the investigation. When enough personnel are available, it is beneficial to assign one agent, at least during the preliminary stages of the investigation, to focus exclusively on the victim in order to conduct the victimology assessment. However, due to manpower constraints of many agencies this is not always an option. This assessment would then become an additional responsibility for each detective—to collect as much information about the victim as possible and then share that information with the case detective.

▶ Assessment Criteria

Information about the victim is routinely obtained during the normal canvass and witness interviews of family and friends, through the regular canvass interviews of neighbors and coworkers, and whenever possible through an examination of the victim's residence to get an idea of who they were and how they lived.

The assessment may focus on both factual and subjective criteria about the victim and the type of information sought for the assessment may be changed or adapted based on different types of crimes and different types of victims. We would want some of the same basic information on every victim but we may include in our assessment other factors based on the specific individual victim and the individual crime. Specific information sought based on the type of victim and crime would include but is not limited to the following examples.

Females—Dating and marital status and history; current and past employment; outgoing personality or shy and withdrawn; confident or uncertain; children or not. If the death was a sexual homicide, then the questions may also have to include their sexual history and sexual interests. Other similar questions would have to be based on the specifics of the crime.

Males—Personality temperament, are they slow to anger or hot tempered; involved in criminal conduct or a criminal history; how would they respond to a challenge or threat; employment current and past; alcohol and drug involvement; military experience; marital status and history; problems at home, work, or personal life.

Children—Dependent or independent personality; outgoing and warm to strangers, or shy and fearful; friends and playmates; living conditions—single parent (which one) or both parents in home; was child's parent living with non-married partner or multiple non-married partners; presence of other children in the home; family economic situation; use of drugs or alcohol in house by parents.

Teenagers—Age-appropriate maturity level; dependant or independent personality; outgoing or shy; age-appropriate friends; information relative to their social networking activities; if they have cell phones with texting abilities; closest friends; any school activities and grades/success in school; disciplinary problems; attendance; dating status; boyfriends or girlfriends or any romance problems; teen age problems at home or with other siblings; what were some recent events in their lives; plans for the future; high-risk behaviors such as drug and alcohol abuse.

These various facts relating to the victim, together with the crime scene examination and other information available, are combined together to paint a picture of the individual victim. As stated previously, the victimology assessment is based on both factual and subjective criteria. The general guideline is—there is **no** unimportant piece of information relative to the victim. Everything is important as we attempt to paint that picture of the victim.

Factual Information

Factual information are those basic facts about the victim that are essentially undisputed. They are what they are and cannot be changed. Examples would include:

Age and sex
Physical features (hair or eye color, height, weight)
Basic family structure (mother, father, siblings)
Marital status
Education level
Criminal history
Physical disabilities and other attributes

Subjective Criteria

Subjective criteria are somewhat different and relate to different aspects, circumstances, or conditions of victims and their lives which may or may not have contributed to their victimization, or elevated risk factors. Factors relating to subjective criteria would include:

Use of alcohol, drugs
Criminal conduct
Socio-economic level

Employment history and type (especially important if public type job such as waitress, convenience store clerk, nurse, salesman)

Sexual preference/orientation (hetero or homosexual)

Sexual history, multiple partners, extramarital affairs

Marital status

Children

Manner of dress

Hobbies

Social activities

Of interest as well is information concerning their residence and how long they have lived in their home or how long have they lived in the same town.

Is their residence located in a high crime area?

Do they have established roots in the area?

Family interpersonal relationships

Friends and acquaintances, support system

Church attendance

Do they engage in any high-risk activity?

Have they been victims of crime before?

Use of the Internet particularly the social networks or dating sites

There are other subjective criteria that are more focused on aspects of the individual's personality and emotional maturity. Examples would include:

Personal aggressiveness or anxiousness

Cool and calm or prone to emotional outbursts

Impulsive or reflective

Self-esteem or self worth, feelings of confidence or uncertainty

Normal style of dress, personal hygiene, overall appearance

Open and friendly to strangers, or shy, non-confrontational, and passive

These facts are considered subjective because of the amount of weight or consideration given to these factors is based on each individual victim and the event dynamics. One factor, such as church attendance, may prove to be relatively important in the lifestyle or personality characteristics of one victim, but play no role in another. Therefore, how much to weigh each factor becomes the responsibility of the detective. Because these factors are subjective, they must be assessed and weighed based on the factual information in the case and the event dynamics. Only then will the assessment become effective as an investigative tool.

▶Gathering the Information

Information concerning the victim can be gathered from a wide variety of sources including official school, medical, or work records, particularly any evaluations of work performance. Much of the needed information will come through interviews of family and friends, coworkers, neighbors, or others that routinely interacted with the victim. Canvass type questions to family members and friends should include not only the basic questions concerning knowledge about the event itself but should also contain personal questions relevant to the victim that might not be readily apparent based on the initial crime scene evaluation.

What is the age, education level, and marital status of the victim?

What is the victim's employment history and current position?

Did the victim have any children?

Did the victim have any physical or mental disabilities?

Did the victim have any fears, anxieties, or phobias?

Did the victim take any medication? If so what type?

Tell me about the victim, what type of a person was s/he?

Did the victim keep any journals or diaries?

Did the victim have an email account or participate in social networks?

How would you describe the victim?

What was the victim's general lifestyle?

Did the victim live alone or with someone? Identify any roommates.

Describe the general area around the victim's residence? (Crime rate, socioeconomic levels)

Tell me about the victim's interpersonal relationships, boyfriends/girlfriends/spouses.

Did the victim recently start dating or recently end a relationship?

Tell me about the victim's interpersonal relationships with his/her family.

What were the victim's best and worst personality characteristics?

What bad habits did the victim have?

Did the victim have any particular routine?

Did the victim smoke cigarettes or drink alcohol?

Did the victim take or abuse drugs? If so what type?

How would the victim respond to a threat or a confrontation?

How would the victim respond to strangers?

What was the victim's general temperament?

What did the victim like to do in his/her free time such as hobbies?

Does the victim engage in high-risk sports or activities?
Is the victim a risk taker or conservative by nature?

Employment history is very important to the victimology assessment because this is where the victim typically spends a third of his/her day. It can be a source of pleasure and satisfaction or a source of stress and frustration. Employment information can be important when dealing with a stranger-on-stranger type of incident. We also want to focus on any job in which the victim is routinely exposed to the public, such as nurse, receptionist, salesperson, or home repair. All of these are the typical public jobs—that is the job involves interaction with the public as opposed to someone who works on an assembly line or works in a small cubicle somewhere out of the public sight. These public jobs, especially those involving money or food and alcohol, put the victim in the public eye which increases the likelihood of interaction with the offender, and witnesses to this interaction. Employment becomes more important when dealing with a stranger-on-stranger type of incident than perhaps some type of interfamilial or interpersonal homicide.

These are just a few of the generalized questions that might provide some good background information on the victim. Based on the particular circumstances of the crime, some of the questions may be unnecessary, or additional questions might be needed. This will be discussed in greater depth in later material as it pertains to suspected suicide cases.

Note that these questions are designed to be asked in an open-ended manner, requiring more than a yes and no answer. This allows the interviewees to expand their answers about what they believe is important about the victim. Be aware that some witnesses may feel obligated out of friendship and loyalty to paint the victim in a positive light or to avoid any negative statements. There is also a natural tendency to not "speak bad of" or criticize the dead. The purpose of these questions is not to criticize or degrade victims, but to develop an understanding of whom they were and if their personality, life style, or other aspects of their lives played any role in what happened. Extra effort may be needed to explain the importance of these background questions in order to obtain an accurate assessment.

In cases of sexual homicide or a stranger-on-stranger type incident, it is also important to ask whether or not the victims ever relayed any concerns about their own personal safety either generally because of the area in which they lived or specifically towards an individual. Many times victims will have discussed problems with close friends and family but declined for many reasons to make a formal complaint to the police. So if there was a problem or issue it might not be found in the police department's database, but may come up during the canvass interviews of family and friends. These types of questions might include:

Did the victim ever talk about any interpersonal conflicts with anyone?
Did the victim report any stalking or unwanted contact with anyone?

Did victim ever believe someone had been inside his/her home or car when s/he wasn't present?

What was going on in the victim's life in the days and weeks prior to the incident?

For female victims, important questions might be "Did she . . ."

Ever report any loss of personal effects such as underwear or intimate attire?

Report any obscene phone calls or other forms of harassment?

Report being followed or being watched by anyone?

Express fear from ex-boyfriend or date?

Discuss any domestic abuse from spouse or boyfriend?

Discuss any pending separation or divorce from boyfriend/husband?

Discuss any unwanted sexual advances from employers, coworkers, or other associates?

As demonstrated in **Case Study 6-1**, because the victim had never reported her feelings or concerns to any authorities, the neighbor had no criminal record or previous contact with the police and the only way the detectives became aware was to ask friends or family members about any concerns expressed by her. This highlights the importance of canvass interviews in the victimology assessment.

There is another important but sensitive topic that should be considered part of a complete victimology, especially when dealing with a stranger-on-stranger type of incident, or when no logical suspects have been identified during the preliminary investigation. This particular line of questioning is

Case Study 6-1

Mid 20s female was found brutally murdered (stabbed and throat cut) and raped on her bed in her apartment. She was found nude, sexually posed, and propped up against the wall. There were indications of forced entry through the kitchen window, but no suspects were immediately identified. During the canvass interview her friends all reported the victim's comments about a male neighbor who lived in the apartment building next to hers that would stand out on the balcony of his second floor apartment smoking cigarettes at night and looking down into her ground floor apartment as she was washing dishes or cooking. She said he gave her the creeps but had never approached her. Based on this information the police turned their focus onto the neighbor. Through investigation and later DNA analysis, he was connected to the scene and convicted of the homicide.

typically reserved for close personal friends and may take additional coaxing or convincing before obtaining an answer.

The line of questioning revolves around "What do you know about the victim that no one else knows?" We all have three sides to our lives and personality. There is a *public side;* this is what we present normally day to day and what most people will use to describe us and our personalities because they see us mostly in public settings and situations. It is the way we typically interact with others, how we handle the normal stresses of work, marriage, family, interact with our children, and all of life's responsibilities and obligations.

The second side is known as the *private side* to our lives. This side is typically shared only with our closest relatives or intimates such as husbands, wives, boyfriends/girlfriends, lovers, or best friends. This private side shared with others may include the victim's own personal fears, phobias, concerns, likes or dislikes, past personal history, any interpersonal conflicts, future plans and goals, personal or romantic relationships, sexual interests and/or sexual history, or other important aspects of his/her private life. Typically the private side relates to the types of interpersonal situations and problems that may affect the victim but may not be well known to others outside the closest inner circle of family and friends (see **Case Study 6-2**).

Lastly, we all have what is known as the *secret side* of our lives. This is the side that few if any are aware of, yet we all have it to some extent in our own lives. The secret side of life refers to those aspects of our lives very few know about, even our own family, closest friends, or even spouses. This secret life may be no more than a brief Internet search for pornography when no one else is around or an email or telephonic correspondence with someone outside a marriage or other personal relationship. It may also be as simple as cheating on income taxes or stealing from the job.

But the secret side of a person may include things no one else would believe. Possible examples would include: housewives or teenagers engaging in prostitution; a husband or wife involved in a secret homosexual relationship; involvement in an extramarital affair; criminal conduct; or the victim's willing participation in some type of dangerous deviant sexual practice such as autoeroticism. The possibilities of what people may be experiencing in their lives are really limitless (see **Case Study 6-3**).

Often the best sources of the secret life type of information can be found in a victim's journals or diaries. Often, in this modern technical era, the best source for this type of information would be the victim's computer and related media. Whether traditional hand written diaries and journals, or computer data, these personal writings often contain the most intimate thoughts and musings of the victim, generally written contemporaneously relating to life events. These writings are a very good source of background information.

The personal computer, if the victim was an avid user, will typically prove the richest source of background information on the victim—personal writ-

Case Study 6-2

A man reported to the county sheriff's department that he, his wife, and his best friend had hiked up the side of a mountain in order to get to the top to view the scenery. They arrived on the mountaintop and noted the far side was a sheer straight drop some 300 feet above a small stream. As they reached the top of the cliff the man reported his wife wanted to take a picture and walked towards the edge. She apparently got too close and accidentally slipped, or the ground underneath her had given way, and she fell all the way down into the creek bed at the base of the cliff and was killed. Suspicions were raised when the husband left the scene even before his wife was brought out of the creek bed and removed by the county sheriff's search and rescue team. He had already returned to his house some 50 miles away. Approximately 30 minutes later he received a visit from his church's pastor. Once inside, the pastor noted the husband was drinking ice tea and had five life insurance policies spread out on the coffee table and was looking at them learning how to file his claim. During a canvass interview with the victim's family, the police learned that the victim was absolutely terrified of heights, to the point of her not being able to even climb a small ladder or even stand on a step stool to hang pictures on the wall. She could not stand to look out of a second floor window because it made her dizzy. So husband's claim of her walking on her own towards the edge of a cliff and looking out over the area was inconceivable. Although the husband's post mortem behavior (leaving the scene prior to his wife's body's removal and then his immediate interest over the various life insurance policies) was suspicious and certainly would have led to a much closer look at what happened, it was the victimology assessment that established clearly, because of her absolute fear of heights, the victim would never have been in a position to look out over such heights as the husband and best friend alleged. Through an event reconstruction, the police were able to show the only way the victim could have landed where she did below the cliff was to be thrown over by the husband and the best friend who swung her by the hands and feet until they launched her over the side. Both the husband and best friend were later convicted of premeditated murder.

ings or correspondence, a history of internet sites visited or searched, chat logs, memberships to social networks, and possible email exchanges. Particularly in cases of stranger-on-stranger and sex-related homicides, the victim's personal computer should undergo forensic examination to see what information might be obtained.

Such computer analysis is also important in missing person investigations. As an example, consider an instance where a victim has told friends s/he was taking a short vacation or leaving for the weekend but was never heard from

Case Study 6-3

Police of a small town were mystified when a young and attractive high school teacher was found brutally murdered in her apartment, the offender leaving her nude and sexually posed at the scene. She had been strangled, stabbed, and both anally and vaginally raped. The teacher was generally known as coming from a good local family, was active in her local church, and considered to be a dedicated and talented teacher, with no criminal background. There were no signs of forced entry into her apartment and the police were unable to identify any potential suspects. During background investigation of the victim however, the police learned some shocking facts. The victim routinely smoked marijuana and a small amount was found in her apartment. It was learned she frequented numerous bars and nightclubs in neighboring towns including gay establishments. She was also very sexually promiscuous, engaging in multiple short-term heterosexual and homosexual affairs. Many of her sexual partners were married men who were taken back to her apartment where they engaged in sexual intercourse. None of these facts were known or even suspected by her family or even her closest friends. This obviously caused the investigation to turn in a completely different direction.

again. In analyzing the victim's secret life through his/her computer, the police noted the victim's interest in deviant sexual practices such as sadomasochism; and that through contact via various social networks s/he contacted a new willing partner. Unfortunately, s/he was lured to his/her death by an offender who was more interested in torture and murder.

Although delving into this type of material may seem like an invasion of privacy, it can provide critical information regarding motive, events, and suspects. We should always exercise sensitivity when investigating a victim's secret life because bringing it to light may interfere with our ability to continue working with the surviving family. No one wants to see a family member dragged through the mud or their memory destroyed, and not all aspects of the secret life are germane to the motive behind the death.

This type of information may not seem to be particularly relevant in certain situations such as domestic or interfamilial type homicides, or suicide, but in actuality a victimology assessment helps paint a picture of what was going on in the victim's life during the time leading up to their death and can be very useful. It may help identify emotional factors or impulsive behaviors that could have had an impact on the decision to resort to suicide. This will be discussed further in subsequent material.

For interfamilial types of situations, a victimology may identify indications or patterns of an abusive relationship between the victim and the offender and/or identify other stressors that may have contributed to the victim's death. More importantly, in most domestic type situations there is a triggering event that takes place in the time immediately leading up to the actual death. A victimology assessment and detailed background investigation should concentrate on the 24 to 72 hours preceding the death.

Although the victimology assessment is all about the victim's particular background and characteristics, it is actually used to tell us about the offender. The victimology assessment essentially is an effort to look at the victim through the eyes of the offender and perhaps determine why the victim was chosen. It may also be able to assist in narrowing the pool of possible suspects through identification of certain offender characteristics through the victimology. Robert Hazelwood, one of the original members of the FBI Behavioral Science Unit, teaches and emphasizes in his many training courses, the concept of "tell me about your victim and I'll tell you about the offender." What he is saying is if we know everything there is to know about our victim, then we can more successfully understand what type of offender could be involved in the incident.

▶ Defining and Assessing Risk Level

Once the background information is collected, the various risk factors and individual personality characteristics pertaining to the victim are identified and evaluated. The victim is then assigned one of three risk categories—high, moderate, or low. The risk categories refer to the likelihood of the victim to become a victim of a crime. The higher the risk category the more likely the victim could come into contact with an offender and thus become a victim. This is not a character judgment of the victim, rather we are learning about the victim to learn about the offender.

A *high-risk* victim is someone who might be expected to eventually be a victim of crime based on residence, employment, or general lifestyle. Examples would include but are not limited to: runaways, homeless persons, drug abusers, criminals, and prostitutes. These are obvious potential crime victims because they routinely put themselves into contact with a criminal element and are often victimized. Engaging in almost any criminal conduct will place the victim automatically into the high risk category because those who are engaged in criminal conduct often associate themselves with others involved in criminal conduct.

Also at high risk are those persons we discussed earlier in this chapter that are engaged in some public type of employment including convenience store workers, bank tellers, waitresses, and nurses. Their employment situation daily places them in contact with many people, hence increased contact with potential criminals.

Another high-risk criterion would be the crime level in the victim's residential or work area. The more time spent in a high crime area the greater the likelihood of coming into contact with the criminal element and thus becoming a victim of crime. In certain situations, the elderly may be considered high risk because of their inability to defend themselves. They are especially sought after by certain muggers and burglars because they generally will offer very little in resistance.

Next, moving down the scale, are the *moderate risks*. These are generally those persons who would have been assigned to the low risk category (and thus very unlikely to come into contact with a criminal element) but mitigating circumstances or events move them into a higher risk category. For instance, a housewife is out shopping after dark and has an automotive breakdown on the highway. Although not normally a risk taker, the fact that she now finds herself alone on the highway with an inoperable vehicle now places her into the moderate risk category. Another example would include a traveler who takes a wrong turn off the interstate and finds himself lost in a high crime area. His normal lifestyle might not place him into such a position, but through circumstances his risk factors are elevated.

A *low-risk* victim is someone who, based on lifestyle and personality characteristics, is unlikely ever to be a victim of crime. Primary factors are the lack of high-risk behaviors and infrequent public exposure. An example of a typical low-risk victim would be a stay-at-home mother and wife, with a stable marriage, who has no outside employment, does not abuse drugs or alcohol, is not involved in any extramarital affairs, and lives in a safe residential neighborhood.

Placement of the victim into one of these categories is a subjective determination based on the facts and circumstances and the individual victim, and is up to the judgment and discretion of the detective.

A further key to victimology is the risk factor of the offender involved in the actual crime commission. From an investigative standpoint, the higher the risk factor of the victim, the lower the risk that must be taken by the offender to commit the crime. Conversely, the lower the risk factor of the victim, then the higher the risk the offender must take to complete the offense. This is why serial murderers often seek out high-risk victims such as prostitutes because they have so many high-risk behaviors; the offender only has to take a small risk in order to commit the crime.

One very important consideration should be determining how much risk the offender was willing to take or what were they willing to do, in order to commit the crime against this victim, at this particular time and place? Along those same lines, how prepared was the offender to commit the offense?

Most high-risk victims may be selected as a matter of pure chance, such as the prostitute plying her trade on the street who comes into contact with an offender looking for an easy victim. Many low-risk victims, however, are specifically targeted by the offender. If the offender did not know the victim personally, then he may have observed the victim at an earlier time and returned later to attack. This is not an absolute rule, contrary evidence notwithstanding; it is a good course of action to pursue until additional evidence can be developed.

TABLE 6-1. Victimology Comparison

Victim 1	Victim 2
35 year old married house wife	21 year old college student
Married 12 years	Single with multiple short termed relationships
Mother of two children 9 and 7	Works as a waitress and as an XXX dancer
College degree	Abuses alcohol and drugs
No outside employment	Recently moved into town
No history of alcohol or drug abuse	Lives in an apartment off campus
Attends church regularly	No criminal history
No criminal history	Unknown to any neighbors
Lives in middle class neighborhood	Few college friends
Knows all of her neighbors	Does not attend church

As an example of how a victimology assessment is used, compare the facts of two basic victim assessments in **Table 6-1** and assign their risk factors and category based on the limited information provided.

Obviously victim number one would be the typical low-risk victim. There are several key factors that make these assessments relatively easy. Factual information includes her age, marital status, children, and social economic status. Subjective factors include attendance in church, known to her neighbors, and lived in the same town all of her life. The subjective criteria is used to provide a flavor of the victim as to who they are. All factors for this victim are indicative at least on the surface, of an emotionally mature and responsible person. Can a victim with these factors still be irresponsible and immature? Of course; but all things being equal we can assume that she is somewhat responsible and at lower risk for becoming a victim during the routine course of her life.

Conversely, victim number two is a classic example of a high-risk victim. Factual information—age, marital status, drug and alcohol abuse and multiple short term relationships—are all indicative of high-risk victims because persons of this age and similar living conditions tend to engage in higher risk type behaviors. Although victim number two does not necessarily engage in prostitution or other criminal acts, her job as a XXX dancer places her into a situation with a high chance of contacting offenders who may frequent that type of establishment. Her recent arrival to the town, nonattendance in church, and being unknown to her neighbors are all examples of subjective criteria that can be used to round out the victim's assessment.

Comparing the two victims, it is clear victim number two is certainly more likely, if her situation does not change, to eventually become a victim of a crime. However, it is important to note that victim number one may actually be more susceptible to an offender's con approach. Again this is based on her overall general assessment that would indicate that although victim number one is older, more mature, and more responsible; she may also be naïve in the ways of the criminal world and therefore more trusting of people, even strangers. She may fall for an offender's polite request to come into her house to use the phone, get a drink of water, or willingly follow the directions of someone impersonating an official.

However, victim number two, the XXX dancer and waitress, has probably heard every story and pick up line and has likely had to routinely confront unruly or drunk customers, thus is more attuned to a con or a pick up line and certainly more self aware of the potential dangers of strangers.

Victimology assessment can also aid in other aspects of the investigation particularly in serial crimes when an MO (*modus operandi*) or signature aspect of the offender might be identified through similarity of victims. This might be a good starting point in linking together what appear to be similar crimes or even linking together what may appear on the surface to be dissimilar.

In **Case Study 6-4**, it was actually the victimology comparison that helped link the sixth case to the same suspect and explain the change in MO or offender behavior. Once the offender was arrested he confirmed that he stayed longer with the last victim because she was so cooperative and never said or did anything to resist him unlike the others. Therefore, especially in serial offenses it is important to not only look at each individual victim but also to be able to compare them to each other for any similarities that may provide a clue as to the goal or motive of the offender.

The victimology assessment can also be used to determine if the victim may have contributed to his/her victimization, by his/her own actions. This concept is known as a *victim precipitated homicide*, first introduced by Marvin Wolfgang in 1958,[1] after his study of 588 homicides in Philadelphia. Wolfgang reported in this study that approximately 26% of the victims in his study appeared to have precipitated their own deaths by escalating a situation through some overt means, such as physical, aggressive, or provocative behavior towards another person. An example would be resisting and fighting rather than giving up valuables; or a person with a quick temper who responds to an insult or perceived slight through a challenge to another person who then responds through physical means or produces a weapon. In either case, had the victim not responded in that manner they may not have been killed. In these types of incidences the victim will likely be described as having a violent or hot temper, a confrontational and argumentative personality, with poor impulse control which of course leads the victim into such confrontations and results. It will probably become fairly clear as you develop your victimology if the victim is the type of person who may have contributed to his/her own death through his/her own actions.

Another example of a victim precipitated death is the so-called *suicide by cop*, wherein the victim intentionally threatens physical harm to another person or moves menacingly towards the police, leaving the police no choice but

Case Study 6-4

There was a series of six early morning burglaries/home invasions in a rural county. After gaining entrance the offender then raped and robbed the elderly females who were all living alone in their homes. In five of these cases the offender entered the residence through a window, accosted the sleeping victim in her bedroom, where he raped them and in several cases inserted foreign objects into their vagina or anus. He then walked them through their house demanding purses, robbing them of whatever cash or valuables they had, and then fled. The sexual assaults were typically of short duration, followed by robbery, and his departure. However, there was some question if the sixth case was by the same offender or a second offender. In the sixth case the offender did not enter through a window but instead jimmied the rear door. He then accosted and repeatedly sexually assaulted the female vaginally and anally, and demanded and received oral sex. But he did not insert any foreign object into the victim. This appeared to be a significant deviation from the normal established MO of the other incidents and there was serious thought of a second offender engaging in the same type of criminal acts against elderly females. However, upon a detailed look of the victimology of the sixth victim and compared to the other five victims it was noted that victim number six reported that she was so afraid for her safety that she had offered no resistance at all and was completely compliant with all of the offender's demands. The other victims all reportedly resisted in some way, either verbally or physically, and some were struck by the offender for their resistance. It was clear that because victim number six was so compliant, the offender was basically free to do whatever he wanted and therefore he did more sexually to that victim than any other victim. The method of entry was also different, but in victim number six she insisted that all of her windows were locked from the inside. The other five victims all reported they were uncertain if their windows were locked or not.

to defend themselves or others by shooting the victim. In reality, had the victim not reacted or responded in an aggressive manner or produced a weapon at the police there would have been no need for anyone to have been injured at all.

A victimology assessment is also an integral part of any Criminal Investigative Analysis (CIA) or the more familiar offender profiling. If a profile or crime analysis is requested, the analyst will spend a great deal of time reviewing the victimology. Victimology assessment is a very important tool in the detective's tool box. It provides a good picture of the victim's activities, lifestyle, and personality. Using this detailed background we might determine his last movements, his character, and any motivations for actions which could lead to determination of the time of death, offender profile, and other insights that will aid in solving the case.

References

1. Wolfgang, M. E. (1958). *Patterns of criminal homicide.* Philadelphia, PA: University of Pennsylvania Press.

Additional References

Geberth, V. J. (2006). *Practical homicide investigation.* (4th ed.). Boca Raton, FL: CRC Press.

Hazelwood, R. B., & Burgess, A. W. (2008). *Practical aspects of rape investigation.* (4th ed.). Boca Raton, FL: CRC Press.

Ressler, R. K., Burgess, A. W., & Douglas, J. E. (1988). *Sexual homicide: Patterns and motives.* Lexington, MA: Lexington Books.

Schlesinger, L. B. (2003). *Sexual murder: Catathymic and compulsive homicides.* Boca Raton, FL: CRC Press.

CHAPTER SEVEN

Autopsy and Interpretation of Injuries

In this chapter we will discuss and describe primarily the four major mechanisms of death—blunt force, sharp force, fast force (which includes gunshot and explosion wounds), and anoxia or death by asphyxiation. Within these four categories we will find cases of homicide, suicide, and accidental death. In some there will be a combination of injuries as typically seen in deaths from motor vehicle accidents where the deceased may have received both blunt and sharp force injuries. In cases where manner of death is difficult to determine, statistical probability may be used—the probability that under a given set of circumstances, history and researched literature indicate to us that a specific type of injury has specific characteristics and will indicate the manner of death accordingly. However, we caution investigators to always seek to validate the information through other means, as exceptions to the rules do occur. This process of validation may include the gathering of more witness statements, scene or event reconstructions, the reconstruction of the wound pattern(s), and the consensus of all investigative parties, including the forensic pathologist or other forensic experts.

▶ Blunt Force Injuries

Blunt force injuries "are produced when energy applied to the body is sufficient to produce disruption of the body's anatomic integrity,"[1] and cover a wide variety of recognizable injuries. These injuries would primarily include abrasions, contusions, and lacerations and can be found in child abuse, assaults (both with and without a weapon), vehicular incidents, and even accidental falls. The recognition and proper classification of these injuries are essential in differentiating whether the manner of death is homicide, suicide, or accident. Forensic pathologists should be well versed in the mechanics of blunt force injury, much more so than clinical pathologists. They should be able to provide information about the manner in which the injuries occurred, the type of weapon or instrument used to cause the injury, and the number of blows or injuries inflicted. This important information will significantly contribute to the accuracy of the findings. On another note, detectives should always be alert for the presence of any trace evidence on the body, the victim's clothing, or in and around the wounds. As a cautionary observation, timing (sequence) of these injuries and/or being able to attribute all injuries to only one object are often problematic and require sufficient evidence to validate the determination.

Abrasions

"An abrasion is a superficial cutaneous injury resulting primarily in damage to the epidermis. It results from tangential or compressive force on the skin."[2] In some situations the direction of the force can be determined as illustrated in **Figures 7-1** and **7-2**.

Contusions

Simply stated, contusions are bruises that occur as the result of blunt force trauma to an area of the body that causes the rupture of blood vessels and the seepage of blood into the surrounding tissue. The extent of bleeding is dependent upon the nature of the tissue involved. Deep tissue contusions may not become readily apparent and could take hours or days to become visible to the naked eye. The utilization of an alternate light source may enhance visibility. Typically we see contusions on skin and tissue over bony structures such as hands, forearms, shins, knees, or face and head. Injuries over these parts of the body are not uncommon even with minor force/trauma (see **Figures 7-3** and **7-4**). Contusions appearing over soft tissue, such as the abdomen, are

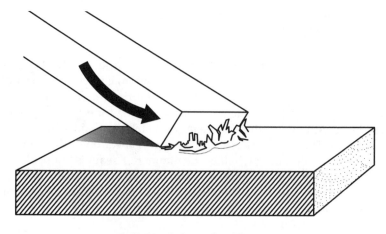

FIGURE 7-1. Illustration of an abrasion.

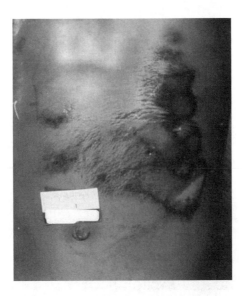

FIGURE 7-2. Photo of an abrasion. See Color Plate 29.

also possible, but are generally the result of the application of a significant amount of force.

After the injury is inflicted and the blood drains into the surrounding tissue a noticeable contusion forms. This is first observed as a reddish area surrounding the impact area but within 1–4 hours the reddish area will turn to a very noticeable bluish-purple color. Over time as the body begins the healing process the contusion will begin to change in color as the injured area is

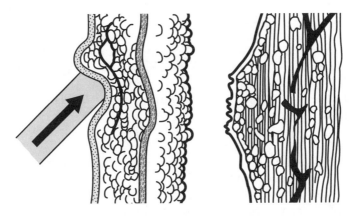

FIGURE 7-3. Illustration of a contusion.

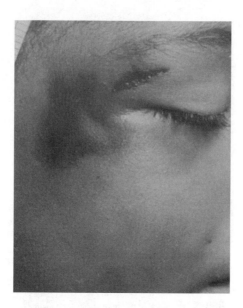

FIGURE 7-4. Photo of a contusion. See Color Plate 30.

repaired and the blood is broken down and removed from the body as waste products.

The color change of the contusion moves along a standard timeline, as indicated below until it is healed and no longer visible.

1. Red   Immediate
2. Blue Purple   1–4 hours
3. Green   4–7 days
4. Yellow   7–10 days
5. Normal   14–21 days

It is these color changes that allow the ME to approximate the time of injury from an observed injury. In the case of children, the ME might note the presence of multiple contusions in various stages of healing. This might be consistent with a very active child, but could be consistent with repeated injuries inflicted during long term child abuse.

Contusions of the Brain

Contusions of the brain can lead to a wide variety of interpretations—an accurate determination needs to be made by an experienced forensic pathologist. There are many variables involved with these types of injuries—the magnitude of the hemorrhage (hematoma), the location (subdural versus epidural, frontal, etc.), the injuring instrument, the age of the victim, presence or absence of fractures, and of course the circumstances under which the injury occurred. The literature describes various categories such as coup contusions, contrecoup contusions, crushing head injuries, diffuse axonal injury, and those that occurred as the result of gunshot wounds or stab wounds to the head.

For the purposes of this chapter we will briefly describe and attempt to illustrate the *coup* and *contrecoup* injury and mechanism. A coup injury occurs under the site of impact with an object, and a contrecoup injury occurs on the side opposite the area that was impacted. For the sake of simplicity we can describe these as "moving object-stationary head", "moving object-moving (rotating) head", and "moving head-stationary object". In the first category, moving object-stationary head, a coup injury is created by the striking of the head with an object such as a baseball bat (see **Figure 7-5**).

An example of a moving object-moving (rotating) head injury might be a victim, struck in the head while walking. Here the head is free to rotate on its axis when a blunt object strikes it (see **Figure 7-6**). In this scenario we could find both a coup and contrecoup injury where, in most likelihood, the coup could be larger than the contrecoup.

Lastly we have the moving head striking a stationary object as in a fall (see **Figure 7-7**). As one can see from the illustration the coup injury is frequently smaller than the rebounding affect found in the contrecoup injury.

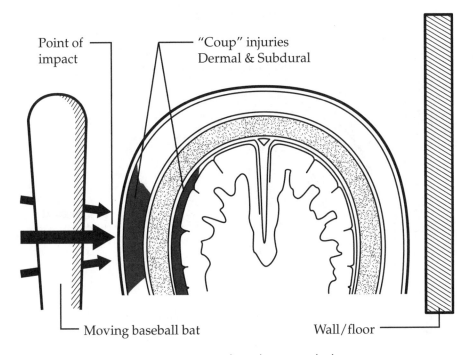

FIGURE 7-5. Moving object striking stationary head.

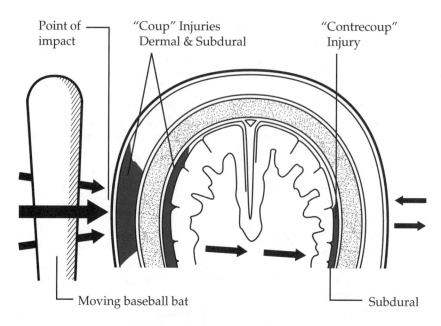

FIGURE 7-6. Moving object striking rotating head.

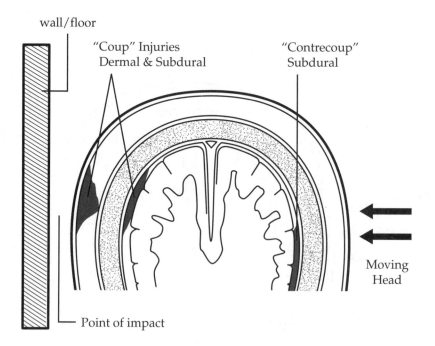

FIGURE 7-7. Moving head striking stationary object.

TABLE 7-1. Coup and Contrecoup Injuries

Case	Injury	Size	Likely Event
A	Coup only	Not Applicable	Moving object striking a stationary head
B	Coup	Smaller	Moving head striking a stationary object
	Contrecoup	Larger	
C	Coup	Larger	Moving object striking a moving (rotating) head
	Contrecoup	Smaller	

The recognition and understanding of coup and contrecoup injuries becomes important in being able to determine if a victim could have died as a result of accident or was a victim of intentional blunt force trauma.

In summary, when these types of injuries are present, please use **Table 7-1** as a guide. Furthermore, keep in mind that these interpretations must be left to the experienced forensic pathologist who will evaluate them in conjunction with witness statements, and information and evidence collected from the scene. An accurate evaluation could be the difference between correctly identifying a homicide or not.

Lacerations

The term laceration is often improperly used to describe sharp force injuries however, "A laceration is a tear resulting from blunt impact that stretches the tissue until it splits. Characteristics of a skin laceration include marginal abrasion, bridging of vessels and connective tissue, contusion, and undermining, especially if the tear is located over bone."[3] With lacerations over bone the separation of the tissue from the bone with shelving may indicate the direction of force.

Unlike sharp force injuries that cut through and separate underlying tissue, a laceration crushes the tissue and the skin is split. It may actually expose blood vessels, nerves, and other tissue in what is known as *bridging*. In a laceration injury a contusion is also present underlying the skin break and at the outer edges.

In dealing with lacerations two other factors need to be considered: (1) patterned injuries may occur that are reflective of the type of object used; and (2) some lacerations and contusions may occur after death. The existence of any post mortem injuries could be very important to the investigator. Remember that once death occurs the heart is no longer pumping blood through the system (see **Figures 7-8** and **7-9**). Therefore, a study of ante mortem versus post mortem injuries is conducted by the pathologist based on appearances and the bleeding or lack of bleeding observed when dissecting the injury location.

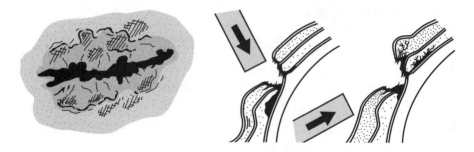

FIGURE 7-8. Illustration of a laceration.

Blunt force trauma to the head may also produce a star shaped laceration that closely resembles a hard contact gunshot entrance wound or an irregularly shaped gunshot exit wound. This has caused confusion in untrained investigators at the scene of the crime who misinterpreted the injury and its cause. A careful examination of the wound however will reveal the absence of burnt skin, abrasion ring, or soot (tattooing) routinely found with gunshot entrance wounds, and the lack of a bullet defect (bullet hole).

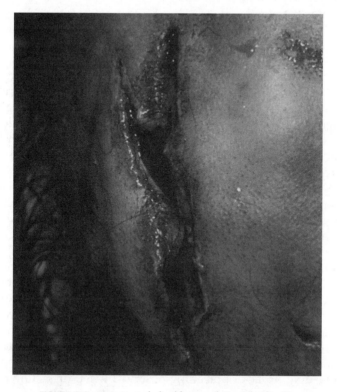

FIGURE 7-9. Laceration to the head from a rock. See Color Plate 31.

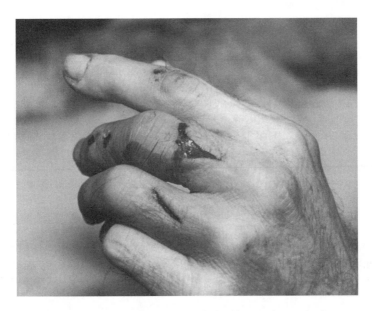

FIGURE 7-10. Blunt force defensive wound to the hand from a rock. See Color Plate 32.

Sometimes with blunt force trauma, as with sharp force trauma, victims may sustain defensive wounds while attempting to defend or protect themselves. Typically, as illustrated in **Figure 7-10**, these will be on the hands, arms, or possibly legs. These injuries could be abrasions, contusions, lacerations, and possibly broken bones.

Deaths Involving Children

Children with obvious signs of trauma are reasonably easy to identify as abused based on the extent of injury, the number and type of injuries, and the many unexplained or "accidental" injuries reported by parents or caregivers. However, one must always be cautious. Many injuries, especially in active children, may appear to be abuse when they are in fact from accidents, normal childhood roughhouse playing, or even from disease processes. In addition to a careful examination of the body, a good medical history of the child is necessary. Of particular import are full body x-rays of younger children. Full body x-rays are advisable for children under 10 years of age, and should be insisted on for any child under 6. The purpose is to determine if there is evidence of unreported injuries or a series of suspicious injuries in various stages of healing, especially those to the ribs or skull.

However, there are a number of circumstances in which the autopsy does not uncover a solid cause or manner of death particularly for infants and children less than 18 months of age who die unexpectedly and for unknown reasons. Some of these cases can now be attributed to Sudden Unexplained

Infant Death (SUID), death of an infant less than one year of age where the cause of death is not obvious prior to investigation. Sudden Infant Death Syndrome (SIDS) is used to refer to the cases in which a cause of death cannot be determined even after investigation (see **Figure 7-11**).

One of the keys to investigating these cases is to ensure a complete review of a child's full medical history looking for verification of prenatal checkups; timely vaccinations; any difficulties at birth; or any history of disease, deformities, premature birth, or other naturally occurring medical problems. The autopsy should also be thoroughly documented with photographs. Even photographs depicting no injury to the body, brain, etc. may be helpful in the cause of death determination and can be used to support any subsequent statements or testimony.

As an example, after the death of a child, photographs of the child's body were taken, but because nothing of evidentiary value was seen in or on the brain (no bleeding or hemorrhages), no photographs were taken of that part of his anatomy. Nearly a year later, a prosecutor had the body exhumed and a non-forensic pathologist claimed to have found a subdural hemorrhage

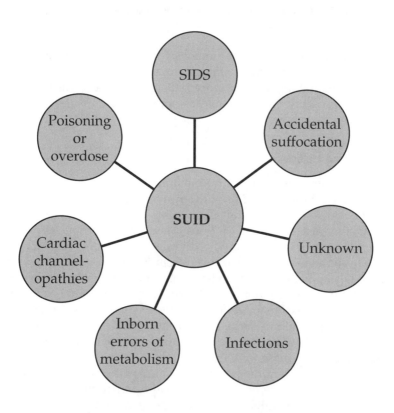

FIGURE 7-11. Types of Sudden Unexplained Infant Deaths (SUID).

suggesting abuse from shaking the child. Both the pathologist and the coroner who attended the original autopsy testified that neither saw the bleeding but without photographic documentation there was no proof. It is strongly suspected the hemorrhage found during the second autopsy was a post mortem artifact most likely created during the embalming process, but we will never know for sure.

Shaken Baby Syndrome is an example of blunt force trauma and injuries typically seen in younger children. These injuries are not inflicted with a blunt force object, but rather are caused by the violent shaking of a baby or infant. As the baby is violently shaken the child's head is moved violently back and forth or from side to side, wherein the brain is injured by impact on the inner skull (both coup and contrecoup), or the shaking ruptures a blood vessel and begins to hemorrhage. With no place for the blood to go in a closed head wound, the blood begins to accumulate and eventually press against the brain causing even greater injury and many times death. Retinal hemorrhages are a marker to look for in Shaken Baby Syndrome, but these may also appear from other non-abusive actions. Therefore the presence of retinal hemorrhages is something to look for, but is not by itself proof that a child has been shaken. The forensic pathologist will need to validate the theory by discovery of other injuries to the child that correlate directly to an incidence of shaking. These may include such things as older or healing bone fractures, other contusions, burns, and brain hemorrhages. Any older injuries, particularly those which were unreported need to be identified and specifically addressed (see **Case Study 7-1**).

Case Study 7-1

A mother brought her 13-month-old child to the emergency room where the child was dead on arrival. The mother stated that her child was playing in her crib and then became quiet. Upon responding to this she noted the child's lips were blue and the child was unresponsive. The mother immediately took her to the emergency room. Upon initial examination the doctors noted retinal hemorrhages but nothing else was remarkable. This prompted the responding coroner to order full body x-rays of the child that revealed numerous rib fractures in various stages of healing. The subsequent autopsy verified the fractures and that the child's brain had been hemorrhaging over an extended period of time. It turned out that the mother's live-in boyfriend was not able to cope with the crying child and had on numerous occasions violently shaken her. The rib fractures were caused by the hands of the boyfriend as he grabbed the child and shook her. These shaking events had occurred frequently and after a short time the bleeding into the brain ultimately caused the child to die.

▶ Sharp Force Injuries

Sharp force injuries are those created by sharp and/or pointed objects in which the object cuts or penetrates the skin. In contrast to lacerations in blunt force trauma, sharp force injuries leave very distinct clean and even margins and do not have the bridging of connective tissue and nerves. Stab wounds and incised wounds are the types most commonly found. Occasionally chopping wounds may occur when a heavier instrument such as a hatchet, a machete, or an axe are used as the weapon. These weapons, due to the weight and structure of the weapons, may cause blunt force as well as sharp force injuries.

Stab Wounds

A stab wound is deeper than it is long and may be inflicted by a knife or any other nontraditional sharp forced instrument including a screwdriver, a fork, or an ice pick. When a sharp force instrument is used to create a stab wound, it punctures the skin and penetrates the body. The depth of the wound depends upon many different factors including the amount of applied force, the instrument used, and where the wound was inflicted on the body. For example, it is very difficult to make an accurate determination as to the length of a knife blade based solely on the depth of the wound, since it is very possible for a 4-inch knife blade to inflict a 6-inch or deeper wound track depending on where the injury was inflicted on the body. If the wound was inflicted on the chest or abdomen with sufficient force, the abdomen or chest of the victim will "give" under applied pressure and allow for a much deeper penetration than the actual length of the blade. One needs to be very cautious in making these types of determinations as there are a multitude of variables involved.

Due to the possible body movement of the victim while being stabbed there are several other injuries/artifacts that may result. For instance, the knife may rock back and forth or get twisted in different directions as it is inserted or withdrawn, as shown in **Figure 7-12**, producing a 'Y' shaped wound.

Stab wounds, and in some cases incised wounds, that cut *across* the lines of tension of the body can produce what is called a "gaping" wound as shown in **Figure 7-13**. If the knife stabs *along* the lines of tension the wound usually takes on a different appearance ("non-gaping") as shown in **Figure 7-14**. Cutting through the tension lines is somewhat similar to cutting a stretched rubber band. If a cut is made across the line the rubber band will snap and separate. But if the cut or stab is made lengthwise, there may be very little damage done because the cut went along the rubber band's tension lines and did not cross them.

In a "gaping" wound it is possible to attempt a realignment of the tissue so measurements can be obtained of the length of the cut to estimate the width

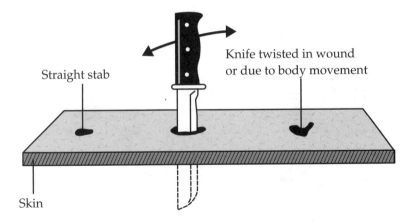

FIGURE 7-12. Illustration depicting injury configurations in knife wounds.

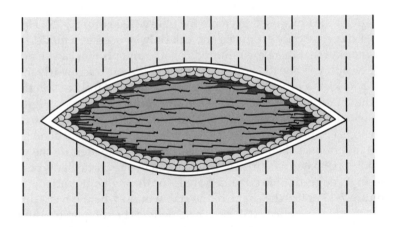

FIGURE 7-13. Illustration of a gaping stab wound.

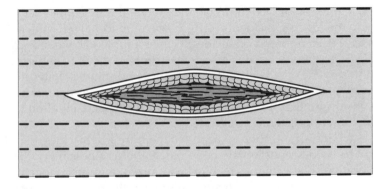

FIGURE 7-14. Illustration of a non-gaping stab wound.

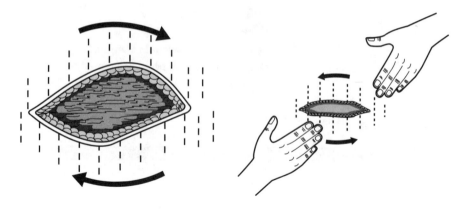

FIGURE 7-15. Illustration of re-aligning a gaping stab wound.

of the blade of the knife used to create the injury (see **Figure 7-15**). However, remember these are only estimates and can only be used as a guide.

Keep in mind that there are hundreds of instruments that can be used as a stabbing weapon. While the knife is the most common, a screwdriver, pair of scissors, a fork, or a broken bottle can produce death if inflicted on the right part of the anatomy or inflicted a sufficient number of times. **Figure 7-16** depicts some of the configurations one may find with different instruments. Note the injuries inflicted and how the entrance wounds may actually form a pattern that mimics their appearance and may help to identify the weapon used. Additional pattern injuries may be caused by the particular type of knife blade—single edge, double edge, serrated—or through hilt marks.

In **Figure 7-17** notice the shape of the stab wound where it has a dull edge and a sharp edge. As reflected these can sometimes be compared to an instrument as indicator that a particular instrument created that injury.

Although not widespread, it is not uncommon for a knife or other sharp force object to be used to self-inflict injuries in a suicide attempt. In these cases it is also not unusual for victims to stab themselves multiple times before succumbing to the injuries. Incidents of 10, 20, even up to 100 self-inflicted stab wounds have been recorded in suicides. These multiple stab wounds can create problems for family and lay persons who find it difficult to understand or accept how anyone could self-inflict such repeated injuries. Later material covers many of these issues in more detail, but from an investigative perspective the sheer number of injuries should not in and of itself eliminate the possibility of self-infliction.

In cases where self-infliction is suspected there are several clues or findings which can be used to substantiate or eliminate this as a possibility. First, the general locations of the injuries tend to be localized or grouped together and within the reach or range of the victim. This generally means the front side of their body; injuries to the back would be inconsistent with self-infliction.

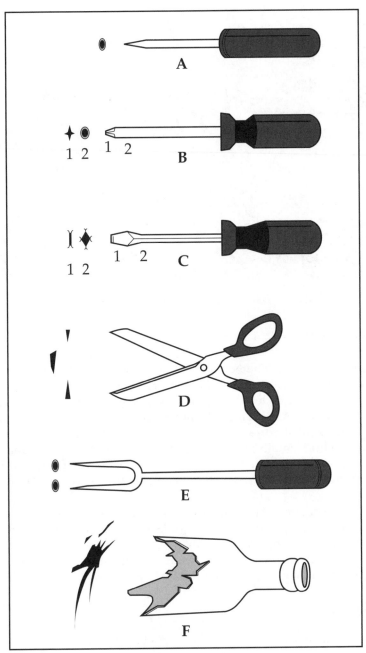

(A) Pointed tool (awl). (B) Philips screwdriver.
(C) Standard screwdriver. (D) Scissors. (E) Barbecue fork.
(F) Broken beer bottle.

FIGURE 7-16. Examples of sharp force wound characteristics.

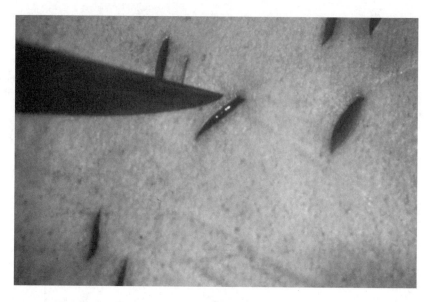

FIGURE 7-17. Shape of stab wound is similar to stabbing instrument. See Color Plate 33.

Another key to a suicide determination is the general orientation of the entrance wounds, whether they are horizontal or vertical. Typically when the wounds are inflicted by another person the weapon is held in the offender's hand and inflicted in a downward motion, resulting in a vertically orientated stab wound. In self-inflicted injuries, the weapon is held in the victim's hand but the motion is more from the side rather than straight down, thus creating more of a horizontally orientated wound. It is important however to note, there may be horizontally orientated stab wounds in homicides, and there may be vertically orientated stab wounds in cases of suicide, but it is the preponderance of the injuries that helps make the determination of what happened.

Lastly, there are often hesitation type wounds present as well. These may be observed as tiny pin prick type injuries or could be very shallow stab wounds, both caused by victims as they work up the courage or resolve to fully stab themselves. It is also not uncommon for suicide victims to exhibit both stab wounds and incised wounds.

Incised Wounds

An incised wound is longer than it is deep and may only affect the outer layers of the skin, whereas stab wounds are deeper than they are long. Like stab wounds, the extent or seriousness of an incised wound is based on a combination of the type of instrument used, the depth of the injury, and the location of injury. A straight razor or sharp knife forcefully drawn across the throat or slashed across the body can produce horrific injuries.

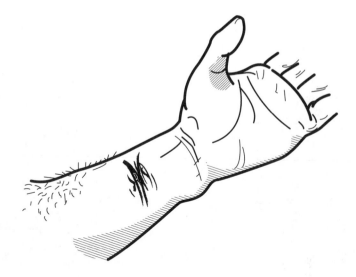

FIGURE 7-18. Illustration of hesitation cuts to the wrist.

Incised wounds are also frequently found with suicide attempts or suicidal "screams for help" in the form of hesitation marks where the individual might cut the wrists or neck but not deep enough to cause death. These are called hesitation marks because it is believed the individual is trying to determine whether or not s/he can withstand the pain of the cutting or are still debating whether to die or not. Compare these (**Figures 7-18** and **7-19**) with the typical homicidal stabbing found in **Figure 7-20**.

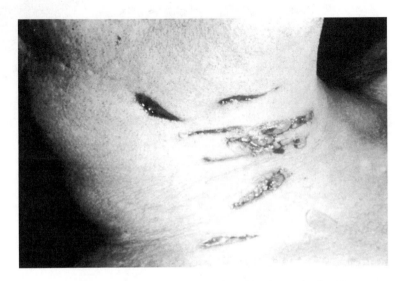

FIGURE 7-19. Self-inflicted hesitation marks on the neck. See Color Plate 34.

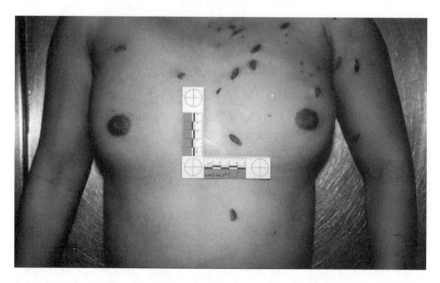

FIGURE 7-20. Homicidal stabbing. This young lady was in her carport getting ready to open her car door to drive to work when her former boyfriend attacked and stabbed her multiple times. Note haphazard nature of the wounds and the vertical orientation of most of the injuries, consistent with a homicidal attack. See Color Plate 35.

Before we leave the category of sharp force injuries it is important to re-member that during a fight, when attacked with a sharp instrument, victims often are moving, and trying to protect themselves, resulting in defensive wounds and widespread distribution of injuries could include the back, the neck, the chest, the arms, hands, or legs (see **Figure 7-21**). The presence of

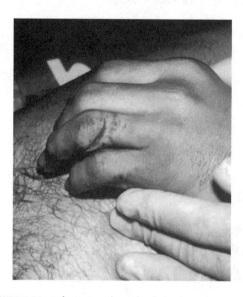

FIGURE 7-21. Defensive incised wound to the hand. See Color Plate 36.

these wounds is a strong indicator that the event is a homicide versus any other manner of death. Many times these wounds are the result of the victim attempting to grab the knife blade and then the offender pulls away, leaving deep wounds on the fingers and palms of the hand.

It is also important to remember that it is not unusual for the attacker to have suffered injuries, particularly in sharp force injuries. Therefore, it is imperative, whenever the cause of death is sharp force injury, to examine any suspects very carefully for injuries to their own hands or for the presence of blood on their clothing.

▶Gunshot Wounds

This section on gunshot wounds will provide only general knowledge and the characteristics that are seen in most shooting cases. No attempt will be made to define, illustrate or describe the numerous types of weapons and ammunition that create different affects on the body. There are far too many weapon and ammunition types to incorporate in the limited space for this text. While the differences between small and large caliber are significant, what is provided here is only a guide and one must consider all possible variations. To be all inclusive would require an entire book which is already available from Dr. Vincent J. M. Di Maio, considered by many as the foremost authority, in his book on gunshot wounds.[4]

Generally speaking, gunshot wounds are categorized as distant wounds, intermediate wounds, close contact wounds or hard contact wounds. These terms are based on the distance between the end of the barrel of the weapon and the victim.

When a projectile is fired it is pushed through the barrel and begins spinning (rotating left or right depending on the rifling) as it travels in the direction fired. The speed of the projectile is dependent upon the type and caliber of weapon and type of ammunition used. The kinetic energy generated determines the gravity of the injury to the body and this energy is relative depending on the weight of the projectile and the velocity at which it is traveling. As a projectile enters the body it produces a very distinctive wound or defect, commonly referred to as an entrance wound. Passing through the body, the projectile produces both a permanent and a temporary cavity. The permanent cavity is the actual path of the projectile as it travels through the body. The temporary cavity is created in milliseconds based on the kinetic energy transmitted through the body, and then returns to normal as the bullet passes through. The temporary cavity is much like a shock wave and thus may actually injure internal organs or rupture major blood vessels in the body. Many times the temporary cavity, created as the kinetic energy is dispersed through the body, causes more injury than the permanent cavity created by the bullet passing through the body. "The location, size and the shape of the temporary cavity in a body depend on the amount of kinetic energy lost by the bullet in its path through the tissue, how rapidly the energy is lost, and the elasticity and cohesiveness of the tissue."[5]

Since this projectile is rotating it creates an abrasion ring around the actual entrance wound as depicted in **Figure 7-22**. It is also important to note that while the entrance wound has the abrasion ring around it, the exit wound does not. Furthermore, while the entrance wound may appear regular the exit wound is frequently irregular because of the tearing of the tissue from both the exiting projectile but also bone fragments it collected while traveling through the body, often causing a very large and irregularly shaped exit wound. A myth that has often been repeated is that the exit wound can be differentiated from an entrance wound because it's always larger than the entrance wound. This is not correct as there are many factors that may influence the appearance of an exit wound.

ENTRANCE

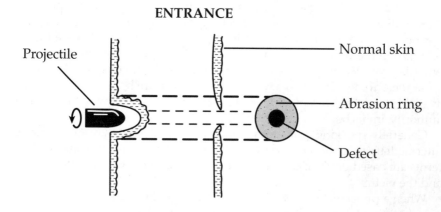

ENTRANCE ANGLE

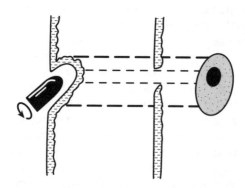

FIGURE 7-22. Illustration of projectile striking the skin straight on and at an angle. In both cases an abrasion is created but takes on an elongated shape in the angle shot.

The difference between the entrance and exit wound are usually very discernible, based on soot, tattooing, presence of an abrasion ring on an entrance wound, and the irregular shape of an exit wound. In shots to the head, the entrance and exit wounds can be differentiated by the beveling of the skull as depicted in **Figure 7-23**. More on exit wounds will be presented later in this chapter.

Distant

Distant gunshot wounds are just that, shots fired at a distance, usually where the shooter is approximately six feet or further from the target. The only marks left behind are abrasion rings created by the spinning of the projectile and the friction it creates on the skin as it perforates the body (see Figure 7-22).

Intermediate

Intermediate gunshot wounds are different. These usually occur where the muzzle of the weapon is a shorter distance away from the target yet the weapon is close enough for the burning powder grains of the ammunition to produce what is referred to as *stippling* or *powder tattooing* as they impact on the target area. This surface could be clothing and/or the actual skin of the person (see **Figures 7-24 and 7-25**). The distance from muzzle to target will vary but is usually 4–6 feet. The only accurate way to determine the actual distance involved in a particular shooting would be for a firearms examiner to fire the questioned weapon with like ammunition at a target with varying distances until he is able to replicate the powder tattooing pattern. Keep in mind that firing through clothing will sometimes alter the appearance of the

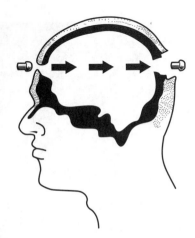

FIGURE 7-23. Illustration of a projectile traveling through the head creating the beveling or cratering effect that helps distinguish between entrance and exit wounds in the skull.

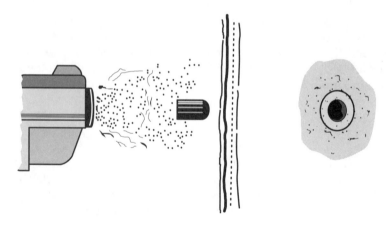

FIGURE 7-24. Illustration of an intermediate gunshot wound.

pattern on the body and may even alter the appearance of the wound itself. This determination has the potential of providing the investigator with valuable information that could position the shooter and his relationship to the victim at the time the weapon was fired.

Close Contact

In close contact wounds the muzzle of the weapon is not in contact with the skin but is held very close to it. A characteristic sign would be the presence of "powder soot overlying seared, blackened skin",[6] versus the distinguishable tattooing pattern seen with intermediate gunshot wounds (see **Figure 7-26**).

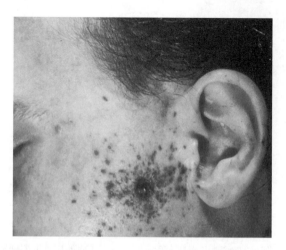

FIGURE 7-25. Photograph depicting an intermediate gunshot wound. See Color Plate 37.

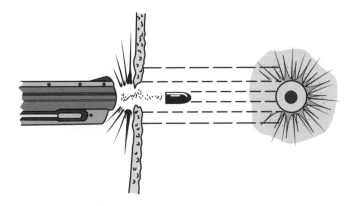

FIGURE 7-26. Illustration of a close contact gunshot wound.

A type of wound Di Maio calls a "near-contact wound" occupies a gray zone between intermediate and contact exhibiting characteristics of both."[7]

The actual position, angle, or trajectory of the weapon can often be determined by an examination of the soot pattern and entrance wound. When the weapon muzzle is tilted to an angle (see **Figure 7-27**) the ending result will

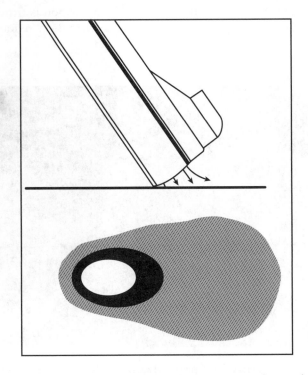

FIGURE 7-27. Illustration of the pattern seen in a close contact wound at an angle.

look like the pattern seen in **Figure 7-28**. In this particular scenario the spouse of the shooter was asleep in bed lying on her left side. The shooter came up behind her and while holding the gun at an angle shot her in the head. He then called 911 and reported that his wife had committed suicide by shooting herself in the head. The trajectory of the projectile was back to front and slightly right to left.

Another example of a close contact wound can be found in **Figure 7-29**. In this scenario, the police officer had been in a high-speed chase where the vehicle he was chasing rolled over onto its side. As the officer approached the vehicle he drew his firearm and cocked it, ready to fire. When he got to the vehicle he reached up to look through the side window and placed both hands on the door edge with his firearm in one hand under his chin. He accidentally pulled the trigger firing the weapon and fatally shot himself. The problem with all this was that the trigger pull to discharge this particular weapon is normally six pounds pressure yet someone had altered the internal mechanisms of the firearm and the trigger pull was closer to two pounds, almost making it a "hair trigger." Without that alteration the weapon probably would not have fired.

Hard Contact

With all hard contact wounds the muzzle of the weapon is firmly pressed against the body. When over bone, such as the head, there is frequently blow-

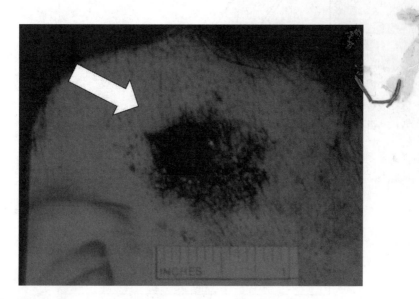

FIGURE 7-28. Photograph depicting a close contact gunshot wound where the victim was shot at a slight angle. See Color Plate 38.

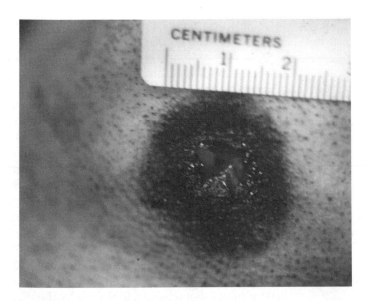

FIGURE 7-29. Example of a close gunshot wound under the chin where the muzzle was very close and perpendicular to the skin at the time the weapon was discharged. See Color Plate 39.

back of gunshot residue, powder, blood, and maybe even tissue (see **Figure 7-30**). These types of injuries should alert the investigator to the possibility that evidence might be found on the hands of the victim as well as suspected shooters. The lack of evidence on the hands of the victim could lead one to suspect someone else other than the deceased pulled the trigger. The absence

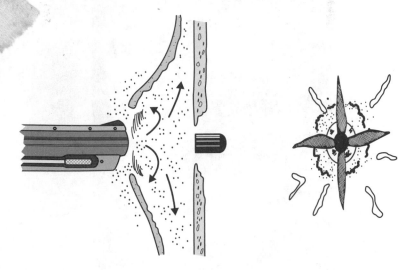

FIGURE 7-30. Illustration of the mechanics of a hard contact wound. To the right is an illustration reflecting how the entrance wound may appear.

of such evidence is not an absolute, however, as there are many factors that may influence the likelihood of blood and tissue being deposited on the shooter's hands. These include the size, type, and caliber of the weapon, how hard the weapon was placed against the boney surface, if there were any intermediate targets such as a hat or head hair that could have prevented the blood and tissue from coming back and being deposited on the shooter's hand. In determining what happened, how and by whom, the investigator is charged with eliminating as well as identifying events and potential suspects.

Figures 7-31 and **7-32** show the classic stellate or star-like appearance of the entrance wound which is typical in hard contact gunshot wounds to the head. In the first case (Figure 7-31) the location is under the chin where the muzzle of the weapon was firmly in contact with the body. The firearm in this scenario, a .357 Magnum, carries a heavy load and creates a great amount of energy, thus the massive devastation to the head area from the projectile gas from the exploding powder. This person was despondent over his battle with cancer and decided to end his pain and suffering. He shot himself twice which caused some concern by the investigators but all the pieces fell together in the end as a suicide. The first, nonfatal shot was declared a test by the victim, like

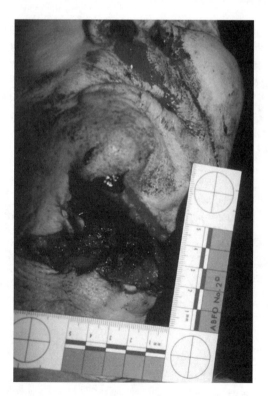

FIGURE 7-31. Hard contact gunshot wound under the chin from a .357 Magnum revolver. See Color Plate 40.

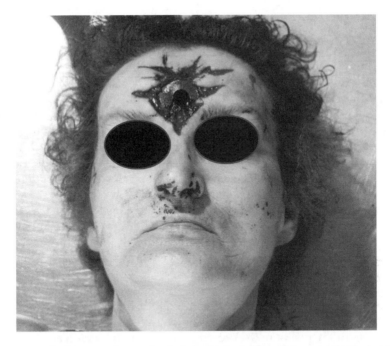

FIGURE 7-32. A hard contact gunshot wound to the forehead with a Bull Dog .44 Magnum, self inflicted suicide. See Color Plate 41.

hesitation marks with sharp force injuries, for the purpose of determining whether or not the suicidal act can be carried out. The authors have seen numerous suicide cases where more than one shot is fired, and while not the norm, it does happen.

In the second case (Figure 7-32) this person fatally shot her husband four times with a Bull Dog .44 Magnum, while he was asleep. She then turned the weapon unto herself. The entrance wound to her forehead is a classic hard contact gunshot wound with the typical stellate or starring effect seen with these injuries. When evaluating these types of wounds (stellate or star shaped) be cautioned that some lacerations to the head may also have similar appearances to gunshot wounds. A close evaluation by the pathologist during the autopsy should clarify any misinterpretations and/or validate the cause of the particular injury.

Other Considerations

It was mentioned this chapter will only be a cursory review of what the death investigator may find with firearm injuries and not an all inclusive documentation relating to everything that can happen with firearms in death investigations. For that reason a supplemental book like Di Maio's should be available for review. However, some additional concepts are important enough to mention here.

The first is the concept of intermediary targets. These are objects that are between the path of the bullet and the body of the victim such as clothing, screening from screen windows or doors, wood or metal frames, glass, etc. Passing through an intermediate target could cause a change in the bullet trajectory, create an unusual or abnormal entrance wound, and/or produce artifacts to the wound and surrounding tissue that could cause an inaccurate interpretation. A good example of this can be found in **Figure 7-33**. The shooter, using a .357 revolver, shot a delivery girl one time through the glass window pane of his house. He was using copper jacketed ammunition. Once he fired the weapon at her, the bullet with the intact jacket passed through the glass window. Passing through the intermediary target of the glass, caused the jacket to separate from the lead core of the bullet creating two missiles that struck the body of the victim creating two different penetrating wounds of the head and neck. The lead struck the head while the copper jacket impacted the neck. The spots seen around these wounds are small particles of glass and not powder stippling as described earlier with intermediate gunshot wounds.

Another important aspect of gunshot wounds is the presence of *shored up* wounds. These can be either entrance or exit wounds depending on the circumstances, body position, the presence of intermediary targets, etc. A lot of

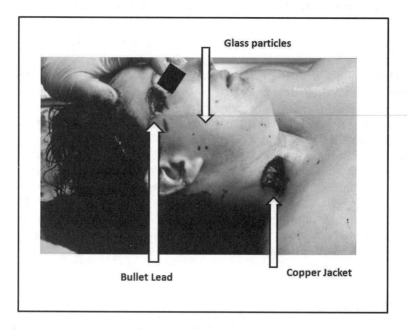

FIGURE 7-33. Example of what can occur when a person is shot through an intermediary target. In this case the victim was shot through a glass window pane with a .357 revolver using jacketed ammunition. As depicted, once the bullet traveled through the glass the copper jacket separated from the lead core of the bullet creating two missiles that impacted the body. See Color Plate 42.

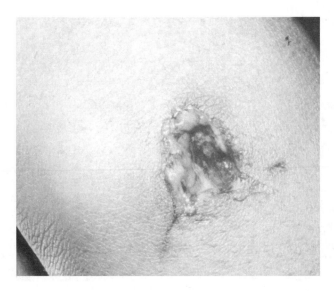

FIGURE 7-34. Shoring up of an entrance wound on the upper arm from a bullet that is tumbling because it traveled through an intermediary target. An examination of the projectile should reveal signs that the bullet struck another object prior to impacting the body. See Color Plate 43.

variables come into play with these types of wounds and the situation needs to be thoroughly investigated to accurately decipher what happened. A classic shored up entrance wound can be seen in **Figure 7-34** where the tissue is shored up (pushed up) by the projectile in its attempt to enter the body. The bullet's trajectory or path has been altered by an intermediary target or is possibly a ricochet. This causes the bullet to either tumble or become totally unpredictable as to the course it will take and may even strike the body base first or sideways, shoring up the tissue accordingly.

Exit Wound Characteristics

Exits wounds can take on a number of variations and if not properly evaluated can be easily misinterpreted. As previously mentioned, the bullet typically travels through the body, and if jacketed, may shed its copper jacket to remain in the body or go off in another direction, while the lead continues to travel through the body. The exit wound is usually irregular in shape when contrasted to entrance wounds and usually does not show an abrasion ring, soot, powder residue, etc. **Figures 7-35** and **7-36**, both show gunshot exit wounds of the head yet they are entirely different in their configuration. Again, note the lack of gun powder deposits and the absence of an abrasion ring. If these had been lacerations due to blunt force trauma one would see abraded tissue and bridging of the tissue.

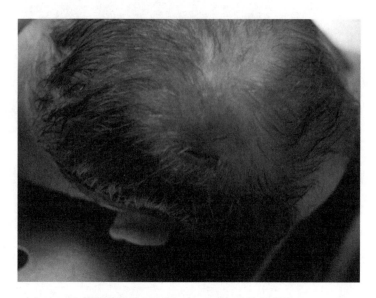

FIGURE 7-35. Gunshot exit wound. See Color Plate 44.

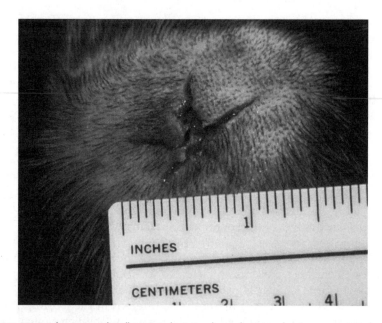

FIGURE 7-36. Gunshot exit wound (Stellate). Typical exit wound—no charring, no burning, no soot or powder deposits and no abrasion ring. Distinguishable from blunt force laceration because there is no bridging of vessels, nerves or other connective tissue, no shelving of the tissue, and no underlying contusion. See Color Plate 45.

There is a misperception or common myth, that exit wounds are always larger than entrance wounds. This is usually true because in addition to the projectile, the copper jacket of the projectile may have separated and might also leave through the same exit wound or bone fragments may also exit the body through the same site, which could cause an exaggerated wound. The best way to identify or differentiate between an exit and entrance wounds is the presence or absence of soot, tattooing, or an abrasion ring.

Laboratory Determinations

In firearm situations the weapon used in the shooting should be collected as evidence and sent to the crime laboratory responsible for performing the forensic examinations. Additionally, evidence from the hands of all potential victims and potential persons of interest (or suspects) should be collected for gunshot residue (GSR) analysis. Furthermore, the clothing of the victim may also prove to have evidentiary value for the firearms and other examiners in the crime laboratory. **Figures 7-37** and **7-38** illustrate the potential evidence that may be available from and around the firing of a handgun.

Making distance determinations of muzzle to target can be very helpful as a means of reconstructing the circumstances of a scene. The process can also validate statements by witnesses and suspects or prove them to be inaccurate. In order to successfully accomplish this task, the firearms examiner needs to have the weapon in question and like ammunition. Therefore, the collection at the scene of extra ammunition of the same caliber as the weapon is paramount.

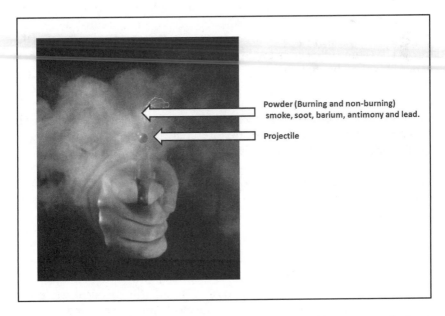

Powder (Burning and non-burning) smoke, soot, barium, antimony and lead.

Projectile

FIGURE 7-37. Photo depicting the powder and smoke that comes out the barrel of the weapon. See Color Plate 46.

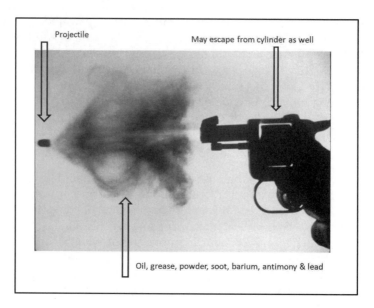

FIGURE 7-38. Photo depicting powder and smoke deposits from gun. See Color Plate 47.

Besides determining the functionality of the firearm, the examiner will test fire it at varying distances in an attempt to replicate any patterns that may exist on clothing or sometimes even tattooing/stippling on skin. GSR determinations may also be conducted and compared with any GSR evidence collected at the scene, from the victim and/or any suspects. However, one must be cautious with GSR results; false positives do occur, and results are only an indication that a suspect has come into contact with certain elements, not proof positive that a weapon was fired by that person.

Many crime labs have stopped conducting GSR examinations on cases of suspected suicide or if the individual has admitted to being present in the immediate area when the gun was actually fired. This is because once the weapon is fired, the GSR elements are thrown into the surrounding area and it is possible to get a positive reading for GSR from just being present when the gun was fired. It is also just as likely that even a suicide victim who shot himself with a hand gun may leave no trace of GSR on his hands. Much depends on the weapon, ammunition, and distance. This makes the reliability of this examination questionable.

▶ Anoxia (Lack of Oxygen) or Death by Asphyxiation

When oxygen to the brain is restricted or occluded, the physical and physiological effects may differ depending on the mechanism or method involved. An examination of these effects can help determine the mechanism that was

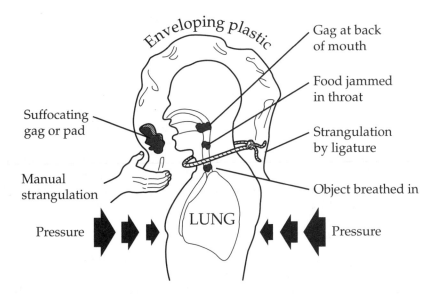

FIGURE 7-39. Some possible causes of asphyxiation.

used. There are four basic mechanisms of asphyxiation: (1) compression of the neck; (2) obstruction of the airway; (3) compression of the chest; and (4) depletion or replacement (see **Figure 7-39**).

Compression of the Neck

Compression of the neck is seen frequently in both homicide and suicide cases and is more commonly known as manual strangulation, ligature strangulation, or hanging. With compression of the neck, death is not necessarily the result of an inability of the victim to breathe, but because the oxygenated blood flow is cut off or slowed down due to pressure on the major arteries preventing blood flow to the brain.

Manual Strangulation

Manual strangulation or *throttling* is the application of pressure to the victim's neck by the offender's hands. Generally this is done with both the victim and the offender facing each other, but it is far harder to strangle someone particularly if the victim is able to offer physical resistance, than often depicted on television. After the pressure is applied to the neck, the victim may actually lose consciousness for a short period of time, the body becoming limp. The offender, thinking the victim is dead, might release pressure from the neck at this point. Once the blood starts to circulate again, the victim may start to recover, at which point the surprised offender may have to continue with the assault in order to finally kill the victim.

Because of the amount of pressure needed and the fact the offender is using his hands and fingers to apply the pressure there are often very distinct contusions and small abrasions observed on the neck which will correspond to the offender's fingers. There may also be seen half moon shaped scratches on the neck from the offender's fingernails. It is also common for the hyoid bone (a small cartilage structure located in the throat) to be fractured and is seen as a marker in manual strangulation situations. Because of the pressure needed there are also frequently deep contusions and hemorrhages in the strap muscles on the side of the neck.

In a manual strangulation, the offender's DNA, in the form of sloughed off skin cells on the victim's neck, may be available. The victim may also have scratched or otherwise injured the offender opening the possibility of finding DNA underneath the victim's fingernails.

Ligature Strangulation

Ligature strangulation or *garroting* is one of the more common forms of homicide by strangulation. It is used perhaps more than any other method for asphyxia type homicides. A ligature is a device, generally a string, rope, twine, or other similar object, that's placed around the throat generally from behind, and is then tightened causing the compression of the larynx, carotid arteries, and jugular veins. Again this method does limit the flow of air into the lungs, but more importantly because of the added pressure it cuts off the flow of oxygenated blood to the brain much more efficiently than manual strangulation.

Ligature strangulation does produce discernible injuries around the neck where the ligature was placed. Because of the amount of pressure and type of ligature used, injuries may produce furrows or indentations and friction burns. Many times as the ligature is being applied to the victim pattern injuries of the ligature are produced and can be observed in the furrows or friction burns on the victim's neck. These furrows and friction burns are generally produced in a horizontal orientation around the throat.

A related method to compress the neck is known as *yoking*, where another object such as a nightstick or even the forearm of the offender is placed around the neck and pressure applied. We might see this when a suspect is accidentally killed by police attempting to subdue a suspect when they place their nightstick or forearm around the suspect's throat and apply pressure. Using this technique the victim will be rendered unconscious relatively quickly and if pressure is not released death will occur. This technique does not always leave contusions or abrasions around the throat that can readily identify the method used.

Hanging

Hanging is the full or partial suspension of the body with a ligature, from a fixed point. Hangings are more typically found in suicide or accidental incidents and use as a method of homicide is rare. It is important to realize that most of the hangings we are confronted with do not resemble the typical judicial hangings or executions that most envision when thinking about hanging. In cases of judicial hangings, death is not supposed to be caused by asphyxia or lack of oxygen but by the breaking of the neck and damage to the spinal column which produces death instantaneously.

Additionally, in most suicidal or accidental hangings the victim is not totally suspended off the ground. There have been many examples of hangings where the victim actually secured the ligature to a fixed point and the victim then positions himself in such a way to induce the pressure against his throat. Many times victims are found in a somewhat vertical position, and if they had actually stood up, they could have relieved the pressure.

Although rope is typically used, it is not unusual for a victim to use whatever material may be available including shoestrings, belts, towels, sheets, and in some cases inside a prison setting, the elastic band from underwear.

Hanging also produces very discernible and recognizable injuries such as furrows and friction burns around the neck, causing what is known as an inverted "V" pattern on the neck. This pattern is readily identified and can be fairly easily differentiated from ligature strangulation (see **Case Study 7-2**).

Obstruction of the Airway

The first type of obstruction of the airway can be described as smothering. This could be as simple as placing a plastic bag over a person's head, or with more force such as placing a pillow over the face and pressing down not allowing the victim to breathe. **Figure 7-40** shows a victim suffocated when an offender applied duct tape completely around her face and head, and closing off her nose and mouth and thus her ability to breathe.

Case Study 7-2

An elderly woman was found hanging in the shed of her garage in what looked like a typical suicide. At the scene detectives could clearly see the inverted "V" pattern on the side of her neck consistent with hanging. But on closer examination they also observed a horizontal ligature mark around the neck which caused them to look at the scene more closely. Later investigation revealed that the woman was killed by ligature strangulation by relatives using a rope. She was then taken to the garage and placed into a noose of a rope hanging from the rafters, as a way to stage the scene to resemble a suicide. Recognizing that the presence of both the horizontal and inverted "V" patterns on the victim was inconsistent with the scene compelled the police to immediately challenge what they were seeing and look more closely at the incident.

FIGURE 7-40. An example of smothering with duct tape. See Color Plate 48.

The second type of obstruction of the airway is through internal means such as a blockage by a foreign object. A good example of this is the very common "Café Coronary", where someone in a restaurant appears to be having a heart attack, and struggling to breathe, when in reality they have swallowed something that has become lodged in their throat and thus blocking air in and out of their lungs. Other examples include elderly who may swallow their teeth, younger children who may swallow any number of smaller objects that can block their airway.

In some homicide cases we see death caused by a gag placed so deeply into the mouth the victim may in panic actually swallow it so it becomes lodged in the throat.

Compression of the Chest

Asphyxia caused from compression of the chest occurs in two basic ways: when the subject's chest is somehow restricted from expanding properly or when the victim's body is placed in or comes to rest in a position which obstructs his air flow.

Typically, deaths resulting from compression of the chest are the result of an accident. However, in the 1820s in Scotland, a serial murderer Brendan "Dynes" Burke used this method quite effectively. Burke would literally sit on the chest of his victim, to compress their chest. Eventually the effort to breathe was too much for the victim and they would succumb to asphyxia. Burke then sold the victim's body, which was otherwise unremarkable and uninjured for use in medical schools. This method of homicide is still known even today as *Burking*.

We also see this type of death in traffic accidents when the vehicle comes to rest on the victim's chest and the weight prevents the chest from inflating. Many times the victims are able to breathe for a short period of time, but eventually the effort becomes too great and they die. Additionally, there are other examples of what are referred to as positional asphyxia. Most often these deaths are also accidental in nature and are the result of the victim being placed or falling into a position that does not allow them to breathe. One of the most unusual cases of this was a victim who was home alone drinking alcohol in his kitchen, when apparently he lost his balance and fell, instead of hitting the floor on his butt, he fell back onto a barstool and literally fell through the barstool legs butt first. As he fell his body was forced into a position where he was literally folded against his own legs. Being unable to break free of the barstool, he eventually died from positional asphyxia when breathing became so difficult in that position.

Another example of positional asphyxia are suspects handcuffed and "hogtied" by police to keep them from fleeing or from further resisting and then placed face down on the ground. Placing them on their chest is essentially the same as placing a heavy object on their chest because in order to breathe they must literally "lift" their own body off the ground. There have been many occasions in the past when this has caused the death of a suspect. Now, police officers are trained to place these subdued suspects on their side to avoid this situation.

Depletion or Replacement

The fourth major mechanism of asphyxia is exclusion of oxygen due to depletion and replacement by another gas or as a result of chemical interference with its uptake and use. Examples include poisoning by carbon dioxide, carbon monoxide, or cyanide. Lividity coloring in carbon monoxide cases is usually cherry red, however be aware that cold environments can also give a cherry red appearance. Another very common example is drowning, where the air in the lungs is replaced by water.

Investigational Considerations in Asphyxiation Death

In some of the mechanical types of asphyxiation deaths due to suffocation, manual strangulation, ligature strangulation, and hanging; petechia (small pin point hemorrhages) may appear in the eyelids and/or the whites of the eyes. One may also see a congested or a cyanotic (blue to purple discoloration) appearance of the face. However, these can occur from other causes as well and therefore should only be treated as an indicator as they are not proof positive.

The terms suffocation and smothering overlap to some degree and are at times used interchangeably. When describing these types of asphyxia, forensic pathologists are advised to include the instrument used, e.g., smothering with a towel or pillow. As we progress into strangulation there are two types that need to be distinguished. They are manual strangulation (throttling or choking) caused by applying pressure that creates constriction of the neck usually from the hands of the offender; and ligature strangulation whereby a rope, belt or other similar object is placed around the neck to occlude the airway and vessels of the neck. "Hanging by ligature is a form of ligature strangulation in which the weight of the body tightens the ligature."[8] Keep in mind that bodies found in hangings can take on many positions and do not have to be fully suspended to cause the death.

While investigating possible hangings it is important to carefully examine the material used along with any marks or abrasions in and around where the ligature is located. In distinguishing the difference between ligature strangulation and a hanging, the ligature strangulation typically has a straight furrow around the neck that is below the larynx (see **Figure 7-41**) while in hangings there is an inverted "V" with the rope placement above the larynx (see **Figure 7-42** and the photograph in **Figure 7-43**). In this last scenario the weight of the body pulls against the rope causing the rope to slide up into the position depicted in the illustration. However, be mindful that if a person is lying

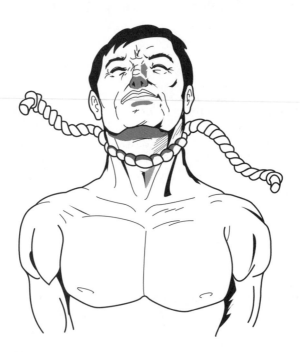

FIGURE 7-41. Ligature strangulation showing a straight furrow around the neck.

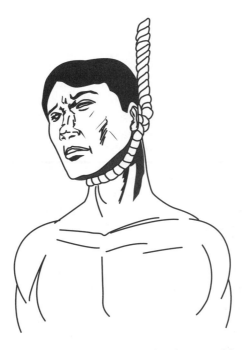

FIGURE 7-42. Hanging showing the inverted "V" furrow around the neck.

FIGURE 7-43. Hanging victim: notice the up and away appearance of the ligature and the protruding tongue due to the pressure from below the chin. See Color Plate 49.

down while attached to a rope around their neck, the configuration and location of the rope and furrow may be different.

As shown in Figure 7-39 note that the mechanism of death in asphyxiation will vary. A thorough victimology must be prepared along with a comprehensive scene investigation and extensive interviews in order to ascertain the correct manner of death. An enveloping plastic film could indicate either homicide or suicide. Manual strangulation, ligature strangulation and/or the utilization of a gag or pillow to suffocate most likely indicate homicides. Ingesting objects or food into the airways are classic accidental deaths while external pressure to the chest and lungs could be either accidental or homicidal depending on the circumstances.

Bodies found in water, while an asphyxia death, present many problems. The longer they are in water the more difficult determination becomes. Everything from aquatic animals to normal decomposition will add to the problems encountered. If at autopsy the body does not show any signs of a struggle or trauma then the manner of death determination will hinge entirely on the circumstances leading up to the discovery of the body along with a comprehensive victimology and the interviews of all involved parties. In the end they could be labeled an accident, a homicide or a suicide.

References

1. Froede, R. C. (Ed.). (2003). *Handbook of forensic pathology* (2nd ed.). Northfield, IL: College of American Pathologists. p. 172.
2. Ibid. p. 140.
3. Ibid. p. 141.
4. Di Maio, V. J. M. (1999). *Gunshot wounds* (2nd ed.). Boca Raton, FL: CRC Press.
5. Ibid. p. 54.
6. Ibid. p. 69.
7. Ibid. pp. 68–69.
8. Froede, R. C. p. 189.

CHAPTER EIGHT

Interviewing Witnesses and Suspects

▶The Interview and Interrogation Process*

One of the most important aspects of conducting any investigation is the ability to acquire information from people. It starts with the ability to listen and hear what others are saying—a good listener is frequently a good interviewer, so pay close attention to what people say, when they say it, how they express themselves, and the words they select. Remember the skill of conducting a good interview is an art and anyone can learn how to do it properly. Therefore, in this chapter, we will describe how to conduct an effective interview of complainants, eye-witnesses, regular witnesses, or significant witnesses; how to conduct a proper canvass that might include eye-witnesses, regular witnesses or significant witnesses; how to conduct a good suspect interview (or interrogation); and ultimately how to properly document the interview process. The basic goal of all interviews is to identify what happened and who did it. We will also explain the Behavioral Analysis Interview and illustrate the value of this technique both in this chapter and with a case example in Appendix A.

In the recent past, the topic of interrogation has come under scrutiny. This text does not reference interrogation in terms of world events or social unrest. The subject has become so controversial that Great Britain no longer uses the term "interrogation" and has renamed the entire process for witness and suspect questioning as "investigative interviewing."[1] Fueling the negative reaction to law enforcement's manner of gaining information from witnesses and suspects may also be the reported "false confessions" found in criminal cases from the United Kingdom as well as the United States. The Innocence Project has reported that of 242 exonerated cases, a false confession was found

---

*Dr. Adcock initially wrote this piece for Chapter 9 of his book *Cold Cases: An Evaluation Model with Follow-up Strategies for Investigators*. Most of it is restated here.

in twenty-five percent (approximately 60).[2] So, is this a real problem? Yes, especially when vulnerable persons of interest or "at risk" types of people (primarily the mentally deficient and/or juveniles) are interviewed by an authoritative figure.

In their attack on the interrogation process, some researchers have unequivocally placed the Reid Technique* at the top of their list as the biggest contributor to the problem of false confessions. There is no doubt that this interrogation process can be psychologically demanding. However, we firmly believe that if fault is to be placed, it is not so much with the technique as it is the person conducting the interrogation. In all likelihood, the interrogator used a variation of the Reid Technique but did not follow the steps exactly as they were taught. As with polygraphs and polygraph examiners, the end results are only as good as the examiner. No one should be convicted on a confession alone as there should always be corroborating evidence, which the detectives are obligated to obtain, to support the confession. The "bad guys" lie to us all the time so why should an admission of guilt or a confession be any different? Any confession needs to be validated through additional investigation or supporting physical evidence. As John Reid once said, "After you obtain a confession the investigation is just beginning."[3]

▶ Conducting the Interview

The meat of any investigation derives from three sources of information: the physical evidence, behavior of the actors involved, and the informational pieces of the puzzle brought together through interviews and interrogations. Proper conduct of interviews is paramount to any investigation, especially in a high-profile case. Many detectives have the ability to conduct a satisfactory routine interview but seriously lack the interviewing skills that are needed for such cases. Courses available to law enforcement are traditionally referred to as "interviews and interrogations," yet the majority of what is taught focuses on interrogation, dealing very little with the actual interview process of victims and witnesses. One needs to be proficient at conducting proper interviews before becoming an effective interrogator. This is another contributing factor to cases remaining or becoming cold and unresolved.

Lack of proper interviewing technique is not the only contributor to failure in these circumstances, but also a lack of proper case management where

---

*The Reid Technique of Interrogation comes from John Reid and Associates at www.reid.com. The technique has come under scrutiny by many social researchers as being too extreme psychologically to the point of causing some to falsely confess. While we do not specifically adhere to or promote the technique it does have some value if properly followed and executed by experienced interviewers. However, the Behavioral Analysis Interview, also taught by Reid is an excellent way to gather information during an investigation and is further described in this chapter with a case illustration at Appendix A.

significant witnesses are totally overlooked and never interviewed. In a particularly baffling murder case, numerous witnesses had told the police and others that actors A, B, and C were involved in the killing. In fact, one of the three had been overheard telling someone he was there and saw it. Yet, none of them were interviewed then or later. Although these witnesses were not the most reliable types, being prostitutes and drug addicts, when there is that much information pointing in the same direction, there is bound to be some truth in what is being said. At a minimum, the information should have been checked out and invalidated if nothing else. It was missed most likely because no one was carefully reviewing the information in the file to ensure all that needed to be done was in fact being accomplished. This is a good argument for ensuring that first line supervisors in detective units review ongoing cases on a regular basis—not to second guess or micromanage the detectives, but to ensure they remain on track, do not form tunnel vision, and economize their time through prioritization of leads and a solid investigative plan.

The object of any interview is to obtain information that will help answer the 6 basic questions: Who? What? When? Where? How? and Why? In order to effectively utilize this tool, the interviewer must have an understanding of the types of questions available, (e.g. open ended, closed/direct and suggestive or leading), and when to ask them. The first of these is the open ended line of questioning. The open ended questions are those questions (or statements) that do not allow a "yes" or "no" response but rather encourage respondents to tell a story of what they saw, heard, etc. An example of this would be: "Tell me everything that happened here." These types of questions elicit a full response from the witness. These are then followed by clarifying type questions to fill in any gaps that may exist in the witness's story.

The closed/direct questions are designed to elicit a specific position or answer from the person. An example of this would be: "Did you have any contact with the victim prior to 1900 hours?" As you can see these questions nearly always receive a "yes" or "no" answer with no clarification until the interviewer asks. Generally, these questions should only be used after the open ended questions have been fully explored and answered, usually near the end of the interview.

The last type is the leading or suggestive question. These can be dangerous because in the process of asking the question the interviewer is telling the witness what they want to hear as a response. For example, "Was the getaway car a red Buick?" versus "What color and type of vehicle was used for the get-away?" These are particularly problematic when interviewing children because the suggestiveness of the questions will act on impressionable minds, putting words in the mouths of the young witnesses or victims that may relate only to the question, not to the facts of the case.

The most important point here is to utilize the open ended questions as much as possible. We need to know what they actually saw and what they actually heard; not what we *think* they saw or heard. When interviewing significant witnesses that probably saw what happened but are either traumatized or reluctant, consider utilizing the cognitive interview. It is especially helpful in assisting an eyewitness to recall what s/he saw during an event. The four step process is as follows:

Step 1. Reconstruct the circumstances of the event—The interviewer begins by asking the witness to reconstruct how the incident began and to describe those circumstances s/he sees surrounding it. This might include the environment, weather, lighting, cleanliness, etc.

Step 2. Instruct the witness to report everything—In this question s/he is asked to relate everything and not omit any details, suggesting to the witness that even the smallest piece could have great evidentiary value.

Step 3. Conduct a recall of the events but in different order—It is here that the interviewer instructs the witness to recall from different points within the time frame in question and may even be asked to reverse the order of events.

Step 4. Change perspectives—In this question the witness is asked to change his/her perspective or role to someone else in the incident to consider what that person might have seen from another angle/perspective.[4]

Although this technique can produce positive results and is widely used in Great Britain, it is, as yet, not popular in the United States, primarily because American detectives sometimes lack the patience necessary to conduct a good thorough interview.

▶ Documenting the Interview

Documenting the interview is absolutely crucial and the investigator has several choices as avenues for this. The best and most accurate would be to document the interview through a video camera equipped with sound. However, video recordings are cumbersome when in the field and not the most practicable solution. The next best thing to video would be audio recordings. These are much easier to accomplish with today's small digital recording devices. Some police departments require all of their officers to record all interviews regardless of the circumstances, and they are adequately equipped to do this with little extra effort involved. Following these two good and thorough methods is the old stand-by process of taking notes where inevitably information is missed or not properly recorded. Much of what is written is frequently in the words of and from the perspective of the interviewer and might not accurately reflect what the witness was trying to say.

Interviews of suspects (interrogations) should be documented with video cameras. Interview rooms in police stations can be easily designed and constructed with video capabilities as well as viewing rooms with two way mirrors where the suspect cannot see who is watching. The greatest advantage to this process is that everything is on tape starting with the rights advisement all the way through the entire interview. It leaves no doubt in the viewer's mind what occurred during the interview and defies courtroom challenges to an admission or confession, or to mistreatment or coercion. This can be especially important when the subject attempts to suppress his confession in court by alleging his request to remain silent, or for a lawyer, were not honored by the police as noted in **Case Study 8-1**.

Case Study 8-1

Two suspects were identified in the course of a murder investigation and were interviewed. One suspect initially waived his rights and began making admissions implicating the other suspect. Then in the course of the interview asked to stop and wanted to seek legal counsel. At this request the interview was stopped and he was taken to another room where he was provided a lunch and a soft drink. Some time later the suspect changed his mind again and asked for the interview to continue, afraid his co-conspirator was going to put the blame on him. Based on his request the interview was continued. However, prior to the start of the interview the suspect was questioned thoroughly concerning how he came about his change of mind. This was needed because police realized his initial invocation of his right to counsel was going to be a centerpiece of his attorney's efforts to suppress any subsequent confession or admissions. The advantage of recording the interrogation can be seen in the direct quotes taken from the appellant court decision found in *State of Tennessee v. Cameron 909 S.W.2d 836* (1995) Court of Criminal Appeals of Tennessee, at Nashville.

"A review of the transcript of the interrogation could lead a trier of fact to no other Conclusion than that the interrogators were scrupulous in protecting appellant's right to cut off questions and that appellant reinitiated the conversation":

CHANCELLOR: Private Cameron, I understand now that you would like to continue to answer questions pertaining to this incident we talked about earlier, is that correct?

CAMERON: Yes sir.

CHANCELLOR: O.K., what I would like for you to do, please, before we go any further or before I will go any further, would you explain to me why, at this time, that you have changed your mind about, if I remember correctly, we stopped the interview because you wished to seek legal counsel, correct?

CAMERON: Yes sir.

CHANCELLOR: O.K. Have you had a chance to talk with legal counsel?

CAMERON: I decided that it would be best just to tell you what I know.

CHANCELLOR: O.K. Did we deny you any chance to speak to legal counsel?

CAMERON: No sir.

CHANCELLOR: Following the interview, following where we stopped with you, did we ask, did we ask you any additional questions?

CAMERON: No sir.

CHANCELLOR: We did about date of birth, place of birth, stuff like that.

CAMERON: Yes sir.

CHANCELLOR: But . . .

CAMERON: Nothing pertaining to the incident.

CHANCELLOR: O.K. While you were out, did we make you any type of promises or anything like that about continuing to answer questions?

CAMERON: Not about questions, sir, just . . . I was made the promise that I could speak to a chaplain or somebody, that was it.

CHANCELLOR: O.K. When did we say you could do that?

CAMERON: He's trying to get hold of my chaplain now, sir.

CHANCELLOR: Did you give him a request by name?

CAMERON: No request by name, sir, just a chaplain.

CHANCELLOR: O.K. Is it your wish to talk with a chaplain after the interview, before the interview, or . . .

CAMERON: Some time before this evening, sir, before bed.

CHANCELLOR: O.K. But it's not necessary that you talk to a chaplain before this interview?

CAMERON: No sir.

CHANCELLOR: O.K. Am I to understand that this is a change of heart on your part?

CAMERON: Not really a change of heart, sir, it's just I've got to tell you what happened for my benefit because I understood and was given the impression that Poe was saying that I'm doing stuff that I did not do so, I'm a good Baptist boy, I may drink and I may smoke but I want to clarify this, not only for that, but for myself, too.

(Poe is the name of the co defendant involved in the murder)

CHANCELLOR: O.K. So, even though you ask [sic] for legal counsel, you do not wish legal counsel at this time?

CAMERON: No sir, not at this time.

CHANCELLOR: O.K. You understand that you, this is part of your legal rights, that you have that right to have a counsel?

CAMERON: Yes sir.

CHANCELLOR: O.K. And you understand that you can have legal counsel present with you now if you wish.

CAMERON: Yes sir, I understand.

CHANCELLOR: And you don't wish that at this time?

CAMERON: No sir, not at this time.

CHANCELLOR: At this time, you are willing to answer questions from Detective Poston and myself?

CAMERON: Yes sir.

CHANCELLOR: O.K. What we'd like to do at this time, understand that this is completely voluntary . . .

CAMERON: Yes sir.

CHANCELLOR: O.K. And this is actually, you brought the subject up, to talk with us, is that correct?

CAMERON: Yes sir.

CHANCELLOR: O.K., we didn't ask you to come back here and talk with us again?

CAMERON: No sir.

"Having reviewed the transcript of the appellant's interviews, we find that the appellant's right to counsel was not violated". . . "Given the trial court's explicit finding on the record before us, we find that appellant's silence was *"scrupulously honored"* and that the subsequent communication was initiated by appellant. Further, we agree with the trial court's Conclusion that the totality of the circumstances supports a knowing and voluntary waiver of counsel. Thus, we find no merit in appellant's argument that his incriminating statements were obtained in violation of his right to military counsel or to civilian counsel."

The appellant court agreed with the trial judge that the suspect's statement was freely given and admissible as evidence.

The above case study clearly demonstrates the advantage of recording of the suspect interview. In this case it was not just the incriminating statements but also the extra efforts to explain the suspect's change of mind that took away any argument the defense might raise to suppress the confession. Instead it helped paint the detectives in a very positive light to the court and to the jury.

Finally, the recorded confession is very powerful evidence especially to a jury pool already exposed to various reality police and detective shows on television. The crime scene examination and the suspect interrogation are both what the jury is expecting to see because this is what they see on TV. It is also a chance for the jury to see the offender in the police interview room where they may appear to be somewhat cocky, uncaring, or arrogant as they relate what they did during the crime, which is generally a contrast with the quiet and contrite defendant sitting in court. One of the better examples was the suspect in the previous case study who made a full detailed confession describing how he and another suspect had robbed and murdered their victim, and then left the body in an open field. The interview was concluded by the suspect's particularly cold comment, "Oh well, I guess I'm not going on my date tonight, huh?" He then chuckled at his own joke which was picked up clearly on the audio tape. When his statement was played back in court, the jury saw another side to the subject who had appeared very docile and timid while sitting at the defense table. Both he and his friend were convicted and one received the death penalty.

▶ The Canvass Interview

One of the most important investigative steps is the canvass interview. Canvass interviews are conducted at the scene, places of business or employment for key actors in the case, or just about anywhere one may find witnesses, significant witnesses or suspects. The purpose is to gather information from those who may not have seen the actual incident, but we think may have heard something, seen something before or after the incident or may know something about the crime, the victim, or perpetrator(s). Some may be or become hostile, reluctant, or uncooperative witnesses, therefore the right approach could make the difference between obtaining information and walking away with nothing. Another important aspect of the canvass interview that cannot be overemphasized is the organization of the process. It is crucial that every house or apartment be contacted and where there is no one home, a follow-up procedure needs to be in place that will insure contact is made with each and every one of these absentees.

Sometimes it is helpful to utilize a predetermined list of questions as found in **Table 8-1**. As one can tell from this list every possible form of information is addressed. As this canvassing process proceeds the interviewers (detectives or uniformed officers) need to understand that when they have made contact with a "significant witness"* a formal written statement is necessary or a recorded interview that delineates the persons on the recording and the spoken words of all those. Some police departments do record all interviews regardless of where they take place, even in the field at individual homes.

Research by Wellford and Cronin shows that one of the key features of successful police departments in solving homicides is the ability of the department to conduct thorough and accurate canvass interviews.[5] One suggestion by co-author Chancellor when conducting a canvass interview in a residential neighborhood is to always look around for a sofa or easy chair, swing, or rocking chair sitting on a front porch as this generally means there was someone (usually elderly) who sat there all day long and probably saw something. This person who probably spends their time watching the happenings of their street and neighbors is generally an excellent source of information. Spend some time with that person to find out what goes on in the neighborhood or

---

*A "significant witness" is one who has specific information that relates directly to the elements of proof for the crime, what happened or information specific to the victim and or suspects.

TABLE 8-1. Canvass Questions

1. Type of structure/area (house, condo, apartment, business, vehicle, roadway, etc.)
2. Record all vehicles description(s), license plates, address where parked, etc.
3. Names and addresses on mail boxes
4. Outdoor lights—do they exist, do they work, are they working now?
5. Can the scene be seen from this address?
6. Could the occupants be seen from this address?
7. Could the suspects be seen from this address?
8. Could the suspects' vehicles be seen from this address?
9. Could the occupants hear any noises?
10. Not home/saw and heard nothing?
11. Names, DOB, address, phone numbers (day/night) of all those canvassed.
12. Description of all people. (Include visitors, guests, past occupants, work issues, etc.)
13. Has anyone left your area in the last couple of minutes/hours/days etc.?
14. Names and descriptions of all people
15. Names and descriptions of all pets
16. Are they renting or owners?
17. Did you see anything (reenact, photo must be taken, witness eyesight)?
18. Did you hear anything (reenact, witness hearing)?
19. Did they receive any visitors recently? If so when?
20. Have you talked with anybody who saw, heard or found anything?
21. Have you found items on your property?
22. Do you know how it got there?
23. Have you located any evidence?
24. What were you doing during the incident?
25. Where were you during the incident?
26. Did you go to the crime scene?
27. If so, what did you see or hear?
28. Did you talk to anyone?
29. Do you know the victim, person missing/arrested, suspect or witness?
30. How well do you know them, for how long?
31. Who else would know them?
32. Do they have any real close friends in the neighborhood/work/area?
33. Tell me everything you know about the incident. . .
34. Have you heard any rumors in the neighborhood about this incident?

(continues)

TABLE 8-1. Canvass Questions *(continued)*

35. Who else should we talk to in the neighborhood?

36. Have you seen anything suspicious or unusual during the past 6 months (or other relevant time)?

37. Has there been any other criminal activity in the area, such as, burglary, prowler, rapes, small fires, thefts, etc.?

38. What usually takes place in this area on a daily basis (all day)?

39. Who are your mail delivery people (UPS, FedEx, USPS, etc.)?

40. Does anyone have daily workers, such as maids, baby sitters, yard care, construction, gas or phone people, etc.)?

41. Any problem families in the area?

42. What other delivery people are in the area?

43. Have there been any carnivals, swap meets, roadwork, flea markets, etc.?

44. What type of vehicles and pedestrian traffic is normally in the area at the time of the incident?

45. Did you see any persons in the area that do not belong?

46. Do kids have any secret hiding places in the area?

47. Are there any of the following in the area: (vacant structures or vehicles, forts, caves, waterways or dangerous areas)?

48. Are there any adults in the area that are always playing with kids, or adults that all the kids seem to like?

49. Name the adults, kids or teens who are out all times of the day and/or night?

50. Has anyone moved into or out of the area recently?

51. Was the move planned or sudden?

52. Do you see any vehicles parked in the area that do not belong?

53. Do you see anything in the area that does not belong?

54. Have you been interviewed by the media or law enforcement officials?

55. If yes, what was their name and description?

56. What did they ask?

57. Is there anything you would like to say or ask?

58. Is there any information you feel is important that we haven't covered?

59. Have we covered everything?

60. Would you please accompany me in walking around all of your property looking for anything that may be missing or has been left on your property that does not belong to you or this house?

At the conclusion of the interview, interviewees should be thanked for their time and asked to contact the detective if they learn of any information or recall any other details.

Any positive responses should be followed up with the times, dates of observations or activities and descriptions of any person or vehicle that was observed. Based on the information determine if a more detailed written statement is needed from the interviewee.

other information about the victim or suspect. Many times the elderly are a wealth of knowledge about their area and the people who live there. This information not only reflects what happened that was unusual but also that which could be considered normal, such as the neighbor's boy friend coming by, the people that walk the street every day at the same time, delivery people, etc. The importance of canvass interviews cannot be overemphasized. Unfortunately, this is often a weak point in preliminary investigations because inexperienced detectives do not understand the value of what is really a fishing expedition to locate other witnesses. This is one of the first areas the case detective or supervisor should review and make certain every effort is made to locate other potential witnesses.

▶The Behavioral Analysis Interview (BAI)

When you have multiple people to interview, utilizing the BAI can be very helpful in narrowing the focus of your investigation. Additionally, as a possible precursor to the interview or interrogation of a suspect it can be extremely valuable. It is one of the better techniques used to assist the detective in determining whether or not a person is being truthful or deceptive in the answers provided.[6] The key to the process is that it provides benchmarks that may indicate a sign of possible deception that needs further clarification and investigation to either validate or invalidate what is being said. As written by Horvath, Blair and Buckley, the BAI is "the only questioning method that has been developed specifically to help investigators sort those who are likely to be 'guilty' from those who are not. In its typical application the BAI is a pre-interrogation interview that is used to focus interrogational effort; however, it also can be used independently in order to circumscribe investigative efforts in those cases in which there is a fixed and relatively large number of suspects."[7]

The BAI incorporates a series of questions geared to elicit responses that may cause the interviewee to provide either verbal or physical behaviors that a properly trained interviewer can evaluate as either being deceptive or truthful. Again, these are only indicators of possible deception, not evidence. The interviewer is taught to ask a set of questions while noting the verbal and physical behaviors exhibited by the interviewee. In the beginning the interviewer asks the usual demographic questions of the person to develop a baseline using neutral issues where one would expect truthfulness to prevail. The interviewer then moves on to a series of questions where the verbal and physical behavioral responses are noted.[8]

1. Start with innocuous questions, e.g. complete name, age, address, employment, etc.
   The purpose is twofold: (1) to acclimate the suspect to the interrogation environment and, (2) at the same time to afford the interrogator an opportunity to evaluate the suspect's normal verbal and non-verbal behavior patterns.
2. A "know why" question. "Do you know why you are here?" or "Do you know why we are here?"
   If the suspect is vague, naïve, or evasive in his reply, such as "I suppose you want to talk about what happened to _____", etc.

that should be viewed in a different light a blunt statement like "You're trying to find out who killed _____." The latter response is more characteristic of that of an innocent person. For the guilty, the words "kill" or "murder" will likely be too emotional and inflammatory.

3. Following the "know why" question it is generally appropriate to say: "We have interviewed a lot of people, the pieces are falling together quickly. If you have anything to do with this you should tell me."

   This offers the suspect an opportunity to readily admit involvement if that be the case. In the absence of the unlikely occurrence of a sudden admission of guilt, the interrogator's statement will nevertheless serve the purpose of inducing a display of behavioral responses suggestive of either guilt or innocence. Compare both verbal and non-verbal behavior.

4. The next step for the interrogator would be to ask a few general questions regarding the suspect's knowledge about the event, the victim, and possible suspects. If innocent, the suspect is thereby given an opportunity to divulge possibly helpful information that might not have been disclosed otherwise. On the other hand, if guilty, s/he is placed in a vulnerable defensive position and may make a remark that would be indicative of guilt or would lead to a specific line of questioning.

   The next series of questions should be asked for the purpose of evoking behavioral responses indicative of either guilt or innocence.

5. "Why do you think someone would do this?"

   The purpose of this question is to ascertain the suspect's perception of the motive for the crime. The guilty individual will be faced with a dilemma when asked this because, in essence, s/he is being asked to reveal why s/he committed a particular crime. In an effort to conceal any indication of involvement s/he may hesitate or else repeat the question as a stalling tactic in order to construct what s/he believes to be an acceptable answer. On some occasions a guilty suspect may even reveal a true motive by offering an explanation such as, "maybe there was an argument, or maybe someone was drinking or on drugs." If the guilty individual does not offer an excuse s/he usually will respond with, "I never thought about it." When someone who you knew is murdered, it is only natural to think about a possible motive or cause for the incident. In conjunction with this type of verbal response, the suspect may engage in a variety of nonverbal gestures suggestive of discomfort and concern over the question.

   The innocent individual may also make similar statements such as "I don't know why anyone would do this, she didn't have an enemy in the world", or "the killer must be insane." In making those comments, s/he would maintain direct eye contact and would probably lean forward in the chair.

6. "Of the people you and _____ knew, who would be above suspicion?"

This question is an implied invitation to the suspect to assist in the investigation. If being truthful, s/he will readily name specific individuals whom s/he feels would be above reproach or for whom s/he would vouch as not being involved in _____ death. S/he will not be afraid to eliminate certain persons from suspicion. If, on the other hand s/he is guilty, the response might be noncommittal. Guilty suspects usually do not want to eliminate any one individual from suspicion because that would tend to narrow the search down to them. They might respond, therefore, by saying, "I don't know, it's hard to say what people might do." Meanwhile, they may shift around in the chair or engage in some other type of movement, break eye contact and display other non-verbal behavior indicative of guilt.

If the suspect names himself/herself as above suspicion, no absolute reference should be drawn, but it must be noted that this type of response is more typical of the deceptive suspect than of the innocent.

7. "Who do you think might have done this?"

Innocent suspects are likely to provide name(s) where guilty suspects usually will not reveal a suspicion about anyone else, no matter how much effort is made to have them do so.

8. "What do you think should happen to the person who did this to _____?"

The innocent person will indicate some significant punishment, such as going to the penitentiary or receiving the death penalty. In contrast, if guilty, the suspect will try not to answer and might say, "It's not up to me" or "Who am I to pass judgment?" or may indicate the offender should be asked the reason for committing the crime. The underlying explanation for this evasion is that were the suspect to suggest a penalty, this would in effect be prescribing self-punishment.

9. "Did you ever think about hurting _____, even though you didn't go through with it?"

If s/he acknowledges s/he has thought about hurting the victim, it is suggestive of possible guilt. Even if the answer is "yes" s/he will probably qualify it by saying, "but not seriously". The innocent suspect will likely answer with a simple "no".

Once a suspect has admitted thoughts about hurting the victim, the interrogator should ask about the kind and frequency of such thoughts. If the thoughts went as far as plans or preparations, and especially an actual attempt, then the interrogator should become even more secure in the belief of the suspect's guilt. Another variation of this question would be, "Have you ever dreamed about doing something like this?"

10. "Would you be willing to take a polygraph test to verify that what you have told me is the truth?"

    The innocent is usually willing. The guilty begins making excuses such as they are not very reliable, etc. Caution must be exercised to avoid attaching too much significance to a person's reluctance (or perhaps even an outright refusal) to be examined.

11. "How do you think you would do on a polygraph test regarding the incident involving _____?"

    The guilty suspect will probably respond by expressing doubt about the accuracy of polygraph tests and may say, "I hope I do alright," "I don't know I'm so nervous," or other such replies. The truthful suspect will usually be very confident of the outcome.

12. "Did you discuss _____ incident with your family or close friends?"

    Experience has indicated that a guilty suspect may say "no" to this question. Not only will s/he want to conceal the fact that an event occurred for which s/he anticipated being questioned, but s/he probably also wanted to avoid actually being asked by a family member or friend any probing questions bearing on possible involvement. Justification for this failure to disclose the event to family and friends may be explained as a desire to not want to cause them any worry or concern. An innocent interviewee, however, has probably discussed the matter with a family member or friend and will acknowledge that fact to the interrogator and also may relate the reactions of those persons.

13. "If we can identify the person who did this to _____, do you think they should be given a second chance?" This is a question similar in principle to the punishment question.

    A truthful person is rarely in favor of giving a guilty person a second chance; the guilty suspect on the other hand will often indicate some type of leniency or be noncommittal about it. Again, verbal and nonverbal communication would be examined to determine the credibility of the spoken answer.

These are not all inclusive but provide a framework for other questions that may assist in determining truthfulness versus deception. These include questions such as: Do you believe anyone else might name you as a suspect? What do you think would eliminate you as a suspect? Have you ever been questioned in the past about this type of crime? Has anyone approached and/or talked to you about this incident? Would you be willing to undergo hypnosis to re-create for the interviewer where you were and what you were doing at the time of the incident? And what would be the easiest way to commit an act like this? Again, all geared towards verbal and non-verbal behaviors.

The behavior analysis interview can also be used as a great screening technique to narrow the focus of the investigation and is used frequently in the military during the initial stages of some investigations such as when sensitive items are stolen and the number of persons with potential access run into the hundreds. The technique calls for the creation of a questionnaire similar to the BAI described previously and it is then given to everyone in the unit and everyone is required to complete the form and turn it in. It is very effective not just in identifying a potential suspect but in cases with hundreds of potential suspects, it is very helpful in prioritizing later face-to-face type interviews. But, it is also surprising to see how many times when offered the chance to provide information in anonymous situations people will respond and actually provide good investigative leads, sometimes even identifying suspects or other persons who should be interviewed.

One real advantage to this approach is the likelihood the suspects will also complete the BAI questionnaire and therefore are aware that everyone in the group unit was offered the same chance to identify the suspect. What they do not know of course is who may have made the identification and what information was provided to the police. This can provide a psychological advantage to use in subsequent interviews.

This technique has been used successfully by the authors on several different investigations and its real benefit comes from the ability to use this technique in nearly every type of crime with just slight modifications to the questions.

▶ Verbal and Physical Behaviors

There are a number of verbal and physical behaviors which can be used to help evaluate the truthfulness or untruthfulness in the interviewee's statement. These are the same behaviors we observe in our children or others that we know very well, and can usually tell us when they are telling the truth or when they are not. We can often recognize an untrue story because of the physical behaviors or body language displayed when telling the story. Some of the more obvious behaviors would include an inability to look you directly in the eye, rapid eye movements, increased swallowing, a weak voice, and other displays of nervous tension. These are all "tells" or things they do unconsciously when they are lying that enables us to see through the story.

As people get older some of the more obvious tells may be consciously suppressed by people based on their experience of getting caught in a lie when they display that behavior. Essentially the more we lie, the better at lying we become and the harder it is for others to tell we are lying. Although criminals may have learned to lie much better, they still subconsciously display behaviors which if recognized by the interviewer can be used to identify a wide range of attitudes and emotions during their interview process. The behaviors may be interpreted as normal human actions, but put into the context of an interview they are seen as displays of tension, nervousness, and efforts to maintain self-control over emotions. Basics of these behavior examples include overall attitude and basic body posture while sitting in a chair. They might be sitting in an open and receptive manner leaning slightly forward towards the interviewer with their hands on their knees and the knees spread slightly; they are relaxed, appear to be cooperative, and although might start off nervous they will adjust in a short period of time. Conversely they are leaning back, legs and arms crossed, are tense, checking the time, and generally only as cooperative as necessary to get the interview over with.

There is no single physical or verbal behavior we can observe and make an assessment of interviewees as to their truthfulness. For instance, nervousness is almost universally recognized as a sign of guilt or untruthfulness, but innocent persons being questioned by the police for the first time, or about a serious offense, would naturally be expected to be nervous as well. Instead we look at a combination of several different things—*clustering*, *timing* and *consistency*. Consistency in this context refers to a series of actions and behaviors that may take place in conjunction with certain questions. *Timing*, or when these behaviors took place within the interview process, such as did these behaviors take place as the question was being asked, or as the question was being answered; or was it several minutes after the question was asked and already answered? *Consistency*, refers to how often they displayed these behaviors? Was it the same cluster of behaviors every time?

The second type of behavior is verbal behavior or what is said and the manner in which the suspect responds to the questions. Examples include the tone of the voice, the volume, the cadence or how fast or slow they answer questions, or even the use of certain phrases. Again there are certain keys to look for but there is no one manner or verbal behavior that can point to the truthfulness or untruthfulness of the interviewee. Again, it is the combination of the verbal and physical behaviors that are considered based on *clustering*, *timing*, and *consistency*.

All behavior noted within the interrogation context is meaningful and although it may seem like an unconscious response by the interviewee, no verbal or physical behaviors occur by chance. Recognizing and understanding the meaning of such behavior takes time, effort, and practice and can be very effectively used. Unfortunately many of the behaviors are not properly recognized and understood which may lead to unsuccessful interrogation results or even worse, false confessions.

Another interesting example of the importance of nonverbal behavior is demonstrated in **Case Study 8-2**. The investigator was actually keying in on the very subtle and certainly unconscious nonverbal behavior of the suspect that he had observed numerous times throughout his career. In this case, the suspect was doing his best to try and remain calm and act as if nothing was wrong. His effort however, was in stark contrast to the behaviors of the others who were irritated at being interviewed, but had nothing to fear because they

Case Study 8-2

A military investigator was working a barracks larceny and had identified six potential suspects but did not have enough information to narrow the list down any further. An older, much more experienced, investigator offered a suggestion to have all six soldiers come to the office at the same time on the same day for interviews. The appointment was made for the following day at nine o'clock in the morning and at the appropriate time all six arrived and were put into the waiting room. Once seated they were all told they were there to be questioned about the barracks theft in question and told to sit and wait for their turn. The young investigator then reported their arrival to the older investigator and was told to just let the soldiers wait. Approximately 30 minutes later the older investigator took the younger one up to look through a door window at the six soldiers in the waiting room. Five of the soldiers were talking and joking around with each other, but one was sitting by himself sleeping. The older investigator confidently identified the sleeping soldier as the suspect and instructed he be the last to be interviewed. Per instructions the sleeping soldier was the last to be interviewed and in a subsequent interrogation did confess to the crime.

were not involved. The suspect's behavior unintentionally made him stand out from the others. This tactic was used many other times by the younger investigator in the case study in his career, and almost always had the same result of identifying the correct suspect.

▶ Suspect Interview (Interrogation)

In the world of criminal investigations, there is no stronger piece of evidence than a confession or admission by an offender to a particular act. In some cases, however, so much effort is directed towards obtaining a confession that some of the more important aspects of death investigation are ignored. When the desire to obtain a confession becomes the main or only goal of the police, the risk of failure to successfully close a case becomes greater. This problem can be explained through an analogy with Babe Ruth's career. In his time, Babe Ruth was the leader in the number of home runs he hit over the years. In reality, Babe Ruth struck out more often than he hit home runs. The same can be said about detectives who rely on the confession as their main source of evidence. Clearly a confession is a highly desirable piece of evidence, but when interrogation becomes the one and only tool in your toolbox and it fails—you strike out.

Suspect interviews are also a chance to talk with offenders or suspects and get their side of events, and obtain important information such as their actions before, during, or after the event; the victim's actions before, during, or after the event; and to obtain and document their alibis. It is especially important because, the suspect interview or interrogation is usually a onetime shot. We probably only will have one opportunity to talk to the suspect, particularly if the suspect was accused by detectives of participation directly or indirectly in the death of the victim. Because of the emotional and psychological stress placed upon the suspects, there are very few persons ever willing to undergo a second police interrogation. Instead, most decline a second interview, and either obtain legal counsel or choose to remain silent.

There are several important concepts in conducting a suspect interview or interrogation. First, there is a difference between an interview and an interrogation. An interview is typically nonconfrontational and although we are seeking possible incriminating evidence it is designed to illicit information from the interviewee in a free flowing type exchange. It is conducted when the guilt or culpability of interviewees is unknown or uncertain and allows them to provide their side of the story as to what happened. During an interview, there are relatively few direct questions asked of the suspect and 80–90% of the talking is done by the offender and 10–20% of the talking is done by the detective. In this stage the detective is asking more open ended types of questions and the offender is responding; the detective exerts very little control over the process except to keep the suspect from wandering too far away from the main issue.

In contrast, an interrogation is undertaken when the culpability of the offender is fairly certain. In circumstances such as an offender caught in the act or immediately thereafter and taken into immediate custody, the police may actually start out with a direct confrontation as to participation in the event. In this instance there is little reason not to proceed directly into an interrogation of the suspect. But generally, interrogations are more successful when they start out as interviews and then move on to an interrogation. Interrogations are both strategic and goal orientated. The strategy comes from knowing the proper technique to use for the particular offender and the main goal is to obtain admissions of guilt from the suspect.

An interrogation once begun is much more direct, accusatory, and controlled—80–90% of talking is by the detective with only 10–20% by the offender. The increased talking by the detective is designed to overcome offender resistance to acknowledging participation in an event. Although we are using direct confrontation type questioning we still want to avoid harsh inflammatory terms such as "murder." Use of such terms are likely to result in an increase of the suspect's fear of legal retribution, therefore it is better to use softer terms like "caused the death" or "killed" to describe the death of the victim.

Offenders must be convinced they are in a hopeless situation and the only way to save themselves is through a confession and that the detective is willing to listen to what happened and get their side of the story. The detective's expression of compassion and sympathy towards the suspect will go a long way to overcome a suspect's resistance. Focus should be on factors leading up to the incident, rather than on the possible punishments or any negative aspects of their conduct. Once the offender has begun to make admissions or finally says, "I did it," the interrogation may revert back to the interview style with the detective asking more open ended questions and the suspect doing most of the talking. Once the offender has begun to make admissions or confess, it is not unusual for him/her to hesitate or begin to resist again, resulting in the detective returning to the interrogation style to again overcome that remaining resistance.

Timing of the Interview

There are no specific rules defining at what point in time a suspect interview is conducted. Common sense says that there is a greater chance of obtaining a confession or useful information from a suspect if s/he is interviewed shortly after the event. So when a suspect is identified or found during the hectic fast paced preliminary investigation period, an immediate suspect interview/interrogation should be attempted; even if all of the potential evidence or information is not yet available.

However, if a suspect is identified after the preliminary investigation there may not be such an immediate need to rush into an interview/interrogation. It may be more effective to slow down and take the time to do a little background research on your suspect, and make certain you are familiar with all of the case facts, witness testimony, and evidence. The reasoning is, after a few days the emotion of the event, when the suspect is at his/her weakest, will have passed. Suspects will have a chance to calm down; perhaps establish a false alibi, or even destroy evidence that could tie him/her to the event. Since the suspect is going to be better prepared, we need to be better prepared as well.

Preparation includes understanding not just the general and specific facts of the crime, including witness statements, results of crime scene examination, and any forensic evidence recovered or already examined, but also a thorough criminal history check to determine any criminal history. Without such prior information the detective does not know which offender statements are consistent or inconsistent with other witnesses or evidence or what experience the suspect may have with police interrogations. An offender's experience becomes very important because they tend to follow a behavioral pattern especially in responses to interrogation techniques. This information is extremely helpful because it gives the detective an idea of possible tactics to approach offenders in the manner they will feel most comfortable with and therefore more likely to talk and thereby give information and hopefully confess.

It is also important to know exactly what information we are attempting to gain during the interview/interrogation. This includes not just the various legal elements of the crime, or to seek admissions or a confession, but also to hear the offenders' versions of events and what evidence or information they have to show they were not involved, to document any alibis, or listen to their justification for their actions. Possible justification generally revolves around issues of self defense or defense of others. From an ethical standpoint it's our goal to establish the truth of what happened and we should be looking just as hard to exonerate the innocent as we do to identify and prosecute the guilty. Therefore, we should also be prepared to listen and see where the interview will go and what information the suspect is going to provide, and not immediately launch into an interrogation.

Another major problem with offender interrogation comes from detectives that are not willing to invest enough time and effort into the interview or interrogation. This is another example of over reliance on the confession and the impatience of the detective to outlast the offender. These interrogations may take hours to overcome the offender's resistance to admitting or confessing to the crime. Therefore, we have to be flexible with the amount of time we may have to expend to successfully complete the interview.

Rights Advisement

There are certain basic constitutional rights that apply when conducting a suspect interview or interrogation. Basically these are the rights established in the Fifth and Sixth Amendments, essentially the right against self incrimination and to remain silent, and guaranteeing the right to counsel.

Each state (and the federal government) has its own rules relating to rights advisement and when the right to counsel applies and some states and jurisdictions are more restrictive than others. For instance, the U.S. military is very restrictive, requiring a formal rights advisement and waiver of rights at the point the person of interest is first considered a suspect or if the purpose of an interview is to collect incriminating information. Other federal agencies rely heavily on a *non custodial interview*, that is they interview suspects or other persons of interest prior to arrest or taking them into custody. Generally, there is an assumed right to counsel as soon as a suspect is taken into custody or when they are no longer free to leave on their own.

Regardless of the state requirement, a suspect must be informed of the constitutional right to remain silent and not answer any police questions, and the right to legal counsel prior to and during questioning. This rights advisement is more commonly known as "reading the Miranda rights." To advise a suspect of these rights is called "Mirandizing." This rights advisement is based on the Supreme Court decision of *Miranda v. Arizona*, in which the requirement to advise a suspect of their right to remain silent was formalized in 1966 by the Supreme Court. After the Miranda decision police departments across the country were certain no suspect would ever again speak with them and their most powerful evidence, a suspect confession, would be lost. In actuality the vast majority of suspects continue to waive their rights and volunteer to talk to police. So, there is no reason to take shortcuts or avoid the rights advisement process. Carefully documenting the advisement and any waiver will take away potential defense arguments to suppress any incriminating statements or evidence.

Interview Outcomes

There are basically three possible outcomes at the conclusion of a suspect interview. The suspect will make denials, make admissions, or will confess involvement. Many times what we end up with is a combination of all three. From an investigative perspective all three of these outcomes can be effectively used in building our case.

Denials

The suspect might deny any involvement in the death or criminal event. For many suspects a complete denial is not unexpected—and regardless of the interview techniques employed or the strength of the evidence of guilt, some suspects are unwilling to make any admissions to participation in any criminal act. This is often the case with career or street criminals who know from previous experience, or have learned from others, ways to defeat a police investigation. For detectives who rely solely on the confession as the main source of evidence, encountering such suspects is problematic to resolving the investigation.

Although frustrating, a denial statement can be as valuable as a confession. Generally when offenders deny knowledge or participation in a criminal event, they will counter any evidence presented by the police with evidence of their own. This evidence is usually some type of "impossibility"; that is, for some reason it was impossible for them to commit the offense in question. One impossibility may be an alibi which establishes their presence at another location other than the crime scene. A person cannot be in two places at the same time, so if they can establish that they were at some other location during the commission of a crime, it would be impossible for them to have committed the crime.

There is a wide variety of potential "impossibilities" such as being physically unable to commit the crime; not having direct access to the scene or the victim; or not having a weapon or other means to commit the crime. One of the weaker types of impossibilities that we see during denials is the claim of a lack of motive to murder the victim. We see this expressed in such statements as "Why would I kill her?", "I had no reason to harm/kill her", "But we loved each other", and other similar statements. Some of these statements are probably true for certain people, but many times they are said automatically as if the suspect can convince another person of his/her innocence because s/he cared for the victim.

Case Study 8-3

A husband was being questioned about the death of his wife he allegedly found murdered inside their house when he returned home late one night. During his interview he provided a detailed alibi as to his whereabouts on the evening in question, including the names of several people that were present with him some distance away from the house during the time of the murder. When questioned about the relationship with his wife or possible motives, he adamantly denied any involvement with her death relating to the police how well they got along in their marriage and how much he was in love with his wife. He even claimed, "The only thing we have ever argued about in our entire marriage was who loved the other one more." The comment of course was not just self promoting, but flies in the face of reality as anyone who is or ever was married can testify. The comment actually caused the police to take a much closer look at the husband. Investigation determined the death actually took place before he left the house that night and the alibi he tried to establish was immaterial. He was charged and later convicted of her murder.

All of these types of self-serving statements are an attempt to demonstrate for the police that there was no reason or motive for the suspect to have killed the victim or be otherwise involved in the crime.

In cases of interpersonal conflicts, having the suspect describe the relationship with the victim can be very revealing as **Case Study 8-3** demonstrates.

Admissions

An admission is when the suspect agrees with certain elements of the investigation but generally denies other aspects. For instance, the offender may admit to being in the area or even being with the victim at some time before, during, or after the incident; but denies any participation or culpability in the actual criminal offense or death of the victim. In cases of multiple-offender crimes the suspect may admit being with the other suspects before or after the event, or acknowledge they were in the area at the time.

Other examples would be admitting to ownership of the weapon used, or possession of some pieces of evidence, even knowingly receiving the evidence after the crime, but again denial of any direct participation in the main crime.

Like denials, admissions can be very useful in developing your case. For instance, if you are dealing with a case involving multiple suspects and one particular suspect admits to being present with the other suspects, then you have established or verified who your suspects actually are or could be. If the suspect admits to being present at the scene before, during, or after the crime or death of the victim, then you have a chance to ask some very detailed questions as to what s/he saw, heard, or did. Even if s/he denies participation in the event, an admission of being present at the scene eliminates the requirement to find other physical evidence or witnesses that place the offender there. The best example of the value of admissions is found during the investigation of rape and sexual assaults. Quite often the offender will admit to having sexual intercourse with the victim but claim the act was consensual. From an investigative perspective we no longer have to prove that the suspect was at the scene with the victim, or if there was actual penetration—the offender has admitted it. The question now becomes one of consent.

Confessions

A true confession is not just an admission, but rather a complete agreement in all of the key elements of the event. It is important to remember, it is not enough to merely obtain an admission, a true confession should include, in as much detail as possible, the suspect's activity, movements, and contacts; before, during, and after the commission of the crime. It should also contain information that only someone who committed the crime would know. Unlike the confession in **Case Study 8-4**.

The confession was taken and accepted by a large and experienced American police department. It was obtained after the suspect's arrest for the murder of his live-in girlfriend some three weeks before. At the time the department was very happy with the result and felt they had a good offender confession. But was this a true confession? The problems with the statement are self evident. What offense was actually committed and when? Tuesday, the offender cites, but which Tuesday—there are generally four of them every month, and about 52 of them a year? What was the criminal offense he admitted to? Kilt? Was this an admission to a criminal act or some offense against Scottish national dress code? Completely unanswered are a myriad of other questions: Where did the crime take place? How did you do it, why did you do it, what did you use, what did you do with the body? Was anyone else involved? Where are the weapons or other items used during the commission of the crime? What is missing are facts about the incident that only the perpetrator or police would know.

By not asking these questions we allow the defense to present their own explanations or excuses, and possibly show the police department in a negative light regarding the thoroughness of the investigation. An investigator

Case Study 8-4

The following is a complete and accurate transcript of the entire written confession provided by the offender to the police: "She came home on Tuesday and started in on me again. It pissed me off so I kilt her."

might ask, "Would this short one sentence confession be well received or badly received by a jury?

A proper confession recounts the activities of the offender and any other participants through all steps of the crime—before, during, and after. Whenever required the detective should walk the suspect through the elements of the crime one at a time to make certain there is no possible way to misinterpret what is being said. The following is a simulated interview between a suspect and a detective where these specific points are covered during the question and answer phase of the interrogation. Imagine the suspect has already admitted to killing his wife; the detective is now trying to get more specific details of the event.

Detective: How did you kill your wife?

Suspect: I shot her with my gun.

Detective: Did you intend to shoot her?

Suspect: Yes.

Detective: Where did you shoot her?

Suspect: I shot her in the chest.

Detective: How far away was the pistol from your wife when you fired it?

Suspect: It was right up against her shirt.

Detective: Are you certain she died as a result of that injury?

Suspect: Oh yes, she was dead, I checked her out after she fell to the ground and started bleeding.

Detective: Where were you at when you shot your wife?

Suspect: We were in the kitchen of her house.

Detective: After you shot your wife what did you do?

Suspect: I just got in my truck and drove back to my apartment. I threw the gun in the fish pond to try and get rid of it.

Dectective: Where is the pond located?

Suspect: Next to my house.

Detective: We found a gun in the fish pond next door to your house, here's a picture of it—is this gun?

Suspect: Yep that's it.

Detective: How do you recognize it?

Suspect: Well, a 9 mm Taurus and those are the hand grips I put on.

Detective: You threw the gun in the pond so the police would not find it?

Suspect: Yeah.

Detective: OK, did you actually plan to kill your wife?

Suspect: Yes, I'd been thinking about it for a number of weeks. I wanted to make it look like someone tried to rob her and then shot her in the process.

Detective: Why did you kill your wife?

Suspect: I needed the $100,000 from the insurance money.

Detective: What did you need the money for?

Suspect: I have a lot of bills, I'm about to lose my truck and house. That money could have paid for them both and I'd be OK financially again.

Detective: Who is the last person you saw before you went to your wife's house and when was it?

Suspect: My girlfriend Sally. I left around 2 p.m.

Detective: Who is the first person you saw after leaving your wife's house after you killed her?

Suspect: My girlfriend and John Smith, my neighbor in the apartment next door. They were standing in the apartment parking lot talking.

In the above rather rough dialog, is part of the question and answer phase of the interrogation. This takes place after the suspect has basically made strong admissions or has confessed to the crime and now the detectives want to clarify certain points of the crime. The suspect is now essentially providing the necessary details to show: (1) the death of his wife was a planned event, thus a case of premeditated murder; (2) he himself caused her death by shooting her; (3) he believed she was dead when he left the scene; (4) he attempted to destroy or otherwise hide evidence; (5) he wanted the police to think it was a robbery; (6) existence of witnesses who saw him before and after the incident; and (8) recognition of the gun which later could be tied to the pond and to the victim through forensic examination.

A good confession will also include as much detail as possible regarding the offender's own actions and interaction with the victim or anyone else before, during, and after the event as well any steps the offender may have taken to dispose of evidence, or otherwise cover up any participation. We must always look for evidence that only the actual perpetrator would know. In the simulated interview the suspect says he put the gun to the victim's shirt and pulled the trigger. Although it may be common knowledge that the victim was shot in the chest, only the real perpetrator could know the gun was actually held up against the chest when it was fired. This could be verified through forensic examination of the shirt. This type of information, that only the person involved in the crime would know, makes a confession valuable and believable. It also diminishes the credibility of later claims of a false confession.

Regardless of denials or limited admissions, if an offender is talking, s/he is providing information about the crime and important investigative leads that need to be followed up. Rather than focusing only on obtaining a confession, gather as much detailed information as possible from the suspect.

Seldom do suspects immediately confess to participation in the crime. Instead the suspect is more likely to initially deny involvement; then make some minor admissions, but continue to deny the more serious aspects of the crime. Eventually, minor admissions lead to major admissions, and then finally to confessions to the crime. The most likely final result of most suspect interrogations is a combination of denial, admission, and confession, wherein the suspect denies certain things, admits to certain things, and confesses to certain things. For instance, a suspect accused of sexually molesting and murdering a child may continue to deny any sexual molestation of the child, but admit to possessing child pornography and then killing the child for other reasons. Although it may seem like splitting hairs, in this example the offender might be more willing to confess to murder, than to be seen as a child molester, considered to be the lowest of the low by prison society.

During the interrogation process there are a few themes we can employ to encourage the suspects to confess known as *rationalization, projection,* and *minimization.* These are also referred to as ego-defense mechanisms because they allow offenders an opportunity to offer an explanation of the event or tell their side of the story in the most favorable light to themselves. This is especially important because the detective must overcome the offender's resistance and fear of arrest, prosecution, and punishment.

Rationalization is basically a face saving opportunity for offenders, allowing them to present or to offer excuses to justify their actions. The process of rationalization allows the transference of guilt from the offender onto someone or something else or to downplay personal involvement. The rationalization used by the offender or offered by the detective, does not have to make sense to anyone other than the offender. Some of the best examples of rationalization come from pedophiles who often maintain their sex with children does not actually cause any harm to the victim; or claiming they are only doing so because they want to educate the child in understanding the joys and benefits of healthy sex. The sex act with the victim was not forced, but rather the victim's own desire to have rough sex; or the knife the victim says was present at the scene was merely a knife they always had and he simply removed it so they would not be accidentally injured. The concept of a sexually aroused man not being able to control himself or not being able to stop once things got started is another good example.

Other rationalizations would include the attempt to save the victim needless suffering or the action was based on self defense, or based on the particular circumstances, the offender was left with no choice but to kill the victim.

Projection is basically allowing offenders to excuse their own misconduct by projecting the blame or fault onto someone or something else. In this case the offender or the detective may offer attempts to blame the victim for the incident, claiming for instance, the victim's own actions actually instigated the incident. Alcohol or drug usage is a very popular excuse for criminal conduct because the suspect is able to blame bad judgment on the intoxicant, which caused them to do something totally out of character. Projecting blame onto co-conspirators, bad living conditions, being poor, under educated, or on society are often very effective. In some extreme cases offenders may also offer excuses such as any number of mental or psychological disorders.

In the case of multiple offenders it is almost automatic for them to each blame the other. In any case, the offender attempts to frame the story around his/her innocence and another's guilt.

Minimization basically allows the detective or the offender to minimize the criminal actions or guilt by playing down the seriousness of the crime and the offender's culpability. Examples would include suggestions such as the victim did not suffer, or the offender didn't really plan to kill the victim, but had to when the victim resisted. Offering a chance for offenders to claim the incident was a one-time bad idea, or the result of a bad temper or the result of the victim making them angry are also effective. Other themes include a case of things getting out of hand and going too far, or the actions were just a momentary, spur of the moment lapse and not some premeditated act or pattern of behavior.

Minimization is basically an attempt to offer offenders some moral relief over their actions by implying many other people have done the same thing they did or others have done far worse. Examples in sexual assault cases would include offering a statement that almost every other guy has used some amount of force during sex and most women just accept that. After all, 99 out of 100 women would never have made a report in the first place. This theme offers a situation where the offender was simply unlucky because the victim was so sensitive rather than implying they actually did something wrong.

Remember, whether these themes are initially presented by offenders or detectives, they are used as a way to explain what happened, or make suspects feel better about what they have done rather than to secure an admission to an actual criminal act. Once these themes are accepted, they are expanded upon and will eventually lead to admissions and hopefully full confessions. All three may be used in the course of the interrogation; many times the detective may have to change to different themes if the offender does not appear to be accepting the defense mechanism.

These themes present detectives with a golden opportunity to develop rapport and in some cases build trust in offenders by appearing as if they are agreeing, supporting, or looking out for the offender or trying to present their side of the incident. By focusing on the resolution of the situation, and their future rather than punishment or consequences, offenders are often more willing to accept that it is in their best interest to confess to the crime. Which theme is going to be successful is dependent upon several factors including the type of offender, age, intelligence, maturity, criminal experience, and the exact criminal acts committed.

Sympathy and Empathy

One of the themes that that often successful is the concept of sympathy or empathy with the victim, wherein the criminal is essentially made to feel bad or guilty over the actions against the victim, particularly if the victim is young or old, or happened to be an innocent bystander. This approach is very effective with most criminals, but generally not so when dealing with sexual offenders who killed as a result of a rape or other sexual assault. This is because typical sexual offenders have no sympathy or empathy for anyone other than themselves. So the concept they should somehow feel bad over what they have done to the victim is not going to resonate with them; the only sympathy or empathy they will really respond to is when it is directed towards themselves.

It is important to remember these rationalizations, projections, minimizations, or other excuses do not have to make sense to us. They only have to make sense to offenders who will often grasp for any possible explanation other than they killed someone.

Alibis

An alibi is evidence or an explanation offered by the suspect to show s/he was not at the scene at the time the offense was committed and should never be accepted at face value. Once an alibi is accepted we have basically eliminated that person from involvement, so it is extremely important we exercise caution in this area. Therefore, each and every alibi should be checked out thoroughly. If a suspect claims s/he was at a particular place or with a particular person at a particular time we must refute or validate that alibi. As a general rule, three independent means should be used to validate the alibi before the suspect can be cleared, but there are some important considerations to remember in this process.

1. An alibi provided by a relative is considered only half as reliable as that of other persons. This is based on the fact relatives often provide alibis to their family members whether they are true or not. Therefore, using the rule of thumb of three independent sources to validate an alibi, if the wife or husband of the suspect provides an alibi for the suspect, this does not count as 1 source, but only 1/2 of one source. An additional 2½ sources are needed to completely eliminate the suspect.

    In many cold cases that have been reopened the new suspect turns out to be the one that had been eliminated too quickly and without proper validation very early on in the case.

2. The alibi must cover the same time period as the event itself or other critical aspect of the crime. Regardless of an alibi before, or an alibi after the event, it is the suspect's whereabouts during the event that is important.

    In Case Study 8-3 the husband had established a very credible alibi for his presence out of town and several hours away. However, it was determined that the wife was actually murdered before the husband left the house, thus making his efforts at establishing an alibi worthless. It almost never matters where the person was before or after the event, but rather where they were during the event.

3. A credible and documented alibi may only mean the particular suspect was not present at the time of the death or criminal offense; it does not necessarily mean s/he did not cause the death or was not otherwise involved in the death somehow. A good historical example

is the St. Valentine's Day Massacre in Chicago. It has been well established that Al Capone orchestrated the mass murder against his criminal rivals. However, at the time the murders were taking place in Chicago, he was conveniently out of state sitting with several well known political figures who could unquestionably verify his whereabouts at the time of the murders. The fact he was out of state did not change the fact he was involved, only that he could not have directly participated in the homicide.

With modern communications via cell phones and text messaging it is quite possible for a suspect to be out of state, even out of the country, and still be actively involved in planning or participating in a homicide or other crime.

There are some instances when it is very difficult to validate the whereabouts of a suspect, for instance, someone who lives alone and claims they stayed home all night and had no contact with anyone else. Canvass interviews of neighbors, possible internet usage, and telephone records may have to be checked, and in some cases a polygraph offered as a means to validate the alibis. In cases where we just cannot validate the alibi, we may have to use other means to eliminate the suspect such as forensic evidence or motive and means. Unless another suspect is eventually positively identified, this person should remain on a possible suspect or person of interest list.

▶ After the Interview

Regardless of the outcome of the interview—denials, admissions, or confession it is wise to obtain a signed written statement. Since this is the one time the suspect has a chance to tell his/her side of the story or at least to provide evidence as to why s/he is not involved, this statement is very valuable evidence. After the suspect has a chance to retain legal counsel or decides to change his/her story or alibis, a written record of what was initially told to police becomes very important, especially if the initial statement is far different from subsequent statements or other evidence provided by the suspect.

If s/he appears in court with a completely different story or denies making earlier statements to police, (or even worse, alleging the statement was obtained through some type of police misconduct) the question becomes "When was the suspect telling the truth—during the initial statement to police or after being indicted or charged with a crime?"

The case or investigation is not over if detectives obtain a denial, admission, or confession. In fact in many circumstances, the results of a suspect interview will dramatically increase the number of investigative leads. Each statement made by the suspect whether admission, denial, or confession must be verified through investigative means.

Once an offender has made admissions or confessed, it is also a good idea as part of the continuing interview to ask the offender to prepare a rough sketch of the crime scene as s/he recalls. We would be interested in the route taken to the scene, movement or activity at the scene, and the escape route. In some circumstances it might be necessary to have the offender prepare several different sketches. In the above simulated statement the offender should be given a paper and pencil to sketch the route he took from the scene back to his house and identify the pond where he tossed the gun. At the crime scene the suspect should be asked to mark a spot where he and his wife were when he shot her. Then write in adjacent to the X, "This is where I stood when I shot my wife. This is where my wife was standing." At the pond, have him place an X at the spot where he threw the gun into the water. Adjacent to the X ask him to write in his own handwriting, "This is where I stood when I threw my pistol into the pond."

Upon the completion of the sketch, it should be signed and dated by the offender and witnessed by the detective. There, in at least two different places he confessed or made an admission to the crime. The value of this exercise is the sketch is really another form of a written confession; prepared in the suspect's own hand and actually helps to demonstrate the voluntary nature of the statement and interrogation process. It is also fantastic evidence to be able to present to the jury.

▶ The Prescriptive Interview

In the realm of interview and interrogation you can never obtain too much information. We feel it is important to include information from the Crime Classification Manual by Douglas, et al.[9] In Chapter Three, "Prescriptive Interviewing: Interfacing the Interview and Interrogation with Crime Classification," it is suggested by the authors that one who chooses to use the prescriptive interview techniques should be certain to interface the interview with what is provided in the manual.

Preparing for this type of interview involves an extensive investigative effort especially considering you may only get one chance to interview/interrogate the suspect. The better prepared you are the higher the likelihood of obtaining an admission and/or confession. With cold cases there is absolutely no reason to even initiate an interview with any suspects until you have successfully prepared yourself by following these four steps:

1. Data Collection—Comprehensive and meticulous data collection system must be implemented to reconstruct each element of the crime. This is a principal factor in determining that all the elements have been met as described by law.
2. Assessment—Assessing the relevancy of the data to the crime is required. Objectively judge the value of the information and if it can apply to the elements of the crime.

3. Analysis—Detectives must do more than just determine that each element is intact. This requires organizing and dissecting the information, thereby observing the complex web of interrelated components of the crime. For example, I may "see" a set of stairs before me; however, I observe that there are exactly sixteen steps covered with a distinctive color and quality of carpet. In addition, the carpet is soiled and cluttered with specific toys and items of clothing, suggesting the presence of children of corresponding ages. The condition of the carpet and disarray of clothing and toys may suggest the house-cleaning habits of the owners and even imply an economic stratum. It is during this phase of preparation that meaning and substance are assigned to the (criminal) act and the actor. Armed with this enhanced understanding, the fourth step is applied.

4. Theorizing—Theorizing assumes the challenges of identifying the motivation underlying the criminal thought process and reconstructing the crime. It attempts to mentally crystallize the interwoven thread or current of thought that the criminal mind uses to justify his crime and general behavior.

The preparatory phase of the interview is preeminent in conducting a successful interview. There is no substitute for this principle, and it should never be sacrificed for convenience or expediency. Preparation is paramount to success.

It was stated that the interfacing of the prescriptive interview process with the crime classification is paramount. Classifying the crime (utilizing the manual) integrates all preparatory steps of the interview. It is the precursor to humanizing offenders and revealing their thought process. It includes the accumulation and assimilation of data compiled during the investigative phase for the purpose of conducting a criminal investigative analysis (also referred to as a psychological profile). It is here where the criminal investigative analyst will review and analyze area photos, maps, sketches, crime scene photos, victimology, and all incident-related reports to formulate a profile of the criminal personality. A close examination of this information will begin to reveal behavioral characteristics of the offender, thereby exposing major personality traits.

The process applied by the criminal investigative analyst may suggest the cause or motive for the crime and offer implications of the offender personality as suggested by the method selected to commit the crime. An assessment of the offender's behavioral patterns can unmask an undercurrent of emotional deficiencies and needs manifested by the offender. An improved understanding of or insight into these emotional deficiencies and needs can provide a solid foundation for the interviewer. This foundation will support the strategic construction of tailored approaches and appeals to prevail upon the offender.

Consider, for example, the advantage interviewers would have if they had in their possession the following personality characteristics of the suspect that were extracted from the analysis of a disorganized lust murder:

- Of average intelligence and a high school or college dropout
- Probably unemployed or blue-collar, unskilled occupation
- Financially dependent on a domineering female
- A previous criminal record of assault-related offense
- Probable voyeuristic activities
- Probable pornography interest and collection
- Alcohol or drugs exhibited in his behavior
- Keen sense of fantasy
- Inability to carry out preplanned activities
- Difficulty in maintaining personal relationships with a female for an extended period of time
- A need to dominate and control relationships
- Sexually inexperienced
- Never married or a brief, combative marital relationship
- Sadistic tendencies
- Controlled aggression but rage or hatred
- Confused thought process
- Feels justified in his behavior while feeling no remorse or guilt
- Defiant of authority
- Low self-esteem
- Frustration from lack of direction or control of life
- Combustive temper
- Impulsive
- Deep anxiety

Douglas et al. go on to write that while considering these characteristics in concert with investigative activities confirming some of the biological and descriptive information provided, an interviewer can begin to observe the offender. The interviewer may recognize and exploit certain personality characteristics and associated emotional deficiencies. In pondering the offender's behavior, thought processes, and aligned emotions, the interviewer is now better prepared to design various approaches to conform to the offender's personality.

This process assists interviewers in stepping out of their world and into the foreign territory of the adversary. If the offender decides to cooperate, it will be because s/he can justify the decision from his/her perspective. There is only one frame of reference that is important in the offender's decision-making process: his/her own. If the interviewer successfully influences the offender to conform, it is because an alliance was forged in the offender's territory.

Although prescriptive interviewing is not a panacea for the challenges in obtaining confessions, it is one more precision instrument to be used in swaying the balance of justice in society's favor. A prescriptive interview will enhance law enforcement's efforts to persuade serious offenders to escort us under the water into the caverns of their torrential minds, surrender their secrets, and expose their culpability. Douglas concludes by writing that it is hoped that the successful use of this method will both promote the cause of justice and deter effects of recidivism.

▶Murder Typologies and Interrogation Strategies[10]

As a prelude to murder typologies and interrogation strategies it is necessary to mention that there is obviously a difference between "hot" and "cold" case investigations as it pertains to interviews and interrogations. Every sound interview should have as much background information on the person being interviewed as is possible. When it comes to suspects this is even more important. In a hot case, little background information is known prior to victim and witness interviews, putting the interviewers at a disadvantage. Time is frequently limited and the pressure is on to interrogate and get that confession. As a result many interviews are conducted without adequate knowledge of the suspect's background, beliefs, behavioral traits or strong and vulnerable areas that could be challenged.

Cold cases present different problems, but also some advantages over hot cases. Due to the time that has passed, the interviews of witnesses can be a challenge to the investigators as they ask people to recall events of years gone by. The advantage, however, is that with the passage of time these witnesses might be more likely to discuss the event than they were 10 years ago. Relationships have changed, people have moved and it is now less threatening and easier. Regarding the interrogation of a suspect, the passage of time is a great advantage to the detective. After the passage of time, the detective has likely obtained all the background information that possibly exists; will know the strengths and vulnerabilities of the suspect; and will know how to approach the suspect, all without the pressures that come to bear in a "hot" case that needs an immediate resolution. Furthermore, due to the passage of time the suspect may feel more confident and comfortable that you had not questioned him/her earlier as a suspect. With cold case investigations, time is on your side.

We have learned that the investigative process consists of three major components—the physical, the informational, and the behavioral. In the behavioral component we need to concern ourselves with (1) pre-offense behavior—stressors that may have pushed the perpetrator over the edge; (2) peri-offense or crime behavior—behavior exhibited by the perpetrator at the crime scene; and (3) post-offense behavior—actions the perpetrator took in the following hours or days after the crime. To help put this in perspective, four typologies will be described along with possible interrogation strategies for each type. (Appendix B is an example of the three components demonstrated by an actual case.) Use the guidelines for interrogation as explained here for the type of personality that you suspect is involved. Remember that these are guidelines, not absolutes.

Research by Keppel and Walter[11] provides a personality type classification model (relating to sexual murders in particular but can be applied to other types of crime as well)—Power Assertive, Power Reassurance, Anger Retaliatory, and Anger Excitation. Certain interrogation techniques are suggested for each type in order to maximize the results. Developing a good suspectology (almost identical to the victimology) is extremely helpful as it puts the investigator into the right position to understand where a suspect may be coming from and gives the investigator the advantage for the interview. So if at all possible, gather as much information as possible about this person prior to the interview. Having this knowledge (suspectology) in hand should lead to a productive interrogation. Keeping in mind the prescriptive interview methodology suggested above, the following procedures are suggested by Keppel and Walter.

Power-Assertive Type (PA)

Characteristics—Rape is planned whereas murder is not. Offender uses aggression and demands to justify his manhood, uses intimidation to maintain a machismo appearance. He targets his own age group and leaves an organized crime scene. He will bring the weapon to the scene and leaves with it. He will also set boundaries to his actions (e.g. he will not entirely remove the head). No mutilation of the body, but may see signs of beating, cutting, strangling.

Who is he?—He's domineering. He takes pride in his image as a man and is likely to be well built. He may drive a pick-up truck or sports vehicle. He's antisocial and a school dropout. If he has a military record, it is likely poor. He'll brag about his crime in a bar for glory points. He has a phobia of being labeled a "pervert." He'll use weapons such as guns, knives, and ropes.

Interrogation Strategies—Approaches: Silent, Fishing, Direct, Accomplice, Degrading, Blame, Pride. The interrogator should establish and maintain control. Challenge the suspect's manhood. Suggest that real men own up to their mistakes, enter prison as a man. Allow suspect to brag. Perhaps, provide suspect with a chair that is lower in height than yours.

The Achilles Heel for the PA is the acquisition and demonstration of the power image. That is, he wants to be viewed as a variant of John Wayne. Dependent upon the amount of threat presented in the interview session, he may attempt to bluff his way through with exaggerated machismo behaviors. Conversely, if he is situationally intimidated by the setting, he will hide the bluff and defer to the power of the police. When opening the interview, you should ask him why he is being interviewed and/or polygraphed. Ask him to explain what the accusations are against him. Ask him about his background, including; age, work history, friendship patterns, group loyalties, values, beliefs, and sexual orientation and behaviors. Although one needs to control for grandiosity and exaggeration, let him brag about his manliness.

With the promise that you will revisit the issues more in detail later, let him give a brief overview of the offense. Upon completion of the review, you should start through the story again with complete detail being given. While doing so, you should jump questions in and out of order. (It is far more difficult to lie under these conditions.) Start showing him inconsistencies in his story. Point out that you would like to believe him man to man, but his role is being challenged. Therefore, if he can explain this/that, there is the potential of being redeemed. (In brief, you are playing the ego games by challenging his masculinity. That is, by locking him into the masculine standards which were implicitly agreed upon earlier, you are corralling him into a small fenced paddock. The next thing is to only open one door for him to walk out unscathed. That is, he needs to admit the truth, like a real man!)

If and when the suspect becomes attenuated and caught up into saving his power image, it might be the time to use one of several approaches to force him into the final gate.

1. Silent Approach—simple eye contact without verbalization
2. Fishing Approach—"I'd like to hear how you planned it."
3. Direct Approach—"You didn't mean to shoot the grocer, or did you? You were having sex and didn't mean to choke her to death, or did you?"
4. Accomplice Approach—fear of partner making a deal, and shifting the blame on them
5. Blame Approach—stupid errors by accomplice
6. Pride Approach—smart crime . . . it took brains to do it
7. Degrading Approach—"Somebody had to do the thinking for you!"
8. We All Make Mistakes Approach—"However, at the end of the day, are you going to be a man or a mouse? Sometimes, a man makes mistakes and stands up and takes the medicine. At least, under these conditions, he has still saved his manhood."

Note: Often, the good/bad cop routine works with this type of offender. However, it can certainly be successful with a single interviewer.

Power-Reassurance Type (PR)

Characteristics—The offender lives in a scripted fantasy world and feels threatened if reality breaks into the fantasy. He acts out fantasies for verbal reassurance from victim. Rape is planned whereas murder is not. Murder is typically a result of a failed rape which leads to overkill and post mortem mutilation. Sexual activity usually occurs post mortem. You would often see wounds to the breasts and groin/thigh areas. The body may have insertions. He avoids women in his own age group and targets those older or younger and chooses familiar locations. He commits attacks during nightly hours and leaves a disorganized crime scene.

Who is he?—He's a loner and a "weirdo." He is likely to conduct stalker activities prior to the attack. He is concerned about his sexual competence and seeks reassurance and the need to justify his power. If he has a military record, the offender was likely a passive soldier who took orders well. Weapon of choice may be clothing, fists, and knives.

Interrogation Strategies—Approaches: Statement, Identification, Social, Religious. Suspect is concerned about power and is impulsive. He'll justify the crime by blaming the victim. You may try approaching suspect by arranging chairs closer together. Like the PA, the PR is concerned about power. However, he wants unconditional affirmation through fantasy driven behaviors. Generally, this type of offender tends to be somewhat disorganized and impulse driven. (Although he may have the plan for the offense in his mind, the particular moment and victim may be opportunistic.) Often, since the offender has already justified the crime in his own mind, when it goes awry, it becomes the fault of the victim. (Nevertheless, do not assume that the crime was unsuccessful for him.)

For the PR, the chairs should be arranged so that the interviewer can close in and touch the suspect. That is, after moderating the suspect's emotional temperature, a review of the facts in chief, the interviewer may need to show care and understanding for the offender. In doing so, the offender can show understanding how the victim helped to mislead him into the situation. The following methods may be helpful in facilitating the PR to admission:

1. Statement Approach—"You just borrowed the items . . . not really stealing them." "It sounds like (the victim) was coming on and tantalizing you."
2. Identification Approach—"I would have done the same thing! Man, when a girl comes on to you!"
3. Social Approach—"Lots of people do what you did. Research has shown that 97% of men feel that women who lead them on . . . need and should be hit!"
4. Religious Approach—"There are no limits to forgiveness."

Anger-Retaliatory Type (AR)

Characteristics—Rape and murder are planned. Typically, the offender commits the attack in a familiar location. The crime is driven by a need to seek revenge against a woman of power or a substitute through anger, sparking a burst of violence. He targets women in the same age group or slightly older. It is a frenzied attack. He leaves a disorganized scene.

Who is he?—He's impulsive, self-centered, and pathologically attached to women. He usually has superficial relationships and becomes estranged from marriage or has a history of domestic abuse. If he has a military record, it may show a discharge for behavioral issues. He usually attacks in areas where he's familiar.

Interrogation Strategies—Approaches: Have knowledge of his history and past relationships. Allow suspect to talk about himself and interrupt him with questions. Bring up women from his past that may have controlled him, which he'll have resentment against. Suspect feels as though he was wrongly victimized by female. Seeks revenge and feels no guilt. He may have substituted a woman rather than attack the actual female figure that "wronged" him.

The critical factor for this type is a catharsis of emotion acted out onto the intended (or substitute) victim. The perpetrator imagines that he has been unduly "victimized" which justifies a retaliatory response. When acting out the crime, the amount of angst is somewhat measured by the pre and post mortem activity. When his appetite has been sated, he emotionally cools and leaves the victim in a position that denotes ultimate contempt and subjugation. After taking a memento, he will exit the crime scene with feelings of triumph, calm and wellness. He can be very socially engaging shortly thereafter; he may develop a sense of maudlin attachment to the victim and display inappropriate sentimentality. The above can be accomplished because he does not feel any guilt.

When preparing to interview this type of perpetrator, you should seek out the female person(s) who have nettled him in the past. Upon opening the interview, let the perpetrator describe himself. Most often, he will embellish his feats of masculinity and relationships with women. Again, ask about all of the different areas of identity. (They were previously listed under PA.) In an overview, let him explain his relationship to or knowledge of the crime. Again, when going through for the second time in detail, the interviewer should jump the question in a non-sequential style which will break the prepared story. This will also frustrate the perp. Also the interviewer can start to challenge his credibility and threaten his portrayed self image by introducing contradictory and challenging comments made by the controlling women in his life. For an example, "You mother said that you never amounted to much because you drank and caroused around. She claimed that you were a bully who just never grew up." These points of reality will start to agitate him and make him relive the anger felt against her. This anger should be built upon. Eventually, he will again feel belittled and trapped by them. Hence it makes it easier for him to explode from within, to save his own face, and claim the crime. In the AR type, the interviewer must NEVER fall into the misbelief that the perpetrator feels guilt. Remember he is feeling aggressive, not shameful, despite the display of emotion and rationalization.

Anger-Excitation Type (AE)

Characteristics—Rape and murder are planned. It is sadistic in nature. The extended torture and killing can be ritualistic. Satisfaction stems from inflicting terror and pain rather than the death itself. It is a crime of luxury. The body may be disposed in an unfamiliar location. A con or ruse may be used to lure the victim. May see signs of cutting, bruising, and ligature marks.

Who is he?—He may appear as an average person, conducting a normal life. He's likely well-educated and financially stable. He can separate a normal lifestyle from his criminal activities. He seeks domination and mastery. There may be sexual or non-sexual emotions. The fantasy fuels the ritualistic attack. He's methodical in his actions.

Interrogation Strategies—Approaches: Most difficult to get a confession. Suspect will try to victimize you. He has a high IQ and will play games. He'll try to size up the interrogator. Therefore you must prove yourself. Probe suspect for facts in a way so that he feels clever. Suspect is sadistic and pleased with what he has done. He feels as though he is better than you and thus you should be in awe of him. He'll reveal partial truth.

The AE type is by far the most diabolical to interview. In brief, he is "satisfied" in the process of administering dependency, dread and degradation. Independent of the perpetrator's level of sophistication, his goal is to achieve a sense of mastery, control and domination. This can also be extended into the interview room with you. It is often acted out in game-playing with the interviewer. Since he feels inherently superior to you, you are the mouse and he is the cat! Accordingly, only when you start to appreciate his greatness will he reward you with partial truths and snapshot bits and pieces.

When preparing to interview the AE, this is the time to do your homework and practice interviewing! You may want to consult an expert. (Even so, the likelihood of a full confession is almost nil.) Consider yourself fortunate if you are able to identify the emotional dead spots. For, despite their upbringing, they learn to emotionally blunt affective feelings which may cause some hesitancy to fully acting out. Inasmuch as the psychopath can only pretend to have common social bonds with others, it is essential for him to "read" the person with whom he is dealing and give the appropriate learned response. He does not feel spontaneous and comfortable in a vacuum. He needs feedback to manipulate the intended target. Therefore, at the interview, you are the intended victim. He will read your body language, words, and flow of logic with the intended goal of measuring and surmounting you. Again, his innate weakness is the pathological need to be superior and master of all. Therefore, use his high I.Q. (average for AE is 119) against him.

Granted there is no guarantee that any of these strategies will gain an admission or confession, but without them the confession is highly unlikely. These must be used as a guide to the events in the interrogation room. Through the victimology report one begins to understand the victim and why this particular victim was selected—to know your victim, is to know your suspect.

▶ False Confessions

Without a doubt false confessions can occur but if the interviewing detectives take the appropriate precautions and heed the indicators, they can preclude a false admission or confession. It should go without saying that almost anyone under extreme conditions where they are not allowed food or water, to go to the bathroom, or are physically battered is more likely to confess just to get away from the treatment. When these tactics are absent, research indicates that those individuals who have the most potential to provide false information are juveniles; those who suffer from mental retardation; those with a low IQ, usually below 70; or are interviewed for more than five hours continuously in one sitting.

The John H. Reid and Associates, Inc. website[12] provides an article in its Investigator Tips section describing why people confess. This article discusses the motives: for tangible gains, protecting a loved one, low intelligence/youthful offenders, coercion, duress, mental illness and faulty memory. It emphasizes that these are not all inclusive, every case must be evaluated on its own merits along with the totality of the circumstances, not just the confession. Reid then suggests that investigators carefully consider the following when evaluating the credibility of a confession:

1. The suspect's condition at the time of the interrogation
   a. Physical condition (including drug and/or alcohol intoxication)
   b. Mental capacity
   c. Psychological condition
2. The suspect's age
3. The suspect's prior experience with law enforcement
4. The suspect's understanding of the language
5. The length of the interrogation
6. The degree of detail provided by the suspect in his confession
7. The extent of corroboration between the confession and the crime
8. The presence of witnesses to the interrogation and confession
9. The suspect's behavior during the interrogation
10. The effort to address the suspect's physical needs
11. The presence of any improper interrogation techniques

The late John Reid once stated "After you obtain a confession the investigation is just beginning" because the investigator needs to validate that confession through other testimony, circumstances, facts and/or physical evidence. It is important to note that not every witness tells the police and not every suspect is lying or guilty.

▶ Conclusion

Because physical evidence, even with the advent of DNA testing, only resolves about 30% of the cases, it is imperative that all investigators learn the art of interviewing both witnesses and suspects. This process of gathering information takes time but is frequently rewarded with sound results. This information can then be substantiated through others and through the reconstruction of the physical evidence. As we have illustrated here many cases are unsolved because of a failing in the interview and interrogation processes. We must do better.

References

1. Shepherd, E. (2007). *Investigative interviewing, the conversation management approach.* New York, NY: Oxford University Press.
2. Innocence Project. Retrieved September 12, 2009 from http://www.innocenceproject.org/ Content/False_Confessions__Recording_Of_Custodial_Interrogations.php
3. Inbau, F. E., Reid, J. E., Buckley, J. P., & Jayne, B. C. (2004). *Criminal interrogations and confessions* (4th ed.). Sudbury, MA: Jones and Bartlett Publishers.
4. Zulawski, D., & Wicklander, D. E. (1993). *Practical aspects of interview and interrogation.* Boca Raton, FL: CRC Press. pp. 160–161.
5. Wellford, C., & Cronin, J. (2000). Clearing-up homicide clearance rates. *National Institute of Justice Journal.* NCJ 181728.
6. John E. Reid & Associates. (2006). *The Reid Technique of interviewing and interrogation.* Handouts provided for the Reid Interviews and Interrogations Course.
7. Horvath, F. Blair, J. P., & Buckley, J. P. (2008). The behavioral analysis interview clarifying the practice, theory and understanding of its use and effectiveness. *International Journal of Police, Science and Management, 10*(1). p. 101.
8. John E. Reid & Associates. (2006). *The Reid Technique of interviewing and interrogation.* Handouts provided for the Reid Interviews and Interrogations Course. p. 33.
9. Douglas, J. E., Burgess A. W., Burgess, A. G. &. Ressler, R. K. (2004). *Crime classification manual.* (2nd ed.). San Francisco, CA: Jossey-Bass. All of the information in this book relating to the Prescriptive Interview is being referenced and reprinted with permission of John Wiley & Sons, Inc.
10. Obtained from Richard Walter with permission in 2007 and from the article: Keppel, Robert and Richard Walter, "Profiling Killers: A Revised Classification Model for Understanding Sexual Murders", *International Journal of Offender Therapy and Comparative Criminology", 43*(4), 1999, pp. 417–437.
11. Ibid.
12. John E. Reid & Associates. Retrieved August 25, 2009 from http://www.reid.com/ educational_info/r_tips.html?serial=12463704263310386

CHAPTER NINE

Reconstruction and Formalizing the Investigative Process

After the initial response, crime scene examination, and the intense activity of the preliminary investigation, things begin to slow down as the investigation enters into the latent or middle stages. Hopefully by this stage the detectives have established a clear understanding of what happened, who was involved, and the motive behind the death. If a suspect has been identified, and the motive established, then this stage is generally used to confirm and validate alibis and other statements by witnesses or the suspect.

Regardless of the status of the case, the detective needs to make time to carry out a task that many detectives ignore. That is to sit down and actually read and understand the investigative file and all of the various reports completed or accumulated thus far. This is a basic step in crime solving that so many detectives do not take the time to complete, or do not understand its importance. The rationale for this seemingly common sense task is quite simple; get organized and stay focused, know what has been completed and what still needs to be completed.

During the initial stages of the investigation there are a multitude of things going on as the detectives respond to the potential twists and turns of events. There are relatively few cases in which the prosecutor is ready to proceed with an indictment and prosecution upon completion of the preliminary investigation. There are cases when this does happen but they are very few and very far between. The best examples are interfamilial conflicts—the husband and wife argue; there is some type of triggering event; a verbal or physical confrontation takes place; escalation to the point where the death of one or the other is the result. Such cases are straightforward with an overabundance of evidence at the scene or from witnesses with which to establish the facts of the crime. Because the offenders in these incidents are not usually criminals, they will most likely truthfully relate the necessary facts and circumstances of the event. Although their statements and other basic facts will have to be followed up and confirmed, and the physical and forensic examinations will still need to be completed, in general terms these are not difficult cases to complete.

Even in those relatively simple cases there is almost always some additional investigative activity needed to complete the case. Sitting down and actually reading the investigative file and all of the documents contained therein, allows the detective to know for certain exactly what facts, evidence, and circumstances have been validated or verified and what facts still remain to be confirmed.

One of the main reasons to read and review the file is also to make sure the detective has received all of the written reports from all of the detectives participating in the preliminary investigation. The more detectives involved in the preliminary investigation the greater the chance of someone not completing reports as required. This is especially true if the investigation involved multiple agencies. Since detectives are notorious for not completing written reports, it is incumbent on the case detective to make sure they are completed and added to the investigation.

The investigative plan initiated during the preliminary stage is likely to have been edited and changed several times as leads were followed up and new information was developed. New information would have resulted in new leads being identified or other previously identified leads being eliminated as no longer needed. Taking the time at this stage to update the plan is especially helpful in complicated cases, those where there is no clear suspect, or when a potential suspect has been identified but evidence is inadequate to make an arrest. This updating of the investigation plan is a continuing process throughout the investigation and will help keep the investigation on the right path.

Studies have shown that in many famous serial murders the name of the offender appeared in the police investigation records, generally within the first 30 days of the investigation, but for one reason or another was not pursued or properly eliminated as a suspect. Whenever we review a cold case, one of the first steps is to review those initial police reports to see if each person who came to the attention of the police was properly vetted and eliminated as a suspect. As the case progresses, it is strongly suggested that the detective sit down at least once a month and review whatever progress has been made or what new information was developed, and again edit and update the investigative plan.

Whenever we review a current or a cold case we begin by placing the documents and reports in chronological order by investigative activity as best we can. This provides the clearest picture of how the case was developed. While reviewing the various reports, make notes—first any names mentioned in any of the documents are noted. Make certain that any person mentioned by name has been interviewed or is placed on the investigative plan to be interviewed. If a person was important enough to be mentioned in the report, then s/he is important enough to be interviewed. We want to especially review the canvass interview reports to note if there was a neighbor, coworker, family member, or friend that has not yet been located for interview. This initial review of the report is perhaps the best time to note these very important interviews and add them to the investigative plan.

Also note the key facts and circumstances, such as recovery of evidence, alibis, testimonial evidence in the form of statements made by witnesses or suspects, and then update the investigative plan to ensure all the testimonial or circumstantial evidence can be validated and that all possible forensic analysis of physical evidence has been requested. It is not uncommon for the case agent to assume that collected evidence had been submitted to the crime lab only to find out much later the evidence was never submitted. This initial review should be used as a means to double check the submission of all evidence to the crime lab.

Case Study 9-1 is a good example of why it is so important to review the case files. Had the facts about the gun in the victim's hand been clearly understood during the original investigation, the detectives may have taken greater interest in the possibility that the incident might not be a suicide.

Case Study 9-1

Information was received by a police agency that a previously investigated report of suicide of a wife may have actually been a homicide, and the scene staged to look like a suicide by her husband. Reviewing the closed file, the basic facts were noted. The responding police officer arrived at the scene and saw the victim lying in bed, as if sleeping, a pistol in her right hand, a close contact wound to her right temple. According to his statement to detectives, the officer said he checked for signs of life and believed he detected a pulse so began CPR. He could not get a good chest compression with the victim in bed and said he was forced to move the victim to the living room floor to allow him enough room to work. He described the gun in the victim's hand as being tightly gripped, but he removed the gun and placed it on the bed. The victim was taken to a local hospital but was DOA. Reading the remainder of the file the very common human phenomenon of *filtering* and *amplification* could be observed and documented as information was passed between witnesses and detectives. Filtering and amplification refers to the changes in the retelling of events as it passes from one person to another. Each person that hears the story filters the information from the person they receive it from based on their own experiences and understanding. As they retell the story to another person, it is then *amplified*, to reflect information about the story they believe is important. As the same story is told and retold by each new person it becomes more filtered and more amplified. The gun that was initially reported as "being gripped tightly" was later described by the responding detectives in their report as being "clutched" in the victim's right hand and was eventually described as a "death grip" in the medical examiners report. The term *death grip* was in turn interpreted as *cadaveric spasm* by the medical examiner. Cadaveric spasm is found infrequently in some homicide cases where the victim is found grasping an object that was being held at the

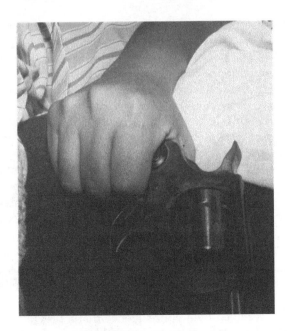

FIGURE 9-1. Gun in hand.

time of death. It is essentially an instantaneous rigor mortis. The importance of this phenomenon is that it cannot be staged, it cannot be simulated or replicated, it is either present or it is not. This was one of the factors the ME used to conclude the victim died from a self inflicted wound. It was only after the case was reopened that the initial officer was finally questioned in person and reported that as he prepared to remove the victim from the bed he raised her right wrist and the gun fell into his hand. It was clear at that point that if the gun fell out of her hand so easily this was not a case of *cadaveric spasm* at all and changed the entire dynamic of the scene. Additionally, the officer described finding the gun in the victim's hand as depicted in a reenactment shown in **Figure 9-1**, with four fingers, including the trigger finger, holding on to the pistol butt. This positioning of the weapon in the victim's hand was more consistent with being placed there after she was shot.

Updating the investigative plan is also an opportunity to prioritize or re-prioritize leads and decide on a clear path of action moving forward. In cases where the victim is not yet identified, the greatest effort should be devoted to this aspect of the investigation. If the victim has not been identified, then the offender or suspect has likely not been identified either.

By this stage the investigative effort should begin to change from the wide net approach used during the preliminary efforts, to a more narrow and focused approach, concentrating on any identified suspects based on their *motive, opportunity,* and *means.* Although we want to begin to focus our effort on a particular suspect, we should be wary of detractors that tend to arise in almost every investigation. These detractors are known as *red herrings* and can cause the investigation to swing wildly back and forth as the detectives run down what appears to be a good lead or a good suspect, but being unable to validate the information, they then swing to another lead or suspect. Reviewing the file will bring these ineffective actions to light. It is not unusual to have five or six or even more persons identified and the investigation shift wildly as detectives try to track down information on one particular suspect, then another.

▶Red Herrings

A *red herring* refers to information or a lead that initially or on its face looks very promising, causing the investigation to focus almost exclusively on that aspect, but which is subsequently determined to be false, inaccurate, or otherwise a dead end. As mentioned before, when we review cold cases we can almost always go back and see exactly where the investigation began to go bad. Generally this starts to happen after one or a series of red herrings has resulted not in a clear and orderly investigative path, but a series of events causing the investigation to first go in one direction and then another.

When teaching this concept we use the analogy that a criminal investigation (regardless of the crime) is like a train rolling on a railroad track. A railroad track is laid out in order and typically goes in one direction only; as the investigation begins to react to new information or evidence, it is like the train hitting a switch and traveling down a spur line headed in a new direction. When the new information or person of interest is eventually eliminated from play, like a train, the investigation must go back to the point where the spur line was taken (or when the investigation started to focus on the red herring) and begin again. Often, instead of returning to the direction they were headed in the first place, the detectives now start off in yet another direction. By responding to another "fire" or person of interest, the focus of the overall investigation is lost and many of the basic questions are left unanswered. Taking the time to go back and review the file should give the detective a chance to note any missing leads or identify what was not checked out prior to a divergence towards a particular suspect or piece of information.

It is a fact of criminal investigation—there are always red herrings. Eventually you reach a point where no matter how good the information sounds or how good the evidence might look, it simply is not enough to derail the "train" of progress that has already been made. This is the time to sit down and review the file again and refocus the investigative effort.

▶Knowing the Offender

Once a suspect has been identified there is an old military adage that we have adapted to criminal investigations and use it as a very important teaching point that is:

Find the suspect, fix them, and then pile on.

This essentially means once we have identified the offender, we want to "pile it on" meaning we want to learn anything and everything about him, including every aspect of his personal life, and if there have been any other criminal offenses committed by the offender. If there are any additional criminal offenses they need to be included in the investigation and also presented to the district attorney.

Conducting a detailed check of the suspect and victim's background was another contributing factor identified by Welford and Cronin[1] in resolving homicide investigations.

The information described in **Case Study 9-2**, provided detectives with another possible victim, a chance to compare the behavior of the husband in each case to see if there were any similarities. The husband increasing the amount of life insurance on his wife before her death is very good circumstantial evidence of premeditation because it was done several weeks before the actual death. Such premeditation is very telling offender behavior because it demonstrates patience, the ability to plan long range, and displays his cold heartedness.

In this case study, the other documents completed while he filled out his loan application were also very important because again it was evidence that showed their marriage was in fact a sham. Friends of the wife provided statements that the husband had insisted he be placed on her insurance policy and she placed on his to conform with the appearance of a married couple. Again, this fact should be seen as another example of the offender's long range planning ability because they were married some eleven months before she was murdered.

Many times the main advantage of this type of information is that it shows the offender lies. It is most damaging if the offender ever decides to take the witness stand to testify because the evidence of this lie is often used to cast doubt as to the truthfulness of his testimony. This information is especially useful in cases where the offender is attempting to use the "good guy" defense. That because of their personality type or history he would be incapable or unlikely to have committed such an offense.

The amount of information that can be developed on the offender is basically limited to the amount of information available and the amount of time detectives are willing to spend collecting it. A detailed background investigation of the offender is one of the most valuable tools in the investigative arsenal.

Case Study 9-2

A woman was murdered and the investigators began to center on her husband, believing the murder was motivated by a large insurance policy. Investigation into the couple determined very clearly that the wife was actually a lesbian, and the marriage was actually one of convenience for the wife to hide her sexuality. Although married, they had never lived together, shared no common bank account, and except for one photo, they had never appeared together. According to the woman's friends, as part of the sham, she had placed the husband on her life insurance policy and knew he had placed her on his company policy as well, thinking that this would be expected from a married couple. When questioned by police, the husband denied their marriage was a sham and claimed instead they just were experiencing a rocky marriage, which caused the wife to temporarily move out of the house and into the home of a female friend. During a background investigation however, police obtained documents relating to the purchase of the husband's own house, which showed it was purchased 3 months after his marriage, but on the loan application and purchase contract the husband indicated he was unmarried, and the wife's name did not appear on any of the documents. The real estate agent also confirmed that the husband made it clear he was single when the house was actually purchased. This of course was additional circumstantial evidence showing the marriage was in fact a sham. A check on his personnel records at his office noted that three weeks before the wife disappeared, the husband had increased her life insurance policy to the maximum amount, but had only paid one increased monthly premium. Additional background showed that the husband had also collected a life insurance policy on another woman a few years before, and the settlement of that policy was used to purchase the house he was living in. This other woman's death was also suspicious in nature, but with little evidence found at the scene it was not vigorously pursued by the police. By concentrating on the husband and his background, an enormous amount of circumstantial evidence was collected.

▶ Investigative Subpoenas

An investigative subpoena is basically a court order directing someone to present himself (*subpoena ad testificandum*) or material items (*subpoena duces tecum*), usually some type of documents, records, or forms. Investigative subpoenas are a way to obtain additional background information about the offender or the victim, identify possible leads and motives, or to confirm or invalidate other allegations and information.

The Latin term *subpoena duces tecum* (or subpoena for production of evidence) can be translated as "bring with you under penalty of punishment." A *subpoena duces tecum* compels the production of documents that might be admissible before the court and not used to obtain oral testimony from an individual. (Summons for oral testimony is carried out through a *subpoena ad testificandum*.) It is essentially a court summons, ordering a certain named party to appear before the court and produce certain requested documents or other evidence for use at a hearing or trial. The subpoena compels those entities whether public or private to deliver the requested documents or face contempt of court violations. Businesses such as banks, other financial institutions, and telephone companies are authorized to charge a reasonable fee for their research and production of the requested information.

There is a wide variance as to how subpoenas are obtained or who is authorized to issue them. In most circumstances the subpoenas are issued by the county or a federal grand jury and obtained through the district attorney or assistant U.S. Attorney. In some states subpoena authority is given to state police agencies in order to assist them in conducting their criminal investigations. Regardless of the authority or how they are obtained, during this stage of the investigative process they may prove to be very helpful in clarifying certain allegations, validating alibis, or identifying a motive.

For example, a suspect may have presented him or herself as financially sound and without a motive to murder for insurance money, but after obtaining his/her business records and personal financial records, quite the opposite may be discovered as demonstrated in **Case Study 9-3**. As the detectives begin to read and review the file they should also make notes regarding what information needs to be verified that might be verified through the subpoena process.

In our modern technological era, in this country, it is almost impossible for us to live a normal life and not leave an electronic record of our existence—lifestyle, personal and professional activities, financial history, and routine comings and goings of daily life. Use of the investigative subpoena will enable examination of those aspects of life of both the offender and the victim.

Case Study 9-3

The suspicious death of a wife cast attention to the husband almost immediately, especially when it was determined during the preliminary investigation the husband had taken out multiple life insurance policies on the wife; many in the weeks before her death. This aroused suspicion, but only after obtaining the couple's financial records was it determined that the premiums for the combined life insurance policies exceeded the available monthly income of the couple, the initial premiums being paid from their savings account. This clearly demonstrated a monetary motive for the husband to murder his wife.

These are a few of the common documents used to obtain information about the offender or the victim. It is not uncommon to get information from one entity and after reviewing the information contained in the documents, request additional subpoenas to obtain additional information.

Telephone records	Cell phone records	Employment records and timecards
Purchase contracts	Email or social network records	Bank records
Security camera recordings	Utilities records	Credit card records
Debit card records	Sales or purchase receipts	Checking account information
Court records	Prior police reports and records	Bankruptcy records
Loan documents	Credit history	School records
Certain medical records	Military records	Business contracts
Financial statements	Insurance policies and claims	Probation reports
Presentence reports		

A suggestion for safeguarding the subpoenaed documents for possible use in court is to make a copy of each document as it is received and place the copy into the investigative file to use it as a working copy. This working copy can be highlighted or written on as needed, while the original is retained untouched in a separate file and can be copied again and again for any future analysis if needed. In this manner the original document can be produced in court as evidence if needed. If the original is ever marked or written on, then an additional subpoena may be needed to get another copy of the same document to use in court.

One of the ways we can best use all of this information is of course through an analysis of the information itself, but also in documenting the various times and dates of events depicted in these documents—a timeline.

▶ Timelines

A timeline is a written report that puts all of the events relating to the crime into proper chronological order. Although it can be used for any crime, its value in homicide investigations becomes very evident when confronted with a complicated series of events, multiple crimes, multiple offenders, especially in serial crimes. Using timelines as an important investigative tool corresponds to the old adage: *"Nothing happens in a vacuum. There is always a before, a during, and an after for every event."*

This is true for every event but especially so when investigating crime. Detectives often want to focus on the event itself, more specifically on the crime scene and witness statements or suspect admissions, and don't always take into consideration very important circumstantial evidence which may have led up to the crime or may have transpired after the crime. Whereas the crime scene does record the "during" aspect, the timeline is really designed to focus on the "before" and "after" of the criminal act. What the timeline also generally establishes is the *opportunity* for the suspect to have committed the crime.

There is no particular format or style for constructing a timeline and there are several computer programs commercially available designed to create a timeline and various link analyses. These special computer programs can produce high quality and very professional looking products, which are very useful especially in court. But, they are also costly to purchase and maintain and may require additional training in order to fully utilize them. However, a workable and useful timeline can be created using a regular word processing program or any one of the spreadsheet programs generally available on most computers.

It depends on what is available for the individual detectives or their agency and how proficient they are with computers. We have found using a simple spreadsheet program produces one of the easiest to use and understandable timelines. The real value of using a spreadsheet program is that little or no additional training is needed and multiple detectives or administrative support personnel can be utilized to update the document as new information is obtained.

The purpose of a timeline is to place all of the various pieces of the investigation into one chronological document. Often the timeline is the only place in the entire case file where all of the facts and circumstances from all documents and statements can be found in one place. More importantly it also is the one place where all of the various events can be seen in context with all of the other facts and circumstances. **Case Study 9-4** demonstrates the value of a timeline.

Case Study 9-4

Following the suspicious death of his wife, a husband received over $150,000 in an insurance policy settlement. During the course of the investigation the husband became very upset at the implication that he had murdered his wife for the purpose of collecting on the insurance policy. He made repeated statements to his friends that he had given the insurance money to his brother to invest for him and had no real control over any of it. He bristled at the implication of murdering his wife for money and his repeated insistence was designed to show his lack of motive for his wife's murder. Later, a subpoena was issued for the bank account where the insurance proceeds were placed, along with telephone records from the suspect and his brother who was supposed to be managing the money. Each and every phone call between the brothers and every withdrawal from the bank account was placed into a timeline. A surprising pattern emerged when all of these divergent facts were placed into chronological order. First, by the time the investigation began to center on the husband, the account had been drawn down from the $150,000 of the original insurance policy settlement to less than $500 in less than a year's time. Second, there were numerous large withdrawals made by the suspect's brother by check throughout the time the account was opened. The most important aspect however was when the phone records were added to the spreadsheet and placed in context with the various withdrawals or checks. It was quickly determined there was a phone call placed from the husband to his brother or from the brother to the husband, before each large withdrawal and after each withdrawal. Although he steadfastly claimed to have no knowledge as to how the money was being used or invested, there was never a check issued or a withdrawal made without the phone call to or from the husband and his brother. Although there was no proof of the context or topic of these conversations, the close proximity of the calls to every single documented withdrawal from the account, argued circumstantially that the husband did in fact have control over the money or had knowledge of how the money was being used. The timeline helped to demonstrate that money was one of the motives behind the murder. The husband was later convicted of the crime.

A second example of the importance of putting events into chronological order revolves around the use of home computers and the internet. For example, a spouse dies from some type of poisoning. A check of the other spouse's internet history log shows numerous searches for that particular type of poison in the days before the death, coupled with an increased insurance policy, or other evidence such as the collection of the necessary chemicals to make the poison. This can be especially damning if telephone calls, emails, or other forms of communication between the suspect and a new boyfriend/girlfriend can be placed into context with other events and perhaps even provide circumstantial evidence that the boyfriend/girlfriend may be an actual co-conspirator to the murder.

The real value of placing these seemingly unrelated events into some chronological order, is the ability to paint a picture of premeditation, establish or destroy an alibi, and to possibly link others to the crime as co-conspirators. In the case of a serial offender, these events could link common cases together with other aspects of the offender's life.

Table 9-1 is a basic example of the simple timeline for a possible serial offender. As noted, by even this small and limited timeline there is already a recognizable pattern to the offender's activity. When further developed it will help to establish his *modus operandi* (MO) and how he selects his victims, perhaps where he deposits the bodies, and other noteworthy offender behavior as well as his opportunity to commit the crime.

In the example we can see that Ricky is already identified as a suspect or at least a person of interest and thus detectives have started to collect information concerning his background and other activity. The general guideline for constructing a timeline is relatively simple. If we can put together a time, date, and an event, then we put it into the timeline. For the timeline there is no such

TABLE 9-1. Timeline

Date	Time	Ricky Timeline
08/01/2009		Ricky residence 325 1st street. (Central City driver license application post office)
3/26/2010	1030hrs	Principal, Central City High, reports Ricky threatened female student (Central City Police report)
4/10/2010	1545hrs	Ricky was served a warrant and arrested for trespassing at the high school (Central City Police report)
4/30/2010	2330	Ricky arrested concealed weapon and traffic ordinance by Central City PD (4th Street Central City)
5/11/2010	1059hrs	Ricky arrested for driving on suspended driver's license in Central City driving black Mazda P/U
6/29/2010	2230	Ricky signs out of work swing shift (Jones Tool and Die time card)
6/29/2010	2335	Ricky arrested for fighting with street prostitute. (Vickie) (Central City Police report) Vickie claims Ricky tried to abduct her. Ricky posts bond and is released
7/3/2010	0030	Ricky withdrew $40 cash from ATM on 4th Street, Central City
7/3/2010	0200	Vickie last seen working as prostitute on 4th Street, Central City
7/3/2010	0900	Ricky's black Mazda logged into Barker Lake Recreation area (Barker Lake sign in register)
7/3/2010	1530	Ricky called in sick to work—swing shift (Jones Tool and Die time card)
7/15/2010		Charges dropped when Vickie did not show up for court. Missing person report filed for Vickie (Central City Police report)
7/20/2010	2330	Ricky received ticket from Central City Police failure to stop. (4th Street Central City)
7/21/2010	0900	Sally, local prostitute reported missing—worked the streets last night never came home Last seen getting into black P/U truck (Central City Police Report)
7/21/2010	0900	Ricky's black Mazda P/U logged into Barker Lake Recreation area (Barker Lake sign in register)
7/22/2010	1330	Rickey observed cleaning vehicle carpet (Jones witness statement)
7/22/2010	1500	Ricky called in sick to work (swing shift) (Jones Tool and Die time card)
7/25/2010	1130	Sally's body discovered at Barker Lake Recreation area. (Central County Sheriff's Office report)
	1345	While processing scene at Barker Lake for Sally, Vickie's body is discovered nearby
7/28/2010	1000	Male tries to pawn gold woman's jewelry—Joes Pawn (looked like Ricky not positive)
7/28/2010	1200	Male tries to pawn gold women's jewelry—Lone Star Pawn (looked like Ricky not positive)

thing as an insignificant event; many times a particular event may seem insignificant when it stands alone but becomes very important when placed into context with other events that were also taking place.

An example would be the timeline entry of Ricky being observed cleaning out the interior of his vehicle. As previously stated, in and of itself the fact could be meaningless. But, when placed into the context of the timeline and other events before and after, it can be seen circumstantially as being very relevant. As a detective, I would assume or believe that Ricky may be trying to eliminate evidence from his vehicle. Later we note Ricky's visits to the lake and recreation site; again in and of themselves this is not incriminating, except when later the bodies of two victims are found at the same general location.

Ricky's use of the ATM machine a short distance away from where the victims were last seen or where they were working late at night, his arrest by police in the company of one of the victims, and her complaint she was being abducted obviously makes him highly suspicious to the police.

Lastly, following each disappearance, Ricky called in sick to work. This is very important offender behavior as it is not uncommon for offenders to call in sick or miss work or school for up to three days following the event because their emotions and anxiety do not allow them to function normally. Having seen this on the timeline, a detective could immediately go back and see how many other days he called in sick or missed work; and then compare to any other missing persons reports for the time immediately preceding his absence to see if there were any other potential victims. There have been multiple occasions when this small fact has lead to the reexamination of other cases or where the suspect was added as a suspect to other cases.

When constructing a timeline, we typically start with some known time such as when the body was discovered, the time the 911 call came in, or if we are lucky enough to establish it, the actual time of death. This first known time is important because this essentially becomes the center of the timeline with other events added as either pre-crime or post-crime events.

Using a spreadsheet program as an example of a timeline, only three columns of information are needed. These columns are identified as time, date, event, and source. The time is whatever time we can identify the event took place; the date of course is the date the event took place. The event is just a short description of the event and as in the case of the example we use just bullets of information. The last column is important because it also identifies the original source of information so if necessary that document or source can be easily retrieved within the file. The timeline can be customized to include as much information as necessary or desired.

The most time efficient method to complete the spreadsheet is simply to sit down and begin to review the file. Look through each individual document including statements, other investigative reports, or other documents such as telephone records, cell phone records, or financial records. Simply place whatever event is noted in the document and place the time and date to that event, identify the original source and then continue on. There are many instances when the date of the event may be known, but not the exact time. For those events without a time we still place them into the timeline but we have to leave the time column blank until we can identify the time. Typically we attempt to determine if possible if it was done in the morning, afternoon, or night time and place the entry in as close proximity to the time as we can. Most of these are educated guesses at best.

When constructing the timeline it will be fairly obvious that times immediately around the time of the initial report to the police or the time of death tend to be more accurate than times of pre- and post-crime events.

There are many instances however when the event may be alleged but not yet verified or there is no exact time or date. As a method to differentiate these uncertain or unverified facts from those facts that have been verified, we suggest placing the information where it would go chronologically in the timeline, but use an italics font. Using that font as a standard for unverified information, we can look at any timeline from any case we have reviewed and note right away the fact indicated is still unverified. Many times this precipitates an investigative lead to be identified and run down to verify the information. In the timeline example, the last two entries report that someone looking like Ricky attempted to pawn women's jewelry, but because this was not completely validated as Ricky, it was placed in italics indicating it is unverified information.

A spreadsheet program is also easy to adapt to fit any particular case or circumstance being investigated. For instance, in cases with multiple suspects or multiple victims you can easily adapt the program to use different colors on the entries to identify the activity of individual persons.

Where we get the information for the timeline is obviously case specific, but generally speaking, we go through all statements and documents, and regardless of how trivial, if a time, date, and event can be found in any statement or report, we place it into the timeline. Again, it is very easy to go through later to delete what turns out not to be important.

▶ NCIC Off-line Checks

One of the more effective tools, especially when dealing with a potential serial offender is an NCIC "off-line check." This is a special request made through the NCIC (National Crime Information Center) to query their data base and determine when and where the offender or his/her vehicle came into contact with police and his/her name or vehicle information was checked through the NCIC. As most know, it is routine for police officers who stop a vehicle for a possible traffic violation to ask for a NCIC check to determine if the vehicle was reported stolen. If the driver of a vehicle or a person is being stopped for suspicious behavior, or whenever someone is arrested, there is an additional NCIC check for any criminal history and to determine if s/he is being sought by police elsewhere or has any outstanding arrest warrants on file. Each one of these contacts through NCIC is recorded in the NCIC database which can be retrieved during the off-line check.

What is provided is the time, date, and agency that requested the information and the reason the individual was checked. If the individual was driving a vehicle, that vehicle information is also provided. Of course for background purposes, it positively places the offender at a specific place at a specific time, which can then be placed on the timeline for later comparison to other events.

What is especially helpful when working on a serial case, is being able to identify the type and description of the vehicle the offender may have been driving at the time of the contact with police. If for instance, the offender is driving a pickup truck at the time of the investigation, but years before there is a contact with police and the offender is driving another vehicle, this could expand the investigation to determine the facts and circumstances behind the purchase of that vehicle or even to determine if that vehicle was ever mentioned in any other offense. It could also identify previously owned vehicles that may have been unknown to police at the time. Identifying previously owned vehicles provides more potential evidence, e.g. when and where it was purchased, financed, and insured.

An off-line check also provides information from Immigration and Custom's Enforcement (ICE) if the suspect ever departed the country or was processed through one of the U.S. points of entry returning to the United States.

Information on a particular offender is readily available on the NCIC server for the preceding six month period. However, information beyond six months in the past up to 10 years can be obtained if specifically requested through NCIC. Although a NCIC check may not be beneficial for every case, for premeditated investigations, or if we are working on a serial offender, it is a very effective tool to use to document an offender's movement and other activities.

▶ Informants or Other Sources of Information

Homicide investigations involving gangs, drugs, or other elements of organized crime are among the most difficult to resolve because they frequently revolve around some type of criminal behavior by either the victim or the offender or both. Additionally, any witnesses or co-conspirators are also likely involved in the same criminal group or involved in some type of criminal activity as well.

In these cases coordination within the agency or neighboring agencies' narcotics, gang, or intelligence units may be beneficial to determine if there are any informants within those criminal elements that may be able to provide any information as to what happened and who was involved.

▶ Criminal Investigative Analysis (CIA)

ViCAP Database

The FBI's Violent Criminal Apprehension Program (ViCAP) database was especially created to assist in tracking down serial offenders who may travel from state to state committing their crimes, or from different locations from within a particular state.

Reconstruction and Crime Scene Analysis

According to Findley[2] reconstruction is the process of applying logic, experience and scientific principles to the sources of information found during an investigation. It is the sum total of the investigation demonstrated in its tangible form. The objective is to form an accurate opinion relative to the events occurring before, during, and after the criminal act. Many times in this book we have mentioned that very little, if anything, is absolute when it comes to death investigations and the same applies to reconstruction. Findley describes how reconstruction decisions should be made based on a continuum as shown in **Figure 9-2**.

"Certainty" is a determination that is rarely attained. "Possible" is a little better, but anything is possible—being "probable" is a different story. "Speculation", at the other end of the spectrum, is a weak determination. The reconstruction process will help the evaluator to at least state with a reasonable amount of certainty, the probability of a certain series of events occurring.

To optimize a reconstruction Findley suggests a series of conditions that if properly met during the course of the investigation will result in a valid reconstruction rather than one full of inaccuracies.

1. Crime scene integrity must be maintained and documented
2. Crime scene must be thoroughly searched and documented
3. All observations by the responding officers must be recorded
4. Forensic autopsy complete with photographs and diagrams
5. Copies of all evidence examination reports
6. Copies of all statements made by victims, witnesses, and suspects
7. Scientific experimentation

Reconstruction Continuum

0 ――――――――――――――――――――――――――――――――――― 10

➡ Speculation
➡ Possible
➡ Probable
➡ Certainty

FIGURE 9-2. Reconstruction continuum.

Pitfalls to avoid include:

1. Relying on insufficient or unverified information
2. Jumping to conclusions before all the data is in
3. Failing to evaluate each piece of data individually than as a part of the whole
4. Inflexibility in considering alternate viewpoints or theories
5. Failure to test the reconstruction

Reconstruction and crime scene analysis are specialized crime scene examinations and according to Gardner and Bevel "it involves evaluating the context of a scene and the physical evidence found there in an effort to identify what occurred and in what order it occurred."[3]

Some form of crime scene reconstruction or analysis takes place as the scene is examined and documented. The goal of the examination and documentation of the scene is to determine the general facts of what happened, and how the various items of evidence relate to each other, to the scene, or to the victim and suspect. Generally speaking this initial review and scene analysis will suffice. Most of the death cases are not very complicated to piece together because they often happened on the spur of the moment without a great deal of planning or preparation. Many times all of the participants are readily identified upon police arrival so there's not always a need for further detailed analysis. But there are those cases when a more detailed examination and interpretation of the physical evidence is needed. These include cases of long term premeditation or instances when the event is part of a staged crime scene. A staged scene is where evidence or the scene is altered by the offender to misdirect a subsequent police investigation. In these instances we are often presented with a more complicated crime scene and it may be quite beneficial to conduct some type of crime scene reconstruction along with a more detailed analysis of what happened before, during, and then after the event.

An event reconstruction and analysis is based on the totality of all physical evidence, scene documentation, results of autopsy reflecting any injuries and cause of death, any statements offered by witnesses, and a great deal of logic by the analysts in attempting to explain how all of the various elements are related. Much of the analysis is based on comparison, contrast, and elimination of various theories or explanations based on a thorough understanding of scientific principals and their application to the reconstruction process.

Two of the more common examinations are bloodstain pattern interpretation and shooting incident reconstruction.

In bloodstain pattern reconstruction we are looking at the blood at the scene to determine some basic facts such as whether the blood at the scene is the result of simple bleeding *after* an injury or was it *caused* as a result of the victim being injured? Examples of this would be the great number of smaller blood stains referred to as "high velocity" caused when a firearm is used to cause the injury; or what are known as cast off patterns generally found on a

FIGURE 9-3. Arterial bleeding. See Color Plate 50.

wall, floor, or ceiling, caused when an object with blood on it "casts" the blood off as it is moved through the air to strike the victim again or when withdrawing the object away from the victim. A gushing or arterial pattern is often found when a major artery is cut during an attack as shown in **Figure 9-3**.

Additional transfer type stains are caused when a bloody object or hand comes into contact with another object such as depicted in **Figure 9-4**. In time sequencing it could be critical to know *when* during the incident blood was deposited at the scene or on a particular target.

FIGURE 9-4. Contact with bloody item. See Color Plate 51.

Case Study 9-5

Detectives asked for a shooting incident reconstruction analysis on an incident in which two vehicles were driving one behind the other at a moderate but unknown speed down an uneven highway, when the passenger of the rear vehicle leaned out and shot a rifle into the taillight of the vehicle in front. The bullet then ricocheted slightly and struck a passenger riding in the rear seat, killing him. The detectives were not certain of the need for the examination, but had seen it done before, were impressed, and were looking for an additional forensic examination to use in court. The problem in this situation was too many variables and too many unknowns to even attempt any type of reconstruction. The vehicles were driving along an uneven and rough roadway, the exact distance between them was unknown, the exact position of the passenger aiming the rifle was also unknown. There was simply no way to replicate the circumstances with any degree of accuracy.

In certain situations an analyst may be able to correctly place the victim and/or offender in their exact three dimensional positions in the scene when an injury was inflicted or the stains were deposited. This is extremely valuable in the reconstruction process and can validate or invalidate witness and offender statements and help formulate the theory of the crime.

Bloodstain pattern interpretation should only be completed by someone who has expertise based on training and experience with a clear understanding of the dynamics involved.

Shooting incident reconstruction is basically an effort to determine the relative position of the victim in relationship to the shooter when the shot was fired or when the victim was struck. Again this is a specialized examination because of the many variables that may be involved including different weapon types and ammunition, and should only be attempted by someone with the proper training and certification (see **Case Study 9-5**).

▶ Reenactment

A reenactment is essentially walking through the events as described by witnesses or by suspects to determine the feasibility of the various statements or claims made by witnesses or the offender (see **Case Study 9-6**).

Another form of reenactment, as illustrated in **Case Study 9-7**, involves the process of trying to replicate injuries or patterns that may exist, in this case on the body. The key to all of these reconstruction processes is that the person conducting them must be able to replicate the environment and items in real situations as closely as possible. If you wanted to validate your hypothesis that a bloody knife had been placed on the carpeted floor and not dropped

Case Study 9-6

During the course of an investigation a witness identified a 20 minute gap in a suspect's alibi. It was during this 20 minute gap police theorized the suspect left the location where he was, returned to the crime scene, murdered the victim and then returned to his previous location. Was 20 minutes enough time go to the crime scene and return? A reenactment was deemed to be necessary, wherein the police would reenact the series of events they theorize happened and time them from start to finish to see if it was possible for the crime to have been committed in the 20 minute time gap. The officers used a similar vehicle to the suspect's and using three different drivers, started at the location of the offender's alibi, drove to the scene, simulated the crime, and then drove back. Three different drivers were used to take into account any variation of driving style and each drove the same route most likely used by the suspect a total of five times each. Also taken into account was the time of day of the event to try and replicate the same general traffic patterns confronting the suspect. The average time of the fifteen trials was seventeen minutes. This reenactment was used in court to validate the possibility that the offender's 20 minute alibi gap could have been used for the offender to travel to the crime scene, commit the murder, and then return.

Case Study 9-7

On a Saturday afternoon, a man with a wife and two young children finished up mowing his yard and entered his home to find his wife covered in blood lying on the kitchen floor. He knelt down beside her to check for a pulse; finding none he immediately checked on his two kids to find both of them stabbed to death in their respective bedrooms. The father then called 911 and the police responded. The autopsy of the wife reflected numerous stab wounds to the chest and a series of cuts on the palm of her right hand that were recorded as defensive wounds. The two children died of stab wounds to the chest with defensive wounds on the hands and arms. In view of the fact that the husband was there and claims he never heard a scream for help nor did he see any strangers; coupled with what were determined to be defensive wounds to his wife's hand, and blood on his clothes, the police arrested the father and charged him with the three murders.

In a subsequent review of the investigation a reconstruction of the wounding was conducted by a forensic pathologist serving as an expert witness for the defense. He concluded that the children, based on the defensive wounds to the arms and hands, were in fact killed by someone. The mother's clothes contained blood from both children. Psychological information showed that she had been suffering from depression and other mental illnesses for sometime. It was determined that the wound patterns to her body were such that she could have inflicted them on herself. A reconstruction to explain the wounds on the palm of her hand was conducted by placing fingerprint ink on the edges of the knife. He then allowed the knife to slip through his hand as if trying to stab someone or an object. This reconstruction experiment produced almost a perfect image on his hand as they did on hers. He concluded that her unstable mental state caused her to kill her two children then she stabbed herself numerous times. Somewhere along the way the knife slipped through her hand creating the wounds on the palm that were initially defined as defensive. Confronted with this information the prosecutor and the police dropped the charges against the husband and he was released.

---

you would need a knife identical to the one in the investigation, real blood and a piece of carpeted floor that is as close as possible to the same carpet in the crime scene. You would then drop the knife at varying heights down to actually placing it on the carpet to replicate the bloody pattern seen on the carpet at the crime scene, photographing and documenting every step taken. Through this process one would be able to determine, with a reasonable amount of probability how the knife got there. It is not enough to speculate, you must be more certain than that.

▶ Behavioral Reconstruction

In order to utilize behavioral reconstruction one needs to have conducted a thorough investigation that includes all activities and information about the crime scene and the behavior exhibited at the scene. This can lead to a typology as described in a later chapter and illustrated in Appendix B. Through a complete suspectology coupled with other interviews, the detective can identify pre-crime behaviors and post-crime behaviors. The disparity found between the pre- and post-crime behaviors tend to indicate and identify potential persons of interest where the investigation needs to focus.

This process of looking at the crime from a behavioral perspective is known as Criminal Investigative Analysis (CIA) or more commonly referred or known to laymen as *profiling* either of the offender or the crime. The process of analyzing the crime scene and/or the offender from a behavioral perspective should only be conducted by someone with the proper experience, credentials, and training to do so. **Case Study 9-8** is an example of what happens when unqualified persons offer expert opinions in an investigation.

Out of all of the disciplines involved in the reconstruction process, behavioral aspects involves the most subjectivity and its analysis is based as much on actual first hand experience in working violent crimes as it is on training

Case Study 9-8

During a review of an unsolved and well publicized serial murder investigation, we noted the police department had received four unsolicited offers to conduct "profiles" of the crime and offender. The department cooperated in each instance hoping for any possible insight into the crime and the offender. Unfortunately none of the so-called experts had the proper training or were qualified to conduct such analysis. The results were four totally different views of the crime and the offender which caused the investigation to go into a different direction each time a new profile was received. If viewed separately, it was as if each "expert" was describing completely different investigations. One analysis was so inadequate we recognized the nearly word for word professional text from which their findings were taken. The result of these efforts was a lot of frustration, wasted time, and wasted resources by the department with no progress towards the outcome. After coordinating with an actual expert on behavioral analysis, all four reports were totally debunked and finally set aside.

and education. It can also be one of the most beneficial analyses to be conducted when at this stage of the investigation no clear suspect has yet been identified. Unfortunately, this is one of the areas in criminal investigation with the most charlatans and false experts mainly because there is no real formal type of certification process. So, it is not uncommon for some so-called experts to have graduated from college on Friday and call themselves an expert in the field of *criminal investigative analysis* or a *profiler* the following Monday. The real problem is these clearly untrained and inexperienced persons are providing erroneous or counterproductive recommendations to detectives that may send them looking in the wrong direction for suspects or evidence.

Even worse when these "experts" are employed as defense witnesses and then testify to this same erroneous information or provide critique of the police in their crime scene examination when they have never actually processed a crime scene themselves in their careers.

Therefore great caution should be exercised in seeking or accepting assistance in this effort to ensure these experts truly have the requisite training and experience to render such analysis.

This stage of the investigation is about staying organized and focused in establishing our theory of the crime. It is also a time to put our theory to the test through any series of reconstruction efforts. If the theory does not stand up to the reconstruction or other forensic examinations, then we have to readjust our theory based on those new facts. Remember, *the theory must conform to the evidence; we do not conform the evidence to fit a theory.* It is also a time to begin to look at our case from the defense attorney's perspective to see if there are any holes in our evidence or in our theory of the crime. It is time for us to play devil's advocate and take a very hard and critical look for potential problems in our case. If we see these holes, then the defense is certainly going to see them and will use them to their advantage if they are not properly addressed. If at this stage we still do not have a viable suspect, then it is time to go back and thoroughly review our case and make certain we have not skipped over any of the basics and there are no missing leads not completed. If there are still several potential suspects but no one that stands out more than others, then try and prioritize the list of suspects and take them one at a time. Continue working until we can finally eliminate them from involvement or finally obtain the evidence to tie them to the crime.

When reviewing cold cases we have generally found the most likely suspect was known to the police during the first 30 days of the investigation and was never considered a suspect or was improperly eliminated as a suspect.

References

1. Welford, C., & Cronin, J. (1999). *An analysis of variables affecting the clearance rate of homicides.* Justice Research Statistics Association.
2. Findley, J. (1997). Personal communication at the Georgia Police Academy, Forsyth, Georgia.
3. Gardner, R. M., & Bevel, T. (2009). *Practical crime scene analysis and reconstruction.* Boca Raton, FL: CRC Press.

CHAPTER TEN

Investigating Equivocal Deaths

The purpose of this chapter is to discuss the investigative processes used to evaluate or analyze an equivocal death.* Most of these cases require consideration of possible suicide, therefore, this chapter will focus primarily on suicide and the differentiation between suicide and other manners of death. As we progress through the types, the circumstances, and the reasons for suicide; and specific investigative procedures we will present a template that can be used to help in determining whether or not the case at hand is a suicide. We have included at Appendix C an Equivocal Death Analysis utilizing an actual case. This case outlines the process and demonstrates how easily a situation can be misunderstood or the information misinterpreted.

Suicide is the 11th leading cause of death among all Americans; the second leading cause of death among Americans age 25–34; and the third leading cause of death among Americans age 15–24.[1] In the United States there are about 14,000 homicides a year while suicides exceed 30,000. Over the past three decades homicides have dropped by 40% yet suicides have remained about the same. As with homicides, a firearm is the weapon of choice for suicides in about 60% of the cases. Men kill themselves far more often than women, although women make more attempts than men, and one should never be surprised to what length a person will go to take his/her own life. Pain of the death process should not be a consideration but rather the totality of facts and circumstances surrounding the person and the event.

Understanding suicide is extremely difficult and no one wants to believe that a loved one has taken his/her own life. It can create a social stigma for the family and others which can cause great harm to the survivors in their subsequent lives. It can be costly as well—most insurance companies have

---

*Equivocal death is any death in which the manner of death is uncertain—homicide–suicide, accident–suicide, or accident–homicide.

suicide clauses attached to their policies and may not pay benefits if the insured commits suicide within a certain period of time from when the policy was initiated. If the deceased person is the main bread winner the costs rise even higher.

Equivocal deaths, especially those that carry the suspicion of suicide, can be more difficult and more problematic for the investigator than any homicides they encounter. It can cause the investigator more grief and concern than anything else in the job and even sometimes in his/her life, yet committing a suicide is not against the law. So why do we care or even pursue these? Because it is our responsibility to the justice system, the citizens we serve, and because "we work for truth." But one must also look at the medico-legal death investigation systems that exist in this country as outlined in previous material. In some cases law enforcement never or hardly ever gets involved, while in others they may remain involved in the investigation until the suicide determination has been substantiated. Either way the charge is to conduct a thorough and accurate investigation that documents everything regardless of what that evidence tells us.

Generally speaking three characteristics[2] are found in suicides: (1) the injuries were self-inflicted; (2) the victim could have inflicted these injuries; and (3) the victim had the intent to kill herself/himself. The first two are usually identifiable and supportable through an evaluation of the scene and the subsequent autopsy but the third characteristic is very problematic. Proving "intent" is difficult because in many cases the victims die carrying the intent with them without any expressions to others about their intentions. Other victims may even intentionally stage the scene and their death to resemble a homicide adding even more confusion to the event. It is also not unusual to have family members attempt to alter the scene to avoid the embarrassment and stigma of a suicide. Therefore, the investigation has to be conducted correctly and thoroughly from the beginning as a homicide until it can be proven otherwise. Utilizing the many processes outlined in this text will aid you in establishing a valid and supportable manner of death. No stone should be left unturned regardless of the potential outcome. In some cases the intent is demonstrated through a collection of numerous different pieces of the puzzle that should also include a psychological evaluation (psychological autopsy) of the deceased person.

The psychological evaluation of the victim is very similar to what we have previously described as the victimology or suspectology. In other words we conduct a thorough review of the person's background, history, life occurrences, education, relationships, work habits, social environment, and mental issues or behaviors that may be relative. All of these help us understand the victim and what may have motivated him/her. While the intent may not be readily identifiable, the totality of the circumstances coupled with the psychological autopsy could very well demonstrate intent.

When conducting the equivocal death analysis the investigator has to keep in mind the three components of evidence: physical evidence, informational evidence, and the behavioral aspects of the victim before and during the event. Begin by reviewing all case reports from investigators; medical records; statements from witnesses, friends, and coworkers of the victim; crime scene information; evidence collected at the scene and subsequent forensic analysis results; and thorough interviews of the victim's most inner circle of family and close friends.

▶ Physical Evidence

Physical evidence includes any injuries to the body. As stated previously, about 60% of all suicides are by firearms, with the fatal injury being found predominantly to the head, followed by the chest. While not the norm, multiple gunshot wounds have been recorded in suicides. In firearm deaths, one should try to answer the following questions: Was it a contact or hard contact gunshot wound to the head or chest? Is the gun still present at the scene? How much knowledge does the victim have about firearms? Can you eliminate everyone else from shooting this person? Does the victim show positive signs for gunshot residue on the hands or other parts of the body (understand that this is not a conclusive finding, only an indicator)? Could the victim have shot himself/herself? The ability of the victim to shoot himself/herself is a confusing point to police as well as family who improperly conclude the injury could not be self inflicted because the victim used their weak hand to hold the weapon or pull the trigger. This probably causes more conflicts between the police and family members than any other factor when firearms are used. In reality it is not unusual for the victim to use either hand to hold the weapon. What we often see is the victim may hold the barrel with their dominant hand against the impact point as if to steady the weapon and then pull the trigger using their weak hand. Therefore, using the weak hand is not really a significant finding unless there is some physiological reason such as the victim's inability to use the weak hand for anything.

Sharp force injuries can be singular or multiple. Frequently, hesitation marks are seen around the neck, wrists, or the inner surface of the arms. As can be seen in the analysis in Appendix C, multiple wounds are not unusual. The authors are familiar with cases with over 100 self inflicted stab wounds of various depths. Our main concern is whether or not the victim could have physically inflicted their wounds, so the location of the wounds on the body is generally more important than the number of wounds.

In sharp force injuries: Were there any hesitation or superficial marks? Where were these located? Is the cutting instrument present at the scene? Is there a pattern of injuries as to location on the body? Does the cutting instrument have the victim's blood or fingerprints on it? Where did this instrument come from? What is the possibility that someone else killed this person (can you eliminate homicide)?

In asphyxiation deaths the most common method is hanging, typically showing the inverted "V" furrow around the neck. However, anoxic death can occur from almost any position with a ligature around the neck, being fully suspended is not necessary. The victim could be lying down, on the knees, etc. The key is whether or not the weight of the body with the ligature is sufficient to occlude the carotid arteries which will, in a short period of time, cause death. In suffocations or depletions, we might see things like a plastic bag over the head or drowning.

In each of these cases, we must answer the following questions: Does the victim exhibit the inverted "V" furrow around the neck from hanging or the straight furrow typically found in homicidal ligature strangulation? Is it feasible that this victim could have gotten into the position on his/her own? Carefully evaluate the position of the body in relationship to the ligature and its connector. Again, is it possible? Does the position of the body, the plastic bag, rope, etc., all make sense or was it possibly staged by a second party?

In a drowning, did anyone see this person enter the water? Did s/he jump from an object such as a bridge or walkway? What was s/he wearing? Were any heavy objects in the clothing or attached to the body? What are the toxicological results? Did the victim have any swimming experience? Can you eliminate the possibility that someone else killed this person? Can we eliminate the possibility of accidental asphyxiation?

In cases of probable suicide by consumption of drugs, alcohol or poisons, we must answer these questions: Is the body position consistent with someone who might have taken a drug overdose? Are there any pill containers or other types of medication nearby whether prescribed or not? Are there any indications of illegal drugs? Does toxicology reflect the presence of any of these drugs, medications, alcohol, or other toxic substances? Due to time and money constraints, most toxicologists only run a few panels in their tests, thus are limited on what can be detected unless asked to search for a specific chemical or substance not in the standard testing modules. Since not all drugs are tested for by the toxicologist what other types of substances did you find in the apartment that if consumed could have killed this person? Can you eliminate the possibility that another person poisoned this victim?

Regardless of the method used, one of the more common findings during toxicology studies is the presence of alcohol. Alcohol as a depressant, can add or magnify the victim's feelings of hopelessness or despair. Since alcohol also tends to lower inhibitions and interferes with logical thinking, it may also provide the fuel needed for victims to actually carry out their plan.

Regarding suicide notes, keep in mind that they are only found about 20% of the time. The presence of a note does not necessarily prove that a suicide took place nor does the absence of a note prove otherwise. Keep in mind that sometimes family members who discover the death may hide or destroy the note to preclude the embarrassment and social stigma, or so they can collect insurance hoping the death won't be ruled a suicide. In searching for notes scan all computers and cellular phones the victim may have had access to at home and at work. All notes should be evaluated as evidence and sent to the crime laboratory for DNA, fingerprint, and handwriting analysis.

According to Holmes[3] there are four general categories of notes that are left behind by victims, these are financial, love scorned, physical health, and mental health. Notes also tend to express feelings of being tired or exhausted, hopelessness, and frustration. They may express their opinion as to their own failings or failings of others on their part and the general expression of not wanting to live. Most will also attempt to apologize or seek forgiveness of their actions to surviving family members or to God and hopes to meet them again in heaven.

Notes are typically written as *explanatory, accusatory,* or *instructional. Explanatory* notes provide a reason or explanation for their actions. These tend to be more self critical often noting some personal shortcomings or failures in their lives, failure to measure up to expectations, or being overwhelmed by life's events. Examples would include:

"I tried to be a man like Dad, but it was too much for me."

"School wasn't hard, but I wasn't smart enough."

"This is no one's fault I just couldn't go on, life was too much."

"I guess I am the failure everyone thought I would become."

Accusatory notes attempt to cast the blame for their actions onto someone or something else. These tend to be very harsh and often personal.

"Mom, you and Bonnie drove me to this. I hope you're satisfied."

"Sally, I hope you and John will be happy now that I am gone."

"I loved you once but now I just hate the thought of you."

"Screwing my friends just wasn't enough, was it? Now you have killed me. Thanks."

"You'll have to live with this for the rest of your life."

Instructional notes typically relate to the final wishes about their funeral, what to tell their children when they get older, relating to insurance or other financial information, or the final disposal of their personal property. These can be very short and simple or complex instructions including which hymns are to be sung, which bible readings are to be recited, where they want to be buried. Examples include:

"I don't want a funeral mass, just put me in the ground."

"Divide up everything between the kids."

Although we use the term 'suicide notes' it is also likely for victims to make their last statement or explanation as to why they are ending their life using video or audio recordings.

▶ Informational Evidence

As in any investigation witnesses can be very instrumental in helping you determine what happened, when, how, why, and who did it. The informational pieces of the puzzle that you collect from them are imperative in making a proper and accurate determination. In collecting the information about your victim ensure that thorough interviews are conducted of all those in the victim's inner circles such as family, social circles, and work groups. Also, during this process creating a good time line is very important. We are looking for what was going on in the victim's life in the preceding days, months, or in some cases even years before the event. Generally we will see a series of events in the victim's past that may culminate to one precipitating event or defining moment when the victim determines that their own death is the only solution to escape their problems. Especially important in the time line are any previous attempts at suicide or any discussion of suicide by the victim. Other important events would include the death of a close friend, relative, any significant other person in their lives, or any well publicized death or suicide of a famous person.

The informational evidence should include any and all medical records searching for physical as well as mental issues or problems the victim may have been going through. Suicide may be precipitated by other suicides especially within family groups due to common stressors, or inability to deal with a loved one's death.* Sometimes disease processes are hidden from relatives. Continue the search into all the victim's financial records and history including tax returns. Review the victim's employment history carefully for any problems that may have been work related. Fully understand the victim's position at work, relations with others, and job performance. The interviews of the victim's inner circles should include all relationships and family members as well. These interviews are extremely difficult—you must proceed carefully with compassion and understanding.

▶ Behavioral Evidence

In earlier chapters we mentioned that the behavioral aspects of the parties involved are critical to understanding what happened, why, and who did it. In most death cases you must collect the information for and evaluate the pre-offense behavior, the peri-offense (crime) behavior, and the post-offense behavior. However, with suicides, post-offense behavior does not exist for obvious reasons. Therefore all actions taken, words spoken, and behavioral demeanor of the victim prior to the event will be the focus, going as far back as possible to look for potential patterns of behavior, changes in demeanor, etc., as illustrated in **Case Study 10-1**.

In the case study we also see another dynamic of behavior as it relates to suicide. It is not just the intent to end their lives but victims may also want to inflict pain, blame, or guilt of their death onto another person. We can see this demonstrated in the location chosen for the suicide, the method used, or in

*As a Chief Deputy Coroner Dr. Adcock had a case where the father committed suicide with his WWII firearm and after the weapon had been examined by the crime lab, the son requested the return of the firearm. It was later released to the son and within six months he fatally shot himself with the same weapon.

Case Study 10-1

A family of four with a nine-year-old boy and three-year-old girl were having dinner one night when the young boy wouldn't eat and appeared to be angry with his parents. The parents told him that if he didn't eat then he would go to his room and stay there without dinner. The boy left and shut his bedroom door. After a couple of hours the mother went to check on her son finding him dead hanging from the inside door knob by his belt. He was only partially suspended with his knees bent and feet on the floor, but as previously mentioned being fully suspended is not necessary to cause death. The subsequent investigation of past events (pre-offense behavior) provided many telltale signs of low self esteem, declining grades, behavioral and acting out problems at school, that all began when the youngest child was born. Further information suggested that the family, unknowingly, had been giving all their attention to the girl and were basically ignoring their son. At this point the boy decided he couldn't take it any longer and hung himself to end his pain and suffering.

---

the notes left behind. While uncommon, it's not unheard of for victims to actually kill themselves in front of the person they are trying to inflict that pain, blame, or guilt on.

Additional victim behavior can be seen in efforts by the offender to arrange the scene in a particular way. Examples include a business man who committed suicide in a hotel room by taking a lethal dose of pills and lying on the bed, placed a plastic bag over his head. On the other bed he had carefully arranged a family photo album and placed his wallet, car keys, glasses, wedding ring, and insurance documents into a large envelope. In another instance a male victim sat on the carpet and leaned against the sofa and shot himself. Arranged in a semi circle around him on the floor were picture frames with photos of his wife and children.

Another victim shot himself in the head in a hotel room, next to him was a bible open to Ecclesiastes 3 with the first two verses highlighted in yellow: [1]To every thing there is a season, and a time to every purpose under the heaven: [2]A time to be born, and a time to die; a time to plant, and a time to pluck up that which is planted. This was interpreted as a symbolic suicide note.

In another instance, a man shot himself in the living room of his ex-wife's apartment, but left a note on the door for his children coming home from school advising them not to come into the house, but to go next door and get the neighbor to come inside first.

In all of the cited examples we see victim behavior to arrange the scene for his/her last act and may help to establish the clear intent to commit suicide.

A crucial part of this type of investigation should include a psychological autopsy performed by a forensic psychologist or psychiatrist. In the performance of this task s/he will need to see all investigative data, reports, statements, etc. Those, coupled with interviews of family and others, will enable the professional to assess the victim's suicidal tendency, based on the totality of the circumstances—particularly the mental and behavioral actions and state of mind of the victim. As an example of how complicated and exhaustive this can be, one of the authors was conducting an investigation into a suicide that may have involved the use of SSRIs (selective serotonin reuptake inhibitors, typically used in the treatment of depression, anxiety, or personality disorders). The forensic psychologist assessing the case had asked him to conduct the interview of the family members—the wife and two sons. He was given a 48 page document that contained 127 questions. The interview of the wife took over eight hours to complete. Needless to say this piece of the puzzle, the psychological autopsy, is critical to a sound determination as to what happened and maybe even why.

▶A Suicidal Determination Template

Over the years many templates have been designed to assist investigators, psychologists and others in making suicide determinations. While none of these are infallible, we felt it is important enough to at least describe one of these that might be useful in determining whether or not a person was at risk for suicide. In an article for the *Investigative Sciences Journal,* Streed reports that in 1983, Patterson, Dohn and Bird created the "SAD PERSONS" mnemonic as a tool to aid in the recognition of a possibly suicidal individual.[4] In this mnemonic, an individual's risk for suicide was determined by assigning *one point* for each affirmative answer from a list of ten yes/no descriptive questions. The descriptive criteria are illustrated in **Table 10-1.**

TABLE 10-1. SAD PERSONS Model

S	A	D	P	E	R	S	O	N	S
Male	Older age person	Depression	Previous Attempts	Ethanol abuse	Rational thinking loss	Social supports lacking	Organized plan	No spouse	Sickness
	The "SAD PERSONS" point-score for suicidal risk was then determined as follows								
	0 to 4 = Low Suicidal Risk			5 to 6 = Medium Suicidal Risk			7 to 10 = High Suicidal Risk		

There are many others that can be of assistance to the investigator in making these determinations. For additional templates it is suggested the reader review the cited reference as found in the *Investigative Sciences Journal*.

▶ Investigative Perspective

Staging Suicide as Homicide

Detectives are far more likely to encounter deaths resulting from suicide or self inflicted injuries than homicides, and investigating suicides may take more time, energy, and professionalism than homicide investigations. From the police perspective our investigation of a suicide is fairly limited to ensuring that the death was the result of intentional self infliction and not the result of a criminal act or omission of another.

It is very important to not jump to conclusions in making a determination of suicide. Suicides are one of the most popular themes used in staging a homicide scene. A staged scene is one in which the evidence or scene is altered in order to misdirect the police investigation. In this instance, into believing the death was a result of self infliction and not a criminal act. Many suspects are actually successful in fooling the police, because many departments do not take the time to conduct an adequate preliminary investigation to validate what the scene is depicting. If a patrol officer that is called to the scene is satisfied after an initial examination, this might be the only police investigation.

It is also not so uncommon for those committing suicide to stage the death to resemble a homicide. There are many reasons behind these attempts including: avoidance of a suicide clause in a life insurance policy; an effort to deflect shame or guilt for their actions onto someone else; they do not want to be thought of as weak by their family; or are concerned with leaving their family a legacy of suicide.

Methods used by victims to stage their own death can be very ingenious and unusual as demonstrated by **Case Study 10-2**.

Case Study 10-2

The body of a mid-30s male was found floating in a small lake by fishermen. Based on the condition of the body it had clearly been in the water for a number of weeks before it was found. Once brought to shore the body was examined and found to have a gunshot entrance wound to the back of the head and an exit wound to the top forehead. A criminal investigation was initiated immediately. This appeared to resemble an execution type homicide—victim shot in the back of the head and then dumped into the lake as a method of disposal.

The victim was identified initially through personal documents in his wallet and later confirmed through dental records. He had last been heard from three weeks earlier and this time frame seemed to match the overall condition of the body. It was then learned that the victim was seen in the area and questioned by ranger personnel three weeks earlier and was asked to leave as the lake was not open for recreational use. Only a few days after this contact with the victim, the rangers returned to patrol the lake area and noted the victim's car parked alongside the road. After a few days it was eventually towed away from the scene.

After discovery of the body the vehicle was located and searched. Inside the front passenger seat was a package wrapped and addressed to the victim's daughter. Opening the package investigators found a number of personal effects including the victim's driver's license, photographs, and his personal cellular telephone. Since the victim did not live near the place his body was found, and no clear criminal motive could be established for his death, a victimology background investigation was initiated. It was learned the victim was estranged from his wife for almost three years, and although he had contact with his daughter on an almost daily basis he had not seen her in over a year.

The victim was essentially unemployed and lived off of various part time jobs and a small amount of money supplied by his estranged wife. He had recently made an unexpected visit to his family, seeing his father, brothers, and other relatives. This had taken everyone by surprise because the victim had absented himself from the family and had had no contact with them for well over ten years. He returned to his hometown and was anxious to repair whatever hard feelings had caused the rift between himself and his family. He stayed at his father's house and by all accounts was becoming reintegrated with the family. Also during his visit it was noted that he began talking about final arrangements if anything ever happened to him and his desires for distribution of his property. He also gave away his hand tools and other property to family members, claiming he was getting other employment and would no longer need them. Just as suddenly as he arrived home he announced he had received employment out of state and would have to leave again, but promised he would remain in contact.

While the family was being investigated the detectives decided to drain the lake to seek any additional evidence. Once they did so, they found a 9mm hand gun and expended shell casing on the bottom of the lake a few feet from the shoreline. The serial number of the weapon identified an owner in another state. The owner was unaware the pistol was even missing and only confirmed the theft after checking the weapons storage box where it was normally kept. Interestingly, the owners were acquainted with the victim and in fact the victim had recently stayed with them for several months while he sought work in the area. Quite unannounced, the victim stated he was leaving and departed, and they had not heard from him again.

A check of his cellular phone records indicated he had been in the surrounding area for a few days, since his cell phone was traced to cellular towers in the local areas. He had made several phone calls back to his family, the last one to his daughter. All efforts to confirm any recent offer of employment for the victim were unsuccessful and it was clear from the appearance of the interior of his vehicle, he had been living in the car for a while. At some point the detectives came to realize there did not appear to be any motive for the victim's murder.

What became more and more plausible was the theory the victim may have killed himself in such a manner to resemble a homicide, perhaps because he did not want to be seen as a suicide victim or perhaps not wanting to have his daughter subjected to the stigma of his suicide. A reenactment was conducted using the same pistol and a person who was the same physical size as the victim. The reenactment showed it would have been relatively easy for the victim to position the pistol at the back of his head and pull the trigger. Once the gun was fired the pistol would fall to the bottom of the lake and the victim would float away; leaving the police to think he had been murdered, execution style and then dumped into the lake. The sudden visit to his family, his giving away possessions, his estrangement from his wife, last phone call to his daughter, and the package containing his personal effects addressed to his daughter were all indicators of someone contemplating suicide. When his estranged wife was contacted and interviewed she told investigators she had been waiting for such a call for a while.

The above case was aggressively worked on for over a year as a homicide, with literally hundreds of hours devoted to the effort before investigators realized in all of their efforts, there wasn't a single suspect ever identified or even a motive for the murder. Investigators began to turn inward towards the victim based on his victimology, and the totality of evidence to make the final determination. Family and friends of the victim can unwittingly hamper an investigation by their refusal to accept the suicide, feelings of guilt for perhaps contributing to the victim's intention, or because they too are "fooled" by usual circumstances or means used by the victim.

Understanding Suicide

There are numerous texts on the subject of suicides written from various sociological and psychological perspectives that help us to understand the reasons behind acts of self destruction. In this text we limit ourselves to a couple of very important concepts we need to understand when investigating suicide or cases of self inflicted injury:

1. You cannot rationalize an irrational act.

Those not suffering personal troubles such as depression or feelings of hopelessness, cannot always understand how a person could end his/her own life—the act is incomprehensible. Suicide therefore, must be seen through the lens of the victim's life and experiences, and not our own. What is unthinkable from our perspective may be totally acceptable and even a welcomed relief for the victim.

This is best explained by Shneidman who saw suicide as a type of psychological pain, which he described as *psychache*. He described it thus: "The suicidal act is both a moving away and a moving toward. Psychache, psychological pain is what the individual wishes to escape; peace is what the person seeks and moves towards. In suicide the two goals are merged as one: escape from pain is relief—that is how peace is defined. The unbearable pain is transformed into peace; the suffering is taken away. At least this is what the suicidal thinks and hopes."[5]

2. There is no such thing as a "too painful" way to commit suicide.

There are as many ways to commit suicide as there are suicide victims. Some are rather painless such as combining alcohol with medications, resulting in basically falling asleep and never waking up. Other common methods include firearms; razors, and knives to self inflict wounds; various forms of asphyxia including hanging, suffocation, or through oxygen exchange such as carbon monoxide inhalation.

There are others however who may choose more violent or certainly more painful methods such as self immolation, suffering what is certainly a most painful death. There are other texts and case studies in which the victim has used somewhat unusual methods of self destruction: an elderly woman who drank caustic liquid drain cleaner; a middle-aged man who straddled a large band saw, turned it on and leaned into the blade, literally cutting himself in half; a female who went to her garage, and using her husband's saber saw pressed it against her neck, nearly severing her head from her body; a young man who walked into the woods with a chain saw, started it and placed it on the ground, then leaned into it cutting his throat. One victim, who actually survived his attempt, had used a large paperback book to hammer a buck knife into the top of his head. These examples of unusual methods can go on and on.

Perhaps the method used has some special significance to the victim or it may simply be a case of using whatever method is available. Regardless of what we might think relative to the infliction of pain on oneself, it is clear this is not always an issue with those who wish to kill themselves. Whenever these issues come up, sometimes the only possible response is to go back to the first concept: You can't rationalize an irrational act.

Sometimes it is impossible to identify a particular reason behind the act of self destruction, but we do know there are certain common factors, based on statistics, recognized as risk factors. Some of the more general risk factor categories include:

Age of the victim

Marital status of victim

Education level

Maturity level

Family or other support system in place

Amount of stress in life

Relative success and failures in life

Socioeconomic living conditions

Employment history

Geberth[6] has identified several other general risk factors which should be taken into consideration when conducting a death/suicide investigation including:

Previous suicide attempts

History of mental disorders, particularly depression

History of alcohol and substance abuse

Family history of suicide

Family history of maltreatment

Feelings of hopelessness

Impulsive or aggressive tendencies

Barriers to accessing mental health treatment

Loss (relational, social, work related, or financial)

Physical illness

Easy access to lethal methods

Unwillingness to seek help because of the stigma attached to mental health and substance abuse disorders or suicidal thoughts

Cultural and religious beliefs—for instance, the belief that suicide is a noble resolution to a personal dilemma

Local epidemics of suicide

Isolation, a feeling of being cut off from other people

It is important to understand some people may have, display, or experience several of these risk factors and yet never go to the next step of taking their lives; while others may only briefly experience some of these factors and resort to suicide. Therefore these risk factors are best used as a guide for what to look for in order to recognize or understand what was going on in the victim's life prior to his/her death.

Geberth[7] has further identified three basic considerations to establish whether or not a death and death scene is consistent or inconsistent with suicide. These three basic considerations are:

1. Presence of the weapons or means of death at the scene
2. Injuries or wounds that are obviously self inflicted or could have been inflicted by the deceased

3. The existence of a motive or intent on the part of the victim to take his or her own life

We agree with these three general considerations, and have developed the acronym of MIA or Motive, Intent, and Ability, as a way to remember the concept.

Motive

Motive, as we have discussed in homicide investigations refers to the general reasons behind the action or why the victim was killed. In the case of suicides, we are concerned with identifying the reasons why the victim might want to kill himself/herself. As stated earlier, there are as many motives for committing suicide as there are suicide victims; unfortunately not all suicide victims provide a clear reasoning for their actions. Instead we are left to look for other bits and pieces of information, in a sense reading tea leaves, in order to conclude with reasonable certainty what happened. We must also depend on family, friends, or other background information on the victim to establish the possible motive.

To develop the motive, a detailed background investigation and a variation of the standard victimology assessment is especially helpful. In suspected suicide cases the focus is going to be even more centered on the victim than in other death investigations.

Intent

Suicide requires a specific intent to ends one's life and without it the death may be more consistent with an accident. The intent or desire to end one's life can be seen in several different ways including examining the lethality of the method chosen such as a firearm. It is not unusual to see victims who may use multiple means in order to ensure their efforts are successful. We see examples many times where victims place a plastic bag over their head and then hang themselves. **Case Study 10-3** demonstrates the use of multiple means where the victim was clearly intent on taking his own life and ensured success through use of multiple means.

Case Study 10-3

A young male was found hanging in his garage, the engine of his vehicle still running and the garage filled up with car exhaust. Toxicology later determined shortly before his death he had also taken a combination of antidepressants and alcohol which would have likely resulted in his death. In this case the victim was so determined to kill himself, he used no less than three methods. Another victim cut both wrists and then stuck his head into a large laundry sink full of water.

Intent cannot be discerned by the victim's actions alone. There have been many occasions when the victim did something wrong, unsafe, or even stupid resulting in his/her own death. Examples include a victim who was killed while trying to unload a newly purchased and unfamiliar weapon. In the military, soldiers are questioned if they are sure they have unloaded their weapons and rendered them safe. One soldier answered affirmatively and then held the weapon to his head to show how certain he was and pulled the trigger. Unfortunately, the weapon was not unloaded. In both incidents the individuals were responsible for their own death, they were holding the weapon when it was fired, but in neither case did the victim actually intend to kill themselves.

Intent refers to the specific goal to end life—not a case of engaging in risky behavior or doing something stupid, but rather a clear understanding of the actions and what the result will be. If suicide was based on risky or even stupid behavior then every parachuting fatality would have to be looked at as a potential suicide because it could be argued the victim by jumping out of a perfectly good aircraft, displayed risky behavior that causes their death. This concept is important and has led to more than one argument with medical examiners or coroners over their determination as to the manner of death.

Ability

Ability refers to the physical ability as well as the means available to commit suicide. It is not always necessary to have experience with weapons in order to load one and pull the trigger. It is also not necessary to have a working knowledge of human anatomy in order to know the best place to cut or stab yourself. We are instead concerned with the overall physical ability for the victim to have self inflicted the wound and the instrument used is at the scene nearby. Contrary to many layman's beliefs, it is not important that the weapon used is found in the victim's hand. Actually it is just as likely for the weapon to be dropped after inflicting the injury as it is to be in his/her hand. The problem is when the weapon is not found at the scene.

In Western culture, there is an inherently negative view towards suicide. The government and society as a whole feel a compulsion to protect people from themselves, as well as from one another. Thus, excepting a limited number of states, suicide and assisting in suicide is illegal, even in cases where there is a compelling individual or medical reason for termination.

Victimology

In cases of suspected suicide, the victimology assessment is a vital piece of the puzzle and is somewhat more focused on identifying the potential motive behind the act. Therefore the questionnaire should be expanded to include specific information on the background of the victim and what was going on in the victim's life:

Are there any financial problems?

Are there any employment problems, layoffs, terminations, loss of pay, or responsibility?

Are there any identifiable health problems?

Any identifiable interpersonal conflicts such as divorce?

Any loss of a family member, close friend, or girl/boy friend?

Did victim have a criminal background or history or pending court action?

Did victim ever actually talk about:

Suicide?

Ending his/her life?

His/her feeling the family would be better off without him/her?

Wanting to get out of his/her situation?

Final plans such as funeral arrangements?

Would death solve any problems for the victim?

Were there any other suicides of friends or family members?

Any recent suicides that were covered or mentioned in the media?

For teenage victims the family dynamic, dating issues, and standing within their peer groups may also prove to be critical background information to establish. This could include possible sexual or physical abuse within the family, difficulties and frustrations with boyfriends/girlfriends, and more common in our modern times their social standing within peer groups. There have been several well publicized teenage suicides which were centered on aspects of the victim's participation in various on-line social networks or other issues relating to conflicts with peers at school. Therefore when confronted with teen victims these are important elements to review for potential motives for their actions or other possible criminal offenses by others.

Staging Homicide as Suicide

One problem for investigators in a suicide case is dealing with family and friends who, regardless of the evidence, remain in denial over what happened. This often leads the surviving family into confrontation with the police over case findings. If the family has the means, it is not unusual for them to seek out and hire their own experts or investigators. If those experts agree with the police, many times the family finds another until they get the answer they want. Theoretically, any police investigation should be able to stand up to any review by another trained professional and come up with the same basic conclusions. Unfortunately, there are other "experts," who, through the use of selective facts and evidence can come to whatever conclusion is sought by their employers.

What often follows is a media assault against the police agency alleging anything from corruption to incompetence, and most certainly a conspiracy to cover up the actual death. Say the phrase "government cover up" and the media will beat a path to the family to get a story, not always concerned with the truthfulness of the story, only the allegation.

This is among the important reasons suicide investigations must be conducted by the police. However, it is important to remember that a homicide might be staged to resemble a suicide. Home invasion/interrupted burglary, sexual homicide, and suicide are the three major themes used when attempting to stage a homicide scene. Staging refers to efforts at altering or changing evidence at the scene to misdirect a police investigation away from the true facts and circumstances. Offenders are aware if the scene is accepted as suicide during the initial police viewing of the scene and a brief preliminary investigation, they can in effect get away with murder.

In **Case Study 10-4**, the conviction of the husband was only possible because the agency first looked at the death as a homicide and conducted a detailed and thorough preliminary investigation. The staging of the evidence was, however, very convincing and it is doubtful if another agency presented with the same type of evidence at the scene would have even bothered sending anything to the crime lab for evaluation in the first place. This highlights the importance of viewing the scene as a homicide until it can be proven otherwise.

There are some instances where the family, regardless of the evidence refuses to accept or consider the victim committed suicide. It is not unusual for them to spend thousands of dollars hiring forensic consultants and private investigators, and legal fees trying to overturn a police determination. This can be extremely frustrating because typically such efforts also include a media blitz criticizing the police and their investigation. The only way to avoid these problems is to conduct a thorough investigation into suicide and equivocal deaths. It will almost always prove to be less expensive in the long run to invest the time and effort to conclusively prove what happened, than to take a short cut and not investigate based on a quick scene examination by untrained personnel. However, as has been stated several times, someone trying to stage a scene and misdirect the police investigation only needs to get through the initial scene observation to get away with murder. In the vast majority of cases a detailed long term investigation is not going to be needed because the facts and circumstances are going to be very evident.

Some professionals believe that sometimes it is better to close out a case as undetermined, rather than as a suicide in order to spare the surviving family members any shame or to cast anything negative towards the victim. After all they conclude, "who does it hurt?" The victim is beyond caring and the concern has to be with the surviving family. Whereas this may be seen as a noble gesture; this flies in the face of proper ethical and professional conduct. As detectives it is our job to report the facts of what happened in the same manner for every investigation we are assigned. If we start making exceptions

Case Study 10-4

Police were called to the scene by a husband who reportedly found his wife in the master bedroom in their house, with a gun in her hand, a single close contact wound to the right side of her head. Three handwritten suicide notes and envelopes were found on the foot of the bed. The responding agency treated the scene as a suspected homicide and it was therefore processed in the same manner including complete photography and collection of evidence. During subsequent preliminary investigation detectives learned the victim had a history of depression and had been prescribed antidepressant medication as part of her treatment. Based on the scene evaluation, the letters, and other factors, the medical examiner listed the manner of death as suicide. Forensic examination of the writing in the letters determined they were written by the victim and her fingerprints appeared on them as well. Although there were some indications from family and friends that the husband was likely involved in her death, with the forensic evidence all pointing to suicide the case was eventually closed as a suicide. All of the evidence collected during the scene examination was actually returned to the husband. Several months later however, after receiving new information primarily based on the husband's pre- and post-crime behavior, and facts about his background which were not known or were not properly vetted during the initial investigation, the case was reopened as a possible homicide with the husband as the main suspect. Major factors including the receipt of $150,000 from a life insurance policy on the wife, the fact the husband had been engaged in a long term affair with another woman who then moved into the house within weeks of the wife's death, and more importantly information from the victim's family. According to them, a previous incident occurred in which the wife awoke at 2:30 in the morning to find their mobile home on fire and filling with smoke. The wife got up and discovered her husband and daughter were both out of the house and the smoke detectors were unplugged. The husband claimed their daughter was not sleeping so he took her for a ride to get her to go to sleep and the fire must have started during the short time he was out of the house. At the time of the fire, the victim had a $100,000 life insurance policy in effect. During the subsequent reinvestigation the evidence released back to the husband was recovered via search warrant and was reexamined at the crime lab. This time the envelop flaps were examined for DNA and on at least one letter the husband's DNA was found. An expert witness would testify the victim likely wrote the letters as a way to gain attention from her husband, leaving them to be found and acted upon. Sufficient evidence was also uncovered on the husband's efforts to establish an alibi and other post-crime behaviors to charge the husband for both the murder and the attempted murder some years before when he tried to set the mobile home on fire. The husband was later arrested, prosecuted, and convicted on all charges brought against him and sentenced to life in prison.

on these cases for the noblest of reasons, will we then begin to make exceptions on other cases?

References

1. American Association of Suicidology. (2007) *Suicide in the U.S.A.* Retrieved from http://www.suicidology.org/c/document_library/get_file?folderId=232&name=DLFE-244.pdf.
2. Geberth, V. J. (2006). *Practical homicide investigation.* (4th ed.). Boca Raton, FL: CRC Press.
3. Holmes, R. M., & Holmes, S.T. (2006). *Suicide, theory, practice, and investigation.* Thousand Oaks, CA: Sage Publications.
4. Streed, T. (2011). *A Template for the Investigation of Suicidal Behavior And Subject Precipitated Homicide,* Investigative Sciences Journal. Vol. 3 No. 1, March 2011. (www.investigativesciencesjournal.org)
5. Shneidman, E. S. (1996). *The suicidal mind,* New York, NY: Oxford University.
6. Geberth, V. J. (2006). *Practical aspects of homicide investigation, tactics, procedures, and forensic techniques.* (4th ed.). Boca Raton, FL: CRC Press.
7. Ibid., p. 397.

CHAPTER ELEVEN

Common Mistakes in Death Investigations

From 1980 to 2008 we accumulated nearly 185,000 unresolved murders across the United States and after looking at literally hundreds of cold cases, it is really remarkable to see how many of these unresolved cases can be directly attributed to one or more investigative failures or common mistakes made throughout the course of the investigation. Many times after reviewing unresolved cases we have been able to go back and point to an exact time, event, or decision when a case started to turn or veer away from the actual facts. Generally speaking these errors are not committed through lack of training or intelligence but most often by a lack of objectivity or discipline to continue through a difficult case rather than seeking out an easier path.

But detectives are human and therefore are ruled by human emotions and weaknesses. Weaknesses can be overcome through discipline and reliance on some of the more traditional investigative methods that have been emphasized through this text. This chapter addresses many of the shortfalls and common mistakes that occur during all forms of criminal investigation but are especially noticeable in death investigations.

▶ Tunnel Vision

Tunnel vision is perhaps one of the most prevalent of the common errors we find in unresolved cases. Tunnel vision is essentially a dogged insistence to focus on one aspect of the case or one suspect regardless of evidence that may point in another direction or to other persons. Tunnel vision can best be understood through a term known as "cafeteria investigation," wherein the detective accepts as truthful any evidence or facts fitting into his or her own theory of the crime but discounts or completely ignores anything that disagrees with that theory. **Case Studies 11-1** and **11-2** are good examples of tunnel vision and the problems it can create.

Case Study 11-1

Upon review of a fourteen-year-old cold case death investigation, it was noted that the agency had identified three very good and likely suspects but had never been able to eliminate any of them. Although all three suspects had a potential motive none of them had the means or opportunity to commit the crime. A detailed timeline of the three suspects' activities was developed, and in combination with other circumstantial evidence already in the file, all three of these suspects could be eliminated from involvement in the death. The assigned case detective agreed with the assessment and conclusions, and based on a new investigative plan reinitiated the investigation in a new direction. Several weeks later a phone call was made to check on the progress of the investigation. It was learned that the detective was actually back to concentrating on the three previous long standing suspects. The detective explained that the original detective had contacted him for an update on the case and despite the timeline and other circumstantial evidence, the current detective had been convinced to refocus on these same three individuals—the new investigative plan had been scrapped. So far the case has not produced any further information on any of the suspects and the case remains unsolved.

Case Study 11-2

A training session at a police academy centered on the importance of sending evidence to the lab. A discussion followed with a local detective announcing he had evidence that he could send to the lab but did not want to because he was concerned with the result. He was convinced he had the right guy and therefore did not want the evidence to be examined at the lab and possibly show a conflicting result. "If they (the lab) tell me he's not the guy, then I'm out of luck so I'm not taking a chance to send it in."

Both of these case studies are good examples of tunnel vision. In the first, although the suspects were clearly eliminated and no other evidence was presented to dispute the facts, the detective was convinced by the previous detectives to continue down the same path that had been followed previously rather than acknowledge that the initial theory was incorrect. The earlier detectives were invested in those particular suspects and were not going to be dissuaded by facts.

The second case study is actually far worse and presents not just an example of tunnel vision, but also of a very serious ethical problem wherein the detective had obviously settled on a good suspect but was not willing to put his theory to the test by sending the evidence to the lab for confirmation. Could this result in a wrongful conviction?

It takes great determination to continue through a difficult investigation, with all of the twists, turns, and red herrings that are a part of every investigation. But we should form our theory of the crime based on the available evidence, not form a theory and then seek out the evidence that supports it. Theories and suspects are good to have but they are always subject to change or refinement as new evidence is collected and evaluated. If we can establish our most viable suspect was not involved with the crime or has an undisputed and verifiable alibi, then we have to look for other suspects.

▶ Lack of Documentation

Perhaps one of the biggest critiques of modern detectives is the failure to complete or provide proper documentation and written reports detailing the results of their investigative efforts. It seems that the general nature of police officers is a love of the investigative process and all the actions associated with being a detective, but a palpable dislike of having to put anything down on paper. Not because they do not know how to write or prepare a report but because it is time consuming and takes away from the "fun" part of investigations—picking up evidence, conducting interrogations, or identifying witnesses.

The reluctance to make a written report or to properly document investigative activity can have severe ramifications in the life of the investigation as noted in **Case Study 11-3**.

There is an old adage we use to explain the importance of documentation that says: "If it's important enough to do, then it's important enough to write a report about it. If it's not important enough to write a report about it, then why did you do it?" The wisdom of this saying is illustrated again in **Case Study 11-4**.

We cannot rely on our memory—if it isn't written down, then it didn't happen. It is just as important to document "non-events" and failures as it is successes, particularly when dealing with interviews and testimonial evidence. One example is an interview with a particular witness who claims not to have seen or heard anything. If no written report is made of the interview, and we later find the witnesses made a statement very favorable to the defense and is on their witness list for court, our case could be in serious jeopardy.

These situations are avoided by documenting every interview and whenever necessary taking written statements from witnesses thereby locking

Case Study 11-3

While reviewing a serial homicide cold case, the detectives were briefed on at least one very good suspect that was associated with at least five of the six known victims. He had lived next door to the first victim; he was seen in the morning hours at a small park a short distance from the residence of victim #2 the morning the victim was found murdered; he had spent the night in his car about a block away from the residence of victim #3 the night before she was found dead in her apartment; he often slept in the woods close by and was observed many times walking by the residence and crime scene location of victim #4; he may have had a personal dispute with victim #5 over the collection and sale of aluminum cans at a local recycling center. During the lengthy briefing prior to reviewing the case documents and scene photographs, the case detectives continued to provide almost a never ending stream of facts and circumstantial evidence they had uncovered. The sum of all of this information clearly painted this particular suspect as the leading person of interest. Later when the case documents were actually reviewed there were no actual police reports within the file documenting any of the previous information supplied by the detectives during their briefing. The detectives were asked about the missing reports and the source of the information they had provided. Sadly the detectives explained they had intentionally not prepared any written reports because the suspect was actually related to someone within the department and they were concerned such information would be compromised. Following this revelation, the detectives were advised to begin to take the time to document all of their information, even at that late date. Unfortunately after some discussion, the detectives could not agree concerning the actual source(s) of information for placement of the suspect at any of these locations. After several hours of honest effort, it was still not clear who exactly had provided the information and what sounded like such a good suspect with very good circumstantial evidence linking him to five out of six homicides was essentially lost because it was not properly documented. Because the information was not documented it is unclear how many times the telling and retelling of this information might have resulted in the inflation of facts, evidence, or event time sequencing.

them into their statements. The earlier statement can be used to impeach the testimony of any witness that later reveals important facts that had been withheld from the police. Police work, particularly detective work, is all about documentation and report writing. It is part of the job—those unwilling to complete these important steps are in the wrong profession.

Case Study 11-4

Upon review of an unsolved case a new detective was brought in to give the investigation some new life. After the initial review of the case file the new detective identified over one hundred additional or new investigative leads that needed to be followed, including the interview of one particular person of interest. During the initial briefing of the cold case, when this person of interest was mentioned as an important interview, one of the original investigating police officers stated that wasn't necessary because he had interviewed the witness already. Since there was no written report reflecting that interview in the file, the new detective asked, "What did he say?" The police officer answered, "Hell I don't remember, but it must not have been important if I didn't make a report." The person of interest was later interviewed and was eventually determined to be the actual perpetrator of the double homicide.

One other common error involving documentation is the failure to collect all investigative reports from all participants in the investigation. This is particularly important when multiple agencies are involved in the same investigation. It is incumbent upon the assigned detective to collect, preserve, and ensure correct filing of all of those reports. **Case Study 11-5** demonstrates the importance of this step.

Case Study 11-5

The original case had been worked by the county sheriff. After a few weeks, they had been joined in the investigation by the state police. Upon reviewing the cold case, it was found that the file from the country sheriff contained only the sheriff's reports although the state police had obviously done some work on the case. The two agencies had never exchanged reports with each other. Each was investigating similar paths, collecting evidence on persons(s) of interest, but neither agency was sharing with the other. Eventually the state police case file was located and reviewed. When viewed separately, both files came up with persons of interest or potential suspects, but neither file was able to identify one particular suspect. However, once the files were combined, one suspect was clearly identified almost to the exclusion of anyone else and the remaining effort focused on this suspect.

▶ Failure to Follow Logical Leads

Clear and logical leads are not always pursued. There are a multitude of reasons or excuses for this failure, but usually the actual reason is not because the lead was not recognized, but rather the detective just did not *want* to act on the lead or did not think it would be beneficial. **Case Study 11-6** illustrates this failure.

Case Study 11-6

An unsolved robbery/murder for a city police department was under review. The armed robbery of a business was committed by two unknown black males driving a small green car. The business owner was shot and killed for not moving fast enough and the offenders fled the scene. There were two witnesses who were slightly roughed up and provided a brief description of the men. During review of the cold case, a document for the TIPS line for the city police department was found. This TIPS line was established so the public could call the police anonymously with "tips," or information on crimes occurring within the city. The TIPS line call sheet documented a call from an unknown female who identified the two suspects as Tyrone (and last name) along with another male she only knew as Tyrone's cousin (no name provided), and that the car they used belonged to Tyrone's sister (no name given). The caller did not provide any other information. The call came in just two days after the robbery and seemed like a very promising lead. The very next document found in the case file was a second TIPS line call sheet reporting a second call two days later (four days after the robbery) by an unidentified male who identified the robbery suspects as Tyrone (last name) and Robert (last name provided) using Tyrone's sister's vehicle. Looking through the remainder of the file, there was no other information about Tyrone, Robert, or the green car. There had been no effort to do any type of background check, or to locate or interview or validate any information on either of the TIPS line information sheets. The case detective was questioned about the TIPS and confirmed knowledge of both Tyrone and Robert confirming that they were cousins and were well known basic street thugs. The possibility of Tyrone's sister having a green car like the one used in the robbery and reported by the TIPS line was also not pursued. In the detective's opinion, he didn't think they had enough information to even talk with them about the incident so they continued looking in other directions for the suspect. The detective had never considered even looking at either of the two men as suspects or as a person of interest. Although the tip was not real evidence per se, it could at least provide a starting point.

Months after it was pointed out to the detective the importance of at least trying to locate and interview Tyrone and Robert, the detective still did not think there was enough information to question them and the case was still unsolved, continuing in yet another different direction.

Understandably, the presence of a citizen's anonymous tip cannot in and of itself amount to probable cause to make an arrest, but without any other direction or suspects coming to your attention what have you got to lose? The reason the department established a TIPS line in the first place was to try to get the public to call in with information. How successful is the TIPS program going to be if we never follow the tips we receive?

The traditional thought process has always been that it is better to run the lead and discover it is not beneficial than to ignore it and find out later that the defense completed the lead and discovered other evidence. Not only could a defense discovery of potential evidence catch you off guard, it can be argued your investigation must be deficient, or your personnel are incompetent. Experience has shown how vital this is—do the lead and document the results—no excuses.

An investigative lead is basically a question, fact, or statement which has come up in the case that needs to be answered, clarified, or verified. If there is an unanswered question or an unverified fact, then it needs to be addressed. Every lead that is run, every fact that is verified, clarified, or discounted has advanced the case. Every suspect who is eliminated has advanced the case. Confirming what did *not* happen, or who was *not* involved is as vital to the case during investigation as knowing what *did* happen and who *was* involved.

As cold case investigators, we might not be concerned initially with what the police *did* do, but rather, what the police did *not* do or what they missed. Leads that were not thoroughly pursued would be the natural starting point in the new investigation. The teaching point is clear—what detectives fail to do or fail to document provides a weak spot for the defense to start poking holes in the investigation.

▶Failure to Validate Alibis or Statements

It is very important to validate information found in the various statements or testimony obtained in the course of the investigation. Regarding any statement made by any person, including a victim, witness, or the offender—believe nothing, verify everything. Any information should be validated by at least two sources, particularly when dealing with circumstantial evidence. If it can be established that A, B, D, and E took place, then we can assume circumstantially that fact C also took place although we may not have any direct evidence that it is true. Because circumstantial evidence is only good when a series of actions can be linked together, if the link between these actions is broken the circumstantial conclusion cannot be established. Therefore, when we seek to confirm our facts we always seek at least two sources to verify the information, so if one source is invalidated, there is still a second source available to establish and maintain that link.

Of particular importance are statements that may seem outlandish, confusing, or doubtful. **Case Study 11-7** demonstrates such an example.

The reconstruction and validation of the victim's statement in this case study played a pivotal role in the offender's later conviction because the offender's identification was based solely on the victim's recognition of the offender, as no forensic or physical evidence was ever recovered from the crime scene. The detectives testified as to their confirmation of the victim's statement that it was possible to both identify a person and see the razor blade through the light coming through the window exactly as she had described.

For alibis, we suggest at least three independent sources be used for confirmation, especially if the alibi is used to eliminate a suspect from involvement in a case. This is a very big step in the investigative process and should not be taken lightly or omitted without good verifiable reasons. Anyone who cannot be eliminated from involvement based on at least three independent sources should remain as a person of interest or at least remain as someone who has not yet been eliminated. When dealing with a suspect alibi, we consider a family member as only one half of a source. Meaning, if a family member says the suspect was at a certain place at a certain time, a full two and one half more sources would be needed to corroborate. This is simply

Case Study 11-7

A young female soldier claimed she was assaulted in her bed by a fellow soldier and was viciously cut on the side of her neck and along her forearm. The victim was eventually able to identify the offender and the weapon used as a double edged razor blade that the offender held between his thumb and index finger. During the initial crime scene examination it was noted the open bay type barracks was absolutely pitch black during the night. The victim insisted, however, that she woke up, saw the offender kneeling beside her bed and that he had shown her the razor blade before she was attacked. While reviewing the earlier case, investigating detectives returned to the victim's area of the barracks during the same time frame of the assault, and lay on a bunk where her bed had been. They immediately noted that a light from the parking lot next door shone through the window above the bed with such brightness you could actually read a normal print book. She would have been able to clearly make out someone kneeling by the bed, and to see a razor blade held in front of her face as she had described. This finding took everyone involved with the investigation by surprise and immediately changed their impression of the crime.

because family members will routinely and unabashedly lie to police in an effort to help a family member.

There are always cases in which no matter the effort, there are only one or two sources that establish an alibi. In those instances, we can revert back to the motive, opportunity, and means rule to attempt to eliminate a suspect.

While reviewing cold cases we have discovered many times the main suspect was eliminated very early in the initial investigations based on a weak or unsubstantiated alibi that had never been checked out or confirmed. Sometimes these alibis are no more than a few weak and unqualified statements such as:

Detective: Where were you when the crime was committed?

Suspect: I was at Johnnies.

Detective: OK.

Following this exchange the detective moved onto other questions. Brief questions and answers like the example may be the only mention of the main suspect's whereabouts in the entire case file. Even worse, based on this statement alone the suspect may have actually been eliminated as a suspect, without even framing the alibi within the parameters of the time of the crime or without establishing "Who is Johnny?". On more than one occasion, during a cold case reinvestigation, an alibi was easily destroyed and the suspect was eventually identified as the perpetrator. These cases typically languish and go nowhere because detectives are out chasing the wrong person(s), because suspects had been erroneously eliminated based on unverified information.

▶ Investigation Stopped Too Early and Failure to Coordinate with Prosecutors

These two common errors often go hand in hand. Whereas the police are responsible for actually investigating the case, it is ultimately the prosecutor that is going to have to present the case to a jury. Therefore, it is imperative the two agencies work closely together. As stated previously in the text, it is advantageous for the prosecutor to be actually present at the scene, getting involved in the case in the early stages. The prosecutor then develops ownership and a personal interest in the case.

But even when the prosecutor comes in later, the police must realize the case or investigation is not over until the offender has been convicted. There are occasions when detectives can expect to be actively pursuing leads and even interviewing additional witnesses who have surfaced during the course of the trial. Unfortunately, there is sometimes a serious disconnect between the police and the prosecutor over duties and responsibilities. **Case Study 11-8** demonstrates these problems.

This case was especially frustrating because although it is very likely the police had identified the right suspect; due to pride, ego, or misunderstanding of their duty and responsibility, they failed to continue with the investigation

Case Study 11-8

A young wife and mother of two was found nude and murdered in the master bedroom of her mobile home. She had been stabbed repeatedly and the mobile home intentionally set afire using lighter fluid on the walls and carpets to destroy the evidence. A suspect was quickly identified as a friend of the victim's husband that was staying at the mobile home temporarily until he could find an apartment of his own. The suspect was the last to see her alive and the fire was determined to have started shortly after he claimed he left the residence for work. After a denial interview, he was offered and failed a polygraph examination. He then invoked his rights and never made any other admissions or confession to the murder. Based on the limited available information the suspect was arrested and jailed for first-degree murder and held at the county jail with no bond. The suspect's attorney declined a preliminary hearing and the case went forward to the grand jury where he was promptly indicted. The prosecutor reviewed the file as the case was coming to trial and realized there had been no other investigative activity in the file since the suspect's arrest, now more than 10 months past. The prosecutor had believed additional work was being carried out, but the police detectives believed they had completed their responsibility by gaining enough evidence for an arrest and indictment and had moved on to other cases. Although there was enough evidence to get probable cause for an arrest and an indictment, there was nowhere near enough information or evidence to proceed to trial. Unfortunately, the evidence was so slim and so much time had passed it was impossible for the case to proceed. Based on speedy trial issues the district attorney was forced to drop the charges and allow the suspect out of jail. Once released the suspect then left the jurisdiction. The police took great offense to the suspect being released, and although asked to reinvestigate, their efforts were so unenthusiastic and lackadaisical the case was eventually closed as unresolved. It remains unsolved to this day.

and gather the evidence needed for a successful prosecution. Sadly, as in so many other cases, there will be no justice for this victim, her husband, or her two children.

The frustration of the previous case study can be matched by the following examples. On reviewing unresolved cold cases we have seen examples of police officers who took it upon themselves to go against the advice of the local prosecutor. Sometimes it was based on a strictly political decision by someone running for public office. Sometimes it was based on conflicts between agencies, where each agency was determined to impose its will upon the other. Regardless of the reasons, the resulting conflict only served to ensure there would be no actual resolution of the case or prosecution of the offenders.

In some of these particular cases, the prosecutor had specifically requested the detectives to either wait on making an arrest until they had completed some additional investigative leads, or had expected additional investigative work to be accomplished after the arrest. Unfortunately, the police decided to ignore the request and made an arrest because they were satisfied with the results of their investigation, or decided their job was finished following the arrest and did nothing more. Unfortunately the police learned the reality of the criminal justice system, that is the police may make an arrest, but the prosecutor must prosecute.

On more than one occasion the prosecutor took this as a direct challenge to his authority and steadfastly refused to prosecute and in several instances refused to even present the case to a grand jury. This of course resulted in the suspect's release from jail and to this day these cases have never been prosecuted. This particular situation played out in at least two incidents on which we conducted a cold case review. In our opinion, the police were right and had centered on the appropriate suspects; but in both cases we agreed with the prosecutor's opinion that there was not enough information or evidence to successfully prosecute at that time and there was no overriding reason to take the suspect into custody. In fact, it would probably have been better if the offender was able to display more post-crime behavior.

Sadly, in the examples of both of the cold cases, the police department compounded the problem by not aggressively continuing the investigation once an arrest was made. Again, there was no justice for the victims or their families. Even worse, at least two murderers were released back into society, perhaps to offend again.

It is imperative that prosecutors and police work hand in hand. It is not enough for the police to be satisfied with their effort; it is up to the prosecutor to be satisfied with the information and evidence that is available. No prosecutor is going to take a case to court if there is not a good chance of winning. It is not merely a matter of making an arrest, it is convincing 12 jury members of the guilt of the offender.

▶ Overdependence on Polygraph or Other "Truth" Devices

The polygraph and other truth detection devices such as voice stress can be useful investigative tools, but are not definitive or conclusive. They should be used as an interrogation tool and not necessarily for determining involvement in a crime, or of guilt or innocence.

The polygraph is designed to measure various involuntary responses from the body including blood pressure, breathing, and the galvanic skin response. The polygraph measures the increases and decreases of responses from the body when put under stress. Since most of us have to think about lying or deceiving and we know when we are lying, this causes responses which are recorded on the graph paper by the three ink pens.

But the polygraph is only a machine; and therefore it's only as good as the individual operator and the operator's personal training and experience. Unfortunately, not all polygraph training is the same. Training can vary from a two week course put together by someone who puts up a shingle claiming to be a polygraph examiner, to a lengthy and formal multi-month course.

There is no such thing as passing a few questions and failing a few questions. The polygraph is an all or nothing type of report, either the examinee passes or fails. The actual results for a polygraph are either deception indicated (DI)—the examinee failed the test; no deception indicated (NDI)—the examinee passed the test; or inconclusive—no opinion can be made and more testing is needed. The results of a polygraph or any other truth verification instrument should never be solely used as probable cause to make an arrest or to charge a person; nor should it be solely used to eliminate someone from being involved in a crime. In our experience we have seen the guilty pass an examination and the innocent fail—not very often, but they both happen. However, it can be used as one of the factors along with other evidence and factors as a method to narrow the focus of the investigation. For example if we have a suspect for whom we can only find one source for an alibi, perhaps we can use the polygraph as a means to fully eliminate them or move them lower down the priority list of potential suspects. The polygraph's real value is in its use as an interrogation tool, where the results of the examination are used as powerful psychological evidence to interrogate the suspect. Although the results of the examination are inadmissible in court; statements made to the examiner are admissible.

▶ Overdependence on Forensic Evidence

If modern detectives have an Achilles heel or weak point, it is in the overreliance and dependence on forensic evidence. Baskin and Sommers[1] have studied the effects of forensic evidence on criminal justice outcomes. They found that forensic evidence was auxiliary and non-determinative while investigative techniques were more powerful predictors of arrest than forensic evidence. This is not to say forensic evidence is not needed or valuable because it is extremely important. We have found that when a detective is confronted with a reported crime for which (1) there are witnesses, (2) physical evidence can be recovered, (3) a suspect confesses or makes admissions to the crime, and (4) forensic examinations are possible, a successful resolution of the case is almost a certainty. Even more important, the detectives know exactly what to do—what remaining leads are necessary, what additional evidence is needed, and how to present the case to the prosecutor. However, when presented with a situation with no witnesses, or a limited amount of physical and forensic evidence, many detectives are lost. It is clear that the modern detective has become spoiled with the dramatic possibilities and has become too dependent on forensic examinations of evidence.

We see evidence of this overreliance as we look through the many cold cases throughout the country. Typically we see this demonstrated by two patterns. In the first, there is an aggressive surge once the case is initiated, including a good effort at the crime scene and initial interviews. The activity quickly dies down, however, if eyewitnesses or forensic evidence is not turned up during the initial hours of the investigation.

The second typical pattern is a near shut down of investigative activity for months at a time because the detectives are "waiting on the crime lab," before they go any further. Whereas on the surface, this may seem like a good tactic and we certainly believe in the importance of submitting evidence for examination; with the backlog of work in most crime labs, it could easily take months or even a year or more before the forensic examination is completed. As the case is stalled pending the lab work, life goes on—witnesses and persons of interest may move away; they might die or get into an accident and be unable to testify; their memories may fade; they may change their mind and no longer want to cooperate with the police.

After a year we find the interest in the case has waned. Although strong during the initial stages, after a year or more, and with other cases to work, it is difficult to dust off this old case and muster the appropriate enthusiasm to continue the investigation. There exists also the very real possibility the forensic examinations will come back with findings that are not helpful to the investigation. At that point, the case is basically cold and there is no forensic evidence to fall back on. The detective would then have to restart the investigation and seek other forms of evidence, a year or more after the events. To a competent and experienced investigator, reading in a file that a detective was or is waiting on lab results before continuing with the investigation is the equivalent of hearing nails scratching across a blackboard.

As we emphasize throughout the text the vast majority of cases are not solved by fantastic new forensic techniques and technologies but through the hard work using traditional methods and techniques. Forensic examination of discovered evidence is imperative and should be initiated as quickly as possible. But, while the evidence is at the lab, the investigation should continue with the expectation the results may not aid in the successful solution of the case. The case must continue to progress, not be labeled as pending.

There are of course exceptions to this general rule. For example, if a good suspect has been identified and needs to be interviewed, but the lab has promised a result within a short period of time, a slight delay is not harmful and positive results would clearly help out in the interrogation. But, if the delay will be numbered in months, we would recommend the interview proceed without the examination results. If the suspect makes admissions or denials during the interview, the laboratory results may be able to confirm or refute them. This evidence might prove to be just as strong as a confession.

The importance of understanding and using the traditional methods of "walking and talking," following investigating leads, developing motives, and verifying statements and alibis can be demonstrated. A study of 798 homicides conducted by Wellford and Cronin[2] noted that physical evidence of some form was discovered in only 72% of the cases and a witness was found in only 80% of the cases. Additional studies documented by Baskin and Sommers[3] tracked the outcomes of 400 homicide cases through the justice system and noted that although physical evidence had been recovered in 97% of the studied cases, there was an arrest in only about 55% of them. Clearly physical and forensic evidence is important, but not the ultimate key to a successful investigation.

Based on these two studies, detectives can expect they must investigate crimes in which there is little if any physical evidence, no witnesses, or the evidence that has been recovered does not produce effective leads or persons of interest. It is incumbent upon detectives to develop traditional investigative skills in order to ensure successful resolution of the case.

▶ Lack of Supervisory Oversight

Supervising a detective unit is not just about scheduling, assigning cases, or monitoring training, supplies, and equipment. These are indeed part of the role of any supervisor. We are referring to another very important aspect of the supervisor's role that represents one of the prime weaknesses in modern American policing—the actual review and oversight of individual cases to make certain detectives are staying on track and accomplishing those things that need to be accomplished.

Much of what we have written about in this chapter—shortfalls and weaknesses in the investigative process—could be mitigated with proper oversight by a supervisor, but this is not a widely held belief among American detectives. In fact, whenever we talk about this aspect of investigations to detectives, there is often open and loud hostility and an attitude of "nonacceptance" of someone reviewing or supervising their work. This could be partially due to the personality type of individuals attracted to detective work in the first place—independent, self starting, logical thinkers. They tend to see themselves as the exclusive determiner of what is important and what is not important in their particular cases and become possessive of their case files.

We see evidence of this during training courses expressed in body language, comments, and definitive statements centering on the theme: "this is my case; and I don't share it with anyone; and no one tells me what to do on *my* case."

We have also seen this concept of "the case belongs to the detective," actually played out as an unofficial but established agency policy. Some agencies have no policy or mechanism for maintenance of the original case file once the detective has concluded the investigation, whether or not it resulted in an arrest and conviction or was closed as unsolved. The case files are maintained by each individual detective at the office or at his/her home. Upon retirement or separation from the agency, the detectives actually take their original files home with them, including photos, negatives, and original statements. Years later when working cold cases, one of the first steps is to go find the original detective (or his widow in many cases) and try to get the original file returned so it can be worked again.

We agree with the general concept of "ownership" of a case—the detectives taking pride in their work, caring about the case outcome, and wanting to see it through until the end. We also realize the importance of having someone outside the investigation look at the work to make sure the important things are being done—evidence is sent to the lab, witnesses are interviewed, alibis are properly checked out, facts are verified, and the detective remains engaged throughout the investigation even after an arrest is made. An active supervisory review process can help ensure that procedures are followed, followed through, and followed up, and that documentation and files are complete and properly maintained (see **Case Study 11-9**).

Literature provides us with a couple of studies that relate directly to this topic of supervisory oversight of ongoing investigations. One by Keel, Jarvis, and Muirhead[4] revealed that while periodic case review did increase the solvability of cases it must be a delicate balance that allows the detective latitude. (As a side note regarding clearances of homicide cases they also noted other important factors that contributed to success: no more than five cases per year per detective; no rotation of detectives; and a minimum staffing of two detectives per unit versus a detective working solo.)

In another study in the United Kingdom, Jones, Grieves, and Milne[5] placed twelve detectives into two groups with three experienced and three inexperienced detectives in each group. While all twelve were to review the same case file one group was allowed to review without any guidance just based on their experiences—subjective method. The other group was given a template to follow for the entire review process—objective method. The results reflected that in the objective approach to case review, observations

Case Study 11-9

In the review of a 15-year-old cold case homicide it was determined that three possible suspects (A, B, & C) were in focus with two (A & B) more prominent than the third. According to many witness accounts these three were involved in the fatal stabbing of a known prostitute. Suspect A was overheard on more than one occasion bragging about how he and suspect B killed this person, yet none of them were ever interviewed. At the briefing of this review to the detectives the more senior detective stated that he thought suspect A may have been involved but admitted he never attempted to make contact for an interview. The supervisor made the observation that the results of these cold case reviews were making her look bad for not reviewing the case for investigative sufficiency, and very possibly she could be correct.

were more constructive; that 70% of the comments were much more positive than negative; that there was a 54% increase in the quality of comments; and that the template closed the gap between experienced and inexperienced detectives regarding their ability to conduct a thorough and meaningful case review.

There are many advantages for conducting a supervisory review of the actual investigation. Perhaps the biggest is one of completeness. If the supervisor can read the file and have no questions or identify no other investigative leads that need to be completed, then there is a good chance the case is going to be acceptable to the prosecutor as well. If the supervisor has questions or concerns, or does not understand everything in the investigation, it is likely the prosecutor or the jury might also have concerns. It is important that supervisors are properly trained and also empowered within their agency to give specific instructions to the detectives.

In conclusion, we have compiled our own Objective Case Review Template consisting of eleven categories that we suggest be used by supervisors to evaluate ongoing investigations and provide comments as needed.

Objective Case Review Template
(Checklist w/comments as needed)

1. Initial response—scene visited
   a. Identification of investigative team and their roles
   b. Proper assignment duties according to talent or capabilities
   c. Obtain briefing from first responders and coordinate with crime scene technicians
   d. Ensure double perimeter and scene security is established
   e. Conduct initial walk through of scene
   f. Next of kin notifications
   g. Eliminate the person that made report or found the body
2. Victim/complainant interviewed
   a. Victim positively identified
   b. Statement evaluated and validated (does it make sense or probable?)
   c. Background and criminal history of victim
   d. Victimology completed
   e. Add pre-crime activity to timeline
3. Scene and evidentiary issues
   a. Crime scene search warrant and return
   b. Crime scene processed and documented (video, photo, sketch, notes)
   c. Staged scene, altered or cleaned up?
   d. Evidence collected

    e. Evidence evaluation (complete list and what does it all mean, what else is needed)

    f. Scene evaluation—organized, disorganized, control (offender behaviors)

    g. Evidence sent to lab

    h. Crime Lab and toxicology results

    i. Review of autopsy determine time and cause of death, compare with other forensic facts

    j. Other forensic experts needed or used

4. Canvass conducted

    a. Double checked for completeness

5. Significant witnesses interviewed and statements obtained

    a. Statement validated and corroborated

    b. Name checks and basic background on significant witnesses

6. Hypotheses formulated

    a. Motive and type of crime

    b. Spontaneous with precipitating event

    c. Premeditated event

    d. ViCAP for similar offenses or suspects

    e. Local MO/Signature check for similar offenses

    f. Criminal investigative analysis (CIA)

    g. Tested and validated or not; repeat as necessary

7. Suspect management

    a. Positively identified

    b. Arrested, clothing seized, fingerprints, and DNA samples obtained

    c. Background and criminal history conducted

    d. Similar cases

    e. Family, friends, coworkers canvass

    f. Interviews of spouse/significant partner/parents/coconspirators

    g. Interviewed w/statements, denials, admissions, confessions

    h. Polygraph

    i. Statement validated, confirmed or discounted

    j. Motives, means, and opportunity

    k. Identification of other witnesses, victims, or other evidence

    l. Other potential information, e.g., telephone toll records, financial documents, cell phone records and texts, life insurance, ATM, checks or employee time cards

    m. Add pre-, peri-, and post-crime activity to timeline

    n. NCIC off line checks

8. Lead management and investigative plan
   a. Identified leads
   b. Followed up
   c. Supervisory review
9. Obtain written reports from all participants
   a. Review for additional investigative leads
   b. Review for any conflicting evidence or statements
10. Reconstruction (validate what you have)
    a. Physical evidence (bloodstain pattern and shooting incident reconstruction)
    b. Informational evidence (denials/admissions/confessions, etc., all validated)
    c. Offender behavior (pre-, peri-, and post-offense behavior)
11. Prosecutor provided all the data
    a. Prosecution presentation
    b. Substantiated elements of proof
    c. List of witnesses and evidence
    d. Respond to DA questions and requests

The common mistakes outlined in this chapter are not the result of a particular lack of technical training, professionalism, or lack of empathy by detectives. Instead, they can be traced to basic procedural and human failures. These include failures to follow basic investigative techniques, an overreliance on technology, and some basic human emotions such as vanity and stubbornness.

References

1. Baskin, D., & Sommers, I. (2010). The influence of forensic evidence on case outcomes of homicide incidents. *Journal of Criminal Justice, 38*, 1141–1149.
2. Wellford, C., & Cronin, J. (1999). *Analysis of variables affecting the clearance of homicides.* Justice Research and Statistics Association, Washington DC. (NCJRS# 181356).
3. Baskin, D., & Sommers, I. pp. 1141–1149.
4. Keel, T. G., Jarvis, J. P., & Muirhead, Y. E. (2009). An exploratory analysis of factors affecting homicide investigations. *Homicide Studies, 13*(1), 50–68.
5. Jones, D., Grieves J., & Milne, B. (2010). Reviewing the reviewers, the review of homicides in the United Kingdom. *Investigative Sciences Journal, 2*(1).

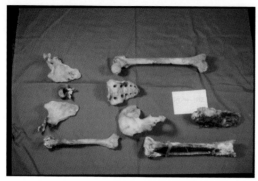

Color Plate 1

Color Plate 2

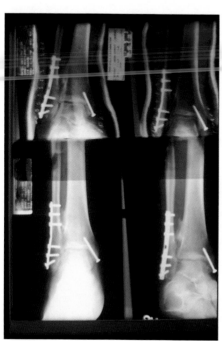

Color Plate 3

Color Plate 4

Color Plate 5

Color Plate 6

Color Plate 7

Color Plate 8

Color Plate 9

Color Plate 10

Color Plate 11

Color Plate 12

Color Plate 13

Color Plate 14

Color Plate 15

Color Plate 16

Color Plate 17

Color Plate 18

Color Plate 19

Color Plate 20

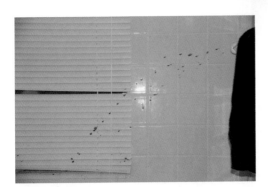
Color Plate 21

Color Plate 22

Color Plate 23

Color Plate 24

Color Plate 25

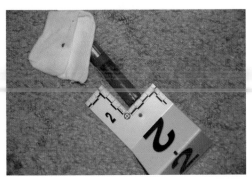

Color Plate 26

Color Plate 27

Color Plate 28

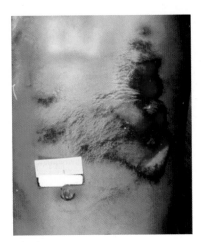

Color Plate 29

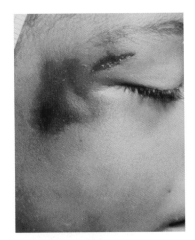

Color Plate 30

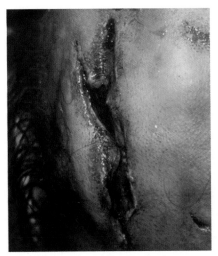

Color Plate 31

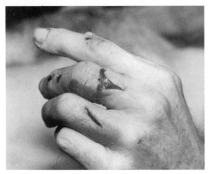

Color Plate 32

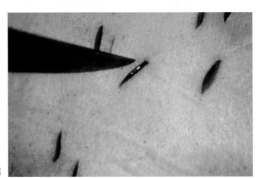

Color Plate 33

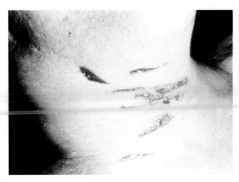

Color Plate 34

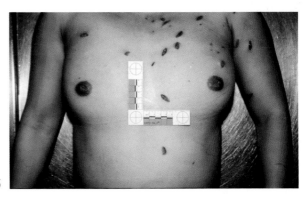

Color Plate 35

Color Plate 36

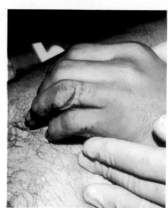

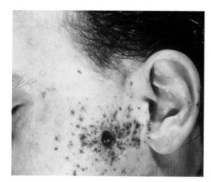

Color Plate 37

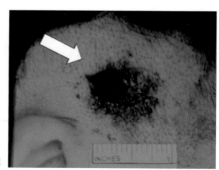

Color Plate 38

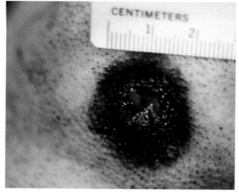

Color Plate 39

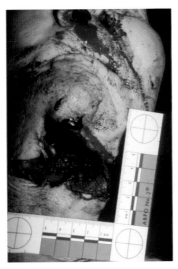

Color Plate 40

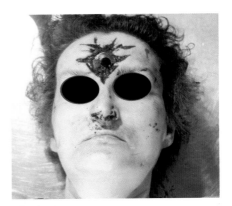

Color Plate 41

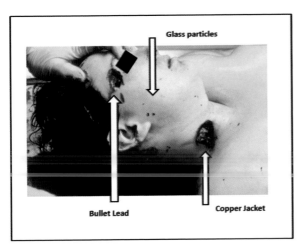

Color Plate 42

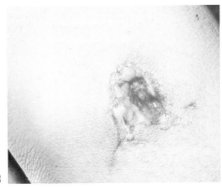

Color Plate 43

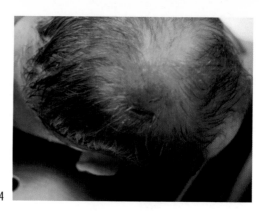

Color Plate 44

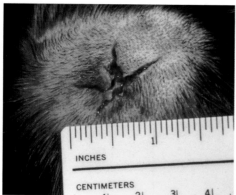

Color Plate 45

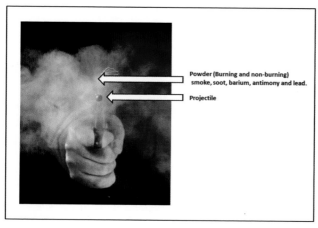

Color Plate 46

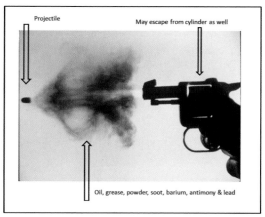

Color Plate 47

Color Plate 48

Color Plate 49

Color Plate 50

Color Plate 51

Color Plate 52

Scene security
Line

Hess' body

Color Plate 53

Leatherman's
Tool/knife

Color Plate 54

Leatherman's Tool/knife

Color Plate 55

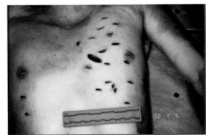

Color Plate 56

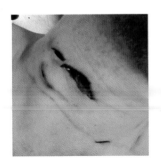 

Color Plate 57

One puncture defect

Multiple puncture defects
That correspond to injuries.

Color Plate 58

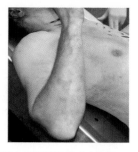

Color Plate 59   No injuries to upper arm as described by second autopsy doctor

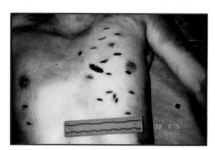

Color Plate 60

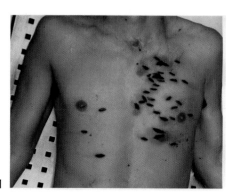

Color Plate 61

Wet/Dirt
markings
On the knees

Color Plate 62

Legal Coordination and Considerations

As with other subjects we have covered, there are literally hundreds of specialized texts and writings on the subject of trial and court procedures. There was actually great discussion between the authors as to the necessity for such a chapter on legal aspects and basic criminal procedure. It is clear from our training, education, and background we are not lawyers. But we have worked very closely with prosecutors over the years in many different jurisdictions and in many different capacities.

Our particular purpose for this chapter is to emphasize the importance of working with the prosecutor to insure we are operating within the law and hopefully to point out some of the difficulties the prosecutor faces in bringing any case to court. Not working with or not listening to the prosecutor is one of the common mistakes leading to unresolved cases. Therefore, in order to bring any offender to justice to answer for their crimes, there must be a good solid working relationship between the police and the prosecutor.

▶ The Prosecutor

Prosecutors are more commonly known in most jurisdictions as district attorneys (DAs). They are elected officials responsible for a specific geographic jurisdiction as determined by state law. They may be limited to a single county or in some states may encompass a multicounty "district" or judicial circuit. There is generally one district attorney who supervises several other deputy district attorneys who generally assist in the prosecution of various criminal cases.

The district attorney (and his/her office) is chiefly responsible for coordinating the government and community's response to crime, from the initial screening, when the prosecutor decides whether or not to charge a case, through all court proceedings, sentencing, and in some cases in the appellate process.

The district attorney's main duties and responsibilities include the following:

- Provide guidance to police agencies on criminal procedures and the law during the course of the investigation
- Assess investigative reports provided by the police within their jurisdiction and determine whether there is sufficient evidence to file a criminal complaint
- Determine if the criminal complaint warrants presentation in criminal court or more appropriately handled through pretrial diversion or other remedy
- Represent the community in the prosecution of offenders in criminal or civil courts
- Direct the county grand jury
- Protection of victims' rights and proper application of victims' rights legislation

There is a very important concept relating to all criminal investigations but especially in a homicide case—the case or investigation is not over until the offender has been convicted. There have been occasions when we have worked investigative leads and interviewed people even during the trial because of new information or allegations that came out unexpectedly during testimony. It is not uncommon for the defense to be secretive about their case and may even introduce surprise information during trial.

If we have conducted a thorough investigation these instances are going to be few and far between, but they still happen. Remember, it is up to the prosecution to present evidence of guilt; the defense however, does not have to present any evidence of innocence. The prosecution has to ensure the evidence they provide to the jury has been validated for its truthfulness and reliability. Theoretically, defense is under the same obligation to present truthful evidence in court, but many times the defense may simply present an alternate theory of events or of the crime without the same burden of evidence.

Homicide cases are among the most complicated of all prosecutions because of the sometimes horrific nature of the crime, the amount of forensic evidence involved, and the number of expert witnesses often needed to introduce and explain the forensic evidence. Because of the complexities of these cases, teamwork between the prosecutor and the police is an absolute necessity. This team work should not just be created as the case is being prepared for court but should be established at the outset of the investigation and reinforced continually throughout the case.

Examples of development of teamwork can be seen in jurisdictions where there is a requirement for a representative from the district attorney's office to respond to all reported homicides in order to provide legal guidance when it is most important during the initial stages of the investigation. This requirement is ordered by the district attorney's office, not the police department, but because prosecution of the offender is always one of the main goals of any investigation, it is to the police's advantage to get the DA's office involved as soon as possible. There are several reasons why this partnership is such an important asset in early stages of the investigation.

The first real advantage is that the DA can: quickly provide legal advice as necessary concerning search warrants or rights advisement; assist in obtaining investigative subpoenas; prepare arrest warrants; and provide input and recommend investigative leads as the preliminary investigation is developed.

This aspect cannot be over emphasized because unlike the police who have a narrower scope, basically to find out what happened, the prosecutor must look at the end product (a prosecution) and what additional evidence will be needed in order to present evidence in a trial. For example, finding a key piece of evidence at the scene is very good for the police and may help to establish some key fact needed to identify the offender. The prosecutor, however, has to determine how exactly that piece of evidence is going to be introduced into the court case, which may require additional witnesses or additional facts that are unrelated to the general police investigation of determining what happened. Therefore the prosecutor often assigns additional investigative leads to the police to help firm up the investigation during the preliminary period when there are likely more detectives involved in the case and the evidence and witnesses are "fresh."

There may be times when the DA's representative might be able to quickly offer a coconspirator or other person on the periphery of a particular crime actual immunity from prosecution in exchange for critical information and testimony as to what happened and who was involved. The concept of offering immunity, particularly during the preliminary stages of the investigation, is more the exception than the general rule, but is possible and much easier when the DA is present on the scene or available at the police station during suspect interviews or interrogation.

Having the DA to respond to the actual scene is the best way for the prosecutor to develop an interest and assume "ownership" of the case by becoming personally involved at the very start of the investigation. By owning the case, the DA (and detectives) will develop a determination and commitment to see it through to the end, especially important in long term cases.

Another benefit of the DA's early involvement is hopefully the development of a good working relationship between the detectives and the prosecutor. This relationship should be based on a general trust between the two agencies. This trust might even kindle the interest of the prosecutor to prosecute an "iffy" or otherwise difficult case, as demonstrated in **Case Study 12-1**.

The value of developing a good working relationship between the two agencies cannot be over emphasized. It is our job as detectives to deliver a well documented and thoroughly investigated case, but there are also other

Case Study 12-1

While working on a very difficult and complicated cold case, a detective invited the prosecutor assigned to the case to lunch meetings. During these informal lunch meetings held in their office the progress of the investigation was discussed, new witnesses were identified, and additional investigative leads were added to the investigative plan. On those days when the prosecutor was in court or the detective was otherwise unavailable, they decided to meet on the weekend on their own time and went over the new details of the investigation together. The result was the development of a good professional friendship and deep trust between the two. The case they were working on was based on a very limited amount of physical evidence and a great deal of circumstantial evidence. It is very doubtful the case would have ever been prosecuted if the prosecutor and detective had not worked so closely together over the length of the case. The offender was eventually convicted but the real importance of the case was the close relationship that actually started to develop between the two agencies. As a result, eventually other prosecutors began to spend more time with detectives going over their cases, providing suggestions and recommendations, and more detectives were asking for advice or asking the prosecutor what else might be needed for the court case. A good professional working relationship was developed between the two agencies that resulted in the prosecutors taking on more complicated cases and the detectives being willing to go outside their normal investigative functions to assist the prosecutors even on cases to which they themselves were not assigned.

tasks prosecutors frequently ask of detectives to assist in the preparation for court such as conducting background checks on potential defense witnesses.

Additionally, because the American jury pool is so inundated with television programs revolving around police, crime scene examinations, forensic evidence, etc., there is often an unrealistic expectation that they are going to see the same fantastic results during a real trial. These high expectations and their influence over the jury are known as the *CSI effect*, and it is a real problem especially when presenting a case with no or limited forensic evidence. This often causes the prosecutor to hesitate to take cases to court without the necessary evidence or forces them to change their tactics or court presentation.

Detectives are especially helpful in these types of cases to help explain the lack of forensic evidence or to reemphasize other evidence that is available. For instance, in the last several years we have been called to testify more often, not just to introduce physical or forensic evidence found during our scene examination, but rather to educate the jury as to our efforts to find that evidence and what a lack of evidence actually means.

As we teach in our college courses, we use the adage "the absence of evidence is not evidence of absence." In other words, if we find a certain fingerprint at the scene, we can state that the person who left the print was perhaps at the scene; but if there were no prints found, we cannot state that the person was not present at the scene. Actually we can only say the person may not have left any prints, or they left prints and we did not find them. So our court room testimony amounted to something like a college lecture and was used to educate the jury on the reality of scene examinations and to counter some of these very unrealistic TV programs and perhaps to lower jury expectations.

As detectives, our understanding of these key principals may in turn provide the prosecutor with a better understanding of how to combat the lack of forensic or physical evidence by using such educational testimony or through the use of expert witnesses.

There must be a clear understanding between the DA and the police; each side must realize how much they need the other. Otherwise we end up with situations (described in previous material on common errors) where the police and DA's office seemed to be intentionally working against each other out of pride, spite, or arrogance.

In many jurisdictions the DA's office also has its own set of trained investigators to assist local police in completing investigations as well as to help in preparing cases for prosecution. These are commonly referred to as district attorney investigators.

▶ District Attorney Investigators

These investigators operate under the direct auspices and legal authority of the district attorney and are often granted full peace officer powers under state law. Essentially this means DA investigators have full powers of arrest and warrant within the state. They are not responsible for conducting routine police investigations but are instead used for a wide variety of functions. DA investigators are often made a part of the critical incident response team called out when an incident involving the use of lethal force by a peace officer occurs within the county.

Generally their duties are focused on providing much of the follow-up investigation in cases submitted to the district attorney by local law enforcement agencies and other county departments. These include such serious felony cases as homicides, sexual assaults, robberies, gang cases, narcotics, insurance fraud, career criminal prosecutions, arson, and child abduction. District attorney investigators also assist other law enforcement agencies upon request when assistance, manpower, or additional expertise may be required. Many of their duties include locating witnesses, serving subpoenas, preparing witnesses for court, preparation of court room exhibits, and proper accounting and securing of evidence obtained from the police.

There are some jurisdictions where the DA investigators by statute also assume *original* jurisdiction over some criminal offenses and therefore may be the primary investigative agency in a wide variety of cases. These include: abuse of judicial process (perjury, witness intimidation, falsification of evidence, conspiracy to obstruct justice), welfare fraud, non-sufficient checks, parental child abductions, election code violations, crimes committed by public officials, corporation code violations, and environmental health violations.

▶ Decision to Prosecute

Prosecution of the suspect is not always an automatic result at the end of the investigation. Since murder trials are perhaps the costliest of all prosecutions, it is not uncommon for the cost of the trial to run into the hundreds of thousands or even millions of dollars, particularly if the offender is a public figure or if the prosecutor elects to seek the death penalty. It is not uncommon for smaller jurisdictions to expend the majority of their annual budget on one trial. It is frustrating to think the administration of justice might be determined by dollars and cents, but the sad fact is many times prosecutorial decisions are based on these hard facts.

Therefore, before prosecutors take a case to court, they must be absolutely certain they have the necessary information and evidence with which to win the case; not just to justify the expenditures, but also because of other very important considerations that might not seem relevant but do play an important part. These considerations include potential double jeopardy—an offender that is acquitted at trial can never be tried again for that same offense. Basically the prosecution gets one shot at taking the suspect to trial for that crime. Other situations that directly influence prosecutorial decisions are cases involving the police as victims or in which police are implicated in a death while performing in the line of duty.

Almost any serious crime involving juveniles, young children, or babies as victims; or whenever juveniles or young children are accused of committing a serious crime is certain to generate a great deal of media interest and be of interest to the public. Additionally, incidents involving rape, sexual torture, or particularly brutal injuries will capture media attention and thus become widely known to the public providing additional pressure to take the case to court. An incident involving a well known local person or perhaps a well known celebrity as either a victim or a suspect will garner additional publicity and media attention and thus add to the pressure on the prosecutor to take on the case.

The case load of the individual prosecutor may also influence prosecutorial decisions. It is not uncommon for prosecutors, particularly in large offices, to be responsible for multiple homicide cases at any one time, dividing their time and attention. Under such stress prosecutors may avoid, or seek other means to dispose of what may seem to be unclear or particularly difficult cases.

Regardless of the potential media pressure, case load, difficulty of the cases, or experience level of the individual prosecuting attorney, no district attorney who must stand for reelection wants to take a chance of losing a major case, thereby suffering loss of voter confidence and media criticism. They will be wary of taking on any "iffy" cases, despite public outcry. If we want them to take our case to a successful conclusion, we must be able to convince them that it is a winnable case.

One effective way to provide the prosecutor with the case facts in an easy to understand format is to prepare a prosecution summary. This may be an informal or formal report outlining general case facts, the evidence, forensic findings if available, and potential witnesses with a brief description of their expected testimony. Essentially we are reducing the entire investigation, (which when presented as a case file or final investigative report, may literally run into the hundreds of pages of written investigative reports, witness statements, or other documents collected during the course of the investigation), into an easily understandable report which can and should be used in combination with face-to-face briefings over the entire investigation.

The following box is an example of what an uncomplicated prosecution summary might look like.

Prosecution Summary

Police Department/Agency
City, State

Case number _____   Investigating Officer _____

Offenses: Violation of _____ (State law citation) _____ ; Premeditated Murder

Subject: Jones, Johnny Albert; Male; (other identifying data deemed appropriate)

Victim: Jones, Mary Lou; Female; (other identifying data deemed appropriate)

Synopsis of event: At approximately 1400, on May 3, 2009, at 2334 1st Street, (This city, this state), Johnny Jones with malice aforethought, did unlawfully cause the death of his wife Mary Jones, residing at 2334 1st Street (this city, this state) by stabbing her in the chest, neck, back, and stomach a total of 10 times; causing her to bleed to death at the scene. Johnny Jones, then partially undressed his wife by opening up her shirt and exposing her breasts and by lowering her pants and underwear exposing her genitals. He then arranged the scene to resemble a burglary/rape type of incident, making it appear that his wife was murdered by an unknown offender.

Motive: Monetary and the desire of Johnny Jones to avoid divorce and to be with another woman.

(continues)

Evidence:
1. New life insurance policy on victim for $500,000 purchased on 30 April 2009
2. Bloody clothing of Johnny Jones observed and collected from floorboard of pickup truck by Detective Smith
3. Blood samples taken from front door at crime scene
4. Cell phone records of Johnny Jones, showing telephone call at 1420, hit cell tower 2 miles from crime scene not at the lake where he claimed to be
5. Small cut on little finger of right hand of Johnny Jones noted at the time of his interview

Forensic evidence/analysis
1. Mary Jones's DNA (blood) found on trousers, shirt, socks, and shoes of Johnny Jones
2. Johnny Jones's DNA (blood) found on shirt of victim and on doorknob of front door

Witness and expected testimony
1. **Marta Smith:** will testify to her involvement in a six month sexual relationship with Johnny Jones; further that she was unaware that he was married and he denied being married. On April 25, 09, Johnny Jones told her he was soon getting large sum of money and asked her to marry him. She called him on cell phone at 1420, 3 May 09, and when Johnny Jones answered, he was out of breath as he talked and said he was at the lake fishing and would call back later.
2. **Oscar Phillips:** insurance salesman who will testify to Johnny Jones's increase of his wife's life insurance policy to the maximum amount on 30 April 09.
3. **Jerome McWilliams:** will testify he is a neighbor of the Joneses; that he observed Johnny Jones leaving from his residence hurriedly at approximately 1415, 3 May 2009; he discovered victim at 1600
4. **Cindy Alexander:** sister of Mary Jones will testify to Mary Jones's decision to divorce Johnny Jones, her efforts to locate a divorce lawyer, and her plans to move out of the house
5. **Officer Murphy:** crime scene technician will testify about crime scene processing and collection of evidence, noted that the rear door window was broken from the inside out
6. **Detective Evans:** city detective, will testify to the arrest and interview of Johnny Jones and Johnny Jones's alibi of fishing at the lake 50 miles away from scene. Also to the examination of Johnny Jones's cell phone records placing him around the scene at the time of the death. Will testify to collection of DNA sample from Johnny Jones.
7. **Detective Smith:** city detective, will testify to the recovery of the bloodstained clothing from Johnny Jones's pickup truck and submission to crime lab
8. **Dr. Luther Edwards:** ME, will testify to the autopsy of Mary Jones and cause of death from sharp force instruments and no evidence of sexual assault. Will offer expert opinion as to the time of death.
9. **Henry Leon:** state crime lab DNA analyst, will testify to forensic examination of Johnny Jones and Mary Jones's clothing and the DNA profiles obtained from both
10. **Walter Patrick:** state crime lab analyst, will testify as expert witness that he examined the window fragments collected at the scene and concluded the rear door window was broken from the inside out not from outside in.

The actual form and substance of the report can be altered to fit individual cases or agencies and is not necessarily limited to homicides, but can be adapted for use in any case. It can also be a good investigative tool when initiated at the start of the investigation with the evidence and witnesses placed into the form as they are developed. This shows the detectives where the investigation might be weak and where they need to look for additional evidence in order to strengthen their case.

▶Multiple Victims and Jurisdictions

One of the key issues for the prosecutor is determining jurisdictions. This can become somewhat problematic when a body is found in one jurisdiction but the crime was actually committed in another jurisdiction; or an offender has crossed state lines. Most of these decisions will be based on state law and court precedence but can prove to be an obstacle that must be overcome.

There is a similar problem in cases of multiple homicides. Even if committed within the same legal jurisdiction, depending on individual state laws, the cases may not be able to be combined into one trial and instead must be prosecuted separately. This of course adds to the overall cost of prosecution and, might force the prosecutors to make some difficult decisions such as limiting prosecution to the strongest case in order to achieve a conviction and then either decline to prosecute the other cases or accept some type of plea bargain by the offender.

▶Plea Bargaining

Plea bargaining is sometimes a necessary evil in the American justice system and is basically an agreement with the offender to plead guilty but for a lesser crime or for a reduced punishment. We see this used in one or two general circumstances.

The first instance is when a reduced charge or a reduced sentence is used as leverage to induce a coconspirator to testify against other coconspirators. Generally this is offered to the person who first comes forward with an offer to assist, or to the person with the least culpability or involvement in the crime. As an inducement for testimony, one of the offenders may be offered a much lower range of punishment and in some cases may escape any punishment at all through an offer of immunity. Immunity, as noted earlier in the text, is essentially an agreement that the person would not be punished for any illegal act s/he may have committed providing s/he testifies truthfully against others. Although we do not like to reward criminals with reduced punishment or even escaping punishment, many times it is simply the price we have to pay to punish those offenders who are more culpable.

The second instance where we see plea bargains used is when the prosecutor may accept a guilty plea by an offender in exchange for a reduction in charge, for example from a very serious felony such as attempted murder, to a relatively minor offense such as assault and battery. This is an extreme example of course, but not necessarily out of line. For the more serious cases involving death, the resulting plea may reduce the charges from premeditated to unpremeditated murder, or even to some form of negligent homicide. An offender may elect to plead guilty in exchange for the prosecutor not seeking the death penalty. We usually see this when the crimes are so horrific and the evidence so overwhelming that the death penalty is a near certainty. In this way the offender receives life in prison instead of the death penalty.

These types of plea bargain decisions are made by the prosecutors and are not always the result of prosecutors trying to ease their case load or their unwillingness to take on a difficult case; many times they are forced into these positions because of the overall cost of the prosecutions, or a lack of the necessary evidence to prove the more serious offense.

Prosecutors do not make these decisions in a vacuum. They are aware of the publicity and how this might play out, they are aware of the evidence they have or lack, they are aware of the feelings of the detectives involved in the case, and perhaps most important they are very aware of the feelings of the victim's family. Plea bargaining decisions are seldom made without prior consultation and agreement of the victim's family and hopefully with the concurrence of the detectives.

We are very familiar with the frustration of detectives and possible misunderstanding of the necessity for the prosecutors to make these difficult decisions. Although this frustration is understandable, it underlines the importance of developing every piece of information, locating every witness, validating every statement or alibi, and presenting the case in a manner which gives the prosecutor enough ammunition to achieve success.

It should also be noted that many states have laws restricting the district attorney's discretion involving plea bargaining during certain crimes or capital offenses.

▶ Stages of a Criminal Case

There are certain steps or phases in every prosecution in which both the police and the district attorney will play very important roles beginning with the arrest of a suspect and ending after acquittal or conviction.

Arrest

Criminal prosecution can actually be said to begin when a suspect is arrested and taken into custody. It is at this stage the government (represented by the police) has taken the first step towards bringing the offender to justice. An arrest may be made under these circumstances:

1. **Direct observation**—if an officer actually observes the offender committing a crime in his/her presence the offender may be taken into immediate custody.
2. **Probable cause**—the best example of this circumstance would be a scene where the suspect is present and admits to the crime or is

immediately identified by the victim or other eye witnesses. The offender may be taken immediately into custody at this point.

3. **Based on an arrest warrant**—an arrest warrant is issued based on the outline of probable cause and by oath or affirmation and authorized by the judge or magistrate. An example is when the offender has been identified sometime during the investigation but not necessarily at the scene. This is a formal process and requires the authorization of a judge or magistrate in order to take the offender into custody.

The entire process of the arrest, taking the offender formally into custody, and the subsequent administrative processing at the police station, is known as the "booking" procedure. Booking actually refers to an old procedure in which arrestees were taken to the supervisor at the police station and their names and other information relevant to the offense entered into a ledger book. The general booking procedure today includes taking fingerprints, photographs, and in some states, DNA samples. After the booking process, offenders in more serious cases such as homicide are generally held in temporary detention inside the city or county jail pending an appearance before the court. In this initial hearing, issues regarding retention or release are settled.

Bail

In most minor or routine cases offenders will secure a rather quick release from detention through a bail system wherein they can put up some type of cash guarantee in exchange for their release until their initial court appearance. Release on bail is essentially the suspect's promise to appear at all future court proceedings with the understanding that failure to appear will result in forfeiture of the bail. In some relatively minor offenses a suspect may even be released on his/her "own recognizance" which is really no more that their promise to show up for their court proceedings.

Bail for homicide cases, because of the severe nature of the crime, is often impossible to achieve because of state law that may prevent bail from being offered, or because the bail is so high (sometimes in the millions of dollars) it is beyond the financial reach of the suspect. Each individual state has its own rules and regulations relating to bail.

Arraignment

The suspect's first court appearance following arrest is known as the *arraignment*. Typically an arraignment takes place at the earliest opportunity but generally within 24 to 48 hours. Many large cities also have night court and thus first arraignments may be conducted even at night.

A timely arraignment, as soon as possible after their arrest, will ensure a suspect is not held incommunicado and is advised of exactly what charges are being filed in the complaint. It is the responsibility of the judge to establish the identity of the accused and to determine if s/he understands the English language and understands the process taking place. The judge will also determine if the person has legal representation and may assign a public defender to the defense. The first issues of bail are discussed and the judge makes an initial ruling.

Lastly, the judge requests an initial plea—the defendant chooses to plead guilty, not guilty or no contest to the charges. Generally, at this stage the defendant pleads not guilty and additional hearings for bail or preliminary hearings are then set as the legal process is initiated.

Preliminary Hearing or Grand Jury Proceedings

The next step in the process is the bringing of criminal charges against the offender. Charges are brought in one of two ways: (1) through a preliminary hearing in front of a judge or magistrate, or (2) through grand jury proceedings. In a preliminary hearing, the prosecution presents a portion of the case to establish sufficient evidence for continuation of the prosecution. This is a mini trial and although the defense attorney may ask questions of the various witnesses there are limitations to what may be presented as defense.

The second way to bring charges is through presentation of the case to a grand jury. The grand jury is a panel of citizens selected from the local community or judicial district to determine whether it is appropriate for the government to proceed with a criminal prosecution. The grand jury is actually meant to protect suspects from inappropriate prosecution by the government. The grand jury members are drawn from the general population and usually serve not for one case but for a certain period of time. During their empanelment they may hear numerous cases or conduct their own investigation into certain matters as guided by the district attorney.

If the grand jury determines that there is sufficient evidence to prosecute it issues what is known in some jurisdictions as a "true bill" or an indictment. In the federal system, cases must be brought by grand jury indictment but states are free to use either process.

If the judge (during a preliminary hearing) or the grand jury is not satisfied there is sufficient evidence or probable cause to bring the case to court, then the charges against the offender are generally dropped at that point. However, because the offender was never in jeopardy, (meaning never in danger of losing freedom during either process), if additional evidence or information is developed it is possible to re-arrest or seek an indictment of the offender at a later time.

Pretrial Motions

Prior to the actual court proceedings, there are often other court hearings that take place. These court hearings are known as pretrial motions and are based on issues or questions that need to be settled before the court and may be brought forth by either the prosecution or defense. Essentially, each side is offered a chance to present evidence or arguments defending their position before the judge. The judge then makes rulings outside the normal court and without the jury being present. The intent is to decide these issues beforehand and lessen interference with the normal flow of the court presentation once the trial has begun.

There are many possible pretrial motions but generally they revolve around obtaining necessary information about the criminal complaint from the police and prosecutor, the defendant's mental competency to stand trial, or around issues of the admission of certain items of evidence or witness testimony.

Discovery

Discovery is one of the standard pretrial motions filed by the defense. It requires the government (prosecutor) provide to the defense all of the evidence they have collected against the accused. This would include both physical and testimonial evidence accumulated during the investigation that could be introduced as evidence at court. This would include all of the police investigative reports, lists of property and/or physical evidence seized, crime scene reports, sketches, photographs, any results of forensic testing/examination that have been requested or completed, and the list of witnesses the prosecution potentially plans to call in their case.

Essentially this ensures the government is not going to use any "secret evidence" and allows the accused to fairly plan the defense against the allegations and to challenge the admissibility of evidence. These type of hearings are so routine, they are now more of a formality rather than any type of real adversarial procedure as with other hearings and the criminal trial itself.

Competency or Sanity Hearings

A competency or sanity hearing is an attempt by the defense or the prosecution to demonstrate the accused's mental condition at the time of the act, which might ensure or prohibit prosecution for that particular offense. Generally the issue revolves around the defendant's ability or capacity to understand or appreciate the nature and illegality of his/her actions at the time the crime was committed, and the ability to participate or assist in his/her own defense.

In these cases the defense will often present expert witnesses to testify as to the incompetence or inability of the accused to understand or appreciate the nature of the crime either based on a temporary situation or because of long standing mental problems.

Each state has its particular laws and procedures for determining competency of an accused to stand trial, but in most cases, if the hearing determines the accused was insane or mentally incompetent at the time the crime was committed, or is incapable of assisting in the defense, it is likely s/he will not be held responsible for his/her actions.

Suppression Hearings

A suppression hearing is an attempt by one side to prohibit or suppress the introduction of evidence or testimony into the proceedings. These hearings are often based on some alleged violation of Constitutional rights. These include but are not necessarily limited to:

- Fourth Amendment issues which generally revolve around the alleged improper seizure of evidence
- Fifth Amendment problems revolving around the alleged improper or lack of rights advisement, and the conduct of the interview or interrogation of the offender
- Sixth Amendment problems regarding the right to legal counsel
- Eighth Amendment issues generally revolving around alleged cruel and unusual punishments or excessive bail
- Fourteenth Amendment problems generally revolving around equal protection claims

Each of these hearings is essentially a mini trial wherein the side seeking to suppress some part of the evidence at the criminal trial presents evidence in support of their claims and the other side has a chance to present counter evidence and arguments in support of their position.

The judge then makes a decision based on the case facts and established precedence as to what evidence is going to be admissible and what evidence is going to be inadmissible or suppressed. Evidence suppressed or judged to be inadmissible cannot be used in court by either side.

Motion in Limine

This is a hearing used to exclude or limit the testimony anticipated by one side or the other. The motion essentially seeks to avoid irrelevant, inadmissible, or prejudicial evidence at any point in the trial. If the judge agrees that the expected testimony may be irrelevant or prejudicial to the case he may limit a particular witness's testimony.

We see this many times when we have statements, admissions, or confessions from coconspirators which might implicate the defendant. Other motions in limine, frequently revolve around the admissibility of expert opinion testimony or attempts to suppress the admission of certain scientific or forensic examinations and techniques. These are commonly known as a *Daubert* hearings.

Daubert Hearings   A *Daubert* hearing is used as a basis to introduce new scientific evidence or forensic techniques, and expert opinions resulting therein. The name is based on the Supreme Court decision rendered in *Daubert v. Merrell Dow Pharmaceuticals* which substantially changed the standards of how scientific evidence and expert witness testimony is evaluated as admissible in court.

Prior to the *Daubert* decision, (and two subsequent related decisions, *General Electric Co. v. Joiner* and *Kumho Tire Co. v. Carmichael*), all federal and most state courts followed the "Frye Standard" or the "general acceptance test" when seeking to admit scientific evidence.

The Frye Standard was based on another earlier Supreme Court Decision, *Frye v. United States*. In the *Frye* decision, the court determined the admissibility of expert opinion on a specific scientific technique was admissible when there was a *general acceptance* by the relevant scientific community of the technique's reliability.

In *Daubert*, the Supreme Court ruled their earlier *Frye* decision was now superseded by changes in the Federal Rules of Evidence, specifically Rule 702 which governs expert testimony. Rule 702 states:

"If scientific, technical, or other specialized knowledge will assist the trier of fact to understand the evidence or determine a fact in issue, a witness qualified as an expert by knowledge, skill, experience, training, or education, may testify thereto in the form of an opinion or otherwise."

The Court determined such a rigid standard initially established by *Frye*, requiring a general acceptance by the scientific community, would be at odds with the new more liberal thrust and general approach of relaxing the traditional barriers to "opinion" testimony as outlined in Rule 702. This new rule establishes a standard requiring a valid scientific connection to the specific inquiry as a precondition to its admissibility.

Rule 702 essentially has two requirements. First, the evidence must be reliable, and supported by accepted scientific methods and procedures. Second, the evidence must be relevant, and sufficiently tied to the specific facts of the case that it will help the jury in resolving a factual dispute. The judge in the trial court is now charged with the role as "gatekeeper" to determine if expert witnesses and their evidence will assist the jury to understand or determine the true facts of a case.

Daubert now allows the judge to evaluate the methodology underlying the expected expert testimony and whether it is scientifically valid and applicable to the facts at issue. This evaluation is based on four basic criteria.

First, whether the theory or technique can be and has been tested.

Second, whether the theory or technique has been subjected to peer review and publication.

Third, to determine the reliability based on the known or potential *rate of error* of the technique or procedure.

Fourth, what is the general acceptance of the theory in the relevant scientific community?

When DNA analysis or bloodstain pattern interpretation was first introduced a pretrial hearing was almost always required for the judge to be satisfied the analysis was reliable enough to be used in court. Because it has been so widely accepted across the country there are seldom any instances where either forensic technique or procedure is challenged.

But with the additional development of new scientific and forensic techniques or the use of non standard type expert witnesses, these *Daubert* hearings are really quite common. Although this is primarily the prosecutor's job to get the evidence into court, it is also one of the detective's responsibilities to assist in locating potential expert witnesses or be familiar with developing forensic techniques which may be invaluable to the investigation and to eventual court proceedings. This is another one of the areas where the detective and the prosecutor should be working together to ensure a successful prosecution.

Trial

Trial is the main event—where the accused is finally brought to court to face the charges, and the evidence collected is finally presented to the jury. Criminal trial procedures follow a set path and distinct phases. The following box is a list of the various stages of a criminal trial.

In the U.S. Judicial System, defendants have a constitutional right to trial by jury, or if they choose, may elect to be tried by a judge alone. Per our beliefs, the accused is presumed to be innocent of the charges and it is the government or the prosecutor which bears the total burden of proof in a criminal trial.

Although the defendant has the right to present evidence and witnesses on his/her behalf, it is not required. A defendant may choose not to put on any defense at all if it is felt that the government has not established guilt.

Stages of a Criminal Trial

Jury selection
Opening statements
Prosecution case in chief
Defense case in chief
Prosecution rebuttal
Closing prosecution arguments
Closing defense arguments
Prosecution rebuttal statements
Charging the jury
Jury decision
Sentencing

Note that the prosecution is allowed to present rebuttal evidence after the defense case and is allowed a second chance to rebut the defense closing arguments. This is because the defendant is assumed to be innocent at the time of trial and it is up to the prosecution to present evidence of guilt.

The prosecutor of course, must prove to the jury the defendant committed the crime, not beyond all doubt, but beyond a reasonable doubt. A jury or judge makes the final determination of guilt or innocence after listening to opening and closing statements, examination and cross-examination of witnesses and jury instructions. If the jury fails to reach a unanimous verdict, the judge may declare a mistrial, and the case will either be dismissed or a new jury will be chosen. If a judge or jury finds the defendant guilty, the court will sentence the defendant.

Sentencing

During the sentencing phase of a criminal case, the court determines the appropriate punishment for the convicted defendant. In determining a suitable sentence, the court will consider a number of factors, including the nature and severity of the crime, the defendant's criminal history, the defendant's personal circumstances and the degree of remorse felt by the defendant.

In certain cases such as death penalty, sentencing is actually a mini trial where the defense is allowed to submit evidence in extenuation and mitigation in order to request a lesser punishment; the prosecutor however is allowed to present evidence in aggravation to emphasize various aspects of the crime justifying the imposition of the death penalty.

In most states it is up to the judge rather than the jury to actually impose the criminal sanction for the crime, the general exception is the death penalty. In most states with the death penalty, it is the jury that decides to impose the death penalty or not. In some cases their verdict is given as a recommendation to the judge who may or may not be bound by the jury's decision.

Appeal

An individual convicted of a crime may ask that his or her case be reviewed by a higher court. If that court finds an error in the case or the sentence imposed, the court may reverse the conviction or find that the case should be retried.

▶ Disposal of Evidence

Even after an offender has been convicted the police are not quite done with the investigation. Generally speaking it is their responsibility to safeguard evidence used in criminal trials. Even after the trial, the evidence must still be maintained until the appeals process is completed. It is very possible for the entire process to be repeated again if the offender is successful in the appeal and an appellate court overturns the conviction and orders a retrial. At that time the evidence will be needed again.

There is also a new school of thought regarding the keeping of evidence, especially in unresolved cases. Because forensic technology is a continually developing science, the current school of thought is to maintain indefinitely all items of evidence until such time the case can be solved and someone brought to trial. This of course can cause some difficulties with the police who now have to come up with some long term storage solutions.

Even in cases of conviction any evidence used is generally maintained by the police until such time as all appeals are exhausted. In death penalty cases generally this evidence is maintained until the sentence is carried out. It is also becoming commonplace for an offender already sentenced and in prison to demand as part of his appellant process retesting of certain evidence based on new forensic technology. This has resulted in many prisoners being released after forensic testing actually exonerated them. Long term management of evidence is going to continue to be a problem for police agencies in the future.

We cannot place enough emphasis on the fact that detectives need to follow through with their investigations by having a good working relationship with their prosecutor and continue to work to achieve the correct outcome. Just because your investigation may be complete and the perpetrator is in jail, your job is not done. In the long run those with good working relationships obtain more convictions and eliminate most of their potential problems at the beginning. It is a team effort.

Additional References

Cook, P. J., Slawson, D. B., & Gries, L. A. (1993). *The cost of prosecuting murder cases in North Carolina*. Durham, NC: Terry Sandford Institute of Public Policy.

Gilbert, D. I., Gilfarb, M. E., & Talpins, S. K. (2005). *Basic trial techniques*. Alexandria, VA: American Prosecutors Research Institute.

The Behavioral Analysis Interview in a Homicide Case

▶ Introduction

The Behavioral Analysis Interview (BAI) is an excellent tool that can be utilized to differentiate between numerous suspects. Some consider it as a precursor to the actual suspect interrogation and in some instances that is the case. But the concept of the BAI is to provide the interviewer with a tool that will help to narrow the field of possibilities. The process utilizes both the verbal responses while carefully viewing the non-verbal behavior which are to be used collectively as indicators coupled with other case information or the totality of the circumstances.

▶ Behavioral Analysis Interview

The following is a case study demonstrating how the Behavioral Analysis Interview technique can be applied to a particular case.

Assume that Mary Jones was found stabbed to death in her apartment at 9:00 a.m., December 7, 2000. All circumstances clearly indicate that the homicide occurred about midnight, and there was no evidence of a forcible entry. Subsequent investigation disclosed that, on a number of recent occasions, Mary and a male friend of hers, Jim Smith, were overheard having loud arguments, primarily about Mary's relationship with several of her male coworkers. There seems to be good reason, therefore, to interview Jim, but clearly there is no basis for an arrest. At the outset of the interview, the investigator should spend a few minutes asking the suspect a series of background questions, such as his complete name, age, address, current place of employment, and other questions designed to establish behavioral baselines and rapport. Following such initial questions, the investigator should ask a "know why" question: "Do you know why you are here?" or "Do you know why we're here?" Since Jim knew Mary and very probably had read or heard about her death, a naive or evasive reply to the "know why" question would be viewed with suspicion. For instance, if Jim states that he had no idea of the purpose of the interview, or if he makes a vague comment such as "I suppose you want to talk about what happened to Mary," that should be viewed in a different light than if he very bluntly states, "You are trying to find out who murdered Mary." The latter response is more characteristic of that of an innocent person.

Following the "know why" question, it is generally appropriate to say: "Jim, we have interviewed many people regarding Mary's death and the pieces are falling together quickly. Jim, if you had anything to do with this, you should tell me that now." This seemingly casual statement will afford him an opportunity to readily admit his involvement, if that be the case. In the absence of the unlikely occurrence of a sudden admission of guilt, the investigator's statement will nevertheless serve the purpose of inducing a display of behavior symptoms suggestive of either guilt or innocence.

If Jim was involved in Mary's death, he may respond verbally to the investigator's statement by saying, "You mean, did I do this? No." Coupled with the verbal response there will probably be a nonverbal response, such as shifting in his chair, avoiding eye contact, or crossing arms or legs. If Jim is innocent, he very likely will immediately say something like, "I had nothing to do with it! I loved Mary. I never hurt her and never would have." As these words are being spoken, he probably would be leaning forward and looking the investigator straight in the eye, using appropriate hand gestures to emphasize his point.

The next step for the investigator would be to ask a series of open ended investigative questions regarding Jim's knowledge about the event, the victim, and possible suspects. If Jim is innocent, he is thereby given an ample opportunity to divulge possibly helpful information that might not have been disclosed if his discussion had been confined to answering specific questions. If guilty, he is placed in a vulnerable, defensive position, because it is very easy to lie when answering a yes or no question, or a question that only calls for a limited response. It is problematic for someone trying to deceive to construct a lengthy answer with details that must be remembered and recalled. He may also make a remark that would be indicative of guilt or would lead to a more specific line of questioning. Listed below are some preliminary investigative questions to ask in this case. Obviously, depending on the suspect's response to these initial questions, appropriate follow-up questions would be asked.

Alibi/Access

- Tell me everything you did from 6:00 p.m. on December 6 until you went to sleep.
- Who can verify your whereabouts?
- When was the last time you saw Mary? What was she doing?
- Did you have keys to Mary's apartment?
- When you were at Mary's apartment, how did you get there (car, bus, walk)?

Relationship with Victim

- Describe your relationship with Mary.
- What kind of person was Mary?
- What were her best/worst traits?
- Occasionally all couples argue or have a disagreement. What did you and Mary most disagree about? Did any of your fights turn physical?
- How did you make up or solve the disagreements?
- On a scale from one to ten, with one being a terrible relationship and ten being wonderful, how would you rate your relationship with Mary?
- What changes would have brought it up to a ten?
- What were your future long term plans with Mary?

Propensity

- Have you ever been questioned before concerning causing injury to another person?
- When was the last time you struck someone in anger?
- When was the last time you had a heated verbal argument with another person?
- What is the worst thing you've done to someone else when you lost your temper?
- What causes you to lose your temper?

Judgment Effectors

- On December 6 did you have anything alcoholic to drink?
- How much? Did you use any drugs that evening?
- Did Mary have any alcohol or take any drugs that night?
- Did anything happen on December 6 that upset you or caused you to become angry?

The following series of questions, which should be intermingled in the investigative questions, are asked for the purpose of evoking behavioral responses indicative of either guilt or innocence.

Jim, why do you think someone would do this to Mary?   The purpose of this question is to ascertain the suspect's perception of the motive for the crime. If Jim is guilty, he will be faced with a dilemma when asked the question because, in essence, he is being asked to reveal why he killed Mary. In an effort to conceal any indication of his involvement, he may hesitate or repeat the question as a stalling tactic in order to construct what he believes to be an acceptable answer. On some occasions, a guilty suspect may even reveal his true motive by offering an explanation, sometimes in the third person such as, "Maybe there was an argument, or maybe someone was drinking or on drugs." If the guilty suspect does not offer such an excuse, he may respond with, "I never thought about it." When a person's spouse, family member, or close friend is killed, it is only natural to think about a possible motive or cause for the incident. In conjunction with this type of verbal response, the guilty suspect may engage in a variety of nonverbal gestures suggestive of his discomfort and concern over the question.

If Jim is innocent, when asked why someone would kill Mary, he might say, without hesitation, that the killer must be insane or "I can't imagine why anyone would do this. Mary didn't have an enemy in the whole world." In making those comments, he would maintain direct eye contact and would probably lean forward in his chair.

Jim, of the people that you and Mary knew, whom do you feel would be above suspicion regarding Mary's death? In other words, who among them would never do anything like this? This question is an implied invitation to the suspect to assist in the investigation. If Jim is being truthful, he will readily name specific individuals whom he feels would be above reproach or for whom he would vouch as not being involved in Mary's death. He will not be afraid to eliminate certain persons from suspicion. If Jim is guilty, his response might be noncommittal. Guilty suspects usually do not want to eliminate any one individual from suspicion because that would tend to narrow the search down to them. They might respond, therefore, by saying, "I don't know; it's hard to say what people might do." Meanwhile, they may shift around in the chair or engage in some other type of movement.

If a suspect responds to this question by naming himself alone as being above suspicion, no absolute inference should be drawn, but it must be noted that this type of response is more typical of the deceptive suspect than of the innocent. An innocent suspect may include his name among other people for whom he would vouch for, but rarely vouches only for himself, because the innocent person may assume they are already above suspicion

Jim, who do you think might have done something like this to Mary? Whereas the previous question called for the elimination of suspects, this one seeks information of an affirmative nature. By asking Jim to reveal his suspicions as to the guilty person, the investigator may thereby evoke a significant and reliable indication of guilt or innocence. This is particularly true of cases where any one of several persons, all acquainted with each other, may have committed the offense.

A guilty suspect usually will not reveal a suspicion about anyone else, no matter how much effort is made to have him do so. In other words, when asked, "From among the people you and Mary knew, which one of them do you think might have done this?" Jim probably would say, "I don't know" or "I haven't the faintest idea." No matter what the investigator says, thereafter he probably will remain adamant in his denial of harboring any suspicion.

On the other hand, if Jim is innocent, he may, after some persuasion, tell of his suspicion, even though it has a flimsy basis or is perhaps based upon nothing more than a dislike or prejudice toward another individual. When first asked the question regarding his suspicion, he may respond, in a rather unsure manner, "I don't know. I can't believe anyone I know could do something like this."

The investigator should then say: *Jim, I'm not talking about actual knowledge or proof. Here's what I mean. There is no question that someone you know may be involved in this. That being so, which one, from among all the people you and Mary ever knew, do you think could or might have done such a thing? Now, let me assure you that I will not reveal to him that you told me anything. My primary purpose in asking the question is to give you an opportunity to relieve yourself of any thoughts along that line, so that your holding back won't make it look like you're the one who's involved in this. If you had no part in it, I want to know that, without having any doubt about it. So let me now ask you, Jim, who do you think might have done this?*

If Jim is innocent, such persuasion will probably cause him to disclose a suspicion about someone else. However, if Jim is guilty and previously had failed to mention any suspicion, he probably will maintain that attitude, regardless of the investigator's persuasion efforts.

Jim, what do you think happened to Mary? I mean how did this happen? An innocent suspect may be emotionally hesitant to even contemplate what may have happened during the incident and tend to speak in generalities of what they have been already told or what they may have seen if they were the ones that found the body. A guilty person typically seems to have more of an insight as to what may have happened. It is also not unusual for them to even volunteer to comment on particular items of evidence at the scene. This is particularly found in those incidents where the suspect may have altered evidence in order to stage the scene and misdirect the police investigation. In these situations they want to make sure that evidence is noted or found by the police.

Jim, do you think the person who did this to Mary was someone she knew? An innocent suspect will offer a realistic explanation of the crime (based on his knowledge of the crime). If the suspect knew the basic case facts, an innocent suspect would be expected to readily agree with this statement by responding, "I'm convinced that this was done by someone who knew her. Her apartment was not broken into so she must have let the person in. She's too cautious to let a complete stranger into her apartment."

A guilty suspect is motivated to open up the investigation and may suggest improbable solutions for its resolution. If Jim is guilty, he may respond to this question by saying, "I suppose that's possible, but she lived in a really bad neighborhood, plus there are stalkers and serial killers out there. It really could have been anybody."

Jim, how do you feel about being interviewed concerning Mary's death? An innocent suspect looks upon the interview as a chance to be exonerated and as an opportunity to help the investigator catch the guilty party. Therefore, he tends to express positive feelings in his response to this question such as, "I don't mind at all. If this will help catch the person who murdered Mary, I'm willing to do whatever it takes." If Jim is guilty, he will likely perceive the interview as a threatening experience designed to detect his guilt. Consequently, the guilty suspect tends to express either negative or ambivalent feelings toward the interview. Characteristic responses from a guilty suspect to the *feel* question include, "It makes me feel like a criminal," "It makes me nervous and scared," "I don't have any feelings one way or another. I know you're just doing your job."

Jim, what do you think should happen to the person who did this to Mary? In responding to this question, if Jim is innocent, he probably will indicate some significant punishment, such as going to the penitentiary or receiving the death penalty. In contrast, if he is guilty, he will try not to answer the question. He likely will say, "It's not up to me" or "I'm not a judge," or he may indicate that the offender should be asked the reason for committing the crime. The underlying explanation for this evasion is that were he to suggest a penalty, he would in effect be prescribing his own punishment. In the event a guilty suspect does indicate severe punishment, any accompanying nonverbal behaviors will likely belie the sincerity of the answer.

Jim, did you ever think about hurting Mary, even though you didn't go through with it? If Jim acknowledges that he had thought about hurting Mary, this is suggestive of possible guilt, even if in his acknowledgment he very likely would have added to his "yes" answer, "but not seriously." If Jim is innocent, his response probably would be a simple "no." This is so even if Jim had previously entertained the thought of possibly hurting Mary. The innocent suspect perceives the *think* question as pertaining directly to the issue under investigation, in this case, the killing of Mary.

Jim, tell me why you wouldn't do something like this to Mary? If Jim is innocent, he is likely to make reference to a personal trait that would keep him from killing someone. Common responses to this question heard from innocent suspects include, "I could never live with myself if I ever did something like that!" or "I've got too much respect for life to ever do something like this!" Conversely, if Jim is guilty, he may offer a third person response such as, "Well, it's wrong." or "That's a serious crime." Some guilty suspects, in answering this question, will make reference to future consequences, such as, "I wouldn't want to go to jail."

Jim, would you be willing to take a polygraph examination to verify that what you have told me is the truth? Both guilty and innocent suspects will generally agree to take a polygraph examination. However, it should be viewed with suspicion when a suspect balks at agreeing to take a polygraph test. In this event it is typical of the guilty suspect to come up with some sort of excuse for not agreeing to take the examination. These include shallow statements, such as that the polygraph is not infallible and that the refusal of courts to admit test results in evidence is proof of its lack of accuracy.

When the suspect does agree to take a polygraph examination, he should be asked, "What would the results of your polygraph examination be if you were asked questions about killing Mary?" A guilty suspect's response to this question often lacks confidence or certainty in his ability to pass a polygraph test. He may respond with qualified confidence such as, "Well, I hope it would show I was telling the truth" or evade a definite response by offering the excuse that he has never had one so he does not know how they work or that he is a nervous individual, even when he tells the truth. He may even say that he might fail the test, adding that he had a friend who failed a test although that friend was telling the truth. While answering this question, the guilty suspect is likely to exhibit poor eye contact, engage in grooming behavior or other anxiety-reducing behavior symptoms. The innocent suspect will confidently predict truthful results when asked this question, such as, "It better show that I'm telling the truth because I had nothing whatsoever to do with causing her death!" During his response, the innocent suspect will maintain direct eye contact and perhaps even lean forward in the chair.

In all instances where suggestions are made about taking a polygraph examination, the investigator should carefully avoid creating the impression that the suspect is required to take the test. Indeed, it is essential that the proposal be presented in a hypothetical way so that the suspect knows that it is only an invitation or an opportunity to establish truthfulness. Upon a suspect's expressed willingness to take a polygraph examination, it may be advisable to ultimately arrange for one whenever the investigator may be uncertain as to guilt or innocence.

Jim, did you discuss Mary's death with your family or close friends? Experience has indicated that if Jim is guilty, he may say "no" to this question. Not only will he want to conceal the fact that an event occurred for which he anticipated being questioned, but he probably also wanted to avoid actually being asked by a family member or friend any probing questions bearing on his possible involvement. He may account for his failure to disclose the event to family and friends on the grounds that he did not want to cause them any worry or concern. If Jim is innocent, he probably has discussed the matter with a family member or friend and will acknowledge the fact to the investigator. He also may relate the reactions of those persons.

Out of necessity, a guilty suspect may have told a family or close friend about Mary's death. When a suspect indicates that he has told a loved one about the issue under investigation, it is often productive to ask, "What was your [friend's] reaction when you told him?" Innocent suspects will probably have initiated the conversation with a friend and will have discussed the crime in some detail. Consequently, the innocent suspect's answer to the reaction question will indicate an in-depth conversation, such as, "He was very supportive and upset just like I was. We talked about who might have done it and why it happened." The guilty suspect's response to the reaction question often reflects that the conversation was shallow or the comment was brought up in passing. A typical guilty suspect's response to this question is, "Nothing really. He was just curious about what happened and stuff."

Jim, if we can establish who the person is who did this to Mary, do you think that person should be given a second chance? This is a question similar in principle to the punishment question. A truthful person rarely is in favor of giving the offender a second chance; the guilty suspect, on the other hand, will often indicate some type of leniency or be noncommittal about it. If truthful, Jim might say something to the effect of "Hell no! Whoever did this should get as much of a chance as they gave Mary!" If Jim is guilty, however, he may respond by saying, "That's hard to say." Again, consideration must be given to the nonverbal behavior symptoms that accompany the verbal response to determine the credibility of the spoken answer.

The examples in this appendex are only a guide to help us look for other behaviors from suspects. There is no single response or behavior, rather it is the totality of all responses combined with other evidence, facts, and circumstances.

Suspect Identification Utilizing Pre-Crime, Crime, and Post-Crime Offense Behaviors*

This appendix will address a method for identifying the primary suspect in a murder investigation and/or corroborate a confession statement which has proven to be especially beneficial in the undertaking of a cold case evaluation. This method requires evaluating the information pertaining to pre-crime events, the facts of the crime, and post-crime behaviors and is wholly comprehensive. As such, the primary benefit to cold case evaluators is this; at the onset of a cold case evaluation investigators have the advantage of having all relevant case information available, whereas during a "hot" case they must rely on a trickle of incoming information. This process is started first by examining the core elements of the crime where a sub-type is identified and subsequently moves outward from a working profile towards identifying like characteristics in identified persons of interest.

While the rule of thumb to work from the inside of the case outward is generally adhered to, this method does have the potential to go awry when leads or tips have been presented that shift the focus away from the thrust of the investigation into a new direction. As a consequence, independent of whether the information provided was relevant to the investigation, the pursuance of these leads can build quickly to a number of *persons of interest* that cannot be affirmed or dismissed. Often, when the potential suspect list exceeds four, eleven, or fifty people, it becomes a major concern when weighing the importance and value of the evidence. Likewise, this is similar in confessions with multiple explanations that are questionable. Here, a method and scheme is offered to resolve this dilemma and use the primary suspect's own

---

*Except for a few small changes and the inclusion of the John List case study provided in this appendix, much of what is here came from Richard Walter's and Sarah Stein's original writings as found in Chapter 8 of Adcock, J. M., & Stein, S. L. (2011). *Cold cases: An evaluation model with follow-up strategies for investigators*. Boca Raton, FL: CRC Press.

behavior to aid the investigation. A case study will be utilized to illustrate the process of identifying the suspect through the behavioral actions of the perpetrator before, during, and after the crime.

In a murder investigation, the pursuit of *who, what, when, where and how* can be difficult, illusive and problematic due to criminal sophistication, lack of evidence, victim selection and/or false confessions. Furthermore, to avoid detection, the perpetrator may have *staged* the crime scene to resemble an accident or suicide. Again, there can be many complexities that can offer misdirection and red herring searches to no avail.

During this time, investigators may receive well-intentioned, *and other's not well intended,* tips regarding the crime. Accordingly, while chasing down these leads it becomes easy to follow the operative theory in front of them rather than consider the actual facts of the case. When this happens, unless there is a major break that shifts the focus back to the crime scene evidence, the odds improve that the investigation will become an unresolved cold case.

In violent crime, murder does not happen in a vacuum. It has victims and perpetrators. To achieve the end result, the perpetrator must actualize a motive with a method when given the opportunity to do so. Here, in part, is the rub for the perpetrator or false confessor. For, despite the self-perceived cleverness of the perpetrator, an examination of the crime scene evidence for what is, *and what is not,* at the scene the perpetrator will ultimately leave a tattletale record regarding the motive and relationship between victim and perpetrator. That is, when the investigator measures the pieces of direct, circumstantial, and physical evidence against known crime sub-types the facts should indicate whether in whole, or combination, the crime was *Power-Assertive, Power-Reassurance, Anger-Retaliatory,* or *Anger-Excitation (Sadism).* Furthermore, the sub-types will provide additional information regarding whether the crime was likely purposeful, fantasy driven, revenge, or pleasure killing.

Power-Assertive Type (PA) In the non-sexual power-assertive type, power is a conceptual term that denotes a process of creating notions, ideas and symbols that reflect thought. Here, the perpetrator chooses to take a criminal action for achieving control and dominance of an individual and/or situation. Commonly, the non-sexual power-assertive murders are committed for greed, investment, contract domestic dispute politics, and/or a simple drive-by shooting. In these instances, the detached relationship with the victim may be minimal and require little or no direct contact with the victim. For instance, the murder could be completed by simply shooting the victim in a place and manner that meets the perpetrator's needs. In contrast, the sexual power-assertive rape/murder, by its nature, has an inherent emotional involvement which increases the probability of percussive injury to the victim. That is, given the increased emotionality, the perpetrator's needs are satisfied only through direct injury to the victim; such as hitting, bludgeoning, stabbing, strangulation, etc.

Power-Reassurance Type (PR)   In the non-sexual power-reassurance type, the acquisition of control, dominance and mastery becomes enhanced through daydreaming and fantasy development. Here, the scripts and usurpation of power is limited only by the inadequacy of imagination. The criminal activity, which may result in the death of the victim, may range from impersonation of heroic and/or professional occupations, stalking the rich and famous, infant kidnapping for a *pretend* family and/or hostilities that make the perpetrator feel important and potent. In contrast, the sexual power-reassurance type uses fantasy to create desired or ideal relationships with targeted or opportunistic victims. Primarily, the victims are either younger, older, or somehow considered "damaged goods" by the perpetrator. Herein, the victim choice, by their age, and/or condition, lessens the inherent challenge and fear to his power that could be produced by a healthy and appropriate aged person. Often, due to his need for validation, the perpetrator will ask the victim for approval and rating of the exhibited performance. Accordingly this type of perpetrator is sometimes referred to as "The Gentleman Rapist." However, when the pre-planned assault goes awry, the loss of power prompts a violent reaction upon the victim. As a result, the crime may show a disorganized scene and possible post-mortem sexual activity.

Anger-Retaliatory Type (AR)   In the non-sexual anger-retaliatory type, the emotional outburst against the target is to punish a perceived wrongdoing, real or imagined, committed against the aggrieved perpetrator. Most often, the violence is percussive (hitting, stabbing, strangulation, etc.) upon the victim until the perpetrator has sated the precipitating hatred. An exception to the percussive violence is the crime of arson. Here, for instance, the perpetrator may burn a rental apartment or home down because of an eviction. Notwithstanding, the goal of the perpetrator is to punish, get even and retaliate against the victim. In this category, the types of victims may be a person, business, group, landlord, child molester, etc. Finally, the non-sexual anger-retaliatory type may convert the more common emotional thrust into a cold and controlled plot against the victim. In these instances, the perpetrator acts out the revenge atypically with detachment and mechanical efficiency in satisfying the condensed emotions. Accordingly, the choice of weapon may be a gun rather than the most common percussive attacks. In contrast, the sexual anger-retaliatory type is often nettled by and attracted to women. Accordingly, while using women to further his dependency/hatred, the perpetrator uses them as foils and scapegoats for explaining his failures. Often, the targeted victims are the same age or older than the perpetrator. For, it is generally this group that has the power to humiliate or scold. An exception to the age range would be a younger woman who may be a clerk in a store that refuses his credit card, step-daughter who threatens to expose sexual abuse, or a female supervisor. Most often, the primary target victims within this group are mothers, aunts, wives and/or girlfriends. However, due to the pathological connection between the perpetrator and victim, the killing of the primary may become unacceptable. Hence, the perpetrator may seek a substitute target for which to act out the crime intended for the primary target. In the crime, the percussive violence may continue into post-mortem activity. Following the emotional catharsis, the perpetrator will position the body with eyes averting egress. Likewise, the perpetrator feels no guilt and exits the crime scene with a feeling of well-being and cleansing.

Anger-Excitation Type (AE)   In the non-sexual anger-excitation (sadism) type, the prolonged and ritualized process of human destruction is the goal unto itself. Here, despite a myriad of methods and schemes, the core elements of sadism are dependency, dread, and degradation of the victim. Although extensive fantasy may be used, it is not required with the non-sexual anger-excitation type. The victims may be known/stranger, male/female and adult/child. Within this subset, the crimes may range from parental torture of children (burning, starving, binding, etc.), male torture of a rival suitor for a love object (humiliation, bondage, beheading, etc.) and war related killing of soldiers (beating, burning, incomplete strangulations, staged beheadings, sexual mutilations, and tossing live prisoners into a fire pit). In contrast, the sexual anger-excitation type increases the fantasy component into elaborate scenarios designed to break the body and mind. Here, operative schemes are devised to confuse the victim by "con games" that offer false hope and then destroy that hope. Again, the satisfaction of these killings is gained in the process of the killing not the death itself. Often, the selections of the victims are from symbolic categories or characteristics; such as, hair color, size, age or fetish interests. Common victims are prostitutes, drug users, nurses, children, students and matriarchs. Methodically, the perpetrator will accommodate the learning curve to exact sexual pleasures through secondary sexual mechanisms like bondage, insertions and etc. The full gambit of this continuum lends with necrophilia and cannibalism.

The information below will provide the reader with additional insight into the four sub-types of offenders that may be encountered during the course of an investigation.

Power Assertive

1. Assault is pre-planned
2. Forceful aggression and intimidation
3. Grasps and maintains control over victim
4. Uses exaggerated machismo over-reaction
5. Search for virility, mastery and dominance
6. Language is directive and commanding
7. Injury to victim is purposeful, not recreational
8. Sexually related violence is percussive: beating, cutting, strangling
9. Brings weaponry to crime scene and takes away after the killing. Often, weapons are part of normal image; a gun, knives, ropes, etc.

10. Although violence may be severe, there is no mutilation of the body
11. Murder does not "count" unless someone knows; feels the need to brag

Power Reassurance

1. Pre-planned rape with unplanned overkill of the victim
2. Prompted by fantasy and over-idealized seduction and conquest
3. Seeks verbal reassurance from victim. "The gentleman rapist."
4. When victim does not yield to planned seduction, the fantasy collapses and an emotional explosion results in killing
5. Often, post-mortem mutilation
6. Tends toward disorganized crime scene
7. Victim selection may be younger or older than the perpetrator. Also, the age range may be similar, if victim is perceived as "damaged goods."
8. Weapons may be clothing, fist and knives
9. If sexual behavior occurs, it is likely to be post-mortem
10. Body may have insertions

Anger Retaliatory

1. Assault is situational-planned
2. Stylized violent burst of attack
3. Violent assault and overkill of victim
4. Victim's eyes away from egress
5. Nettled by poor relationships with adult women
6. Assault precipitated by scolding from woman
7. Victim is often a scapegoat/substitute for the intended victim
8. Victim is chosen because she lives or works in area near offender
9. Victim may be pre-selected pending the perpetrator's impulsive reaction to an anger/challenge
10. Although perpetrator may drive to the crime location, he approaches the last 200 feet by foot

Anger-Excitation (Sadism)

1. Homicides are pre-planned and designed to inflict terror and pain upon the victim
2. Satisfaction is found in the killing continuum, not in the death
3. The insatiable appetite is predicated upon dependency, dread and degradation
4. In the search for domination and mastery, the overt sexual dynamics may become delayed and muted. Instead, there is a rise of secondary

sexual mechanisms which allow emotionally laden power concepts to become activated and satisfy the crushing of the prey.

5. The victim selection may be male/female that fits the perpetrators needed symbolic category; such as, prostitutes, nurses, children, students, matriarchs

6. Complementary fetish interest may be long blond hair, specialized shoes, large breasts, or tawdry clothing

7. Once a victim has been encountered by con and/or ruse, he will attempt to isolate for control

8. As fantasy system is implemented, the perpetrator may show vacillating mood shifts with a methodical approach at terrorizing the victim

9. Prior to killing, there may be evidence of burning, cutting, washing, bruising, and ligature marks

Unlike natural, accidental, or suicide, homicide is the only manner of death that has post-crime behavior. That is, although the victim's body is dead, the perpetrator still derives satisfaction from the killing. Ergo, unwittingly, the perpetrator's post-crime behavior continues to leave evidence for the investigator to capture and use for identification and eventual prosecution.

Inasmuch as the crime scene evidence is the beginning and nexus for the investigation, the evidence, by presence or absence, compared to the appropriate crime sub-type becomes the "gold standard" for evaluating the relevance of other data, information and understanding on the case.

Given that the homicide/murder was committed with a motive, in a particular method at a specific time and location, these factors indicate the perpetrator had sufficient cause to target and kill the victim. Whether the perpetrator may have had a great deal or limited exposure to the victim, he/she found cause, method and time to aggress against the target. These actions prior to the killing are pre-crime behaviors. That said, given the nature of the victim, it is possible that three to fifty people may have wanted the victim dead. Accordingly, while looking into each of these possible suspects, the investigator can write down the victim/suspect relationship, conflict between the parties and the intended benefit to the suspect for killing the victim. Again, using the standard created by the crime scene, one can match the crime scene crime sub-type to that of the pre-crime behavioral suspect list. In fact, the crime sub-type of the crime and the suspect should be the same. In particular, if the crime is determined to be Power-Assertive, so should be the motivational and relationship structure of the suspect.

Again, contrary to conventional thought, the murder is not over when the body dies, but when the perpetrator stops deriving satisfaction from the killing. *In some instances, this may be days and/or years!* Accordingly, since these behaviors follow the killing, these actions are called post-crime behaviors.

Here, the investigator can take the same subjects listed in the pre-crime behavior suspect list and fill-in for each suspect whether they benefited with greed, power, silencing a secret, sexual gratification, or hatred. Again, as in the pre-crime behavior analysis, the investigator uses the crime evidence and sub-type of the crime to measure against the post-crime suspects. When completed, the primary suspect's pre-crime and post-crime behaviors should match to the crime description and analysis. For example, if the crime was Power-Assertive, the primary suspect should show Power-Assertive for both pre-crime and post-crime behaviors. In addition, if the primary suspect is within the pool examined, the pre-crime and post-crime entries should contain a number of weighted linkages to the crime. If not, this could indicate a direction for further investigation and/or the primary suspect has not been included in the list.

Perchance, given a list of five possible suspects, one particular person has numerous entries that are significant to motive and the relationship with the victim, the same person should be examined on the post-crime behaviors to determine the quantity and quality of perceived or real gain made by that person. Often, dependent upon the type of killing, these items could range from 25–40 entries. Alternatively, if none of the other four suspects on the list have any pre-crime or post-crime issues beyond possibly disliking the victim, because of a bad car deal, they can be algebraically crossed off to clear the field of extraneous clutter. *Note: it is possible that one or more persons may have been involved in the killing. If so, each of the persons should have listed key items and a relationship with one another.*

In reference to the primary suspect, once the data has been collected and properly entered into the schematic diagram, directional vectors can be drawn from the pre-crime behavior through the crime standard and transverse into the post-crime behaviors. Ergo, the vector represents the connection *before*, *during*, and *after* the crime. Accordingly, this can be done a number of times at different points of congruency. In effect, this means that the primary subject, through actions and words, helps identify themself at the exclusion of all others.

▶ Methods

As previously mentioned the first stage of the process is to identify the crime characteristics and behaviors. Generic examples can be seen in **Table B-1**.

Peri-crime Behavior—The crime behavior exhibited and performed at the crime scene is pivotal to all behavior preceding and following it. Accordingly, as the standard, it is first established between the pre-crime behavior and post-crime behavior. The data for crime behavior should include; time of notification, location and position of body, injuries sustained (blunt force trauma, gunshot wounds, stabbings, strangulation, etc.) post-mortem manipulation of the body, presence or absence of collateral evidence (clothing,

TABLE B-1.

Pre-crime behavior	Peri (crime) behavior	Post-crime behavior

	Notification:
	  Date
	  Time
	  Location, etc.	

	Scene:
	  Organized
	  Disorganized
	  Items missing, etc.	

	Body position:
	  Normal
	  Staged or posed	

	Unusual findings or potential signature issues	
	Autopsy findings	

	Cause of death:
	  Gunshot wound
	  Stabbing
	  Strangulation, etc.	

	Wound pattern(s)	
	Etc.	

money, body parts, etc.). Finally, this section should include the autopsy findings for the primary and secondary causes of death.

Pre-Crime Behavior—This category extends to all persons reported or developed by investigators that may have had conflict with or, in fact, caused death to the victim. Dependent upon the type of risk factor for the victim, this number may vary from one to ten or more. For the purposes of data entry, this section should be located on the left of the crime behavior column. Each suspect should be listed individually across the top of the section with room to enter significant points of interests below the name.

Often, the information listed here is circumstantial and in need of documentation. Accordingly, it is wise to note the source of the information.

Most often, the supplied information refers to relationships between the victim and mentioned suspect. Sometimes, it can be relationships gone awry, jealousy, fear, hatred, love, control, greed, sexual behavior, business conflict or a myriad of other potential reasons. Again, it becomes extremely important to note whether the tip/witness knows first person of the alleged facts, or whether it came via an undocumented route through the rumor mill.

Note: Commonly, the witness's observation, heard conversation, or tidbit of information would not stand alone as a piece of evidence. However, when linked with other pieces of collateral evidence into a network, it can become relevant and upgraded into a credible statement.

Predicated upon the above comments, it still remains that one, two, or three unkind remarks regarding the victim does not . . . a killer make! In fact, done correctly, the primary suspect should have overt and/or underlying angst, motive or reason to benefit from the victim's death.

Post-Crime Behavior—Following the crime, the killer may act with stealth and/or unwitting brashness to benefit from the miscreant deed. *Frequently, despite being alert and having made attempts at being cautious, the perpetrator will yield intelligence and knowledge to the underlying psychopathology underwriting the crime. Hence, dependent upon the sub-type style, the perpetrator, by behavior, may have with cavalier bravado revealed the true nature and identity of themself.*

Again, dependent upon the sub-type of murder, the post-crime behaviors may vary from bragging about the killing, inappropriate behavior at the funeral, and diminution of the victim and exaggeration of their own importance, attempt to establish an alibi, attempted interjection into the investigation, creating false scenarios, new relationship or marriage, money or insurance gains, silencing secrets known by victim, improved power base as a result of the victim's death, disconnect between affect and word content (smiling while stating that they are devastated at the loss of their wife), change in lifestyle and/or satisfaction that the victim is dead.

▶Case Illustration

Now, as a means of illustrating this method of suspect identification and/or corroboration of a confession, we are going to use a case from Westfield, New Jersey. On November 9, 1971, John Emil List, an unemployed accountant and father of 3 children shot and killed his mother, wife and three children in their 18 room home. He left a long letter to his minister and attempted to explain his reasoning for the killings. Subsequently, after making arrangements with notes to avoid early discovery of the bodies in the ballroom, he vanished with the bodies being discovered approximately one month later. John List remained at large for the next 18 years. Contrary to the self-serving statements in the letter to the minister that he sent them to heaven because their errant ways were leading to damnation, the crime scene revealed evidence for a non-sexual anger-retaliatory type crime. In brief, the primary targets were his strong mother, wife and developing daughter. The two sons appeared to be simply collateral damage. All victims were shot in the head. This indicated the cold conceptualization of the condensed anger. Further, the faces of the bodies were covered. In addition, his personal failures including unemployment and lack of relevance to the family created hostility against the women. In search of an excuse for personal failure, he chose to blame and punish and justify their deaths. Once the murders were completed, he felt free to start a new life and reinvent himself. Accordingly, given the confession with the old identity, he created a new identity of Robert P. Clark and started to repeat many of the earlier behaviors which led to the murders of his family. Per List, he did not experience any guilt for committing the crime. Atypically, he was the only suspect who had confessed to the crimes in the letter. That said, although he admitted to the crimes, his confession of fact was predicated upon a preferred lie rather than the anger-retaliatory nature found at the crime. Eventually, he was caught and prosecuted for the crimes. He was found guilty of 5 murders and died in prison on March 21, 2008.

Utilizing this case study as an illustration of the suspect identification process an abbreviated array of crime behavior concerning this case followed by pre- and post-crime indicators have been provided. Table B-2 places all the information together in one table so correlations can be made. Then, Figure B-1 shows the vectors of relationships and correlations while Figure B-2 should be used in court to make the process easier to understand by a jury.

Utilizing the murders perpetrated by John List as an example, the process of pre-crime, peri-crime, and post-crime analysis for the purposes of subject identification will be explained. The task of identifying a subject, or, conversely, the elimination of persons of interest based on the analysis of pre-crime, peri-crime, and post-crime behavior is an intricate process that involves two primary components. The first of these is the identification of personality attributes and behaviors that can be ascribed to the subject from prudent observation of crime scene characteristics. This is to say that the elements of behavior presented at the crime scene itself will tell investigators the typology of offender; from this broad classification, a specific individual with behavioral characteristics similar to those found at the scene of the crime will reveal himself. For example, in examining the John List case, it was determined that the elements of the crime scene satisfied the behavioral elements ascribed to an anger-retaliatory offender; violent, targeting close family members, covering the victims eyes, etc. Once the crime was classified as an anger retaliatory offense, investigators were able to identify John List as the perpetrator via behavioral parallels that indicated his involvement in the murders.

The second element of pre-crime, peri-crime, and post-crime behavioral analysis involves the disparity between pre-crime and post-crime offense behaviors; that is, the greater the difference between pre-crime and post-crime offense behavior on the part of a subject, the greater the likelihood becomes that he or she was involved in the commission of the crime. For example, a specific subject of interest prior to the crime may have been employed, did not abuse either drugs or alcohol, and was in a stable relationship. However, following the commission of the crime, this same person of interest may have been fired, began drinking and or abusing other substances, and disengaged himself from a significant relationship. These radical lifestyle changes, while not wholly indicative of guilt, can prove to be valuable indicators to investigators regarding a subject's potential involvement in a given crime.

Both of these elements of pre-crime, peri-crime, and post-crime behavior analysis have a single element in common: if executed correctly, the perpetrator of the crime will distinguish himself from other possible subjects in the sense that his personality will be closely aligned with the behavioral elements depicted at the scene of the crime. Additionally, his pre-crime and post-crime behavior will most likely be disparate as his life, both physical and emotional, was altered by the commission of the crime. That being said, this investigative tool can prove invaluable; especially in death cases where the victims are no longer able to recount what transpired during the course of a crime.

The John List case, while not difficult in the sense that the subject had already spoken to his guilt in a letter written to his Priest left at the crime scene, remains an excellent example of how the analysis of pre-crime, peri-crime, and post-crime behavior can lead to subject identification. Additionally, investigators in any instance, whether or not a subject has professed his guilt, must confirm the validity of any statements to avoid faulty or all together incorrect prosecutions. As such, the analysis of pre-crime, peri-crime, and post-crime behavior can provide supplemental circumstantial evidence to bolster the merit of a case in regard to motive, means, and opportunity.

As stated earlier, this process is initiated at the scene of the crime. The elements within the confines of the crime scene itself will broadly classify the type of offender being sought by investigators. That is, is the offender a power-assertive, power-reassurance, anger-retaliatory, or anger-excitation individual? In the case of John List, the peri-crime characteristics were as follows:

Peri-Crime Behavior

1. December 7, 1971, the Westfield Police Department, New Jersey, provided a welfare check on the List home and found the dead bodies of List's wife, Helen, 46; daughter, Patricia, 16; sons John, 15, and Frederick, 13; and his mother, Alma, 85. The entire family of victims had been shot to death. The weapons used were his father's 9mm Steyr automatic handgun and his own .22 caliber revolver.
2. While funeral music played on the intercom system, the investigators discovered an unsent letter written on November 9, 1971 to the local Lutheran minister. The letter detailed the events of the day.
3. After the children had gone to school, he shot his wife, Helen, in the back of the head as she ate breakfast. With the aid of a sleeping bag, he dragged her body to the ballroom in the mansion. He cleaned up the blood with newspapers.
4. Subsequently, he then went to the third floor apartment of his mother, Alma, and shot her above the left eye. Due to her weight, he left her there.
5. When the daughter, Patricia and youngest son, Frederick returned from school, he shot each one of them in the back of their heads. Like their mother, they were transported to the ballroom on sleeping bags.
6. List had lunch at home.
7. In the afternoon, List drove to watch his eldest son, John, play a soccer game and drive him home. Upon arrival, he shot John who began to struggle with him. Subsequently, he shot John at least 10 times. John was removed to the ballroom and lined up in a row with the other siblings and mother.
8. List covered each victim's eyes with a cloth.
9. Again, feeling hungry following the final killing and clean-up, List fixed himself a dinner before leaving the home.
10. The discovered crime scene did comport with the description offered by List in the letter.

Based on the behaviors described above, List can be classified as an anger-retaliatory killer. That is, he harbored immense anger towards his family, particularly the matriarchal figures such as his mother and wife, Helen, demonstrated by the fact that he chose to shoot them first. With the broad classification of an anger-retaliatory personality, the discovery of pre-crime behavior assisted investigators with corroborating the motive, means, and opportunity for John List to murder his family. The pre-offense behaviors of List were as follows:

Pre-Crime Behavior

1. John Emil List was an only child born on September 17, 1925 to strict parents in Bay City, Michigan. At age 19, his father dies and he was in the total care of his controlling and penurious mother.
2. He served in World War II in the U.S. Army and was later given an ROTC commission as a second lieutenant. He developed an interest in guns.
3. Due to financial support from his mother, he attended the University of Michigan in Ann Arbor, Michigan, where he earned an undergraduate degree in business administration and a master's in accounting.
4. During the time at the University of Michigan, it was purported that he had a superior attitude with others and pursued a prestigious position in banking.
5. In 1951, he met and married his wife who had similar goals of financial and social success.
6. Due to an unwillingness to modernize in the banking business, he began to fail with repeated lower pay and status positions. Eventually, he became unemployable which he hid from his family and friends.
7. Meanwhile, while the family means dwindled to emergency levels, he spent his time in the park waiting during the time that would normally coincide with the hours of a regular job.
8. Given the strong demands of the strong matriarchy of his mother, wife, and emerging daughter, the sense of financial and social impoverishment was cause for many arguments and conflicts.
9. Inasmuch as his mother was aged and lived in the third floor of the List mansion, she gave her son, John, the legal authority to do her banking though a joint account. This money is what John List used during the period of unemployment. However, while unknown to his mother, these funds had been almost completely exhausted by John.
10. Although capable, he had little interest in friends, particularly male. He was a loner except for his guns and dreams of escaping the pending doom and collapse of the former life.
11. In preparation for change, he created a new identity, Robert Clark, selected a new area to live, (Denver, Colorado) and made strategic plans for the murders.
12. Amongst the plans were notes to the children's schools indicating that they were on vacation, cancelled the milk order, etc.

The pre-crime behavior above revealed to investigators several pieces of behavioral, circumstantial evidence that corroborated behavioral elements found at the scene of the crime. The primary theme that reoccurred in pre-offense behavior was that of a domineering matriarch. John List's mother exercised complete control over him in regards to financial security. This power held by the mother undoubtedly emasculated List and reduced him to feelings of inadequacy and shame. When List was commissioned as a second lieutenant in the U.S. Army and developed an interest in guns, it was most likely his first experience with autonomy and a sense of power and control. The association between firearms and this renewed sense of power would continue throughout his life and therefore, the use of firearms to dispose of his family is a logical behavioral link. Further, when List enrolled in the University of Michigan, where he earned his undergraduate degree in business administration and a master's in accounting, it was clear that he was struggling to detach himself from the fiscal power exerted over him by his mother. However, shortly after List married is when the pre-crime behavior becomes telling that tragedy was not far behind. That is, List's career began to fail; he once again became reliant on his mother for financial security and stability, forfeiting his job and depleting her financial resources to make ends meet. This resentment for his masculine inadequacy and the strong matriarchs that caused the feeling of ineptitude, as well as the knowledge that his secret failures would soon be exposed when money ran out pressured List to devise a plan to escape. That plan involved utilizing his passion for firearms, psychological surrogates for power and control, to murder his family and flee to Denver, Colorado as Robert Clark.

The pre-crime behavior described above was very much aligned with the crime scene characteristics of the John List case. The first element of pre-crime, peri-crime, and post-crime behavior analysis was therefore successful in subject identification; that is, the subject partially revealed himself to investigators in the sense that pre-offense behavior indicated his behavioral typology (anger-retaliatory), which matched the crime scene classification. However, the second element of pre-crime, peri-crime, and post-crime behavior would also be invaluable to investigators in confirming John List as the murderer of his family. That is, the disparity between his pre- and post-offense behavior indicated beyond a reasonable doubt that List was the perpetrator of the murders. The post-crime behaviors attributed to List were as follows:

Post-Crime Behavior

1. Following the murder of his wife and mother, John List needed cash to put into effect his new life and travel. List went to his mother's bank and withdrew the last $2,000.00. During the process, he requested that the teller put the money into a bank envelope and seal it with her initials across the seal so that his mother would know that he had not taken any money.
2. Once all of the victims were dead and arranged in the ballroom with cloths covering their eyes, John List cleaned the kitchen, ate a meal, wrote a letter of admission and excuse to the family minister, wrote notes to the mailman and school officials, tuned the stereo to organ music for a mock funeral and walked out the door into a new life, as Robert P. Clark.
3. Following the discovery of the bodies, his car was located in a parking lot at Kennedy International Airport. He had vanished into thin air with only speculations of possible suicide, escape to possibly Germany, or hiding out in the United States.
4. *Following an 18 year hiatus of no investigative information, the television show, "America's Most Wanted", featured the case which resulted in his identification and capture. Then, it was learned what had happened in the intervening years.*

(continues)

5. Prepared with a new identity and fictional past, he flew from Kennedy International Airport to Denver, Colorado to hide and activate the new persona. (Although he did not experience any guilt for the murders, he was aware that he had done legal wrong and the police were looking for him.)

6. In the effort to establish protection and living arrangements for himself, he became a night auditor in a hotel . . . which provided limited daytime exposure for possible recognition. Nevertheless, he still, within a month, rejoined the Lutheran Church and was helping them as an auditor.

7. Through church activities, he met a divorcee and told her that his first wife had died with cancer. Later, they were married.

8. Purportedly, after the first year as Robert P. Clark, he forgot about the previous John Emil List and felt no threats of discovery.

9. In Denver, like Westfield, New Jersey, he had difficulties with employment and these issues were starting to cause strain in the second marriage.

10. In an effort to start anew, somewhat close to home, he and the second wife moved to Richmond, Virginia and assumed a quiet life.

11. On May 21, 1989, AMW featured the List family murders on the show with 22 million people watching. One woman and her daughter recognized their former neighbor, Robert P. Clark, as John E. List. They called the television show and the information was passed on to the FBI. It was learned that he now lived in Richmond, Virginia and the FBI arrested him shortly after the airing of the program. He denied that he was John E. List, however, fingerprints from earlier gun permit applications proved that he was John E. List.

12. He was convicted in New Jersey of 5 counts of murder.

13. Later, when asked about his wife, he referred to her as a "syphilitic bitch." (In fact, he claimed that unbeknownst to him at the marriage in 1952, she was infected with syphilis from her first husband.)

14. Prior to his death on March 21, 2008, he gave an interview with CBS commentator Connie Chung. During the interview, he recanted the claims that he had made in the letter to the minister left in the house. Now, he indicated that he had simply got tired of the financial and personal issues presented by the women in the family. Ergo, he murdered them because he wanted to reunite with them in heaven.

15. When asked why he did not commit suicide, he responded because it was a mortal sin that would have kept him out of heaven and the reunification with his family.

The post-crime behaviors listed above contributed in two unique ways in confirming John List as the sole perpetrator of the murders of his family. In one sense, the erratic and disparate post-offense behaviors as compared with pre-crime behaviors indicated to investigators List's involvement in the crime. Conversely, the meticulous and consistent behaviors as compared with pre-crime characteristics also lent credence to List's involvement. The erratic behaviors of List following the commission of the murders can be seen in post-offense behaviors one (1) through three (3). That is, going to the bank, withdrawing the last of his mother's savings, writing hasty notes to the mailman and school officials, and fleeing the state via a flight to Denver, Colorado. The rapid succession with which these behaviors transpired are not indicative of a grieving husband, father, or son, but rather suggest the actions of a guilty mind.

Conversely, the actions List carried out once commencing his life as Robert P. Clark were consistent with pre-crime behaviors and demonstrate his underlying pathology of egoism, narcissism, and cowardice which contributed significantly to the murders of his family. That is, despite his prior failures in his chosen vocation of finance, List attempted to revive his career, which was again unsuccessful. Additionally, he rejoined the Lutheran Church and remarried, demonstrating his need for matriarchal reinforcement and support. Finally, when interviewed about his wife that he had murdered, he accused her of being a "syphilitic bitch," thereby confirming his resentment for domineering females.

The post-crime behavior described above, both the erratic behavior and the actions taken by List attributable to uncontrollable psychological pathologies, confirmed to investigators that he was indeed the sole perpetrator of the murders of his family. That is, the disparity between pre-crime and post-crime behavior in the rapid succession of behaviors displayed following the commission of the crime versus the meticulous and deliberate actions taken prior to the murders demonstrated List's guilt knowledge and his desire to escape apprehension by authorities. Additionally, his more pathological actions following the commission of the crime were indicative of his hatred for strong matriarchal figures and confirmed the behaviors observed at the scene of the murders. Given this fact, it is important for investigators to remember that there is value in both spontaneous post-offense behavior, and post-offense behavior that is consistent with pre-crime and peri-crime psychological needs of an offender.

To effect a successful suspect identification or elimination via the analysis of pre-crime, peri-crime, and post-crime behaviors, there are two primary methodologies available. The first method is particularly useful to investigators to either identify or eliminate a person of interest. The second method can be especially helpful to prosecutors in explaining the process of subject identification to a jury. The underlying premise of these two visual techniques is to identify as many like behaviors as possible within the three sectors of pre-crime, peri-crime, and post-crime behavior. The more commonalities in behaviors between the three categories that are observed, the greater the likelihood that a particular individual is involved in the crime as taken from **Table B-2**.

The first method that can be used by investigators is most helpful during the preliminary investigative phase where there are several persons of interest and subjects must be eliminated. This technique first involves listing all peri-crime behaviors relevant to the case; that is, all of the physical and behavioral elements of the crime itself. Following the listing of all pertinent crime scene facts, pre-crime and post-crime behaviors for each person of interest are listed in chronological order. What results is a separate diagram for each person of interest with pre-crime, peri-crime, and post-crime behaviors included. The behaviors may either be verbally described on the diagrams, or numbered for convenience. Following the construction of a diagram for each person of interest, lines may be drawn between behaviors that are consistent. The more lines drawn between the three sectors of pre-crime, peri-crime, and post-crime behavior, the greater the likelihood that the person of interest being considered was involved in the commission of the crime. An example of this type of diagram derived from the behaviors presented in the List case can be seen in **Figure B-1**.

TABLE B-2.

Pre-crime behavior	Peri (crime) behavior	Post-crime behavior
1. John Emil List was an only child born September 17, 1925 to strict parents in Bay City, Michigan. At age 19, his father died and was in the total care of his controlling and penurious mother.	1. December 7, 1971, the Westfield Police Department, New Jersey provided a welfare check on the List home and found the dead bodies of List's wife, Helen, 46; daughter, Patricia, 16; sons John, 15, and Frederick, 13; and his mother, Alma, 85. The entire family of victims had been shot to death. The weapons used were his father's 9mm Steyr automatic handgun and his own .22 caliber revolver.	1. Following the murder of his wife and mother, John List needed cash to put into effect his new life and travel. List went to his mother's bank and withdrew the last $2,000.00. During the process, he requested that the teller put the money into a bank envelope and seal it with her initials across the seal so that his mother would know that he had not taken any money.
2. He served in World War II in the U.S. Army and later given an ROTC commission as a Second Lieutenant. He developed an interest in guns.	2. While funeral music played on the intercom system, the investigators discovered an unsent letter written on November 9th, 1971 to the local Lutheran minister. The letter detailed the events of the day.	2. Once all of the victim's were dead and arranged in the ballroom with cloths covering their eyes, John List cleaned the kitchen, ate a meal, wrote a letter of admission and excuse to the family minister, wrote notes to the mailman and school officials, tuned the stereo to organ music for a mock funeral and walked out the door into a new life, as Robert P. Clark.
3. Due to financial support from his mother, he attended the University of Michigan in Ann Arbor, Michigan, where he earned an undergraduate degree in Business Administration and a Master's in Accounting.	3. After the children had gone to school, he shot his wife, Helen, in the back of the head as she ate breakfast. With the aid of a sleeping bag, he dragged her body to the ballroom in the mansion. He cleaned up the blood with newspapers.	3. Following the discovery of the bodies, his car was located in a parking lot at Kennedy International Airport. He had vanished into thin air with only speculations of possible suicide, escape to possibly Germany or hiding out in the United States.
4. During the time at the University of Michigan, it was purported that he had a superior attitude with others and pursued a prestigious position in banking.	4. Subsequently, he then went to the third floor apartment of his mother, Alma, and shot her above the left eye. Due to her weight, he left her there.	4. Following an 18 year hiatus of no investigative information, the television show, "America's Most Wanted", featured the case which resulted in his identification and capture. Then, it was learned what had happened in the intervening years.
5. In 1951, he met and married his wife who had similar goals of financial and social success.	5. When the daughter, Patricia and youngest son, Frederick returned from school, he shot each one of them in the back of their heads. Like their mother, they were transported to the ballroom on sleeping bags.	5. Prepared with a new identity and fictional post, he flew from Kennedy International Airport to Denver, Colorado to hide and activate the new persona. (Although he did not experience any guilt for the murders, he was aware that he had done legal wrong and the police were looking for him.)

6. Due to an unwillingness to modernize in the banking business, he began to fail with repeated lower pay and status positions. Eventually, he became unemployable which he hid from his family and friends.

7. Meanwhile, while the family means dwindled to emergency levels, he spent his time in the park waiting during the time that would normally coincide with the hours of a regular job.

8. Given the strong demands of the strong matriarchy of his mother, wife and emerging daughter, the sense of financial and social impoverishment was cause for many arguments and conflicts.

9. Inasmuch as his mother was aged and lived on the third floor of the List mansion, she gave her son, John, the legal authority to do her banking through a joint account. This money is what John List used during the period of unemployment. However, while unknown to his mother, these funds had been almost completely exhausted by John.

10. Although capable, he had little interest in friends, particularly male. He was a loner except for his guns and dreams of escaping the pending doom and collapse of the former life.

6. List had lunch at home.

7. In the afternoon, List drove to watch his eldest son, John, play a soccer game and drive him home. Upon arrival, he shot John who began to struggle with him. Subsequently, he shot John at least 10 times. John was removed to the ballroom and lined up in a row with the other siblings and mother.

8. List covered each victim's eyes with a cloth.

9. Again, feeling hungry following the final killing and clean-up, List fixed himself a dinner before leaving the home.

10. The discovered crime scene did comport with the description offered by List in the letter.

6. In the effort to establish protection and living arrangements for himself, he became a night auditor in a hotel . . . which provided limited daytime exposure for possible recognition. Nevertheless, he still, within a month, rejoined the Lutheran Church and was helping them as an auditor.

7. Through church activities, he met a divorcee and told her that his first wife had died with cancer. Later, they were married.

8. Purportedly, after the first year as Robert P. Clark, he forgot about the previous John Emil List and felt no threats of discovery.

9. In Denver, like Westfield, New Jersey, he had difficulties with employment and these issues were starting to cause strain in the second marriage.

10. In an effort to start anew, somewhat close to home, he and the second wife moved to Richmond, Virginia and assumed a quiet life.

(continues)

TABLE B-2.

Pre-crime behavior	Peri (crime) behavior	Post-crime behavior
11. In preparation for change, he created a new identity, Robert Clark, selected a new area to live, (Denver, Colorado) and made strategic plans for the murders.		11. On May 21, 1989, AMW featured the List family murders on the show with 22 million people watching. One woman and her daughter recognized their former neighbor, Robert P. Clark, as John E. List. They called the television show and the information was passed on to the FBI. It was learned that he now lived in Richmond, Virginia and the FBI arrested him shortly after the airing of the program. He denied that he was John E. List, however, fingerprints from earlier gun permit applications proved that he was John E. List.
		12. He was convicted in New Jersey of 5 counts of murder.
12. Amongst the plans were notes to the children's schools indicating that they were on vacation, cancelled the milk order, etc.		13. Later, when asked about his wife, he referred to her as a "syphilitic bitch". (In fact, he claimed that unbeknownst to him at the marriage in 1952, she was infected with syphilis from her first husband.)
		14. Prior to his death on March 21st, 2008, he gave an interview with CBS commentator, Connie Chung. During the interview, he recanted the claims that he had made in the letter to the minister left in the house. Now, he indicated that he had simply got tired of the financial and personal issues presented by the women in the family. Ergo, he murdered them because he wanted to reunite with them in heaven.
		15. When asked why he did not commit suicide, he responded it was because it was a mortal sin that would have kept him out of heaven and the reunification with his family.

The second method of demonstrating the process of subject identification is one which is most helpful to a prosecutor when explaining behavioral analysis to a jury. While the method described above, depicting lines between behavioral vectors, is helpful to investigators in visualizing commonalities between pre-crime, peri-crime, and post-crime behaviors, it can also be overwhelming to the general public. As such, a simpler method is depicted in **Figure B-2**. This method also involves charting pre-crime, peri-crime, and post-crime behaviors numerically, but in a more comprehensive and organized fashion:

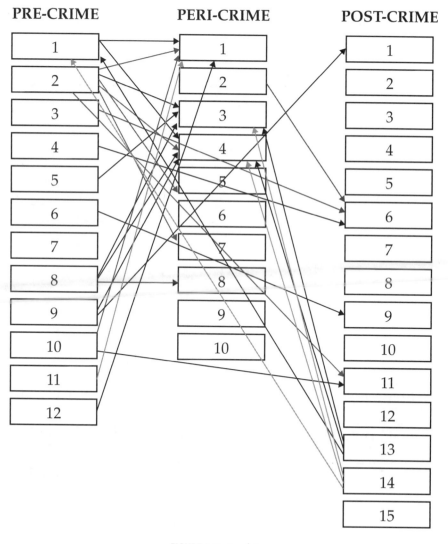

PRE-CRIME   **PERI-CRIME**   **POST-CRIME**

FIGURE B-1. Correlations.

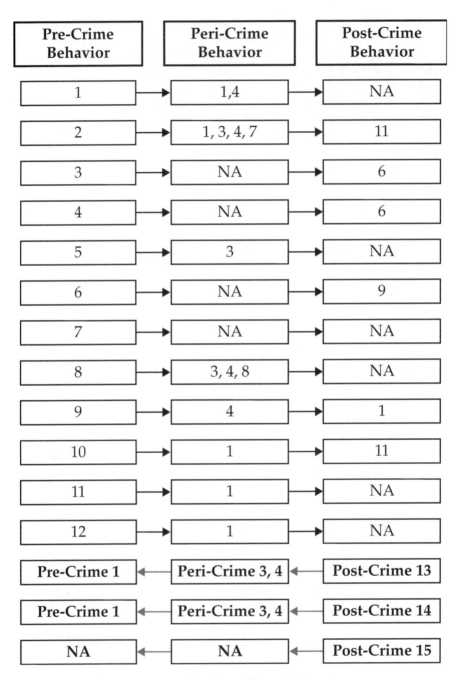

FIGURE B-2. Correlations illustrated for ease of understanding.

This chart shows the pre-crime and post-crime behaviors listed numerically (1–12 and 1–15). As can be seen from the arrows pointing towards the right, for pre-crime behaviors one (1) through twelve (12), the chart is read left to right. That is, pre-crime behavior is correlated with peri-crime behaviors one (1) and four (4), and is not correlated with any post-crime behaviors. From the verbal descriptions of the behaviors above, it can therefore be said that pre-crime behavior one (1), "John Emil List was an only child born September 17, 1925 to strict parents in Bay City, Michigan. At age 19, his father dies and he was left in the total care of his controlling and penurious mother" is correlated with the peri-crime behaviors one (1), the murder of his entire family, and four (4), which was the specific killing of his mother.

In the latter portion of the chart where the arrows are shaded and are drawn from right to left, the reading of the chart is reversed. That is, given that there were more post-crime behaviors that may have correlated only with pre- or only with peri-crime behaviors, it may be necessary to add another portion of the chart. Therefore, from post-crime behavior thirteen (13) to post-crime behavior fifteen (15), the chart is read from right to left. For example, post-crime behavior thirteen (13) is correlated with peri-crime behaviors three (3) and four (4), and pre-crime behavior one (1). That is, the post-crime behavior of List referring to his wife as a "syphilitic bitch" and demonstrating his resentment for domineering females is correlated with the peri-crime behavior three (3) of killing his wife, and four (4) of killing his mother. Additionally, this post-crime behavior is correlated with pre-crime behavior one (1), which is the death of his father and being left solely dependent upon his domineering mother.

▶ Conclusion

While the task of subject identification or elimination via the analysis of pre-crime, peri-crime, and post-crime behaviors is somewhat daunting, it is essential to the process of death investigation. The underlying premise of subject identification through inspection of pre-crime, peri-crime, and post-crime behaviors is that the subject will reveal himself through both commonalities and disparities between behaviors. That is, commonalities between pre-crime, peri-crime, and post-crime behaviors speak to the underlying psychological, pathological needs of an offender that are unchanging over time. The psychological and physical elements present in a crime scene will allow investigators to classify an offender typology (e.g. anger retaliatory, power assertive, etc.). From this broad taxonomy, individual persons of interest will either be included or excluded based on personal proclivities and pathologies. Conversely, disparities between pre-crime and post-crime behaviors as can be seen in List's erratic movements following the murders of his family speak to guilt knowledge of an offender; the interruption of a usual routine by the commission of a crime which he or she must then conceal.

The physical depiction of a pre-crime, peri-crime, and post-crime analysis in the form of diagrams can also be infinitely helpful to both investigators and prosecutors. For investigators, the visual representation of linkages between behaviors can assist in either identifying or eliminating a person of interest. For prosecutors, the simple pictorial representation of the information derived from the behavioral analysis can provide an avenue to explain an otherwise extremely intricate process to a jury of laypersons.

The formulation of a detailed and accurate behavioral analysis is essential to a successful death investigation. Beginning with the elements of the death scene itself, classify an offender type. Following this, with meticulous investigative work, the perpetrator will reveal himself via the connections between pre-crime, peri-crime, and post-crime behaviors.

Equivocal Death Analysis

▶ Introduction

The purpose of this case study is twofold: (1) to define equivocal death analysis, identifying the process one should go through to conduct a proper and accurate analysis and (2) to use the death of Captain Gordon Hess as the backdrop (case example) that will demonstrate the key characteristics of an equivocal death analysis and show the reader how easy it is for information to be misinterpreted, ultimately adversely affecting the lives of many, especially the surviving family members and instill distrust in the investigative system.

In the course of describing this incident, the evidence, the information, the behavioral issues, etc., there were many exceptional and well respected experts (about 12) that became involved providing their advice and rendering conclusions on the manner of death of Gordon Hess. However, none of these persons are going to be named, because this evaluation is not about who did what, said what, or wrote what, but rather how and why this case became so misinterpreted and convoluted. In the end you are welcome to agree or disagree and if anyone wants to discuss this further and/or see my references and documentation, I will gladly provide them. Remember: "We work for Truth."

▶ What Is an Equivocal Death Analysis?

Equivocal death is a death where there is uncertainty as to what happened. To be more specific, "What was the manner of death?" These are cases where we are tasked to determine between suicide and homicide, accident and suicide, or homicide and accident. Vernon Geberth[1], one of the foremost authorities on homicide investigation, makes a very profound statement:

"... Suicide cases can cause more problems for detectives than homicide investigations." In my 30 plus years of experience, if there was ever a true statement, that is it.

Therefore we are frequently faced with this dilemma and need to be able, to the best of our ability, make the correct determination. People's livelihood may depend on it. Family members need to know the truth in order to reach a point of acceptance and move on with their lives, not to mention that our legal system requires it as well. So, while discussing the Hess case I will outline the process that should be incorporated into any death investigation team or unit protocol. However, keep in mind that not all cases can be resolved to the satisfaction of all concerned.

The tough decision of making an accurate manner of death determination needs to be made without bias and prejudice. While it is the responsibility of the medical examiner and/or coroner to make this final decision, no one should make it in a vacuum without full knowledge and consideration of all the facts. You must consider everything known to the case, and armed with that knowledge, apply your experiences to the decision-making process. Your decision must be made with a reasonable amount of certainty that is supported by the evidence, not just your supposition. Remember that nothing in death investigation is absolute. We have to work with probabilities—coupled with our knowledge and experiences we make life altering decisions.

When conducting an equivocal death analysis I think it is important to consider the steps listed in my design of the Scientific Method for Investigators, especially Steps 4–7.

▶ Scientific Method for Investigators

1. Obtain from witnesses the accounts of what happened
2. Based on these accounts anticipate the questions you will be asked by others so you can properly collect and record the physical evidence
3. Collect and record the physical evidence
4. Formulate hypotheses about the events that occurred and anticipate the questions you will be asked
5. Determine whether or not the witness statements are consistent with the physical evidence; gather more information or evidence as needed
6. Through the process of verifying witness statements, admissions/confessions consider the evidence at hand and disprove as many hypotheses as you can
7. Formulate an assessment (final hypothesis) to a reasonable degree of certainty, recognizing the existing limitations

While conducting an equivocal death analysis it would be prudent of the investigator or evaluator to consider this method. Go to step four and start off by formulating hypotheses about the events and anticipate questions that you may be asked or that may arise. Can you answer those questions? Does the evidence support your answers? Then move on to whether or not the witness statements are consistent with the physical evidence; gather more information as needed. Through the process of verifying these statements, consider the evidence at hand and attempt to disprove as many hypotheses as you can; understanding that it is impossible to disprove all of them. Finally, formulate an assessment (final hypothesis) that is supported by the evidence to a reasonable degree of certainty, recognizing the existing limitations. Adhering to this process will solidify your evaluation and will help you present conclusions that are supported by the evidence while addressing possible alternatives.

Keep in mind that before anyone can take on the daunting task of conducting a reliable equivocal death analysis s/he must have access to copies of the entire case file, without exception. Making a determination in lieu of all the documents or just on a few is just plain wrong and reckless with no regard for the actual truth. It is unfair to the surviving family members and unfair to the system we support and serve.

I also warn you that there are many "consultants" who claim to have all the requisite knowledge and experience to conduct an equivocal death analysis, when in fact they may not be what they say they are. A valid consultant will admit his/her weaknesses up front and will not hesitate to seek the advice of other experts with more knowledge in a particular area. In addition to having access to the entire case file s/he must review all photographs, sketches, crime scene processing documents, a listing and status of all evidence and laboratory work, copies of all interviews, all records collected during the investigation, etc. In short, everything must be viewed and considered. Personally, I have declined to review cases where the documentation was lacking or non-existent or I didn't have critical information that I knew should be in the file. As I said earlier, to have reviewed them anyway and provided a conclusion would have been reckless of me.

During the course of conducting the analysis remember that investigations are comprised of three major components, the physical evidence, the informational pieces, and the behavioral aspects; and that we consider what happened before, during, and after the incident. The process begins with a comprehensive review of all the police supplemental reports or agent reports starting with the first notification and continuing to the most recent date of investigative activity. These reports will help set the tone of the investigation at the time it was conducted as they will frequently contain telltale signs of objectivity or the lack of objectivity. All investigators are humans and as humans they make mistakes; but if their system is properly structured they correct these potential problems in stride while investigating the circumstances of what happened. Then a review and analysis needs to be performed concerning all evidentiary issues from the scene, to the lab, etc. Additionally the equivocal death analysis reviewer needs to evaluate all other pieces of information in conjunction with the behavioral aspects of the primary persons involved. It is the totality of the circumstances that should guide one to a proper conclusion.

▶ Case Study and the Scene

In March 1998, Gordon Hess, a captain in the Army National Guard from the state of New York, was conducting his annual training at Ft. Knox, KY. At about 0445, March 3, 1998, Hess was seen by his bunk mate leaving their area dressed in his army physical training gear consisting of sweat pants and a hooded gray U.S. Army sweatshirt. He had stopped by his wall locker and grabbed his wallet as he left the building. He then went to another building for a cup of coffee but it hadn't been made yet; he exchanged a few words with a few other soldiers and then walked outside. That was the last time Hess was seen alive. It was also noted that this rising at 0445 hours was totally out of character for him as he was known to be a late sleeper. Hess then failed to show up for breakfast and failed to report for training that day. When he did not show up for training, a close colleague spent most of the day searching for Hess at nearby hotels, train stations, hospitals, airlines and even called home. About 1600, he officially reported to his superiors that Hess was missing. The military police and the unit began a search for Hess until darkness had set in to no avail.

The following morning, they reinitiated the search that resulted in Hess's body being located about 0800 face down in a small creek bed or ravine with shallow water, only a few hundred yards from his barracks on Ft. Knox. He was dressed in the same sweatpants and PT hooded sweatshirt as previously mentioned when he was last seen alive. The soldiers turned Hess over and pulled his shoulders and head out of the small pool of bloody water. He was placed on his back and one soldier covered his head with a field jacket out of respect for Hess in what is considered to be a typical human reaction (see **Figures C-1** and **C-2**). In Figure C-2 note that the crime scene perimeter was well delineated some distance away from the center of the scene where Hess's body was located. Security was quickly established after the discovery and was maintained throughout the scene processing.

The army CID (Criminal Investigation Command) was the lead investigative agency charged to conduct the death investigation and from the onset the death was treated as a homicide. With this charge they began the crime scene processing; detailed agents to canvass the area; interviewed all those in the unit that knew Hess; collected any information that would help prepare the victimology report; while all along looking for reasons why Hess's death occurred that would lead to potential suspects. During the course of the canvass of all unit members no interpersonal conflicts or grudges or motives to hurt Hess were uncovered, in fact he was almost universally well liked and respected. Only one significant event was noted by many of his fellow soldiers who commented that Hess's demeanor significantly changed after one of their

FIGURE C-1. Body location. See Color Plate 52.

training exercises. This particular exercise was one of several training events involving Captain Hess's unit which consisted of computer simulations of combat operations. In this particular incident Captain Hess lead his unit in a very aggressive and devastating attack on the enemy. However, during their debriefing he learned his attack was actually a "fratricide" incident. (A fratricide incident is defined as the employment of friendly weapons that results

Scene security Line

Hess' body

FIGURE C-2. Area surrounding the scene. See Color Plate 53.

in the unforeseen and unintentional death or injury of friendly personnel or damage to friendly equipment. In this particular case, during a computer-based battlefield simulation, Hess's unit, at his direction, killed the members of two friendly companies.) During the next exercises Captain Hess was criticized for being noticeably unaggressive and hesitant which was out of character for him.

Ultimately there were no signs of a struggle anywhere near the body site in the ravine. Some soldiers had walked in and around the scene prior to the arrival of the CID, in fact one of the soldiers that found Hess left his coffee mug on a nearby rock (see **Figure C-3**) while another one threw his cigarette into the water. While this is not acceptable it happens; in fact there are very few crime scenes that have not been altered or contaminated prior to the arrival of the investigative agency. This is something we deal with every day and while we attempt to minimize the intrusions they will and do occur.

Besides Hess's body the crime scene search resulted in the recovery of a bloody Leatherman's Tool (knife) from under the edge of a nearby rock (see **Figures C-4** and **C-5**). This later became critical because the crime lab was able to identify his blood on the knife blade portion of the tool. Closer views of the tool/knife can be seen in Figures C-4 and C-5. No other blood types were detected. Furthermore, Hess still had his wallet, with all its contents including money; his keys, ring, and the case for a Leatherman's Tool with the instructions in his pockets. The investigation learned that Hess had bought the Leatherman's Tool the previous evening to replace the one he lost sometime in the past. The plastic covering to the tool and case were found discarded in a nearby dumpster. A latent print examination of that container found Hess's prints on it.

Coffee mug

Leatherman's
Tool/Knife found
Under rocks edge

FIGURE C-3. Relationship of Leatherman's Tool and coffee mug to the body.

Leatherman's
Tool/knife

FIGURE C-4. Location of Leatherman's Tool. See Color Plate 54.

Leatherman's
Tool/knife

FIGURE C-5. Closeup of location of Leatherman's Tool. See Color Plate 55.

Nearby it was interesting to note that some tree branches were broken. The first question that comes to mind is whether or not they were broken in a struggle? As it turns out an analysis of those branches by the crime lab indicated the branches were initially cut with a sharp instrument before being broken, further they also identified wood fragments collected from the hands of Hess. Speculation is that Hess may have cut them while pondering his future actions. Are there other possibilities? Maybe, but the evidence strongly supports this hypothesis. Bottom line, the scene showed no indications of a struggle or that a robbery occurred and the possible death weapon was close at hand.

Over the past few years the army and CID have been criticized for allowing the scene to be covered with two tons of dirt based on the belief that Hess's blood created a bio-hazard. Actually that really did happen but it was two days after the scene was processed and released. The implication of the criticism was the dirt somehow damaged or destroyed the scene perhaps making any future examinations difficult. However, the scene was a creek bed and after a few rains the dirt washed away leaving the bedrock intact and undamaged. I would wager a guess that any city or jurisdiction would not wait even a day to hose off human blood from their street or sidewalks after a bloody incident.

▶ Autopsy of Captain Hess

While the investigative process continued, an autopsy of Hess was conducted by a forensic pathologist from the Armed Forces Medical Examiner's office. This process was witnessed by other members from the Armed Forces Medical Examiner's office and CID agents. The physiological changes of Hess's body were consistent with him dying during the early morning hours of the previous day, soon after leaving his barracks. The autopsy revealed that Hess had sustained 26 stab or incised wounds, 6 to the neck and 20 to the chest, many of which were superficial (see **Figures C-6** and **C-7**). Two of these penetrated the left ventricle, four penetrated the lungs and two penetrated the liver. None of these wounds were out of the range of Hess. There were no defensive wounds found anywhere. And there was no evidence to support Hess had been sexually assaulted. Cause of death was cardiac tamponade, not exsanguination, not trauma to the heart or lungs. The wounds were serious but not incapacitating, were fatal but not instantaneous. Based on the scene, the injuries and the initial background information the forensic pathologist ruled that Hess's injuries appeared to have been self-inflicted and that the death was tentatively being listed as a suicide. However, this was subject to change after toxicology and further investigative measures had been accomplished to either validate or refute the initial findings.

Hess's clothing was also collected at the autopsy. It was interesting to note that there was only one defect (possibly a knife puncture) through the hooded

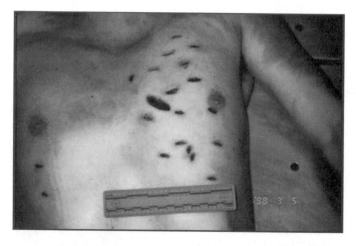

FIGURE C-6. Stab wounds on victim's chest. See Color Plate 56.

sweatshirt that was unzipped. Underneath Hess had on a dark colored t-shirt that bore multiple defects that were consistent with the wounds in his chest (see **Figure C-8**). Speculation is that he may have tried to stab himself through the sweatshirt finding it to be too difficult, therefore opened (unzipped) it and continued to stab himself the other 20 some odd times. Unzipping or opening the sweatshirt is not the action of a person trying to kill you. However, sufficient information has not been gathered to allow a final manner of death determination to be made. Note that the temperature in the early morning hours was around 30 degrees.

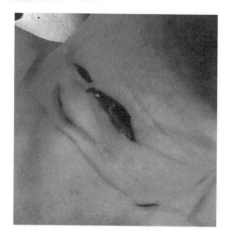 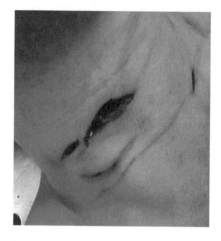

FIGURE C-7. Neck wounds. See Color Plate 57.

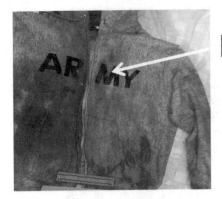

One puncture defect

Multiple puncture defects
That correspond to injuries.

FIGURE C-8. Sweatshirt and undershirt. See Color Plate 58.

On March 4, after the discovery of Hess's body, Mrs. Hess received a death notification from army representatives. Unfortunately these representatives made statements that were not appropriate at this point in time. They stated, without a proper basis of knowledge that "person or persons unknown had assaulted her husband." While it was true that the CID was investigating the death as a homicide these representatives were not acting in accordance with proper death notification protocol, especially since the criminal investigation was in its beginning stages. To add insult to injury, a couple of days later, after the autopsy, the Public Affairs officer for Ft. Knox, without consulting the CID first, and definitely without consideration for the family, made a press release in which he stated that the autopsy results reflect Hess's injuries were self-inflicted, implying the death was a suicide. To make matters worse, this occurred near the time the funeral was to commence and set the Hess family into an emotional spin that should never have happened. They deserved better, but admittedly our system is not perfect.

The criminal investigation was still in its infancy and no one had received or documented enough information to formalize such a finding. All leads have to be exhausted; all potential hypotheses of what happened have to be explored; and then, with the totality of circumstances at hand, a final determination can be made. Ultimately it took the CID over a year before they concluded their investigation. From the beginning and well into all interim reports to the very end the CID had the death listed as "undetermined." Only others outside the investigation labeled it or inferred otherwise.

As I understand it, the family, at the suggestion of an attorney and through the attorney, stopped the funeral and requested a second autopsy be conducted by another forensic pathologist from New York. This pathologist mentioned that the body showed evidence of being embalmed; that nine injuries to the chest were superficial in that they did not penetrate the chest cavity and with one exception basically supported the findings of the initial autopsy. That exception was described as a one inch superficial wound to Hess's upper right arm. This pathologist suggested that it was a defensive wound and thus strongly indicated a violent struggle. Based on this he concluded Hess's death was a homicide. However, photographic documentation from the first autopsy of the area in question clearly reflects there were no injuries to Hess's upper arms, right or left (see **Figure C-9**). Furthermore, there were no defects or blood stains on Hess's clothing that would coincide with an upper arm injury caused during an attack. One can only assume that what this second pathologist saw on Hess's upper arm was a post mortem artifact. It is also important to note that the second pathologist was not provided with any of the background information or was aware of any other case facts obtained by the CID during their preliminary investigation. He further did not examine the clothing or speak to any of the investigators. His decision was based solely on the examination of the body.

 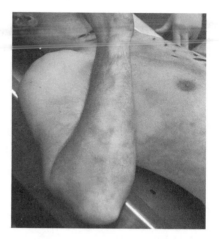

No injuries to upper arm as described by second autopsy doctor

FIGURE C-9. Victim's right arm with no injuries. See Color Plate 59.

▶ Victimology*

In time, the historical aspect or victimology relating to Hess began to unveil itself to the investigators. That coupled with the psychological autopsy provided much needed data. Gordon Hess was dedicated and devoted to his family, friends, and community. He loved his family and children and was a dedicated father and husband. Hess had been described by many as a perfectionist. He consistently strived to be the best and to do things better. "He was competitive and struggled to be number one while he begrudgingly tolerated second best."

According to the report his career path was erratic and frustrating. For a competitive and dedicated man he struggled early in his career after leaving the army, (he was a prior enlisted soldier) working at several rather menial jobs before becoming a fireman. Although he was personally successful, this all led to financial strain due to the failures of several employers. He always wanted to be on a winning team, which finally seemed to have happened when he became a fireman. Hess appeared at this time to excel at all his endeavors and likely expected nothing less from himself. It was indicated that earlier in his life Hess loved the army and initially did not want to get out but family issues and concerns made it necessary. Therefore, his affiliation and participation with the National Guard was probably one of the most cherished endeavors in his life. He enjoyed status and achievement in a structured environment that was team oriented and was a respected leader.

It also reflected that becoming a company commander was viewed by him as a significant achievement. The army and this status was a big part of his identity; one that he did not just turn off after a training cycle because he continued to be involved by being at the armory frequently well beyond the expectations of his supervisors and his stated responsibilities. The army was a part of him. Yet he was not depressive and did not appear to suffer from any psychiatric disorder or medical problem. While he had conquered much adversity in the past, Hess was a man who struggled with feelings of inferiority that "fueled his drive to prove to others and to himself that he was competent and worthy of his achievements." He strongly identified with his roles as a fireman and an army captain. However, he had difficulty tolerating self-perceived failure in the audience of those from whom he sought and received affirmation.

▶ Psychological Autopsy

The psychological autopsy report was prepared by a forensic psychologist. According to his report, "A psychological autopsy is a reconstructive study

---

*Taken from investigative case file documents and the psychological autopsy report.

of a decedent's behavior, personality, motivation and frame of mind at the time of death."* This report, without benefit of interviews of the Hess family, who either refused to be interviewed or did not return the doctors calls, fully outlines the psychological observations and provides findings that directly relate to Hess's demise.

In the evaluator's opinion, ". . . there appears to have been a tragic series of events beginning on March 1, 1998, following the simulated fratricide (previously defined) incident that led to a rapid regression and loss of control for Cpt Hess. A series of events that were distorted beyond their realistic boundaries led to a loss of perspective and a feeling of complete and utter desperation for Cpt Hess."

"Despite positive feedback and reassurances from peers and seniors, Cpt Hess became very fixated on the fratricide incident. In the days and hours that followed there were numerous observations that Cpt Hess was painfully preoccupied with the incident and may have been losing perspective." Once Captain Hess learned of the fratricide he reportedly took the criticism more harshly than intended. During the night and day that followed, Captain Hess was observed:

1. During the day that followed Cpt Hess was quiet and showed little emotion.

2. During the next training simulation Cpt Hess seemed apprehensive and reluctant to engage the enemy.

3. The commander was critical of all the companies but did not single out one commander. Later Cpt Hess approached the commander, obviously concerned over his actions causing the fratricide, and asked the commander how he was doing. He assured Hess he had nothing to worry about.

4. During that next evening Hess had dinner and some beer with fellow soldiers, watched training videos and went bowling. At 2300, when his bunk mate went to bed, Hess was reading a training manual.

5. The following day he arose earlier than usual. After the last mission of the day, Hess was seen entering the after action area with his face "flush, blood shot eyes, and dripping with sweat."

6. That evening while talking to his wife (she reported later) Hess sounded frustrated and felt that he was not getting enough practice and was being rushed. Further, that another company from New York was blaming him for everything that went wrong. She told investigators that during that phone conversation Hess frequently sighed and couldn't complete several sentences.

---

*Psychological autopsy report of Gordon Hess, February 26, 1999.

7. That same evening, after a few beers, Hess was observed as being despondent, lying in bed in his PT outfit, reading a book on tank operations. He allegedly told another captain that he was upset and blamed himself for the failed exercises.

8. At about 2340 hours a senior officer saw Hess pacing the floor outside his room. As he approached Hess, Hess said he again wanted to discuss the fratricide incident. They went outside the building where Hess was observed as being visibly upset and shivering. According to him Hess looked exhausted, nervous and emotional.

9. On the following day, after learning of Hess's disappearance, this senior officer feared Hess might have killed himself.

10. Another captain, a detective with the New York State Police, told the evaluator, that he found it odd that the bunk mate searched hotels, airports and bars for the missing Hess instead of looking for him on base where he was known to run and could have injured himself.

In conclusion, the doctor/evaluator writes that there is ". . . some evidence to suggest that Hess was agitated and distressed, unable to tolerate the stress of continued training, in combination with his own self perceived failings. He subsequently self inflicted numerous lethal and non-lethal stab wounds using his Leatherman Tool to his neck and torso resulting in death, either to relieve his stress or punish himself."*

In reading all this one needs to understand that this report was not submitted until the end of February 1999 and only after the evaluator had thoroughly reviewed the entire investigative case file, autopsy reports, photographs and after conducting numerous interviews of the actors involved. It is not something that is taken lightly and like everything else in a death investigation it is just another piece of the puzzle that has to be considered in order to see the totality of the circumstances.

▶ Review of Literature

In December of 1998 I was asked by the army CID to conduct an independent equivocal death analysis of the Hess case. In order to accomplish this I received copies of the entire investigative file consisting of four large folders, all photographs of the scene and autopsy, and copies of reports from outside experts for the family and for the government. In addition to what I am provided I always try to search outside the box a little to see what else may be out there because no single person has all the knowledge or experience necessary and as a result needs to either confirm beliefs or refute them.

*Psychological autopsy report of Gordon Hess, February 26, 1999.

TABLE C-1. Homicide v. Suicide Stab Wound Direction

Direction	Suicide	Homicide
Vertical	20%	75%
Horizontal	80%	25%

Therefore, after a careful review of the documents and photographs I conducted a review of the literature to see what else might be out there that could influence my decision. Specifically I was looking for studies, research articles, etc. that dealt with homicides and suicides where sharp instruments were utilized. In this search I located a study by Karlsson et al.[2] from Sweden that was directly related to the topic at hand.

One of the first things that caught my eye was their comparison of homicide versus suicide in regard to the distribution and angle of the stab wounds (see **Table C-1**). Notice that with suicide the predominance of horizontal wounds is about 80%, while in homicides they are predominantly vertical. Now if you look at **Figure C-10** count the vertical versus the horizontal wounds. On the left chest area Hess has 2 vertical and 16 horizontal stab wounds. On the right side of his body he has 2 horizontal stab wounds.

Figure C-11 is of a man who committed suicide by stabbing himself more than 33 times. This occurred in his house in July 2000 in Camden, NJ. He also had hesitation cuts on his neck. Notice that these are localized in the left chest and that approximately 31–32 of those stab wounds are horizontal with only about 3–4 being vertical. This is one of many that I have seen since the Hess case in 1998.

The Karlsson study also reflects that the most self-inflicted stabbings was 31 by a female while Hess had 26. The above New Jersey suicide exceeded

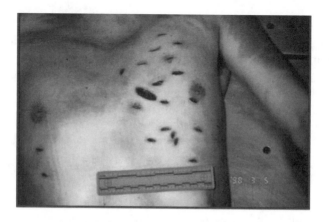

FIGURE C-10. Stab wounds on victim's chest. See Color Plate 60.

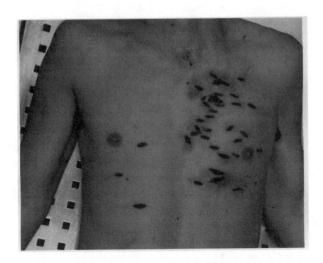

FIGURE C-11. Suicide case from New Jersey. See Color Plate 61.

that with at least 34–35. As to the location of injuries, the concentration of the injuries on Hess was also consistent with Karlsson's study and with the New Jersey suicide. They focused on the left side and primarily upper left side. And when considering clothed versus not clothed only 6% stabbed themselves through their clothing.

I couldn't conduct this analysis without reviewing the authoritative piece on homicide investigation by Vernon J. Geberth. In his book, Geberth[3] provides some very valuable information especially in Chapter 13, "Suicide Investigations." In the "Investigative Considerations" portion of his book (p. 363), Geberth writes the following: "The investigator should be aware of three basic considerations to establish if a death is suicidal in nature.

1. The presence of the weapon or means of death at the scene
2. Injuries or wounds that are obviously self-inflicted, or could have been inflicted by the deceased
3. The existence of a motive or intent on the part of the victim to take his or her own life."

Geberth goes on to write, "It should be noted that the final determination of suicide is made by the medical examiner/coroner after all the facts are evaluated."

As we look at the Hess case the knife with only Hess's blood on it was found at the scene. All of his injuries were well within Hess's reach and therefore could have been self-inflicted. Motive (or intent) is always the most difficult thing to prove. In one of his books Maris[4] writes that some victims suffer from "unbearable psychological pain" that could correlate to Hess's perception of himself as rejected, deprived, distressed, and boxed in, in that everyone was blaming him for what went wrong with the simulated exercise. Another expert, David Lester[5], suggests that " . . . suicidal behavior may follow anger, disappointment or frustration." This may only be temporary, "but for an impulsive person it could be very dangerous." However, I would suggest that the psychological autopsy in conjunction with information from the writings of Maris and Lester, coupled with the fact that it can be shown within a reasonable amount of certainty that Hess did inflict those injuries to his body, he therefore demonstrated his intent.

In further review of Geberth's book[6] I found the following to also be informative and relative: Under the classification of "Wounds" Geberth writes "Most suicidal stab wounds involve the mid and left chest area and are multiple in nature." Then ". . . investigators should not presume homicide based merely on the extent of injury, they should not be fooled by the method." He also writes that ". . . some people's motives never *surface*; the motive died with the deceased." Under the heading "Investigative Considerations *Evaluation of the Wounds*", Geberth provides some very sound advice for those evaluating potential suicide cases (Note that at least 5 of the 7 correlate with the Hess case):

1. Could the deceased have caused the injuries and death?
2. Was the person physically able to accomplish the act?
3. Are the wounds within reach of the deceased?
4. Are the wounds grouped together?
5. Is there more than one cause of death?
6. Describe the nature and position of the injuries.
7. Are there any hesitation marks?

Additionally, Geberth addresses depression as a clinical perspective in suicidal behavior. Under his category of "Cognitive Symptoms" he writes "The depressed individual thinks or perceives of himself or herself in a very negative way."; "The individual may feel that they have failed in some way or that they are the cause for their own problems."; "They believe they are inferior, inadequate, and incompetent. Their depressed cognitive functioning causes them to have intense feelings of low self esteem."; and "The depressed individual actually believes that he or she is doomed and there is no way out." There seems to be a noticeable correlation between Geberth's writings and the facts and circumstances of the Hess case.

▶Bloodstain Pattern Analysis

As a part of this review I also considered the bloodstain pattern analysis report prepared by an expert for the government. The evaluator concluded,

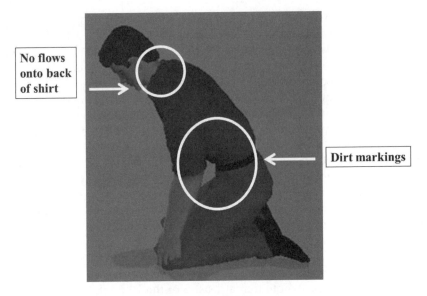

FIGURE C-12. Possible body position.

based on the bloodstains and the condition of Hess's clothing that for the most part Hess was on his knees during the infliction of the wounds as illustrated in **Figures C-12, C-13, C-14,** and **C-15.**

For example in Figure C-13 there was a V-shaped blood flow pattern down the front of Hess. Also there was blood spatter on the front of his right thigh along with concentrated dirt stains on his knees.

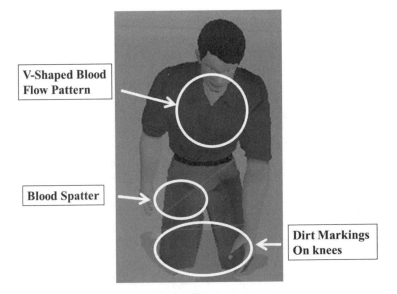

FIGURE C-13. Frontal view.

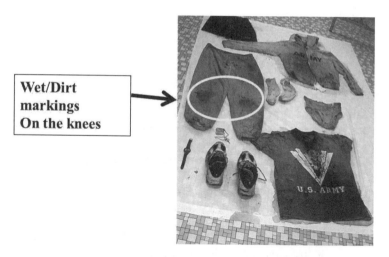

FIGURE C-14. Victim's clothing showing knee stains. See Color Plate 62.

Plus in Figure C-15, there were no blood spatter or drips on the lower portions of his legs or on his shoes. All this becomes critical because it counters any supposition that he was attacked standing up and then became incapacitated lying on his back from his injuries while the assault continued.

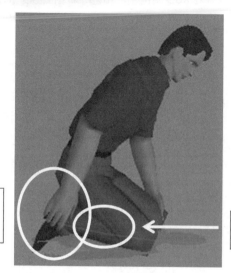

FIGURE C-15. Blood spatter study.

▶Outside Experts

Because the army has a policy to not release their investigative products until after the investigation has been completed and the report has been finalized, only the experts for the government had access to the entire investigative file. As a result those who were asked by the family's representatives to review and comment were given limited access to investigative information and were consequently at a great disadvantage.

In addition to the doctor who conducted the second autopsy, the family, through their lawyer, had obtained the services of at least one expert who in turn brought others into the equation. Most of these were doctors or forensic pathologists who are well respected within their fields of study and work but, as previously mentioned, were given limited information to work with. All three of them affirm that the Hess case should be labeled a homicide not a suicide. But the usual caveat is found at the end of these reports. Basically that with the receipt of additional information they reserve the right to re-review and/or change their opinion(s) accordingly. But in my experience, even when presented with information to the contrary, they still may refuse to change their initial opinions.

To my knowledge all points raised by these representatives have been countered with sound facts, evidence and circumstances as reflected in the final investigative report. These are enumerated below:

1. Two pathologists for the family commented that the Y-shaped stab/incised wound on the chest of Hess could have been caused by Hess's attacker (homicide) but neither seemed to consider that it could have also occurred during a suicide attempt. In other words there were other possibilities that needed exploring and all the wounds were within Hess's reach.

2. Another observation was made that viewed Hess's wounds as haphazard with no similar orientation to each other. I would suggest that if one looks at the wounds to Hess's chest (Figure C-10) that they do have a similar orientation by being anatomically in the same general area of the left upper chest and that they were predominantly horizontal versus vertical. This is also consistent with the New Jersey case seen in Figure C-11.

3. There was also a comment made about not having any hesitation wounds therefore this should be listed as a homicide. This turns out to have been a misinterpretation of the terminology reported in the initial autopsy report. The initial autopsy report did reflect the term "superficial" and when asked by the investigators to clarify this, the doctor said they could also be labeled as "hesitation" cuts.

4. An expert forensic pathologist for the government who reviewed not only the investigative files but Hess's clothing and the Leatherman's Tool, found many correlations between the wound patterns, and the

t-shirt, and the Leatherman's Tool. This person concluded that all injuries to Hess could have been self-inflicted and that there was no evidence to the contrary; especially no defensive wounds.

5. A question that was raised was how could a 2.5 inch blade on a knife create a stab wound with a depth of three inches? Those of us who have had medico-legal death investigation training have always been taught that due to the compression of the chest or almost any body part the depth of the wound is not a reliable indicator for the length of the knife blade. This is further described and clarified in Froede's Forensic Pathology Handbook.[7]

6. A well respected forensic pathologist that supported the homicide conclusion cited a series of reasons why Hess's death was not a suicide. Some of this goes back to the misinterpretation of the terms "superficial" versus "hesitation". This doctor also was not aware of the incised wound of the upper right arm observed in the second autopsy as being an artifact. The number of wounds (26) while large is uncommon but possible; that thought also applies to the self-inflicted stabbing through clothing, uncommon (6% by Karlsson's study) but still within the realm of possibility. Last but not least this person did not know that Hess's blood had been found on the knife blade of the Leatherman's Tool.

7. Another observation reportedly made by one of the family's experts was that the Karlsson study isn't applicable because it occurred in Sweden versus the USA. Further that many of those in that study were either under the influence of drugs or alcohol and/or had mental issues whereas Hess had neither. It is true that Hess's toxicology was negative but based on the investigative report and the psychological autopsy Hess was suffering emotionally, albeit self imposed. As to the self-inflicted multiple stab wounds it is also true that they are seen more often with those who are either drugged or intoxicated; but other cases have been documented, especially when no defensive wounds are found. Furthermore, homicidal multiple stabbings are more likely than not to be erratic as in a frenzy attack with wounds scattered over the body.

▶ Conclusion

"Can We Believe What We See, If We See What We Believe?"[8]

Personally, I feel that this quote speaks a lot to what happened in the Hess case. At the onset, especially with the misstatements by the army, this case got off on the wrong track for the family. In a time of high emotions they did not know who or what to believe. This in itself was a tragedy that the family should never have had to endure. They did what I probably would have done not knowing how the system functions, thinking a "cover up" etc. This led to the hiring of a lawyer who in turn engaged the services of other experts to find out what happened and who was responsible—the answers that everyone would like to have and deserve to receive in these situations.

Any civil law enforcement system can be complicated and the armed forces are probably worse. As previously mentioned they do not allow any part of their investigative files to be released to the family until after the entire investigation has been completed. In some respects I understand that position but in this case, if the army had been a little more forthcoming, I think this whole matter of debating over the correct manner of death would have been avoided and resolved early on, saving everyone time, emotional pain, and tax dollars. Hopefully we have learned from this. But the sad part of those comments and the position taken to not release the information sooner is that it kept the truth from coming out in a timely manner.

The nature and sequence of events—death reported as possible homicide, then shortly thereafter changed to suicide; then a second autopsy says homicide due to what was later determined to be a post mortem artifact; numerous reviews of only limited documents and information—promulgated the homicide hypothesis. I am confident that all of these experts rendered what they believed at the time to be a correct conclusion based on the limited information they were provided. I think it is important to note one more thing—we can disagree with forensic findings if we have an expert of equal stature to perform analysis and come up with a different result; but we cannot discount or refuse to consider forensic examinations from a reputable examiner, just because they don't agree with our theory of the crime.

In one of the opening paragraphs I wrote: "Keep in mind that before anyone can take on the daunting task of conducting a reliable equivocal death analysis s/he must have access to copies of the entire case file, without exception. Making a determination in lieu of all the documents or just on a few is just plain wrong and reckless with no regard for the actual truth. It is unfair to the family of those who survived and unfair to the system we support and serve." It is paramount that we follow this rule as closely as we can.

"We work for Truth"

References

1. Geberth, V. J. (1996). *Practical homicide investigation*. Boca Raton, FL: CRC Press. p. 359.
2. Karlsson, T., Ormstad, K., & Rajs, J. (1988). Suicidal sharp force injury in the Stockholm area 1972–1984. *Journal of Forensic Sciences. 33*(2).
3. Geberth, V. J. p. 363.
4. Maris, R. W., Berman., A. L., Maltsberger, J. T., & Yufit, R. I. (Eds.) (1992). *Assessment and prediction of suicide*. New York, NY: The Guilford Press.
5. Lester, D. (1997). *Making sense of suicide*. Philadelphia, PA: The Charles Press Publishers p. 5.
6. Geberth, V. J. p. 345.
7. Froede, R. C., (Ed.). (2003). (2nd ed.). *Handbook of forensic pathology*. Northfield, IL: College of American Pathologists.
8. Nordby, J. (1992). "Can we believe what we see, if we see what we believe? Expert Disagreement". *Journal of Forensic Sciences, 37*(4), July 1992.

INDEX

Page numbers followed by *f* refer to figures; page numbers followed by *t* refer to tables.